THE INDIAN CHRISTIANS OF ST THOMAS

THE INDIAN CHRISTIANS OF ST THOMAS

AN ACCOUNT OF THE ANCIENT SYRIAN CHURCH OF MALABAR

BY

L. W. BROWN

BISHOP OF UGANDA

Formerly Principal
Kerala United Theological Seminary, Trivandrum, Travancore
Sometime Chaplain, Jesus and Downing Colleges
Cambridge

CAMBRIDGE
AT THE UNIVERSITY PRESS
1956

PUBLISHED BY
THE SYNDICS OF THE CAMBRIDGE UNIVERSITY PRESS
London Office: Bentley House, N.W. 1
American Branch: New York
Agents for Canada, India and Pakistan: Macmillan

Printed in Great Britain at the University Press, Cambridge
(Brooke Crutchley, University Printer)

To

WINIFRED

CONTENTS

LIST OF ILLUSTRATIONS

PLATES

MAP

LIST OF ILLUSTRATIONS

PLATES

MAP

ACKNOWLEDGMENTS

MANY people have encouraged me to write this book, none more than Mr P. C. Joseph, Principal of the Church Missionary Society College, Kōṭṭayam, who gave me many books at the start of my research. I am grateful for the generosity of the Rev. Fr Placid, T.O.C.D., D.D., who has not only given me advice, especially in the matter of Part Two of this book, but allowed me to read his unpublished History of the Church in manuscript; Mr K. N. Daniel also generously allowed me to read his Church History in manuscript; to both these manuscripts I make frequent reference. The late Fr H. Heras, S.J., was always ready to discuss my conclusions and to put me in touch with source material. His Grace Mar Theodosios taught me much when I stayed with him in his *āśram* and made helpful comments on Part Two, which he read in manuscript.

I am grateful to the Leverhulme Trustees for a research grant which enabled me to visit Syrian churches I should not otherwise have been able to see.

The Master of Selwyn College, Cambridge (Dr W. Telfer), and Dr G. P. T. Spear kindly read Part I at an early stage in its preparation and I owe much to Dr Telfer's suggestions. The Rev. Henry Chadwick has kindly verified patristic references for me. I wish to thank Mrs E. O. Shaw, who prepared the map, and Mr K. K. Kurien who did much of the typing at an early stage. Mrs Gay Swabey helped me prepare my manuscript for the Press with great generosity and perception.

Plates II and III are reproduced from photographs by the Rev. H. R. Ferger. I am grateful to Professor H. W. Bailey for his note on the Pahlavi signatures on the Copper plates (pp. 89, 90) and to the Rev. J. C. Winslow for permission to reproduce the description of the Kiss of Peace from *The Eucharist in India*.

The Cambridge University Press has given me much help in the preparation of the manuscript for printing.

Lastly I must express my deep and affectionate gratitude to His Holiness the Catholicos and his Church, and to many other members of the Syrian Christian community, including my former Bishop, Dr C. K. Jacob, for their friendship and kindness to me from the day I first set foot in their country in 1938.

LESLIE UGANDA

LIST OF ABBREVIATIONS

Asseman	J. S. Asseman, *Bibliotheca orientalis Clementini Vaticana* (in qua manuscriptos codices syriacos, arabicos, persicos, turcicos...Bibl. Vat. addictos recensuit), (Rome, 1719–28); 4 vols.
Cheriyan	P. Cheriyan, *The Malabar Syrians and the Church Missionary Society, 1816–1840* (Kōṭṭayam, 1935).
Ferroli	D. Ferroli, S.J., *The Jesuits in Malabar*, vol. I (Bangalore, 1939).
Gouvea	*Histoire orientale des grans progres de l'eglise catholique en la reduction des chrestiens de S. Thomas par le reverendissime Don Alexis de Menezes, archeveque de Goa* (composée en langue portugaise par A. Gouvea et tournée en français par J. B. Glen) (1st ed., in Portuguese, 1606; French ed., Antwerp, 1609, used here).
Hosten	Fr H. Hosten, S.J., *Antiquities from San Thome and Mylapore* (Calcutta, 1936).
Hough	James Hough, *The History of Christianity in India* (London, 1839); 4 vols.
Ittoop	Pukadiyil Ittoop, *Suriāṇi Kristyanikaḷuṭe Sabhacaritram* (Church History of the Syrian Christians) (2nd ed., Kōṭṭayam, 1906).
Mackenzie	Col. G. T. Mackenzie, *State of Christianity in Travancore* (Trivandrum, 1901).
Mackenzie MSS.	A large collection of MSS. on South Indian history and affairs in the Madras Museum.
Mingana	A. Mingana, *Early Spread of Christianity in Asia* (Rylands Library Bulletin, 1926).
Whitehouse	T. Whitehouse, *Lingerings of Light in a Dark Land* (London, 1873).

INTRODUCTION

THE existence of an ancient Christian Church on the Malabar coast in south-west India has been known to Europeans since the time of Marco Polo. Although Chancellor Geddes had published a book in English in 1694 about this Indian Church,[1] it was virtually discovered by the Church of England in 1811, when Claudius Buchanan, a chaplain of the East India Company, published his *Christian Researches in Asia*.[2] Since that time many have taken in hand to write about the Malabar Church, or 'Syrian Church', as it is often called, but no book is really satisfactory, either because it depends entirely on previous writings, with no new facts to present, or because it is polemical in tone, not really interested in the Church for its own sake.

Geddes never went to India, but drew his information from the Portuguese writings made available to him while he was Chaplain in Lisbon. He was as much concerned to show the iniquities of Roman Catholic behaviour as to describe the Indian Church; indeed, his sources of information were too restricted for that. Hough[3] relied on Geddes and La Croze[4] and indulged in many paragraphs of comment on Roman behaviour. In this he was followed by Whitehouse,[5] though his book includes much valuable first-hand description. Buchanan was more interested in the antiquity of the Church than in the details of its struggle with the Portuguese, and he calls special attention to practices shared by the Indian and the English Churches, when these differ from Roman use. Howard[6] elaborated this theme. Rae[7] gave a more impartial account than most of his predecessors, but neither he nor Keay[8] (who wrote a summary history) knew Malayāḷam, the language of Travancore, Cochin and Malabar, where the Church is found. Their sources of information were therefore very limited. One of the best general accounts of the history is the description

[1] M. Geddes, *History of the Church of Malabar* (London, 1694).
[2] C. Buchanan, *Christian Researches in Asia* (Cambridge, 1811).
[3] J. Hough, *History of Christianity in India* (London, 1839).
[4] V. La Croze, *Histoire du christianisme des Indes* (La Haye, 1728).
[5] T. Whitehouse, *Lingerings of Light in a Dark Land* (London, 1873).
[6] G. B. Howard, *Christians of St Thomas and their Liturgies* (London, 1864).
[7] G. M. Rae, *The Syrian Church in India* (Edinburgh, 1892).
[8] F. E. Keay, *History of the Syrian Church in India* (Madras, 1938).

of Christianity in Travancore contributed to the *Travancore State Manual* by Col. Mackenzie.[1] It is unfortunate, but inevitable, that none of the contributions made to the subject by Indian writers so far has been written from an impartial standpoint. The outstanding Indian writers are the Rev. Fr Placid, T.O.C.D., D.D., K. N. Daniel and T. K. Joseph.

There is therefore need for a fresh investigation of the history of the Malabar Church, written from a standpoint which is both sympathetic and, in the assessment of responsibility for schism, as impartial as possible.

This book is concerned with the section of the Church now called 'Orthodox'; it has therefore to leave out of consideration the various groups which live apart from that section, once the occasions of separation have been noticed. Thus we shall see that the Indian Church had a loose-knit unity until 1653, for the last fifty years of that period under Roman obedience. Then about half of the Christians became Jacobite in allegiance (if not at once in liturgy or theology). The work of English missionaries in the nineteenth century, concurring as it did with personal rivalries and factions among the Indians, led to the secession of the Mar Thoma Church, and the conversion of a few families to the Anglican faith. The continuing body of Jacobites has been torn asunder by disputes arising, not from doctrinal differences, but from the clash of persons and their struggle for power. By 1950 the two factions apparently gave up hope of reconciliation and now exist as separately organized churches, the Jacobite, acknowledging the supremacy of the Jacobite Patriarch, and the Orthodox, under the (Indian) Catholicos of the East.

It will be suggested in this book that the founders of the Church were Christian 'East Syrian' traders, from the Persian Gulf area, and it will be apparent that a most important feature of its history is the succession of contacts with foreign Christians, drawn to the Malabar coast by trade. This was possible because of the geographical situation of Malabar. It is now established that at least from the first century A.D. there was regular trade between the eastern Mediterranean and southern India by way of the Nile and the monsoon winds which blow regularly and strongly from the Red Sea to Malabar. There was also coastal shipping coming down the west coast of India from the Persian Gulf. Successive foreign

[1] G. T. Mackenzie, *State of Christianity in Travancore* (Trivandrum, 1901).

visitors, with the possible exception of the Dutch, have had considerable influence on the life of the Indian Church, and outside contact has been too regular and sustained for thought and worship ever to become, *sui generis*, an expression of Christian faith in distinctively Indian form. From the earliest times the language of worship has been Syriac, and so deeply rooted was this tradition that the Portuguese in the sixteenth century, while anxious to reform the Indian Church in accordance with Roman customs, quickly abandoned as impolitic their endeavour to latinize the worship. The worship of the Jacobites and Orthodox is still unaffected by Indian thought, except that both sections have begun to use the vernacular more in public worship. But the theology and ritual derives wholly from the Syrian church, though the Syriac words are written in Malayāḷam characters.

The third part of this book is concerned with the worship and faith of the Church. It was written before the publication of *Studies of the Syrian Liturgies* by H. W. Codrington[1] and has been rendered unnecessary, in part at least, by the appearance of that brochure. I have therefore reduced the matter considerably, but retained enough to give an outline picture of this side of the Church's life.

Although the worship of the Church and the theology expressed in its liturgical books (for there are almost no other writings which express the official theological position of the Church) remain entirely foreign, in social life and custom the Church is completely Indian. There was no interest in recording history in Hindu India until the nineteenth century, when western scholars initiated some concern with the subject. Scientific history was indeed irrelevant to scholarship whose chief concern for centuries had been with the Vedanta. For this reason we cannot tell how early the Christians became completely assimilated to local society and were no longer thought of as foreigners, but there is no doubt that this took place many centuries ago. The assimilation of the community to its environment is certainly one of the reasons for its survival through the centuries. This topic is examined in the second part of this book. The literature on the subject is very small and references to such as there is will be found in the relevant context.

The Christians of St Thomas appear to have lived in two worlds at the same time, but with no consciousness of tension between

[1] *Studies of the Syrian Liturgies*, H. W. Codrington.

them or of disharmony within themselves. They were Christians of Mesopotamia in faith and worship and ethic; they were Indians in all else. In church they professed belief in one Almighty God, out of church they observed omens and propitious days and were content to recognize the existence of Hindu gods, though they did not worship them. Perhaps two chief factors contributed to this *modus vivendi*. On the one hand the Syrians had an intense pride of race and tradition, summed up in their claim to St Thomas as their apostle, which made them exclusive. On the other hand, the unit in Hindu society was the caste, and the Christian desire to continue as a separate closed community was to the non-Christians not only acceptable but inevitable. Hindus expected the Christians to conform to the general conventions which governed caste society and would not have understood it at all if the Christians had practised evangelism, a means of adding to one's own community entirely unknown among Hindus. Western Christians, beginning with Menezes, could not accept this compromise, and tried to arouse an evangelistic spirit in the Christians, but until very recent times they met with no success. One reason why things are now a little different is that the younger generation's education and participation in enterprises with other Christians, like oecumenical conferences, have weakened or destroyed the conception of their community as a caste.

The two worlds of cultus and culture inter-penetrated and influenced each other chiefly on socio-religious occasions such as marriage. Here we see the church service completely foreign in form, except for perhaps two ceremonies which are not counted part of the rite but which most Christians would consider indicate the actual moment of marriage—the tying of the marriage thread round the bride's neck by her husband, and the investing with the marriage cloth. In the house the proportion is reversed—here all the customs and observances are indigenous, except for the prayers said by the priest attending.

Although the cultus was foreign and in an unknown tongue it did keep the community, all down the ages, authentically and deeply Christian. The centre of community life was the parish church, where Sunday by Sunday all the people gathered to see the drama of redemption and Christ's reign in glory shown forth even if they could not understand the words of the service. The people lived through the events of Christ's life as the special ceremonies of the Christian year were observed in cycle, and all the great occasions of their lives were pointed with purpose in the Church. But the cult had an ethical fruit. There are many European witnesses, from Gouvea onwards, to the very high moral standard of the St Thomas Christians in business dealings and in family relationships. The history of the community points to the freedom with which a culture can be accepted by Christians, provided that the dominant factor in their lives is the worship of God through the Incarnate Son. The importance of a liturgy expressing and impressing the facts and meaning of God's acts in Christ and bringing every time of life to its hallowing by God cannot be overemphasized. It is a matter for speculation how much vitality would have been added had the Indian Church received at an early stage the Scriptures in its own tongue, as its Syrian mother had done.

There seems no doubt that it was the cultus which enabled the St Thomas Christians to remain authentically Christian down the ages. But there were other contributory factors. The Hindu rulers of Kēraḷa[1] were justly noted for their tolerance, and the barrier of the Western Ghats kept the country from invasion by the Muslims.[2] Perhaps their Persian Nestorian background disposed the first Christians to walk warily with their princes, and made them unlikely to approve of, or mingle too freely with, 'idol-worshipping' Hindus. Then also there was the frequent, if not continuous, contact with the Christian Church outside. At times this might be concentrated in the person of a single bishop, and at times there might be long periods without even a bishop, but the Church prayed constantly for its Patriarch and never lost the consciousness of itself as part of a greater whole. Perhaps it is always necessary for the well-being, and even the survival, of a Church to have this vision.

It must not be supposed that Western Christians from the sixteenth century tried to come into closer relations with the St Thomas Christians for purely spiritual or ecclesiastical reasons. That is true of the missionaries; the motive of the rest was not altruistic. After the Synod of Diamper in 1599 a distinguished Jesuit wrote to his Father-General that the effect of the action there taken would be of immense service to Portugal, as the Christians

[1] Kēraḷa is the ancient name for the Malayāḷam-speaking area.

[2] When Tippu Sultan in the eighteenth century did get as far as north Cochin the Christians suffered very severely. Thousands were killed and the churches destroyed.

could put thirty thousand trained soldiers in the field.[1] The Dutch officer Visscher suggests it might be a good idea to train young Dutchmen in Syriac and Malayāḷam and then bring them out to convert the Syrians to the reformed faith. 'Perhaps, too, the Company's interests might really be furthered by the course suggested; seeing that these people, besides being numerous, are generally speaking of a martial turn, not to mention that the principal merchants who supply the Company are to be found among them.'[2] The Carmelite Vicar-General, Paul of St Bartholomew, writing at the close of the eighteenth century, explains that the Indian Christians are the chief supporters of the Dutch East India Company at Cochin, because the Company protects them. He says: 'If the English and the Dutch, therefore, do not endeavour to secure the friendship of the Christians in India, on whom can they depend? How can they hope to preserve their possessions in that remote country?'[3] A few years after we find Col. Munro, the first British Resident, referring to his endeavours for the St Thomas Christians as equally important to the interests of humanity and the stability of British power.[4]

The life of the St Thomas Christians conformed to the pattern sketched in the second part of this book until the first or second decade of this century. Then there came changes which have been revolutionary, caused by the very rapid supersession in the great cities of traditional Indian culture by the commercial and educational pattern of the West. Syrians were particularly fitted to take their place in the new order, and were not slow to seize the opportunities offered by the new conditions. Many of the younger and better educated members have left their homes and their rural, church-centred way of life and gone all over India, and to many other places, in the professions and in commerce, and the religiously serious among them begin to see their Church in its true context. Some of the clergy have been educated abroad, mostly in Anglican colleges, and have attended oecumenical meetings. One result has been to strengthen their consciousness of the Church's ecclesiastical position and feelers have been put out towards closer relations with other 'monophysite' Churches. At the same time

[1] See p. 39.
[2] Visscher's *Letters from Malabar*, Letter XVI; Engl. trans. by H. Drury, p. 105.
[3] Fr Paul, *Voyage to the East Indies*, Engl. trans. p. 207.
[4] See p. 133.

knowledge of, and interest in, the old social customs are dying. A Syrian bishop who kindly read through and criticized the second part of this book in manuscript, remarked that most of the ceremonies described were now unknown to young men and women, except in a few country districts. The very rapid spread of Western education and the extension of country bus services will hasten this abandonment of the old culture and soon the St Thomas Christians will be united only by ties of relationship, community self-interest, and their cultus.

The St Thomas Christians have already made a great contribution to India and to the World Church. If they could drive out the devil of litigiousness and come together once more as a united body the old dream of the first English missionaries might become reality, and the Syrian Church of Malabar become a most powerful instrument for the evangelization of India, and the immeasurable strengthening of the whole Christian body in that great country.

PART I

CHAPTER I

THE CHRISTIANS OF ST THOMAS IN THE SIXTEENTH CENTURY

MOST of the considerable number of books written about the St Thomas Christians of Malabar attempt to trace their history from its beginning, starting with an examination of the tradition of St Thomas's mission to south India. But such a method is unsatisfactory because the sources for our knowledge of the first fifteen centuries are of very different degrees of historical worth, and the reader cannot easily get an unconfused picture of the events which certainly happened because of the entanglement of legendary, or only doubtfully probable, incident.

This study starts therefore with an account of the Church as it was when European Christians first came to Malabar at the beginning of the sixteenth century. Just before and for some time after the turn of the century Portuguese explorers had been very active, and friars, in particular, seem to have wandered singly or in small groups all over the eastern trade routes. Some of these men wrote accounts of their travels, and these form the main source of our knowledge of the state of Indian Christianity at the time, together with the journals of the administrators who worked in the Portuguese centres which were established on the west coast of India. These accounts give us only one side of the picture and there is, unfortunately, hardly anything from the Indian side of the encounter, except one or two Syriac letters, and even these are written, not by Indians, but by the Syrian prelates who were ruling the Church when the Portuguese arrived.

The period under review is not only well documented from the Portuguese side; it forms a very convenient unit for consideration, as it begins with the landing of the Portuguese on Malabar soil in 1500, when the Admiral Peter Alvares Cabrol came to Cranganore and first met many Christians of St Thomas, and it ends with the Synod of Diamper in 1599 when it seemed as if the whole community had been brought securely under Portuguese control and Roman obedience, assimilated in doctrine and ceremonial to the customs of the Christian West, with the local peculiarities that it had acquired during the centuries largely done away.

The Portuguese set out on their voyages of discovery in the fifteenth century with a twofold motive. First they wanted to expand their trade and to enrich themselves and their nation as quickly as possible; and there was also a genuine religious motive. The enthusiasm for religion which animated their king and ensured that every ship that sailed carried with it priests to minister to those on board made the Portuguese regard the evangelization of the natives wherever they settled as a governmental and national responsibility. When Vasco da Gama first landed on Indian soil he was concerned first with commercial possibilities, but he also expected to find fellow Christians and was eager to discover relics of St Thomas, venerated then as Apostle of India. This expectation led to an incident which has often been recounted.

Vasco da Gama reached Calicut in May 1498. There he and his party visited a Hindu temple and, thinking an image of Kāḷi represented the Virgin Mary, began to pray to it. The account says that the people called out 'Mary', which led to this confusion. The people were either saying the goddess was *Māri* (Kāḷi) or else saying *Māṛi* ('Get out of the way')—addressed to the crowd of small boys who would inevitably have accompanied the party. Probably also the dark atmosphere of the temple, with its twinkling lights before images and its garlands of flowers, and possibly worshippers signing themselves with the swastika, which does look very like the sign of the cross, may have contributed to their confusion. 'Only one, Juan de Sa, who had some doubt of the matter, in making his genuflexions said, "If this be the devil, I worship God", which made da Gama smile.'[1]

In 1500 Peter Alvares Cabrol landed at Cranganore and found many 'Christians of St Thomas' [*sic*] there.[2] He took one man, Joseph, an adventurer who had already been to the Patriarch of Babylon ten years before, back with him to Europe. Joseph went to Lisbon and thence to Rome (where the Pope received him), Venice, Jerusalem and back. A book was later published, usually described as *Novus Orbis* or *The Travels of Joseph the Indian*, which contains a description of the Malabar Church. The value of

[1] Faria de Sousa, *Portuguese Asia* (Engl. trans.) I, p. 16.

[2] Diogo do Couto, *Da Asia*, decadas I–LVI, cap. VIII, quoted in *Some Elucidations* by Bp Matthew de Oliveira Xavier of Cochin.

the book is vitiated by the fact that the editor admitted he could hardly understand Joseph's speech. The description of the Church as having a supreme head, twelve cardinals, two patriarchs and many other high hierarchs cannot be taken seriously.[1]

Vasco da Gama arrived in India for the second time in 1502. This time he came to Cochin and was visited by a deputation of Christians living near Cranganore who said they wanted protection against Muslims and heathen so that the remnants of Christianity left there by St Thomas might not entirely disappear. They submitted themselves to the admiral as representative of the King of Portugal and handed over a staff of authority. This was a red-coloured stick decorated with silver, with three silver bells on top. Da Gama seems to have accepted it as of far more significance than it actually was, as do Couto tells us he received it with great pomp, dressing his ships and saluting with all his guns.[2] The Portuguese connected the incident with the Christian dynasty the Pope thought was extant in 1439,[3] and considered they had thus taken over suzerainty of the Christians. Gouvea[4] says that in former times the Christians had elected a king to act as their overlord and get justice for them from the petty kings in whose territory Christian groups were settled. 'Acting upon their resolution, they chose as their first king one Beliarte, whose title was King of the Christians of St Thomas, and for some years they were in this power of having a distinct king', until the dynasty came to an end and the local King of Diamper took over his jurisdiction and properties, and then, when these rajas ceased, the King of Cochin 'claimed to have more jurisdiction and right on the Christians of St Thomas than the other kings in whose lands they dwell'.[5]

[1] Translated by Simon Grynaeus (Basle, 1532). Thomas Astley, in his *Voyages* (London, 1754), I, p. 48, dismisses Joseph's book as short and not very satisfactory; Asseman, *Bibliotheca orientalis*, however, treats him as a serious authority. According to Ferroli (p. 68), it is 'an unreliable translation of *Paesi nuovamente retrovati et novo mondo de Alberico*, by Fracan-Montalboddo (Venice, 1507).

[2] Do Couto, *Da Asia*, decada XII, cap. V, pp. 289, 290. Maffei (in 1589), Gouvea and Faria de Sousa repeat this story.

[3] See p. 84.

[4] Antony de Gouvea was an Augustinian monk who was entrusted by his Order with the preparation of an eulogy of Menezes's work in the Serra. He was studying the *Prima* in Goa at the time, and had not accompanied Menezes. He made a careful record based on three main sources: (i) a treatise by Roz describing the Archbishop's visitation; (ii) a fuller account by Mechior Blas, who accompanied Menezes and wrote a daily journal; (iii) consultation with Fr Blaise of St Mary, the Archbishop's confessor on the journey.

[5] Gouvea, *Jornada*, p. 22. The references are to Glen's French translation of 1606. There has been discussion about the historicity of this statement. T. K. Joseph seems to accept the Christian dynasty as a fact (*Malabar Christians and*

We have a document which tells of this meeting of Portuguese and Indian Christians from the Indian side, and shows how glad the Indians were at the prospect of an alliance which would strengthen their hands. This document is a letter written by four bishops sent to India by the Patriarch of Babylon. It tells in some detail the way in which the Franks (Portuguese) first came to Malabar. The first ships took a year to reach India but the next fleet that came used the monsoon and got to Calicut in only six months. The Muslims of Calicut, jealous of their monopoly of trade,[1] incited the Samorin against them, so that he killed seventy Portuguese and five priests who were with them. The rest took refuge with the Raja of Cochin and were rescued from the armies of Calicut, which had followed them down, by the timely arrival of other Portuguese ships, whose forces defeated the invaders and drove them back. The Portuguese then established forts at Cochin and Cannanore. The four Nestorian bishops on arrival in the country (1503) went first to Cannanore and were hospitably received. They remained with the Portuguese two and a half months and one day celebrated their liturgy after the Portuguese priests had said mass. After this, they went south, eight days' journey, to their own Christians.[2]

We are not concerned here to follow the Portuguese attempts to secure the support of local kings in their struggle against the Moors

their Ancient Documents, p. 8). K. N. Daniel does not; he quotes de Souza (*Oriente conquistado*, I, pt. II, cod. II, p. 17) who says that King Beliarte was not a Christian but a Hindu who ruled from Koyoor. There was trouble between Muslims and Christians, the former supported by the Cochin raja and the latter by Beliarte. The Christians were successful; and as the price of his protection Beliarte demanded not only an annual tax from them but also declared himself 'Defender and Protector and King of the St Thomas Christians'. The successors of this dynasty would naturally wish to take over such an assumed authority, but apparently they were not powerful enough to enforce it or to be of any service to the Christians. So when the Portuguese came, the St Thomas Christians were delighted at the prospect of getting a new protector who was also a Christian like themselves. Daniel conjectures that the rod, which has often been called a 'sceptre' by writers on the subject (forgetful perhaps of the fact that this is not a usual ornament of a petty king) was perhaps the 'parkkol', mentioned as a permitted ornament in the copper plates. At the end of the fifteenth century only three kings, the Koḷatiri of Cannanore, the Samorin of Calicut and the Tiruvaṭi of Venāṭ (the district from Quilon to Cape Comorin) had sovereign rights. There were nine minor kingdoms, including Cochin (K. M. Panikkar, *Malabar and the Portuguese*, pp. 5–7). See also *Kēraḷa Society Papers* (1932), series 10, p. 34.

[1] The Arabs had treaties with the State of Venice. The coming of the Portuguese threatened this joint monopoly.

[2] Asseman, III, p. 590; translated by Mingana, *The Early Spread of Christianity in India*, pp. 36ff. There is another Syrian MS. (25 of Paris. R.O.C. 1912) which repeats some of the facts given in this letter; Mingana, pp. 82, 83.

(Muslims), but the insecurity of the newly built Portuguese forts made the enlistment of local allies of cardinal importance and the obvious allies were their fellow Christians. Both sides realized that a firm alliance would be of the greatest benefit. The Christians by themselves were not always strong enough to get their rights from local kings. Yet they were a powerful community, fairly prosperous, with a good part of the pepper trade in their hands, and enjoying a considerable status in society. Moreover, they were trained fighters. We find their bishop, Mar Jacob, writing to the Pope about 1523, explaining why the Christians at that time had not committed themselves fully to the Portuguese cause. He said that the Muslims had grossly deceived his people about Portuguese intentions but that a priest, Master Joam Caro, had now told them the truth of the matter. The bishop had accordingly gone with the Malabar Christian leaders to meet the Portuguese in their fort and factory at Cochin, where they were well received. 'This I did many times until I had brought them [the Malabar Christians] to love thee, and then they agreed and swore to me, never more to sell the pepper to the Moors and to bring it clean and dry to thy factory, as indeed they are doing, as thou canst see by the shrinkage, which thou shalt see of this and the last two years. And further I have won all these Christians of this country for thy service, so that when thou shalt be in need of them, thou shalt find in it over twenty-five thousand warriors.'[1]

Gouvea said that the Christians supplied the Raja of Cochin with an army of fifty thousand gunsmen, and so the severance of this connexion would weaken that king very greatly. He said further: 'The main strength of the rajas consists in the Christians of St Thomas they have. They are fine gunsmen and so good shots that they rarely miss fire, and from early age they are brought up gun-in-hand and thus turn out splendid hunters.'[2] He said that all went about with swords and shields, and some with guns and lances, which they left at home only when going to church, or when moving about in their own lands.

The way of life of the Christians is described by Gouvea and other Portuguese writers, and some of the information they give will be found in Part II of this book. Here it is enough to say that there is no evidence at all that the Christians were considered

[1] The letter is quoted in full in Ferroli, *The Jesuits in Malabar*, pp. 110–13.
[2] Gouvea, book I, chapters 15, 19.

a foreign community. They were a recognized part of Malabar society and that society had coloured their understanding of Christianity. At the same time they were not a wholly isolated Christian remnant. Some Portuguese writers say that for long periods the Indian Church was without bishops, but there is no evidence that this was their normal state. The document already quoted which gives the story of the first encounters with the Portuguese from the Indian side was written to the Patriarch of Babylon[1] in 1504 by (Chaldean or East Syrian) bishops who had arrived in India. They had been sent in response to a deputation from Malabar received by the Patriarch and Catholicos Mar Simeon in 1490. The document tells the story as follows:

'In the year one thousand eight hundred and one of Alexander (A.D. 1490) three believing men came from the remote countries of India to the Catholicos Mar Simeon, Patriarch of the East, in order to bring bishops to their countries. By the will of God, one of them died on the way, and two of them reached the Catholicos alive. The Catholicos, who was then in the town of Gazarta of Baith Zabdai[2] was greatly pleased with them. One of them was called George and the other Joseph. The Catholicos ordained both of them priests in the holy Church of St George at Gazarta, because they were well instructed, and sent them to the holy monastery of St Eugenius. They took from there two monks, the name of both of whom was Joseph, and the Catholicos ordained both of them bishops in the Church of St George. He named one Thomas and the other John, and he wrote to them admirable letters patent signed with his own seal. After having prayed for them and blessed them, he dispatched them to India in the company of the Indians. By the assistance of Christ, our Lord, the four of them reached there alive.

'The faithful were greatly pleased with them, and went to meet them joyfully with Gospel, Cross, thurible and candles, and ushered them in with great pomp with psalms and canticles. They consecrated altars and ordained many priests, because the Indians were for a long time without bishops. Bishop John remained in India,

[1] It is disputed whether this Patriarch acknowledged Roman supremacy. The Romo-Syrians maintain that he was under the Pope, but this view is entirely opposed to the view that the East Syrian Church, whatever it was doctrinally, was formally in schism by the recognition of the Catholicos as Patriarch at the Synod of Makarbte in 424 during the catholicate of Dadyeshu, 421–56. Vine, *The Nestorian Churches*, p. 48; see Fortescue, *Lesser Eastern Churches*, p. 51.

[2] Jezireh on the upper Tigris.

and Bishop Thomas, his companion, returned after a short time to the Catholicos.[1] He was succeeded by Mar Elijah, the Catholicos and Patriarch, who also took from the monastery of St Eugenius three pious monks, one of whom, David Arrika, he ordained Metropolitan and renamed Mar Yabh Alaha. The next one, called brother George, he ordained bishop and renamed Mar Jacob. He ordained all of them and sent them to the country of India, to the islands of the sea which are inside Java and to China. The four[2] of them reached there in peace and safety, by the assistance of Christ, their Lord, and they saw Mar John, bishop of India alive. The latter, and all the blessed believers who were there, were greatly pleased by the arrival of the fathers. A year after they sent a letter to Mar Elijah, the Catholicos (but before its arrival the Catholicos Mar Elijah died and was succeeded by Mar Simon). In the letter they said...:

'"Now we would inform thy love that by the assistance of God, and through thy accepted prayers, we arrived in the blessed country of India in good health. Thanks be to God, the Lord of all, who does not confound those who trust in Him! All the Christians of this side were greatly pleased with us, and our Father Mar John is still alive and hale and sends thee his greetings. There are here about thirty thousand families of Christians, our co-religionists, and they implore the Lord to grant thee a long life. They have begun to build new churches, are prosperous in every respect, and living in peace and security: may God be praised! As to the monastery of St Thomas the apostle, some Christian men have gone into it, have inhabited it and are now busy restoring it; it is distant about twenty-five days from the above-mentioned Christians; it is on the shores of the sea in a town called Mylapore, in the country of Silam, one of the Indian countries. The countries of India are very numerous and powerful, and their distance is about six months' journey. Each country has a special name by which it is known, and our own country in which the Christians are found is called Malabar. It has about twenty towns, out of which three are renowned and powerful: Karangol, Pallur and Kullam,[3] with others that are near them. They contain Christians and churches, and are in the vicinity of the large

[1] Catholicos Simeon died in 1502.

[2] Mar Yahb Alaha, Mar Jacob, Mar Denha and another, possibly Mar Thomas, but we do not know.

[3] Cranganore, Paṛavūr or Pālayūr, Quilon.

and powerful city of Calicut, the inhabitants of which are idol-worshipping pagans.'"[1]

It is plain from this letter that while the Malabar Church was truly Indian, it depended on the East Syrian Church for its theology, its liturgy and its bishops.

Gouvea truly says that the greater part of the questions and debates which the Portuguese had to raise with those ancient Christians did not concern the faith and law of our Lord Jesus Christ but rather their spiritual and temporal government.[2] The Portuguese held the Roman obedience to be an essential mark of the Church and they therefore were compelled to persuade their new allies to accept the Pope as their true Patriarch, and in the event of persuasion failing, to force them to it. This was not an easy task, since the Indian Christians were very conservative and had no wish to transfer their allegiance from the Patriarch of Babylon to the Pope, although at the same time their commercial sense warned them it would be politic to appear to accept the Portuguese demands. They therefore promised more than once that they would abjure all heresies and submit to the Pope of Rome as the true pastor of all Christian people, as this seemed a condition of keeping the very profitable pepper trade in their hands. But it is clear that they had no intention of keeping these promises, and they reckoned that no Portuguese other than a few religious would be likely to penetrate far from territory protected by garrison and guns into the Serra, the hilly country where the majority of Christians lived. For nearly a hundred years their estimate of the situation proved correct, until a new and very determined young archbishop was appointed to Goa, Alexis de Menezes, who, against all advice and the pleading of his ecclesiastical subordinates and his civil governor, came to Travancore and carried out a thorough visitation. But for nearly a century their methods of procrastination worked. Trade was maintained and their old ways were undisturbed, except by occasional preaching friars or the activity of the Jesuit College at Vaippikkoṭṭa.

Mar Jacob, whom we have already met, remained at his post from 1503 until his death in 1549.[3] His first contacts with the

[1] Asseman, III, p. 590; translation from Mingana, pp. 36ff.
[2] Gouvea, p. 24.
[3] Mar John seems to have died shortly after the arrival of the four bishops. Mar Yahb Alaha and Mar Denha seem also to have died soon after. Ferroli, p. 103.

Portuguese had been friendly and they seemed to have remained so for the next twenty years. In 1506 the Portuguese governor of Cochin made a treaty with the Rani of Quilon, one clause of which provided for the rebuilding of the church of the St Thomas Christians and the restoration of their ancient privileges. Similarly, in 1510 the viceroy gave the bishops of the St Thomas Christians one thousand *fanams* to restore the church at Cranganore. In 1517 Portuguese and St Thomas Christians went together on a pilgrimage to Mylapore, where the King of Portugal was restoring the ruined church. But after this the tone of the documents changes, and the explanation is given in the letter of Mar Jacob of 1523. The Arab traders had influenced the Christians against their new allies by stories of dishonest dealing and ulterior motives and difficulties in trade transactions arose. Also friars had begun to penetrate into the Christian churches and there had insisted on saying mass according to the Latin rite. This might not have caused offence in itself, but soon they began to attack the local way of doing things, to accuse the Christians of being 'pestilential Nestorian heretics', and to say that the baptism they administered was invalid. One of these friars was said by his own vicar-general to have 'a hard head and a very hot temper' and by another 'to know very little and be very dissolute'.[1] But others were more tactful. Fr Joam Caro, O.P., seems to have lived for some time with Mar Jacob and was the bishop's secretary when he wrote to the Pope, and also when he wrote to the King of Portugal about the same time, 1523. This letter reveals that the king had been paying the bishop a salary and had succeeded in procuring his complete subservience. He says that Fr Caro is writing to defend the rite he and his church use in baptism, and that he would prefer the Portuguese priests not to baptize his people with the Latin rite, as the people are accustomed to their own rite and bishop. But if the king insisted, he would allow even re-baptism. 'In the meantime he takes these Portuguese priests with him to get the people accustomed to them, and that they might instruct his Christians in the matter of faith, that after his death they might accept them in his place.'[2] It is clear from other letters still extant that all the Portuguese clergy who had dealings with him were by no means satisfied with Mar Jacob's orthodoxy or good intentions, but the Franciscans stood by him

[1] Ferroli, pp. 103–4.
[2] *Kēraḷa Soc. Papers* (1932), series 10, p. 274.

and travelled about his diocese with him.[1] St Francis Xavier writes to the King of Portugal in 1548 praising the 'good and holy old man' and complaining of the want of courtesy shown him by the king and almost all in India. He says 'He has been working much among the St Thomas Christians, and now in his all but decrepit old age he is very obedient to the customs of the Holy Mother the Church of Rome'.[2] The fact that the Franciscans alone were caring for him suggests that his own people, in spite of their usual great reverence for a bishop, felt he had deserted the faith, and had left him alone. Mar Jacob died in 1549.

At about this time the mother church of the St Thomas Christians, or at least, since we should not prejudge the issue, the East Syrian or Chaldean Church from which its bishops had been coming, was split by family feuds. The Patriarch Simon bar Mama died in 1551 and a number of bishops duly elected his nephew, Simon bar Denha, to succeed him, as had become the custom. But others thought a monk called John Sulaka more suitable and elected him. To strengthen his position Sulaka favoured the Franciscan missionaries who had come among them and with their aid went to Rome where he made a confession of faith before Julius III and was ordained Patriarch in 1553, and was given a bishop, Ambrose Buttigeg, and a priest, Zahara, to help him in his work. Sulaka returned to his country but was arrested by the civil power and murdered in prison in 1555. Another bishop, Abdiso, was chosen by his party to succeed him and received the pallium from Pius IV.[3] Abdiso immediately set about consolidating his position and establishing his claim to be lawful Patriarch of the whole East Syrian communion (which was of course disputed by the other Patriarch, Simon bar Denha) and so appointed two bishops for the Indian Church, Mar Joseph and Mar Elias, and sent them with Buttigeg and Zahara.

Abdiso overlooked the fact (or may have been ignorant of it) that all Indian Christians had been placed by Rome under the patronage of the King of Portugal, and so the arrival of the party at Goa in

[1] See Mar Jacob's letter to the King of Portugal 1530; published in *Kēraḷa Soc. Papers* (1932), series 10, pp. 274, 275 and Ferroli, p. 113. In 1545 the Franciscans established a seminary at Cranganore to train men for the priesthood, but all the education was in Latin and the Church never allowed any of the students to be ordained in the Serra. Fr Vincent de Langes was Principal.

[2] Ferroli, pp. 149, 150; *Life and Letters of St Francis Xavier* (1872), by H. J. Coleridge, II, p. 82.

[3] 1555–67.

1556 was not greeted with marked enthusiasm. On the contrary, the Portuguese put them into a monastery at Bassein and kept them under observation for eighteen months. They made a great impression by their piety and earnestness and were taught to say mass in Latin according to the Roman rite. They wanted to go to Malabar but were dissuaded on the ground that the Bishop of Goa was the only lawful bishop of Malabar and of the whole of India and of all parts of the Orient conquered by Portugal. The writer of the report, Fr Antonio, suggested that the King of Portugal should procure a bishop for Cochin with special jurisdiction over the Malabar Christians and should ask the Pope to instruct the Patriarch that on no account should he send any more Chaldean bishops.[1]

In 1558 Mar Joseph was allowed by the Portuguese to go south to Cochin, probably to try to deal with another Chaldean bishop who had arrived in the Serra, presumably from the other party in the East Syrian Church, which had not come under Roman obedience. He was accompanied by Buttigeg and Zahara, Mar Elias returning to Mosul. Buttigeg died almost at once, but Zahara accompanied Mar Joseph and a report of their work is extant.[2] They introduced confession, confirmation and extreme unction into the Malabar Church, which seems to have been ignorant of these rites. They also communicated with the other bishop, of whom nothing else is known, and persuaded him to return home.[3]

But Mar Joseph's attachment to the old way of faith was apparently revived by his contact with the Indian Christians, and according to the Jesuit historians he began to change his ways and later on contradicted the teaching he had been giving, said that confession was not essential, image worship was idolatry and the Virgin should be called Mother of Christ, not Mother of God.[4] Perhaps this change of attitude was influenced by resentment at the fact that the first Jesuit missionary to the St Thomas Christians, Fr Carneyro, had arrived and was also working among them. This

[1] Letter of Antonio da Porto to the King of Portugal; reproduced by Ferroli, pp. 158ff.

[2] Report to Pius IV; see G. Beltrami, *La Chiesa Caldea nel secolo dell' unione* pp. 47, 48, quoted by Ferroli, p. 153.

[3] Ferroli, p. 153.

[4] The Sulaka line eventually ceased to be uniat and is the modern Mar Shimun line. It is clear that the link with Rome was always rather nominal, which would explain the very slight attachment to Roman doctrine and obedience shown by the uniat bishops, Joseph and Abraham, in Malabar. See Vine, *The Nestorian Churches*, pp. 171–3.

man soon detected heresy in the bishop's teaching and tried to confront him in public disputation, which the bishop always managed to avoid. Fr Carneyro went so far as to persuade a raja, with whom the bishop had taken refuge, to arrest him as a disturber of the peace. The bishop evaded this, but was eventually caught by the Portuguese and taken to Cochin, where the Jesuits forced him to make public confession and retraction of his errors. Not content with this, they sent him to Goa, and from Goa to Lisbon. Here, however, he met the queen and Cardinal Henry and charmed them by his courteous behaviour and his professions of faith. They sent him back to India in 1565, but he again began to preach the doctrine of the East Syrian Church, unmodified by the Roman connexion. Again he was arrested, and tried by the First Council of Goa in 1567, which found him guilty of heresy. Sent to Portugal again he satisfied the authorities of his complete innocence. From Portugal Joseph went to Rome, and it was reported that he would have been created cardinal had he not died.[1]

Portuguese action against their bishop and the novel teaching which had come to the Serra through the Portuguese (who did not agree with the go-slow policy previously adopted by the friars and who made no attempt to hide their abhorrence of much of the faith and practice which the Indians had for centuries accepted as orthodox) made the Indians despair of seeing Mar Joseph again when he was first deported and they sent to the Patriarch, asking for another bishop. The Patriarch of the non-Roman line received the deputation and sent Mar Abraham back with them.[2] This bishop managed to avoid Portuguese detection on his journey and arrived in Malabar, where he was warmly welcomed. But, contrary to expectation, Mar Joseph did return, armed with a brief from the Pope giving him authority and commission to teach the doctrine which his Patriarch (Abdiso) had professed.[3] The two bishops both claimed jurisdiction and the Indian Church was divided in its loyalty. Mar Joseph, on the strength of his brief, now asked

[1] Fr Roz, *De erroribus Nestorianorum* (1586), introduction, p. 7 (edited in *Orientalia christiana*, XI (1928), pt. 1). On the other hand Beltrami, quoted in *Subsidium ad bullarium patronatus Portugalliae* (1903), by Dom Mattheus, pp. 33, 34, says that the Acta of the Council of Goa make no mention of heresy in connexion with Mar Joseph.

[2] Fr Ferroli and the other Roman historians must be wrong in supposing that Mar Abdiso sent Mar Abraham. The later history is inconceivable on this supposition.

[3] Brief of 27 June 1564 of Pius IV.

Portuguese help, and they arrested Mar Abraham in his turn and shipped him to Europe. On the way he escaped and reached Abdiso, who wrote to the Archbishop of Goa that Abraham had become entirely obedient to the great Church of Rome and that he had consecrated him metropolitan and sent him to Pius IV. The Pope discovered that the consecration was invalid as he was not previously in priest's orders and so had him re-ordained privately, up to consecration as bishop, after receiving his profession of faith. He then sent him back to India, requesting the Patriarch to divide the Serra (or territory of the St Thomas Christians) between Abraham and Joseph.[1] This was done by Abdiso who informed the Archbishop of Goa of the new arrangement. A strange feature of the correspondence is the acknowledgment by the Pope that the diocese of the Serra belonged to the Patriarch, as the Portuguese claimed it was a part of the Portuguese patronage and so came directly under the jurisdiction of Goa.[2]

Abdiso's arrangement was never carried out: for, before his letter reached Malabar, Mar Joseph had been arrested again and sent to Rome, where he died in 1569. Mar Abraham arrived in Goa from Rome with his letters in 1568, but the Portuguese were unwilling to allow him to enter his diocese, holding that he had tricked the Pope into misunderstanding his true position. He escaped, however, and reached Malabar, and the authorities of Goa took no further action. He re-ordained all the priests he had ordained during his previous stay in the country, but had as little contact as possible with the Portuguese. He refused to go to a council at Goa in 1575, fearing further imprisonment, but seems to have trusted the Jesuits at Cochin to understand and interpret his position.

The Council of Goa resolved that the diocese of the Serra should be governed by a bishop appointed by the King of Portugal, and not by the Chaldean Patriarch, or if this transfer of authority was not expedient, that the Archbishop of Ankamāli (the traditional title of the Bishop of the St Thomas Christians) should be bound to attend the Council of Goa.[3] Any bishop coming to the Serra must first present his papers at Goa. The Portuguese knew that both

[1] Ferroli, pp. 162ff.

[2] Letter of Pius IV to the Archbishop of Goa 23 February 1565. See Ferroli, pp. 152, 153, etc.

[3] In 1598 the Portuguese king presented a Jesuit as Bishop of the Serra, but no action was taken because the church of Ankamāli was not then in the king's patronage; Ferroli, p. 291.

Patriarchs of the East Syrians would try to assert their authority over the Indian Church. It would be difficult to know which party a bishop belonged to, and even the uniat Patriarch was not, in Portuguese eyes, as orthodox as could be wished. Mar Abraham realized that if the Pope agreed to the resolution he would become more or less a suffragan of the Archbishop of Goa. So he sent a correct profession of faith to the Pope (Gregory XIII) and wrote to the Patriarch warning him that his jurisdiction and his revenues were in danger. He also said that five bishops were necessary for the Serra, but that they must be Easterns and not Latins. Mar Abraham also strengthened his friendship with the Jesuits and in 1577 a residence for them was built at Vaipikkoṭṭa, which developed into a seminary for the education of priests. The Jesuits, in return, took the part of Mar Abraham and obtained from the Pope a brief naming the Indian, Archdeacon George, administrator of the diocese, in the event of Mar Abraham's death, and nominating him as Bishop of Pālayūr.[1] He was never consecrated by Rome but the appointment was to cause the Portuguese a good deal of trouble in after years. Mar Abraham himself had written to the Pope in 1575 explaining why he was not going to the Council of Goa. A letter written a few years after complains of what he had suffered from the Portuguese and says how helpful the Jesuits were.[2] The Pope wrote to Goa and to the King of Portugal about the complaints, but told Mar Abraham that he must go to future Councils, with the Pope's own promise of safe conduct.

Meanwhile Portuguese fears were realized and a bishop named Mar Simon arrived from the Nestorian Patriarch. This man won some support, and seems to have been encouraged by some Franciscans. He was caught eventually by the Portuguese and appealed to Rome. At Rome he was instructed and there was some idea of sending him back to India, but instead he was sent to Lisbon, where he died in 1599.[3] Before Simon left, he had appointed a vicar-general, a priest called Jacob, who carried on the fight against Mar Abraham and the Portuguese. He died in 1596, of a strange disease which took him off in three days and which

[1] Ferroli, p. 164.
[2] 3 January 1579.
[3] Ferroli, p. 169. See Mackenzie, *State of Christianity in Travancore*, p. 21. Mar Abdiso in a letter to Gregory XIII, 13 January 1584 says he had no credentials from anyone and was a simple priest (Fr Bernard's *Mar Thomma Kristyānikaḷ*, p. 42).

Gouvea says was a miraculous punishment for his blasphemous denial of Mary's perpetual virginity.[1]

From the Portuguese point of view these irritations were offset by the remarkably rapid progress of the new Jesuit seminary at Vaipikkoṭṭa. There seemed every prospect that it would contribute greatly to the conversion of the Church to Roman ways because the mistake of the 'foreigners' of the Franciscan seminary at Cranganore had been avoided. About fifty students were living in the seminary, studying Latin and Chaldean, morals, theology and liturgy. Fr Francis Roz, afterwards to be Bishop of the Serra, was teaching and perfecting his Malayāḷam and Syriac, and acting as general adviser to Mar Abraham. Worship was celebrated in Syriac, according to the old rites, as well as in Latin. In 1583 a provincial synod was held at Ankamāli, at which many reforms were accepted by the bishop, his clergy and lay representatives.

In 1585 Abraham had enough confidence in the Pope's safe-conduct to go to Goa for the third Provincial Council, where a number of reforms, largely relating to the conduct and maintenance of the clergy, were decreed. Fr Roz was appointed to help Mar Abraham carry out the reforms, including the correction of the Chaldean books used in the diocese. But a year after Fr Roz wrote his treatise *De erroribus Nestorianorum* and there says in the preface that Mar Abraham had fallen away from the truth. He had re-ordained his priests for the third time (for the Council of Goa had said the previous ordination was invalid because there was no wine in the chalice at the *porrectio instrumentorum*), but made no move to correct the books or to do the other things he had promised. Roz accused Abraham formally in this book of being a Nestorian heretic.[2]

[1] Gouvea, p. 54. He was buried in the church near Muṟṟucira which he had built.

[2] The doctrinal position of the Church before the Portuguese found it has been much disputed in Travancore. Fr Panjikaran and other Romo-Syrians maintain that it was Catholic and that Mar Jacob was a Roman Catholic bishop (*The Syrian Church in Malabar*). But the book of Fr Roz seems to me to establish beyond doubt that the St Thomas Christians were formally Nestorians. This question is examined, however, in Part III of this book. Some of Fr Panjikaran's arguments are answered in 'Rome and the Malabar Church', by K. N. Daniel in *Kēraḷa Society Papers*, series 10, with note by T. K. Joseph (see Ferroli, p. 173). Cf. also a letter of Fr Abraham di Giorgio, S.J., saying that 'the Archbishop here is a heretical Nestorian, and lives worse than a pagan, a beastly and carnal life' (Ferroli, p. 173). Gouvea (p. 42) says that a letter from Abraham to the Patriarch was intercepted, where he speaks of yielding to the Portuguese demand for ecclesiastical supremacy under duress and says they were like a hammer over the anvil; he says that the bishops of India had accepted his profession of faith at Goa.

A crisis developed in 1590 when Mar Abraham refused to ordain the students of the Vaipikkoṭṭa seminary, and came to a head when he was summoned to the fourth Provincial Council at Goa, and refused to go. All the papers about him were sent from Goa to the Pope, who issued a brief ordering the newly appointed Archbishop of Goa, a man of thirty-five named Alexis de Menezes, to inquire into the case and keep Mar Abraham in custody if found guilty, pending orders from Rome.[1]

But the Portuguese never brought Abraham to trial in person. He was kept at Ankamāli, the old headquarters of the diocese, which was away from the sea coast, far from effective Portuguese power. In 1595 he had fallen ill, and apparently been reconciled with the Jesuits and professed allegiance to Rome, but he fell ill again and died in 1597. He was the last Metran or Metropolitan of the undivided church of the Christians of St Thomas. Before the death of Mar Abraham the authorities at Goa had received another brief from the Pope ordering that on his death a vicar apostolic be appointed to rule the see, apparently ignoring the previous order appointing Archdeacon George to this work.[2] Mar Abraham is said also to have nominated the archdeacon as vicar on his death-bed, and to have sent to the Patriarch for another bishop. Menezes had heard of this move and had sent strict orders to Ormus, to the Portuguese there, to intercept any cleric coming from Chaldea or Persia.[3] It is said that a bishop and a priest coming from the Patriarch were stopped and sent home again.[4]

On Abraham's death Menezes, who was touring north of Goa, at once issued letters patent appointing Roz vicar-general of the Serra, but this was considered unwise by the more experienced Jesuits at Goa and the document was not published. The archbishop was persuaded on his return to issue another order appointing the archdeacon vicar-general, with Fr Francis Roz as his assistant; but this proved unacceptable to the people of the Serra. Menezes gave way to pressure on this point also, and appointed the archdeacon sole governor, on condition that he made an acceptable profession of faith. The archdeacon agreed to this condition, but said it would be better to defer this action until Easter time, when a great concourse of the people would assemble, and the action

[1] Brief of 27 February 1595 of Clement VIII.
[2] 21 January 1597. [3] Gouvea, p. 52.
[4] Geddes, *History of the Church of Malabar*, p. 41.

could be performed fittingly in their presence.[1] Menezes agreed, but it is clear that both he and the archdeacon, who was also a young man, were feeling their way, and taking the measure of each other. The course of events following this is told at length in Gouvea and most of the histories. It is a story of the European's determination to see his will carried out, a will he firmly believed to be the will of God, and the Indian's intense dislike of this threat to the whole way of life which the Christians of St Thomas had inherited from their fathers. The Christians were told that their faith and their forms of worship were unsound, that their rejection of images, which was derived from their mother Church but was also a mark of their separation from their Hindu neighbours, was heretical, and that many of their social customs were unacceptable.

The local rajas who had for centuries recognized that they were bound to maintain the honourable social position and ancient privileges of the Christians disliked the quarrel but were more afraid of offending the Portuguese, with their power and wealth,[2] than of upsetting their Christian subjects; and strong pressure was brought upon them by Menezes to assist his plans. The history of Portuguese dealings with their bishops was well known to the Malabar Church. If they had failed to persuade the Syrian bishops to submit by money and flattery, they had used force and imprisonment, and Archdeacon George and the leading Christians were afraid of similar treatment. So the archdeacon for some time tried a policy of making easy promises, but not keeping them, and of staying in the inland parts, away from the Portuguese. After four months he called the clergy together at Ankamāli and discussed the situation with them, making them promise to obey him alone, to reject any bishop unless he came from Babylon, and to resist all change. He was frightened, however, by news of the archbishop's intention to come to the Serra in person, and so made a confession of faith before Franciscans. He refused to do so before Jesuits, knowing, as is clear from their writings, that they already distrusted him, and possibly thinking it easier to deal with foreigners who had not learned Malayāḷam so well as the Jesuits. It may be observed here that rivalry and mistrust between Portuguese

[1] Gouvea says that this procrastination was in the hope that a bishop would arrive from Babylon before the date proposed for the profession; p. 59.

[2] All through this period Portuguese squadrons were active on the sea, and States which did not fall in with Portuguese wishes were attacked and their towns sacked.

Jesuits and Italian friars undoubtedly assisted the archdeacon's policy of procrastination. The archdeacon's profession made no mention of the primacy of the Pope, and of the Church of Rome as the sole mistress of all Christian Churches in the world. Menezes required him to make it again, and he did so, but spoiled the effect by saying that he had not understood what was said, as he knew no Latin, and that he acknowledged the Pope as head of the Latin Church, but not of the universal Church. This was profoundly unsatisfactory to Menezes, who saw that the reforms he desired in the Indian Church, and the authority he claimed over it as archbishop of the East, could be based only on acceptance of this fundamental tenet. He decided therefore to come to Malabar himself, though his advisers, both civil and ecclesiastical, did everything in their power to stop him. But it is clear from Gouvea's *Jornada*, even though it was written as a tribute to Menezes by one of his own Order of Augustinian friars, that the archbishop was a man of great determination and personal courage, and that he allowed the arguments and pleadings of his colleagues no more to deflect him then from what he believed to be his duty, than later, during his visitation, did he allow the frequent threats to his life from both Christians and Hindus to deter him.

Menezes landed in the Portuguese settlement of Cochin on 1 February 1599, and after settling various civil matters, he sent for the archdeacon. The story of this first meeting between the two men, as it is recorded by Gouvea, shows well the attitude of each.[1] No marked difference in their attitudes is to be seen until the end of this part of the story, which is the complete capitulation of the archdeacon and the pro-patriarch party at the Synod of Diamper. The archdeacon received the summons and decided with the clergy that they would treat the archbishop with courtesy, but make clear to him that they regarded him only as a visiting bishop, having no jurisdiction over the St Thomas Christians. As a safeguard against possible Portuguese treachery he took with him two *paṇikkars*, or teachers of the art of warfare, with three thousand armed men. The archbishop received the archdeacon in a small pavilion with great courtesy, even though the *paṇikkars* stationed themselves on either side of his chair with drawn swords, apparently desirous of the honour of being near the archbishop but really ready to deal with him at the smallest sign of hostility against the archdeacon. No

[1] Gouvea, pp. 139–50.

occasion for violence arose, though the crowd outside got restive when the conversation, which was general and did not deal with any points of disagreement, seemed somewhat prolonged.

The archbishop thought that there was a prospect of overcoming the Indians' fears and suspicions only if he conducted his negotiations within their own territory, so he arranged to go to Vaipikkoṭṭa next day and meet the archdeacon there. He travelled by water accompanied by a considerable suite of Portuguese and was welcomed by the students of the seminary (carefully coached by their Jesuit teachers) with speeches begging him to free their Church from error. The archbishop, in reply, began the work of teaching which he had come to do. Standing with his primatial cross in his hand, and his mitre on his head, he delivered a long sermon on the obedience due to the holy Roman Church, and the great danger they were in from their connexion with the errors of Babylon. He alone was their true pastor, and those who trusted in bishops sent by the Patriarch would finish up in eternal fire. The next day he led a penitential procession and then delivered two sermons, one on purgatory, and the other on confirmation, as the Christians of St Thomas had no knowledge of either. Then he confirmed all members of the parish. This rite, which the archbishop celebrated wherever he could, was much misunderstood both by the Christians and by the Hindu rajas, who interpreted the signing with chrism and the buffet on the cheek as outward signs that the Portuguese had taken Indian subjects under their jurisdiction and had made them their slaves.

The archdeacon was not in the place during these ceremonies but arrived two days later. The archbishop continued to treat him with courtesy and attended the office and the Eucharist he celebrated, but was scandalized to find that the Patriarch of Babylon was referred to both in the office and the mass as the universal Pastor of the Catholic Church. The Jesuits, of course, had been aware of this, but had thought it unwise to press for a change until the seed of truth they were sowing had taken firmer root among the people. But the archbishop felt his silence about such a reference would be a tacit blasphemy, so, without telling anyone of his intentions, he called together the staff and students of the seminary, the archdeacon and his priests, and the Portuguese who were there, and preached to them a most powerful sermon about the obedience all churches owed to their mistress, the Church of Rome, and all

Christians to the Pope. Then he pulled a paper out of his pocket and excommunicated any who called the Patriarch of Babylon universal pastor, or who named him in any act of public worship, as he was a Nestorian heretic, schismatic and outside the Church. This fulmination took everyone by surprise and the archdeacon and the two senior priests with him were at once made to sign the document, which was posted on the church door. The archdeacon and his party then went off, and set up such a lamentation that all the Christians gathered to know what was the matter. They said they wept because the archbishop and the Portuguese were forcing them to leave the law of St Thomas, in which they had been brought up and nourished, and had insulted their Patriarch by whom they had been governed more than twelve hundred years. The crowd was easily inflamed and wanted to go at once to take revenge on the archbishop, but the archdeacon stopped them, pointing out that they could not molest the archbishop in the territory of the Raja of Cochin, the ally of the Portuguese, and that for the time being they must hide their feelings. He said he had signed the excommunication document under duress, and he denied that there was anything in common between the law of St Thomas, to which they belonged, and the law of St Peter. This distinction was afterwards widely canvassed among the people and was still accepted, for instance, at Pālayūr, even after Diamper, where it had been specifically condemned. The archbishop, meanwhile, was being reproached by the Portuguese for his hastiness, but he said that his conscience did not allow him to do anything other than come at once to the principal point of the errors of the Serra. Unmoved he prepared to proceed on his visitation the following day.

In some places, especially in the north, the archbishop was in grave danger, *amouques* vowing to kill him;[1] but he showed no sign of fear and preached everywhere about the one law of Christ which required submission to Christ's Vicar on earth. Some churches he had to force open, and to others the people would not come. He was apparently not satisfied with the progress he was making; for after some time he met the archdeacon and agreed to go to the churches only as a visitor, and to perform no function other than blessing the people pending the calling of a synod, to consider all

[1] 'Amouques' are described by Gouvea as men who take a vow to do something, like killing anyone who has insulted the Christians, and who keep their vow, even at the cost of their own lives.

outstanding questions. But his pastoral compulsion was stronger than his diplomacy and almost immediately he was confirming the people at Purakkaṭ, whose king wished to come into alliance with Portugal and so had threatened punishment if the people did not present themselves to the archbishop and submit to his demands. The archdeacon and his party naturally had full reports of all the archbishop's activities. Their indignation came to a head when the archbishop went to Diamper and then gave notice he would confer orders, summoning the archdeacon to be present. He replied that this was a breach of the agreement they had made, but the archbishop replied that he would exercise jurisdiction according to the brief sent him by the Pope, whom all the world ought to obey. The archdeacon persuaded the local raja to forbid entrance to the church (by the customary mark of sticking a bough within a circle, which Gouvea says was a ban always obeyed), but the archbishop and his ordinands were already within, and the following morning, after examination and vows of loyalty to Rome and abjuration of the Nestorian heresy, thirty-three young men were ordained. The opposition to Menezes increased, and many times his life was threatened by Hindus or Christians in various places, but he was also winning adherents by the dignity and pomp with which he celebrated the sacraments, by presents and courteous behaviour and also by his complete fearlessness. Gouvea says that one reason the Indian priests resented Menezes was that he would not sell the sacraments, while they were accustomed to receive dues when a man came to communion, and they largely depended on such fees, which the Portuguese said was simony. The archbishop spent Holy Week 1599 in Kaṭutturutti, where the ceremonies, carried out in full pontificals and a choir brought from Cochin for the occasion, greatly impressed everyone, especially the veneration of the cross on Good Friday, which appealed to the sense of great reverence the people had for the cross. As a result all the parish came over to his side. Fr Roz arrived on Holy Saturday and was overjoyed to see the change in the people—for on a previous occasion he had had to get the civil authorities to open the church door for him to say mass, and when he had showed them an image of the Virgin they had cried: 'Take it away, we are Christians and do not worship idols or temples.'

The archdeacon's chief instrument in blocking the archbishop's progress was the suspicion of the Hindu kings that Menezes's object in working for the union of the Christians with Rome was to secure their allegiance to Portugal, instead of to their native rulers. He tried to stimulate this fear, so that the rajas were willing to coerce the Christians and prevent them obeying the archbishop. This stratagem was quickly realized and Menezes went to see the most powerful ruler, the Raja of Cochin, and spoke to him harshly, without allowing him to answer a word, insulting his gods and threatening him with hell. The raja apparently swallowed these insults, though he must have been furiously angry, and did all the archbishop wanted. Thus the archdeacon's chief support was taken away and he could hold out no longer. He came and threw himself at the archbishop's feet. He was made to sign a profession of faith and abjuration of Nestorianism, anathematizing his Patriarch as a heretic.[1] He promised to summon all the priests to a synod and to deliver up all church books for correction. This profession was not made publicly, as the archbishop first required, but privately, in the presence of the archbishop and Fr Roz only.

From this time the archdeacon appeared to co-operate loyally with Menezes. He signed the summons to the synod and travelled about meeting the principal men of the Church and explaining the intention of the meeting, while the archbishop was at Paṛavūr, working hard preparing the decrees of the synod, and making other preparations, such as consecrating altar stones for distribution to all the churches. He had already consecrated the holy oils on Maundy Thursday. He ordained fifty young men at Paṛavūr, with the archdeacon assisting, having first taken from them a profession of faith and an oath of allegiance to the Pope and the Church of Rome. At last all was ready and the archbishop left for Diamper, where the synod was to meet.

The synod was opened with great solemnity on 20 June 1599 with the celebration of the mass *Ad tollendum schisma* by the archbishop in the presence of many Portuguese from Cochin, as well as the priests and lay representatives of the St Thomas Christians.[2] Fr Roz preached a sermon on the duty all Christians have of obedience to the Pope. Then the office *Ad incipiendum concilium* and the Pope's briefs authorizing the synod were read. Inter-

[1] See Ferroli, p. 183. His account does not wholly agree with Gouvea.

[2] The synod is fully described in Hough, II, pp. 23–132, who follows Geddes's translation of Gouvea's account. Geddes gives this translation as a kind of appendix numbered pp. 89–443 to his book of 109 pp. J. F. Raulin, *Historia ecclesiae Malabaricae*, gives a full account of the synod. There were present 153 priests and 671 lay proctors (Ferroli, p. 185).

preters were then appointed, since the proceedings were to be in Portuguese. All were invited to contribute anything they could to the discussion, by informing the archbishop beforehand, and priests could propose amendments to the decrees. The discussion lasted from early morning until evening, with a break of three hours in the middle of the day. 'At every meeting first the doctrine was stated, then the discipline determined, and finally the decree was settled upon and read out.'[1]

On the first day the clergy were called upon to make a profession of faith according to the formula of Pius IV, with some points added to deal with local errors, particularly contradicting the archdeacon's former contention by affirming that there is only one law of Jesus Christ. The archbishop first made this profession, ending with an oath never to receive any bishop not sent by the Pope and an anathema against the Patriarch of Babylon. There was some murmuring about this last clause, but nevertheless, led by the archdeacon, all the priests present accepted the profession and signed it. The deacons and lay representatives followed suit. A decree was passed at this meeting requiring all priests not present at the synod to make the same profession, and ordering that no one could hold any office in the Church until he had done so. The archbishop had thus made sure that the measures which were to follow, for the reformation of the Church and of some social customs, would be accepted, for all had accepted the authority by which they were to be announced. To give the Christians encouragement in this course, Menezes called the civil governor of Cochin Fort and publicly entrusted the Christians of St Thomas to his care as representative of the King of Portugal, charging him to protect them in all things, except such matters as were the proper responsibility of their local kings. This he added because his actions were being followed with close and anxious attention by spies of the rajas, who naturally very much resented Portuguese efforts to transfer the allegiance of their subjects. The governor accepted the charge, and the members of the Cochin council who were present at once passed an act confirming this pledge. Menezes then retired to rest, but the prime minister of the Cochin raja was soon waiting on him, to express his concern at what had taken place. He went off apparently satisfied with the archbishop's explanation that none of his actions, nor the decisions of the synod, would affect in any way

[1] Ferroli, p. 185.

the relationship between the Christians of St Thomas and their local rulers.

The business of the synod was done in two sessions every day and the decrees prepared in advance were passed. Many objections were raised, but in every case the archbishop's partisans rose to speak in support and the opponents of the measures, leaderless as they were, lacked ability and courage to sustain their objections. On St John Baptist's day (24 June) most of the Portuguese went off to another church to celebrate the feast there and so on that day the synod proceeded to deal with the reformation of the faith of the Church, a proceeding which was painful to the Christians of St Thomas and which the archbishop, to spare their feelings, had agreed to deal with when only the local Christians were present. Altogether eight days were spent in passing the decrees. After they had been read the diocese was divided into seventy-five parishes and Menezes appointed vicars for each. This was another innovation, for in most Syrian Churches then (and, in many, now) the priests were drawn from one family and the senior priest was considered the vicar. Each of the newly appointed vicars came to kiss the archbishop's hand and he then delivered a charge to them, which contained detailed directions about their behaviour, instructions in various parts of the pastoral office, and rules for ministering the services of the Church. After this the new vicars, the archbishop, all other clergy, the lay deputies and the Portuguese present all signed the decrees. The *Te Deum* was then sung in procession, some singing in Latin, some in Syriac and others in Malayāḷam, but all, we are assured by Gouvea, with one voice and great joy. The archbishop blessed the people and so the synod ended on 26 June 1599. All that remained was to instruct the new vicars in their duties, to arrange for all the clergy not present to subscribe to the decrees, to provide altar stones, holy oil, vestments, wine, books and other things necessary for the conduct of worship in the churches and to settle various disputes and quarrels which had been brought to the synod for arbitration.

The decrees of the synod deal with the abuses which Menezes had found during his visitation and which had been attacked before by the friars and by the Jesuits.[1] But they also provide a corpus of positive teaching about the faith, and detailed regulations for the ordering of Church life.

[1] E.g. Roz, *De erroribus Nestorianorum*, written in 1586.

The positive teaching was decreed and accepted in the third session of the synod (held on 24 June). Fourteen decrees give a conspectus of Christian doctrine, starting with the Holy Trinity and going on to deal with the Incarnation and the place of the Blessed Virgin as Mother of God. Salvation is affirmed to be through Christ alone, and the fact of original sin and its removal by baptism is explained. The next five decrees deal with the Last Things, heaven and hell, purgatory (of which the Indian Church had not known), the resurrection of the dead and the last judgment, the fate of the faithful and unfaithful angels, the veneration and invocation of angels and saints, and the honour due to the relics of saints. Other decrees teach the doctrine and worship of Christ, the Virgin and the saints through images, the work of the guardian angel, the supremacy of the Pope as successor of St Peter, Vicar of Christ, and the inspiration of Scripture, with a list of canonical books. The synod dealt with other matters of faith at other sessions, prefacing every set of decrees aimed at reformation with a statement of doctrine. In this manner baptism, confirmation, the sacrament of the Eucharist and the sacrifice of the mass, penance, unction, orders and matrimony were dealt with.

The decrees directed at the reformation of the Church arose out of the statements of faith and were concerned with two principal sets of errors, those connected with Nestorians and those, far fewer in number, which were Hindu in origin. So the synod provided for the copies of the Scriptures found in the Serra to be corrected and certain omissions supplied and arranged that all prayer books, missals and other Syriac literature should be collected. Detailed directions were given for the revision of the liturgy.[1] If correction was not possible all books were to be destroyed, and it was specifically provided that the anaphoras of Theodore, Diodore and Nestorius should be cut out of the missals and burned. In the mass a ceremony of breaking the host so that the wine could soak into it was condemned. Errors connected with Christ, for example reluctance to speak of his Passion, were made plain and the use of the crucifix and rosary enjoined, and another decree exposed the error of speaking of the Blessed Virgin as mother of Christ rather than as Mother of God. Veneration of saints connected with Nestorianism was condemned, the Roman calendar

[1] J. B. Glen published the liturgy as amended at the synod in *La Messe des anciens chrestiens* (Antwerp, 1609), 123 pages.

was imposed instead and the dedication of churches changed where necessary.[1] The whole matter was summed up in a decree which accepted the decisions of Ephesus (the two hundred fathers), anathematizing Nestorius and rejecting his errors, acknowledging the faith of the Roman Church as true and accepting Cyril of Alexandria as a blessed saint.

The decrees against Hindu practices were aimed only at customs which the Portuguese felt inimical to a true Christianity; they did not attempt to change the whole social structure, assimilated though that was in many respects to the non-Christian society of Malabar. Thus certain ceremonies at marriage and the attendance of Hindu musicians in church during mass were forbidden.[2] So also, while it was permitted for Christian children to attend schools conducted by Hindu masters, no reverence must be paid to any idol, and heathen shrines in Christian schools, kept for the use of Hindu children, were forbidden. The last action of the synod, in the ninth session, dealt with various matters, including the extirpation of superstition, Christian belief in omens, laws of inheritance, dress, drink and such-like things. A decree of the third session[3] dealt with three errors which were said to be found among the Christians—transmigration, the determination of men's lives by fate or fortune (presumably horoscopes and *karma* were in mind here), and the belief that everyone had to follow his own *d-harma*, or way of life, all of which would lead men to salvation. Attached to the statement on each of the sacraments was a number of decrees regulating the conditions of its use. They aimed at the assimilation of the Indian or Nestorian custom to the Roman in all disputed matters, and enable one to build up a fairly comprehensive view of life in the Church at that time, if taken with the forty-one decrees of the eighth session, which dealt specifically with the reformation of church affairs.

A few other decrees, most of them enacted at the third session, dealt with errors peculiar to the local situation. The archdeacon's thesis, of an essential difference between the laws of St Peter and St Thomas, was condemned and all oaths taken against submission to Rome were declared cancelled. No universal Pastor save the Pope was to be acknowledged and anyone speaking against him was to be punished. The decisions of the Council of Trent were

[1] Menezes changed the dedication of several churches from Mar Aphrod and Mar Prodh to that of All Saints, and the church at Ankamāli from Hormusius to Hormisda, orthodox Persian martyr.

[2] Session III, decree 20.

[3] Session III, decree 4.

declared binding on the Church of the Serra, and no one was to preach unless he had first subscribed to them, and been licensed by the bishop, or the rector of Vaipikkoṭṭa. All priests who had taught errors or fables had to recant publicly. The Syrian Church was declared subject to the Inquisition at Goa, which had had, however, no previous dealings with the Christians of St Thomas, and which was petitioned to authorize priests in the Serra to administer absolution in the special cases reserved to it. The final decrees of the synod asked the King of Portugal to take the Christians under his protection and ordered all vicars to keep a copy of the proceedings of the synod to be read regularly to the people so that the Church might be governed by them in all things.

After the synod the archbishop resumed his interrupted visitation. It is unnecessary to follow his journey in any detail. His procedure at each church followed the same general pattern. He was met on arrival by the people and taken from the parish boundary to the church in procession, listening to welcome songs which praised the Church of Rome and the archbishop himself and all he had done since coming to their country. Welcome songs of this descriptive and laudatory character are still a feature of most public meetings in Travancore. When they reached the church the archbishop would vest himself and give a general blessing to the parish. Then he would grant indulgences, and then order all books in the people's possession to be brought for correction, on pain of excommunication for disobedience. He then arranged for all the unbaptized to be brought to the church the following day, visited the sick of the place and had a conference at night with the priests and chief laymen, to settle difficulties and abuses. The following morning the archbishop said mass, but before doing so confessed publicly to his confessor, to encourage this practice, ordered by the synod, among the people and to disprove their theory that if a man made his confession he would die soon after. Then the archbishop handed all books brought in to Fr Roz and others for correction or, if necessary, destruction. Though this was done everywhere, the destruction was especially great at Ankamāli, where the diocesan archives were kept. Probably most of the books were of foreign origin,[1] as the local records were usually made on

[1] Mingana, pp. 67–72, gives a complete list of all the Indian Syriac MSS. now known to be in Europe. Most are in the Vatican Library. Some MSS. in the University Library, Cambridge, show traces of the erasures made by order of the synod (e.g. Oo. 1.8.22 Missal, fos. 106, 109).

ōḷas, or strips of palm leaf. The archbishop always gave a long sermon explaining some of the decrees, he administered the oath to all priests not at the synod, baptized, confirmed, and installed the vicar of the place. He tried to recall the Church to its evangelistic duty and took every opportunity of preaching to the Nāyars who had come to see his vestments and the ceremonies he performed. In his sermons, however, he often spoke insultingly about their gods, and thus enraged some of them. He was able during his journey to instruct and baptize a few Hindus.

The archbishop took steps, during this time, to obtain from the Pope and the King of Portugal permission to transfer the see from Ankamāli to Cranganore, where there was already a Portuguese church and fortress. He found that a good deal of instruction would be needed before the decrees became operative in the ordinary life of the Church: for example, at Tēvalakkara the priests were living a secular life and the Christians would not approach the archbishop and his party, for fear of pollution which would affect their free intercourse with the Nāyars, and in Pālayūr a farce was performed between characters representing St Peter and St Thomas, who debated the jurisdiction of the Churches of the Serra. St Cyriac, patron of the Church, acted as umpire and decided the dispute in favour of St Thomas. The archbishop was apprehensive of the results of such propaganda, and sent a priest to exorcize the actors—a move which seems to have had an immediate and impressive effect.

The visitation ended at Paṛavūr, where the archbishop appointed the archdeacon as administrator of the diocese until the Pope should choose a bishop for them. He gave him two assistants, Fr Roz and the rector of Vaipikkoṭṭa, ostensibly on the ground that his learning was insufficient for the work of literary reformation. Menezes then asked the clergy and people if they had anyone in mind for their bishop, and was told that all would welcome him. The archbishop said he would gladly come and executed a document, to be sent by the people to the Pope and to Portugal, resigning from Goa and accepting the diocese of the Serra. He asked them if they could nominate anyone else, in case he was not set free to come, and they then asked for Fr Roz. An interesting and rather inexplicable light on this is thrown by a letter sent to the Pope by the archdeacon in November 1599, in which he speaks of the great work of the archbishop for the St Thomas Christians,

PLATE I

MONOLITHIC STONE CROSS AT KAṬUTTURUTTI CONSECRATED BY ARCHBISHOP MENEZES IN 1599

says that they have sworn never to receive another bishop from Babylon, and asks for the archbishop to be sent as their own bishop. Failing this he asks that the Pope should appoint Fr Francis Roz, S.J., who knows the diocese, has preached and taught everywhere; and, besides being learned and holy, he knows Syriac. 'As to Malayāḷam and Malayāḷam customs, he knew them as well as they.'[1]

The archbishop's resignation was not accepted, and the next year he consecrated Fr Roz as first bishop of the Serra (not archbishop). The archdeacon remained loyal for some time but later rebelled and caused great trouble. The archbishop's achievement was recognized throughout the Western Church, and its hoped-for effect is thus described in a letter from the Visitor in the south to the Father-General of the Jesuits: 'at the Synod assisted the Governor of Cochin, Dom Anthony Noronha, and the chief dignitaries of the city, who on behalf of the King of Portugal had assumed on themselves the task of the protection of these Christians. How important was the step and how greatly it was in the future to promote the interests of the Portuguese Crown, none can gainsay who is aware of the effect of binding this race, which from the days of St Thomas had alone in India held the faith and could place in array thirty thousand armed men, to the cause of Portugal, and of bringing them under the obedience of the Roman See'.[2]

We take up the story of Bishop Roz's episcopate and the events which followed in Chapter IV. In the next two chapters we examine the origin of the Church which the Portuguese found in Malabar and attempt to reconstruct its history until the dawn of the modern period in the sixteenth century.

SOURCES

DR A. MINGANA translates Syriac MSS. relevant to our study in *The Early Spread of Christianity in India*. Most of his material is from Asseman's *Bibliotheca Orientalis*. I have made extensive use of Mingana's work. The Buchanan Collection in the University Library, Cambridge, includes Syriac MSS. collected in Malabar. Our main sources are the Portuguese records and journals of men connected with the administration in Goa, and letters and reports of ecclesiastics.

[1] Ferroli, p. 206. [2] Ferroli, p. 208.

K. M. Panikkar in *Malabar and the Portuguese*, Introduction, pp. xiii–xv, describes the collection of translations and transcriptions of Portuguese documents which is preserved in the India Office Library, London. He makes use of them in his book, which, however, has only passing references to the Christians. He cites the following Portuguese histories which are of importance for this study:

John de Barros was connected with the India Office in Lisbon and wrote *Da Asia*; decadas I, II and III are relevant.

Gaspar Correa was secretary to Albuquerque (whose *Cartas* in four volumes are in the India Office collection) and wrote *Lendas da India*. The chapters relating to Vasco da Gama were translated in 1859 for the Hakluyt Society.

Faria de Sousa, *Portuguese Asia*, a book translated into English in 1695 by Capt. J. Stevens. There is a copy in the University Library, Cambridge.

Duarte Barbosa, *A Description of the Coasts of East Africa*, was translated and published by the Hakluyt Society in 1866.

Diogo do Couto, *Da Asia*, decadas IV and XII.

Other books which are relevant, though not of great importance, are *Portuguese Dependencies in Asia*, D'Orsey (London, 1893), *The Portuguese in India*, Danvers (London, 1894) and *The Rise of Portuguese Power in Asia, 1447–1550*, R. S. Whiteway (London, 1899).

La Croze mentions *Asie*, Battoli (Rome, 1667), *État présent de la religion*, Cerri, and J. B. Gemelli Careri's *Voyage autour du monde*.

The ecclesiastical sources are numerous. The most important, which has provided the basic material for Chancellor Geddes's *History of the Church of Malabar*, La Croze's *Histoire du christianisme des Indes*, and all subsequent books, is *Histoire orientale des grans progrès de l'église catholique en la reduction des chrestiens de S. Thomas, par le rvme Don Alexis de Menezes, Archeveque de Goa*, (composée en langue portugaise par A. Gouvea, et tournée en français par J. B. Glen). This was published in Antwerp in 1609. Gouvea was a member of the Augustinian Order and the book was written at Goa soon after the archbishop's return from Malabar, by command of the Order, in honour of their famous son. The Portuguese edition was published in 1606, then followed a Spanish translation and then the above-mentioned French, which has been used in this book. It is a faithful version of the Portuguese.

The Acts of the Synod were published separately in 1606 at Coimbra by Gouvea. Geddes had a copy of this and has given a complete (and, according to La Croze who worked on it independently, a trustworthy) translation in his book, from which Hough reprinted the decrees in *The History of Christianity in India*, II.

There are two pamphlets not generally available which were lent to me by the kindness of the Bishop of Cochin. The first is *Subsidium ad bullarium patronatus Portugalliae* by Dom Matthew, Bishop of Cochin. The other is *Some Elucidations*, written on the occasion of the Right Rev. Dr Medlycott's article which was published in the *Voice of Truth*, 11 and 21 June 1902. This uses Portuguese MSS. and works like de Barros's and is really a defence of the Portuguese (the nationality of Bishop Matthew).

Il Viaggio all' Indie orientali by Fr Vincent Mary of St Catherine of Siena, Procurator General of the Discalced Carmelites, Rome, 1672. This was written by one of the Pope's Italian Carmelite mission sent out in the time of Archbishop Garcia and is very critical of the Portuguese Jesuits. It is used extensively in La Croze.

Fr Paul of St Bartholomew, C.D., for some time vicar general in Malabar, wrote a number of books, of which *India orientalis christiana* is the best known.

A very useful book which makes use of all these sources is *The Jesuits in Malabar*, by D. Ferroli, S.J., I. I have made considerable use of this book in this chapter. It is sometimes unreliable in identification of places, but otherwise clear and constructive. Ferroli naturally uses Jesuit sources most of all. The 'Litterae Annuae' of members of the Society working in India have never been published, but Ferroli was able to get access to many. Fr Saulière, S.J., printed some extracts from the British Museum Coll. (4785) in translation in the *Indian Athenaeum* (August–September 1923). P. du Jarric, S.J., published three volumes of *Histoire des choses plus memorables adventues tant ez Indes orientales, que autre pais de la descouverts des Portugais, en l'etablissement et progrez de la foy chretienne et catholique*, in 1600, 1610, 1614. He used earlier works by Jesuits. A Latin translation was published in 1615 under the title *Thesaurus rerum indicarum.*

A book used by Mackenzie in his *State of Christianity in Travancore* is *Oriente conquistado a Jesu Christo pelos padres da Companhia de Jesus da provincia da Goa* by Francis de Souza. This was written in 1698 (with the help of the MS. of a monk who had come to India in 1593) and published in 1700 at Lisbon. A reprint was made in Bombay in 1888.

I quote from Ferroli passages from *Nova relatio de rebus in India orientale a patribus Soc. J. anno 1598–9 gestis*, by Rev. P. Nicholao Pimenta, Superior of the Jesuit Mission in India, and Rev. P. Cl. Aquaviva, General of the Society (Mainz, 1601). Another collection of Pimenta's letters was published in Rome in 1602.

It will be seen how heavily loaded all this evidence is on the foreign side. In the absence of any evidence we can only conjecture the reaction of the Indian Church to their confrontation by an organized, intelligent and determined body of men, capable of producing all this literature about it.

CHAPTER II

THE ST THOMAS TRADITION

THE Portuguese in the sixteenth century knew the tradition of St Thomas's apostolic work in India and did not stop to ask whether the India in question was in fact our India. They had read in Marco Polo's book and later heard, from friars who had passed through South India, of the Indian Christians who claimed a connexion with the Apostle, and their keen interest was aroused. The two kings of Portugal whose reigns covered the first half of the sixteenth century sent their sea captains to India and directed them to search for apostolic relics, while they carried out their primary task, the capture of the spice trade.[1] The Indian Church had held its foundation by St Thomas as an article of faith for centuries before the Portuguese came, and in December 1952 all Syrian Christians joined in celebration of the nineteen-hundredth anniversary of the Apostle's landing. In this chapter we shall consider the earliest records of this tradition, and then examine the local forms of it found in Malabar. It is convenient to look at the story of St Thomas's death separately. The chapter ends with an evaluation of the evidence.

The earliest account we have of St Thomas's missionary work is in the *Acts of St Thomas*,[2] a popular romance, probably written in Syriac in the fourth century and later translated into Greek, Latin, Ethiopic and Armenian. The purpose of the *Acts* was to call attention to the necessity of virginity and poverty for the truly Christian life. The writer says very little of church life and fellowship, he is concerned with the salvation of individual souls, and for this reason some have thought that the work originated in Greek gnostic circles. The great stress on celibacy as a way to salvation, and the emphasis on the miraculous are not in themselves proof of a non-Catholic origin for the *Acts*, as even in the time of Aphraates only the unmarried could be baptized in Edessa.[3]

[1] Dom Manoel, 1495–1521, Dom Joas III, 1521–57; see J. Charpentier, *St Thomas the Apostle and India*, pp. 27, 28.

[2] M. R. James, *The Apocryphal New Testament*; see also E. J. Goodspeed, *History of Early Christian Literature*, pp. 119–24.

[3] F. C. Burkitt, *Early Eastern Christianity*, p. 125.

It was probably not until the fifth century that this rule was relaxed.

The *Acts* tells the story of the Apostles dividing the regions of the world by lot, and each going to his allotted place to preach the Gospel. Thomas was given India as his field of work, but he complained that a man with his Jewish background could not evangelize the Indians. The Lord himself then intervened. He met Abbanes, the factor of an Indian king, Gundaphorus, who was searching for an architect to take back with him to his master, and sold him Thomas who was a carpenter, afterwards returning the slave-price to him. Abbanes and Thomas sailed to Andropolis and thence eventually to Gundaphorus's royal city. Here the king treated Thomas kindly and showed him the site on which he wished his new court and palace to be built. Thomas undertook the work and received an advance payment for materials, which, however, he gave away to the poor, travelling round and preaching and ministering in the name of Christ. After some time the king came back to the place and naturally wanted to see the progress of the work. Nothing had been done and the king's anger was not assuaged by Thomas's assurance that he had built him the palace not on earth but in heaven. Thomas, and Abbanes who had brought him, were thrown into prison. But just at that time the king's brother Gad died and saw in heaven the glorious palace Thomas had built. He was then allowed to revive and tell his brother what he had seen. Both Gundaphorus and Gad were converted to the faith by this miracle and received chrism, baptism and the eucharist. The next chapters of the *Acts* tell of a series of miracles, with dead people raised and animals speaking. At the end of the seventh Act we read of Thomas committing his infant Church to a deacon called Zenophus or Xanthippus and going in a chariot to another city, in another king's dominions. No indication is given of the distance. Some ladies of this court came to hear Thomas's teaching and were converted, much to the annoyance of their husbands, as they would no longer live in the ordinary marriage relationship. Then the queen herself was converted and joined the Church, which brought to a head the royal resentment against Thomas and led to his imprisonment and eventual death by a lance thrust. Before his death, however, Thomas was able to ordain a presbyter and a deacon and to organize and consolidate the Church. After Thomas's death King Misdeus was worried about his sick son and thought he would use a relic of the Apostle to cure him. When the tomb was opened the king found that the body of the Apostle had already been taken to Mesopotamia (presumably to Edessa) by a believer, but dust from the tomb worked the required miracle. The son was healed and the king became a Christian.

Plainly, no confidence can be put in the historical reliability of these stories. They are written to magnify St Thomas, so that reflected glory would come on the Edessene (Chaldean) Church which claimed him as her founder. There were two reasons why this was necessary. In the fourth century there was bitter war between Parthia and Rome and it was essential to the safety of the Edessene Church that she should show her independence both in origin and administration of the Church of the Western Empire. Not only that; for some time Eastern Christians had been conscious that they were not reckoned orthodox by the Church of Antioch and the West, and the claim to apostolic foundation—made in the Abgar legend where we read of Judas Thomas himself sending Addai (Tatian) to Edessa—was a claim to be on an equal footing with the great Church of the West.[1] When the *Acts* was written there were known to be Christians in India and the story here told of their origin linked them with the Edessene Church and demonstrated its apostolic outreach.

Those Fathers who mention St Thomas all rely on the *Acts* for their information; no independent tradition remains. Origen, the *Clementine Recognitions*, Eusebius of Caesarea, Rufinus of Aquileia and Socrates say that St Thomas preached the Gospel in Parthia.[2]

A little later we find another tradition among writers in touch with Edessa.[3] Ephraim of Nisibis, who died in 373, says that Thomas worked in India and he is followed by Gregory Nazianzus, Ambrose and Jerome. Some writers tried to reconcile these accounts by postulating a long land journey through Mesopotamia

[1] W. Bauer, *Rechtgläubigkeit und Ketzerei im ältesten Christentum*, chapter I.

[2] I owe much in this section to Fr Heras, S.J., *The Two Apostles of India*. Cf. Origen, *In Genesim* III (Migne, *Patrologiae Cursus, series latina*, XII, col. 92 A) and *Recognitiones Clementinae* IX, 29; Eusebius of Caesarea, *Historia Ecclesiastica* III, I (Migne, *Patrologiae Cursus, series graeca*, XX, cols. 213–15); Rufinus of Aquileia, *Hist. Eccl.* I, 9 (Migne, *Pat. Cur. ser. lat.* XXI, col. 478); Socrates, *Hist. Eccl.* I, 19 (Migne, *Pat. Cur. ser. gr.* LXVII, col. 126).

[3] Ephrem. *Carmina Nisibena* (ed. Bickell, Leipzig, 1866), p. 163; Gregory Nazianzen, *Oratio XXXIII contra Arianos II* (Migne, *Pat. Cur. ser. gr.* XXXVI, col. 227); Ambrose, *In Psalmum XLV*, Enarratio 21 (Migne, *Pat. Cur. ser. lat.* XIV, col. 1143); Jerome, *Ep. LIX ad Marcellam* (Migne, *ibid.* XXII, col. 589).

to Parthia and Persia and finally India.[1] The difficulty is more apparent than real, because Edessa was under Parthian rule until the end of the century, and so was northern India. While the Parthians were ruling Persia, Jewish influence was very strong, as is apparent from the hero story of Esther, and from the fact that Aramaic or Pahlavi inscriptions occur on coins and monuments right down to the time of the Sassanian king, Shapur. The Parthian empire had spread into India and in the middle of the first century B.C. a new Parthian kingdom, centred on Taxila, had been founded in north-western India. Orosius in the fifth century said that generally the country (from the Indus to the Tigris) was called Parthia.[2]

After the fourth century the ecclesiastical writers (except Rufinus and Socrates) are unanimous that Thomas's field of mission was India, but again they do not specify any particular district.[3] So also with the tradition handed down by the Nestorians. Mar Solomon, Metropolitan of Bussorah, says that Thomas taught the Parthians, Medes, and Indians until the king of the Indians stabbed and killed him with a spear because the Apostle had baptized the king's daughter. The Jacobite tradition is the same.

In the early writings, however, the name India is used very loosely. Thomson notes that by A.D. 200 Axum and southern Arabia were thought of as a sort of nearer 'India'.[4] In the fourth century we find Abyssinia spoken of as India Minor, and so is the Yemen. Abdias, about A.D. 600, said that there were three Indias, the first bordering Abyssinia, the second on Persia and the third 'which extends to the edge of the world'.[5] Mingana has examined the causes of this confused usage, especially in Syriac writings, and has come to the conclusion that for many Western and West Syrian

[1] Pseudo-Dorotheus, *Index Apostolorum* (p. 155, ed. Schermann, Bibl. Teubneriana, 1907); Pseudo-Hippolytus (*ibid.* p. 166); Bar Hebraeus, *Chron. Eccl.* I, 34; so the Roman Martyrology (21 Dec.).

[2] Orosius, *Historiae* I, 2 (Migne, *Pat. Cur. ser. lat.* XXXI, cols. 676–7).

[3] Gaudentius of Brescia, *Sermo* XVII (Migne, *Pat. Cur. ser. lat.* XX, cols. 962–3); Paulinus of Nola (Migne, *ibid.* LXI, col. 514); Beda, *Martyrologia* XII, Kal. Jan. (Migne, *ibid.* XCIV, col. 1137A).

[4] In the eighteenth book of *Greek Chronography* of John Malda, eighth-century India seems to be Ethiopia and Arabia. 'Citerior India and extra Indian Indias', T. K. Joseph, *Journal of Indian History* (Trivandrum, Aug. 1947), pp. 175–87; Thomson, *History of Ancient Geography*, pp. 300, 361, 368.

[5] *Expositio totius mundi* XVIII, 35. Hosten notes that this 'India' would be India Ulterior, including Coromandel, the 'India Superior' of the *Passio*; the 'Upper India' of Archbishop John de Monte Corvino, *c.* 1292; the 'Greater India' of Marco Polo, *c.* 1292–3 and of Jourdain de Severac, 1322. See *Antiquities from San Thome and Mylapore*, p. 301.

writers India was a convenient term to use for the little-known lands of the East. East Syrian and Nestorian writers, on the other hand, had much more contact with the real India and knew more about it from traders as well as from their Church connexions. 'For them', says Mingana, 'India is nearly always our modern India.'[1] On the other hand, we have to remember that many Alexandrians would have at least a superficial knowledge of our India, for their city was the terminal port of the Roman trade until it broke down in the fourth century. Indians were common figures in the streets and Clement knows about the Brahmans and the *vanaprast-han* stage of life, lived in religious meditation.

There is evidence that in the *Acts* 'India' refers to our India, or rather to the area of the North-west Frontier Province now contained in Pakistan. King Gundaphorus and his brother Gad are now known to be historical figures, ruling over the Scytho-Indian empire east and west of the Indus from about A.D. 19–45.[2] There was a considerable Jewish colony in north-western India in the first century, which might have attracted the attention of the first Christian missionaries.[3] There are other facts which seem to indicate a northern locus for St Thomas's work. Bardaisan in his *Book of Fate* (A.D. 196) speaks of Parthian Christians living among pagans, which might be a result of the destruction of the Indian Parthian empire by Kushan invaders about A.D. 50.[4] There are also said to be Christian tribes still living in north India, but holding their faith a secret from all others. For example, at Tatta in Sind (the ancient port of Pattala at the mouth of the Indus) there is a fakir community which calls itself by an Aramaic name, something like 'Bartolmai', and claims to have been descended from St Thomas's converts and to have books and relics to prove it. Unfortunately no outsider has ever been allowed to see this alleged proof.[5]

[1] Mingana, pp. 11–14.

[2] W. R. Philipps, *Indian Antiquary*, XXXIII, pp. 10ff., 'Trans. of Notes on the Indo-Scythians by Sylvain Levi'; *Camb. Hist. India*, I, pp. 563–78; Arch. Survey of India, *Annual Report* of 1902–3, p. 167. Some scholars, however, do not now regard the date of Gundaphorus as firmly established.

[3] The Kharosttic (Sanskrit in a Semitic script) inscriptions on coins and an Aramaic inscription of one of Asoka's edicts found at Taxila establish this fact; *Journal of Asiatic Studies* (1915), pp. 340–7; Herzfeld, *Epigraphia Indica*, XIX, pp. 251–3; see also N. A. Faris, *The Arab Heritage*.

[4] *Camb. Hist. India*, I, pp. 580–5.

[5] R. A. Trotter, 'The history of Christianity in Sind', *Conference*, February 1947.

We can reasonably conclude that the passages in the Fathers and in the *Acts* do refer to our India, but no indication is given of south India—in fact the balance of probability is that they refer to the Parthian India of the north-west.

This discussion is the necessary background for the question which really concerns us, the apostolate in south India. It is possible to maintain this on the ground of the *Acts* only by extending the waggon journey to another city into a long journey from north to south. Farquhar[1] does this and ascribes to Abbanes considerable trade connexions and wide knowledge of shipping, making him very influential as the king's *rajavaikehaka* or trade commissioner. 'This man', says Farquhar, 'without doubt selected the new field for Thomas and sent him, on the Kushan invasion becoming threatening, down the Indus to Pattala and thence to Socotra, which he evangelized while waiting for another ship to take him down to Muziris in Malabar.'[2] Farquhar states the south Indian tradition in one form and seeks to show that this is original and the story in *Acts* secondary. Arguing from this premiss Farquhar says that the author of *Acts* supplied fictitious names[3] and tried to assimilate Thomas's story with that of Christ, especially in the details of his death, presumably following on the line of thought involved in speaking of Judas as the Lord's twin brother.[4] He stresses the single spear of the local tradition which is mentioned also in the Nestorian liturgy and was found among survivors of the Nestorian Church in Mylapore by the Portuguese in the sixteenth century. According to the *Acts* four soldiers stab Thomas. This, however, seems a very small point on which to place importance. Farquhar's imaginative reconstruction is entirely conjectural, lacking any solid foundation in the evidence available. The local traditions, as we have them now, are all post-Portuguese, and ultimately dependent on the *Acts* or on its derivatives, the Latin

[1] J. N. Farquhar, *The Apostle Thomas in North India*.

[2] Francis Xavier says that the Christians in Socotra claimed to have been established by St Thomas.

[3] He notes that none of the names is Indian. Two of them are Mesopotamian —the lady Mygdonia sharing her name with a district near Nisibis. It is much simpler to note that all the names are from Syriac-speaking countries bounded by the Euphrates and Tigris. Burkitt says that in the only extant Roman deed of sale of a slave from Mesopotamia the slave's name is Abbanes.

[4] The Twin cult at Edessa is examined in Burkitt, *Early Eastern Christianity*. It may be noted in this connexion that in the astrological division of the world among the signs of the zodiac India falls to Gemini, and it may be that this affects the description, in the Edessene *Acts*, of the division of the world and the sending of Thomas, the Twin, to India.

works called the *Passion of St Thomas* and *Concerning Miracles*. They are recorded here, since there is no book in English in which they are easily accessible.

The first account of the tradition is contained in the words of a song, sung on socio-religious occasions like marriages. This is called the *Thomma Parvam* or Thoma's Song and describes 'the coming of the Way of the Son of God' to Kēraḷa.[1] It states that Thomas left Arabia and reached Malankara (not far from Cochin and Cranganore) in December A.D. 50. He made converts in Tiruvancikuḷam (Cranganore) from Jews who were living there as well as from natives of the place. The king also became a Christian and was given the name of Andrew, and his nephew Kēppa was ordained priest. Thomas later went south and preached the Way (*Margam*) for a year in Quilon, where he baptized fourteen hundred persons and set up a cross for them to worship. This is said to be the Apostle's ordinary practice, for a little later he is at Pālayūr in the north where he 'set up a cross of beautiful fashion that all of them might worship and carry out the rituals'. Thomas then went east to the territory of the Cōḷa kings, where at Mylapore he gave away money paid him by the king to build a palace, and was about to be killed by his angry client, when the king's brother rose from the dead and described the splendid palace built by Thomas for the king in heaven. Thomas then returned to Travancore and visited the churches he had established, and preached the Gospel in other places as well. He built churches in these places, appointed teachers, and 'finally gave them the gifts of the Holy Spirit in a regular manner'. This apparently refers to holy orders and confirmation, since at Malayāṟṟūr and five other places we find him giving the gifts to priests (*ācāryas*) and to laymen. Then follows the

[1] Italian translation published at Rome, 1938, by Fr Rocca in 'La leggende de S. Tomaso Apostolo', *Orientalia Christiana*, XXXII, 89, pp. 169ff.; published in Malayalam for the first time in 1916 in *Mar Thomma Kristyanikaḷ* (The Mar Thoma Christians) by Fr Bernard, part I. Zaleski, *The Apostle St Thomas in India*, gives an account of the song sung in 1912. MSS. of the song are in the Mannānam monastery. T. K. Joseph says that the first known use of the song was by one Vargese of Pālayūr, in 1892. The song is said to have been composed for use in the church of Niraṇam by Thomas Ramban in 1601, who claimed to base it on a prose account handed down for forty-eight generations from his ancestor Maliyēkkal Thoma Ramban. Internal evidence is against the song being of seventeenth-century date. The Malayāḷam vocabulary does not seem to be early; and the years are given in the Christian reckoning, introduced by the Portuguese only in 1498, but not widely used until modern times. The Portuguese found the Christians observing 3 July not as the anniversary of Thomas's death, but of his arrival in Malabar; Gouvea, bk. I, chap. 19, p. 60.

description of the appointment of Kēppa (who had already been ordained priest) as Thomas's successor. Thomas invested him with his own robe and laid his hands on his head. He entrusted to Kēppa the government of the believers and commanded them to accept Kēppa as himself. St Thomas won over seventeen thousand souls because of the supernatural virtue which shone in him. An exact account is given of his converts: 6850 Brahmans, 2590 Kshatriyas, 3780 Vaisyas and 4280 Sudras. Two kings were converted and became metropolitans, seven Nampūtiri Brahmans, heads of villages, became *gurus* or bishops and four became monks. Thomas ended his days in Mylapore rather dramatically. He was ordered by Brahmans to worship Kāḷi in a sacred grove, but refused, making the sign of the cross. The grove was immediately consumed by fire and the image of Kāḷi removed, whereupon the enraged Brahmans stabbed Thomas with a spear so that he died on 3 July. Twenty-seven days after his death Thomas appeared to his disciples and instituted a *dukhana* or feast of remembrance, observance of which would carry with it special favours through his intercession in heaven.

The next record of the local tradition which is available is contained in a letter written in Syriac in 1721 by Mar Thomas IV (1688–1728) to a Dutch scholar of Leiden who had asked for some account of the Malabar Church.[1] The bishop tells the story of an Indian king who wanted a palace built and sent Habban, his major-domo, to Jerusalem in search of a descendant of Solomon's builders. He was met by our Lord who miraculously brought Thomas from Edessa by the ministry of an angel and handed him over to Habban. So Thomas arrived in India and converted the king and many Indians, giving them baptism and the priesthood, and building seven churches. Then he went to Mylapore, where he was speared to death in A.D. 52 and his body carried to Edessa by an angel. The foundation of seven churches is a constant element in the local tradition, but the ones named in this account, 'Mylapore, Corignalore, Parakar, Irapalli, Kothamangalam, Niranam, Tiribancore', are different from those in the usual list.

A certain priest Mathew wrote a Syriac letter in 1725 which mentions the arrival of the Apostle at Malankara from Mylapore, his foundation of the churches and his death at Mylapore.[2]

[1] English translation in Mingana, pp. 48ff.

[2] Land's *Anecdota Syriaca*, I, pp. 24–30. The letter is translated by Mingana, pp. 42–8; also translated by H. Drury, *Letters from Malabar*, pp. 105ff.

The best-known expression of the local tradition is the *Margam Kaḷi* song, which was composed and sung for the first time in 1732. It was written to accompany a dance depicting in dramatic form the foundation of the Malabar Church. The song tells the story of how our Lord sold Thomas to Avan (Habban) to build a palace for the Cōḷa king, as in Mar Thomas's account. Thomas accepted the work but said he must go for his tools, and would be back in a year. He received an advance payment and went off preaching first in the Cōḷa country and then outside. In the course of this work Thomas was in touch with local ruling houses and performed many miracles. Thomas went far afield, to Malacca and China, but came back and stayed in the Cōḷa kingdom for another year. He then heard of Kēraḷa and went there, arriving at Malankara, preaching to the Brahmans of Cranganore, and ordaining two of them priests. Then he went south, erecting crosses at Quilon, Niraṇam, Kōtamamgalam, Kottukkayal, Cāyal and Pālayūr. At this point of the story we hear of the anxiety of the Cōḷa king to see his palace. He sent for Thomas and put him in prison when told he must wait till after his death to see the new palace, and was so mortified by the deception that he wanted to abdicate. However, his brother died at that time and saw the palace in heaven. He revived and told the king of its glory. The king, his brother, Habban and others were baptized, and the faith spread apace, arousing Brahmans to jealousy. They ordered Thomas to worship Kāḷi in her sacred grove, which Thomas refused to do. Then the grove was consumed by fire, but, while it burned, one priest in his anger seized a pointed stick and killed Thomas. The king took the body and buried it in Mylapore. According to this story Thomas died on 21 December 52.

It seems that these forms of the tradition depend on the *Acts*, modified by local Christian traditions of the foundation of particular churches and legendary stories of Hindu holy men.[1] For an example of this last possible influence we may compare the stories

[1] There exist other records of the local tradition, but they add nothing to what has already been given. Mar Thomas VIII (1809–16) sent a description of the origin and life of the Syrian Church in reply to an inquiry from the Madras Government (quoted in Whitehouse, appendix D, p. 304); and one of the early Church Missionary Society missionaries, Benjamin Bailey, translated a Malayāḷam account of the tradition in 1818, but they give no further details. In 1869 Joseph Ittoop wrote a history of the Church in Malayāḷam (*Malayāḷuttuḷḷa Suriyāni Kristyanikaḷuṭe caritram*); he quotes the *Margam Kaḷi Pāṭṭu* but does not use the *Thomma Parvam*.

of St Thomas paying his workmen in sand, which turned into rice, and drawing to land a large floating tree trunk which all the king's horses and all the king's men had failed to control, with similar stories told of Hindu heroes.[1] St Thomas is also credited with all kinds of miracles in the traditions of the seven churches he is supposed to have founded. The emphasis on the veneration of the Cross and many other details in the stories are decisive against an early date being attributed to them.

The identification of these seven churches varies from writer to writer, but the churches of Malankara near Cranganore, Quilon, Paṛavūr, Kokkamamgalam, Niraṇam, Pālayūr and Cāyal are those generally accepted as of apostolic foundation. Most of these places are on the Periyar river estuary, or on channels or canals associated with it, or on the sea coast. Only one, Cāyal, seems to have been inland in the mountains. It is likely that Jewish colonies also existed near most of them, as is the case to this day at Paṛavūr.

Malankara, from which the Church is often called the Malankara Syrian Church, is the place where St Thomas is supposed to have landed. It is an island now, with no church, but the next village is significantly named Paḷḷippuram, or 'church-town'. The anciently important town of Cranganore was very near. It is now silted up, with only an old Portuguese tower remaining to show any sign of former greatness, but once it was one of the major ports of the world, mentioned by Ptolemy and other authors as Muziris; it was also called Mahodayappaṭṭaṇam, Tiruvaṇcikuḷam and, by the Jews, Shingly. The modern name is Koṭuṅaḷḷūr. The Portuguese had an important factory in Cranganore, and moved the seat of the archbishopric of the Serra there in 1609. Gouvea describes a chapel in Cranganore which contained a cross erected by St Thomas, which moved Christians to repentance when they venerated it, and to which Hindus, as well as Christians, brought offerings. This cross was said occasionally to become radiant with light or even to levitate itself, and to work miracles. Cranganore is said to have lost much of its importance before the Portuguese came, from 1341, when a great flood changed the course of the river. It may here be remarked that the configuration of the land has changed frequently

[1] Duarte Barbosa, *A Description of the Coasts of E. Africa*, p. 161, describes the sand miracle in 1516. Their are similar Hindu stories, cf. G. U. Pope, *The Sacred Kurral*, p. 11.

in this coastal area, and it is clear that many places now inland, like Niraṇam, were once on the coast.

Quilon shared with Cranganore the distinction of being a famous Christian centre and indeed, until land registration was modernized at the beginning of this century, Christians were always described in official documents as belonging either to Cranganore or Quilon. The ancient town of Quilon has long been covered by sea, but fifteenth-century writers mention the church founded by St Thomas, and a cross he is said to have set up.

The ancient church of Paṛavūr is said to have been damaged or destroyed by Tippu Sultan, but a small church incorporated into the great modern Romo-Syrian church building is still reckoned as built by St Thomas, and a small incised cross is venerated as his.

Kokkamamgalam is in the same area and still a Christian centre. The church, however, does not still remain. The church at Kōtamamgalam, thirty miles inland at the foot of the mountains but on the Periyar river, is sometimes claimed as a church founded by St Thomas; it is an ancient and impressive structure crowning a hill, but much restored in the last century. On the whole the identification of the 'apostolic' church with Kokkamamgalam rather than Kōtamamgalam seems more likely.

Niraṇam church has been rebuilt, but many stories of St Thomas's connexion with it are cherished locally. In 1900 at Niraṇam T. K. Joseph heard the legend that while St Thomas was there the new-born child of a low-caste barber died and people accused the Apostle of being its father. To vindicate his purity he at once brought the child to life again, and the baby declared that Thomas was not his father. The father and his family were converted by the miracle and the man became sexton of the church. The sexton in 1900 claimed to be a direct descendant. This is clearly an aetiological legend to show why a low-caste man was sexton of a Syrian church. The details of this story remind one of the other popular story of the Brahman who killed his son and then accused St Thomas of the murder. The Apostle vindicated himself by restoring the child to life, who then pointed to his own father as his murderer.[1]

[1] See Tamil story about St Thomas and Kandappa Raja translated from the Latin by W. Taylor, *S. Indian Christian Repository*, I, pp. 263–6. Zaleski, *The Apostle St Thomas in India*, pp. 170, 171, takes this story from de Barros, *Da Asia*, VI, p. 231. There are other references in Portuguese writings. A similar story is told of Thomas of Cana and also of St Francis Xavier at Kottar; Fr Hosten, *Antiquities from San Thome and Mylapore*, p. 255.

Pālayūr near Caukkāṭ in Malabar, formerly connected with the sea by a canal and with the site of a former Jewish settlement not far from the church, is still a great pilgrimage centre. In the churchyard are images formerly belonging to a Hindu temple, and adjoining it are sacred tanks. The tradition concerning this church is contained, as are those of the other churches, in songs sung at festivals. It is hard to form any judgment about the age of these songs of welcome, for the writing of such songs is a common art. Pālayūr is said to have been a Nampūtiri (Kēraḷa Brahman) village when St Thomas visited it. He converted some of the Brahmans by a miracle: the water which he threw into the air while bathing in the tank remained suspended in the air or became flowers.[1] (A similar incident is told of all the other six places and of Mylapore in the Kandappa Raja story.) Some Christian families at Kuravilaṅāṭ trace their descent from these converts and for proof point to their house names, which they share with Malabar Brahman families. (From two of these families, Pakalomaṟṟam and Sānkarapuri, St Thomas is said to have ordained the first priests.) The other Brahmans cursed the place and left it for good and to this day no Brahman will live or even drink water there. (Caukkāṭ may mean 'cursed wood'.) The tradition says that the temple was converted into the church. The present building replaces one destroyed by Tippu Sultan in the eighteenth century, which was built by Fr Fenicio in 1516, replacing the ancient wooden building he found there.

The exact whereabouts of the last church, Cāyal or Nilakkal, is not known. Ward and Connor in their *Memoir of the Survey of Travancore and Cochin* say they found the remains of buildings in the forest about thirty-six miles east of Ṛānni. The Christians are said to have been driven from the place by a plague of poisonous spiders, and four families from there are said to have founded the Ceṅannūr church in 1244–5.

We turn now to consider the tradition which places the death of St Thomas at Mylapore, near Madras. The local Malabar tradition of St Thomas's death follows the account given in the Latin *Passio*. It speaks of his death from the lance thrust of an angry Brahman, his burial and the translation of the body to Edessa, either by the agency of an angel or the devotion of one of his followers. There are

[1] Kuriakose Kaṭṭanar, *Malabar Kristyānikaḷ*, and Fr A. F. Wellanikkaran in *Caritas*.

many references in early writings to St Thomas's burial place, but its identification with Mylapore is much disputed. John Chrysostom (d. 407) says that the place of St Thomas's tomb is as much known as those of St Peter, St Paul and St John and while he presumably means that people do know where these tombs are, and not the contrary, he unfortunately says no more.[1] Gregory of Tours (544–595) said he had learned from Theodore the Indian that there was a great monastery in India where Thomas's body lay before being transported to Edessa, with a lamp which burns continuously, though never replenished by any human hand.[2] In 636 Isidore of Seville, basing his account on the *Passio*, says 'Therefore, this Thomas preached to the Parthians and the Medes, up to the furthest eastern parts, and there preached the Gospel and suffered martyrdom. Indeed, being pierced with a lance, he died at Calamina, a town of India, and was honourably buried there on the twelfth before the Kalends of January' (21 December).[3] Others like Usuard and later writers echo this tradition.[4] It is not confined to western writers. Yesuyab, Bishop of Nisibis (consecrated 1190) boasts of the sacred sites of the East and refers to 'the corpse of St Thomas the apostle in India'.[5] Mar Solomon of Basra (1222) says that some 'say the apostle was buried in Mahluph, a city in the land of the Indians', implying that there were other theories current at the time.[6] Gregory Bar Hebraeus (1246) speaks of St Thomas's preaching in India, his martyrdom at Calamina and the translation of his body to Edessa. Avur, son of Mathew, in 1340 gives more definite information and says 'his tomb stands on the peninsula Meilan in India', while four Mesopotamian bishops writing in 1504 made the identification final and say 'the houses as well as the tomb of the Apostle St Thomas stand on a city on the sea named Meliapor'. On 3 July the Syriac breviary celebrates St Thomas's martyrdom and says 'Thomas was transfixed by a spear on the sea shore in the land of India' and again 'glorious Apostle St Thomas, who didst pitch thy tent near the sea, pray the supreme Lord to make us

[1] John Chrysostom, *Comm. ep. ad Hebraeos*, hom. XXVI (Migne, *Pat. Cur. ser. gr.* LXIII, col. 179).

[2] Gregory of Tours, *De gloria martyrum* XXXII (Migne, *Pat. Cur. ser. lat.* LXXI, col. 733).

[3] Isidore, *De ortu et obitu patrum*, 74, 132 (Migne, *ibid.* LXXXIII, col. 152). See Zaleski, *The Saints of India*, pp. 139–40.

[4] 'Auctarium martyrologii Usuardi Lubecliae et Coloniae' (Paul, *India orientalis christiana*, p. 144).

[5] Asseman, p. 306.

[6] Mar Solomon quoted in Medlycott, *India and the Apostle Thomas*, p. 38.

rejoice with thee in heaven'. The identification of Calamina or Mahluph with Mylapore is not made definitely by any of the above writers until the sixteenth century, but Hosten considers it proved, not so much on philological or other grounds as by the fact that pilgrims came to Mylapore to the Apostle's tomb, apparently even before the coming of the Portuguese.[1] Paul summed up this point of view when he said 'All the Christians of the East, Catholics and heretics like the Nestorians, Jacobites, Armenians, the Catholics of Bengal, Pegu, Siam, Ceylon, Malabar, and Hindustan, came to make their devotions and this alone is sufficient to confirm the ancient and universal tradition that St Thomas died at Mylapore'.[2]

There is, however, other evidence which must be taken into account in any consideration of Mylapore's claim to be the place where St Thomas was martyred and buried. The first European traveller to arrive there was Marco Polo in 1293. He found the tomb there, in Malabar, at a certain little town having no great population, with little merchandise and not very accessible, and said it was a place of pilgrimage for Nestorian Christians and Muslims, who used red earth from the tomb to cure fevers.[3] Marco heard that the saint's death was accidental, as he was shot by an arrow aimed by a low-caste archer at a peacock.[4] The Muslims who venerated the tomb are said to have claimed that it was the resting place of a Saracen holy man and great prophet of their own who came from Nubia, and T. K. Joseph points out that the tomb excavated by the Portuguese in 1523 lay north-south, the usual Muslim position. It is not impossible, however, that the Muslims who venerated the tomb were carrying on an old practice derived from their ancestors before the rise of Islam, and that these ancestors were, in fact, Christians. Hosten gives some suggestive

[1] The story told by de Barros, *Da Asia*, III, pp. 7, 11, and by Camões, *Os Lusiades*, X, pp. 114–16, is that Thomas was stoned by jealous Brahmans while preaching or praying. Then he was pierced with a lance while lying wounded on the ground. His disciples brought his dead body to the church he had built and there buried it. These writers were relying on contemporary local tradition.

[2] Paul, *Viaggio alle Indie orientali*, I, p. 61.

[3] Yule, *Book of Ser Marco Polo*, revised by Cordier, II, cap. XVIII, pp. 353ff. This use of earth from Thomas's tomb is noticed in the sixteenth century by Gouvea, p. 299.

[4] The connexion of St Thomas with the peacock (Mylapore probably means 'Peacock town') is constant and requires investigation. Marignolli (Hosten, *Antiquities*, p. 279) wrote that St Thomas was painted in the Indian churches dressed in a white tunic and a cloak of peacock's feathers. In the *Margam Kaḷi* the dancers wear peacock feathers and the peacock is commonly carved on the churches, often one on either side of a cross. See page 203.

references which would support this theory and also quotes the story told by Correa of Muslims captured by a Portuguese ship off Calicut in 1502. Before these men were executed they asked for baptism and called on the name of St Thomas.[1] It is not unlikely that the ancestors of the Muslims from Iraq and the Persian Gulf who controlled west coast trade at the beginning of the fifteenth century, and for ages before that, had Christians among their number. If this theory is correct, then the tomb held to be that of a Muslim *pir* in the thirteenth century may in fact have been that of a forgotten Christian leader, if not the Apostle himself.

John of Monte Corvino visited Mylapore at the same time as Marco Polo and speaks of a church of St Thomas there. In 1324 Odoric speaks of fifteen houses of Nestorians living beside the church which he describes as full of idols, two statements difficult to reconcile. Marignolli in 1349 speaks of the church which he had built with his own hands. De Conti in 1449 said there were a thousand Nestorians living in the city who worshipped the body of St Thomas, but in 1504 Duarte Barbosa found the church in ruins and occupied by a Muslim fakir who kept a lamp perpetually burning.

It is clear that the identification of the Mylapore tomb as the burial place of St Thomas the Apostle, and the ascription of special sanctity to various places in the locality—St Thomas's Mount and the Little Mount—were entirely the work of the Portuguese, whose known attitude towards the saints, and eager desire to find apostolic relics do not induce confidence in their historical judgment or critical examination of the facts.[2] All later Portuguese writing on the subject seems to be based on a deposition made on oath by one Diego Fernandez in 1543.[3] He said that

[1] Correa, *Lendas da India*; see *Three Voyages of Vasco da Gama*, p. 334.

[2] Xavier remarks: 'There are at San Thoma more than a hundred Portuguese all married; they have a very devout church and all think that the body of the Apostle is lying there.' *Monumenta Xavierana*, I, p. 387. When the Portuguese first landed at Pulicat near Madras they at once claimed to recognize the site of St Thomas's tomb (Luigi Rancinotto in *Gubernatis: storia dei viaggiatore italiani*, p. 128). At Vijayanagar, a city not founded until the thirteenth century, they said 'Here St Thomas preached'; letter of a Venetian traveller to Ser Zuane di Santi written in 1511, *Gubernatis*, p. 382. See Heras, *Journ. Bombay Hist. Soc.* (Sept. 1929), pp. 284–9.

[3] *Esplendores da religio* (Goa, April 1930), pp. 152–6; this periodical cites *Vida de St Francis Xavier* (by Fr John de Lucena), *Asia Portugesa* (by Fr Faria de Sousa, I, pp. 222–4), and *Oriente conquistado* (by Fr Francis de Souza, I, p. 152), as relying on this deposition; it also cites O. Gabinete, *Historia chron.* I, p. 13.

in 1517 he had gone to Mylapore with an Armenian, and visited the tomb of St Thomas. The people living there had been afraid to meddle with the tomb, but it was eventually opened and some bones and a lance head were found. These were solemnly placed in a coffer and are now venerated in San Thome Cathedral at Mylapore. In 1547 the movement to make Mylapore a holy place was quickened by the discovery of a stone slab with a cross in bas-relief and an incised Pahlavi inscription, while foundations were being dug for a larger church on St Thomas's Mount. The Portuguese could not read the inscription, but an old Brahman scholar was persuaded to do so, which he most obligingly did, as follows: 'In the time of the Lord Jesus, Thomas a man of God, was sent by the Son of God (whose disciple he was) to these parts to bring the people of the nation to the knowledge of God, and he built there a temple and wrought great miracles and that finally praying he knelt before that cross and was transfixed with a lance by a Brahman; and that that cross remained stained with the blood of the saint for everlasting remembrance'.[1] This remarkable effort of course confirmed the faith of the Portuguese and this was immeasurably strengthened by the miracle which happened on alternate years on 18 December when the cross changed colour and sweated during the Gospel at mass. This miracle ceased with the end of the Portuguese control. It must be added that the diocesan authorities of Mylapore are now cautious in the claims they make for the tomb and the other sites.[2] In 1950 the Roman Catholic bishops in Malabar resolved to try to get back for their Church the bones of St Thomas from Ortona in Italy, to which place they had been taken from Edessa in 1258, thus making plain that they do not regard the bones now kept at Mylapore or Goa as those of the Apostle.

It is clear that this evidence is quite insufficient to establish the death and burial of St Thomas at Mylapore as an historical fact. Indeed, a Jesuit historian, writing of the story of the finding of the tomb, says, 'these details are quite enough for disclosing the untruthfulness of the discovery';[3] for they were not content to

[1] See p. 80 below, for a modern translation.

[2] F. A. D'Cruz, *St Thomas the Apostle in India*, p. 112; quoted by T. K. Joseph, 'St Thomas in Parthian India', *National Christian Council Review* (Jan. 1952), 'Catholics who venerate the tomb are not compelled to believe in its genuineness'.

[3] H. Heras, S.J., review of *St Thomas the Apostle in India* (D'Cruz) in *J. Bombay Hist. Soc.* (Sept. 1929).

identify the tomb as one that had contained the body before it was taken to Edessa, but found white bones and a broken lance and placed these articles in a coffer to be kept next to the altar, where they are still. It is not impertinent to add that in the Mylapore area, as in other parts of south India, Iron Age burials are exceedingly common, and the tombs excavated by the Portuguese in 1522 and 1523 may very likely be of this period, perhaps even coeval with St Thomas. But, even if we cannot accept the claims made for the Mylapore tomb, the tradition of St Thomas's death in south India is not entirely disproved, and no other place in the world claims the event. We cannot prove that the Apostle worked in south India any more than we can disprove that fact; but the presence of Christians of undoubtedly ancient origin holding firmly to the tradition, the proof of very considerable commercial contact between the western world and the Malabar coast in the first century of our era, and the probable presence of Jewish colonies at the same time, may for some incline the balance to belief that the truth of the tradition is a reasonable probability. The evidence we have cannot do more than this.

There is no doubt that an apostolic mission in the first century, whether or not it actually happened, was perfectly possible from a physical point of view. Evidence can be adduced to show the commercial importance of Malabar and its trade connexions with Babylon and the Hebrews. Many claim that the Ophir from which Solomon's ships obtained apes, ivory and peacocks was in Malabar, but this cannot be proved.[1] There were three main routes between India and the western world: first, from the mouth of the Indus to the mouth of the Euphrates and thence up the river to the point where roads branched off to Antioch and the Levantine ports; second, an overland route over the mountains to Balkh and thence to the Caspian or entirely overland; and a third route from India to the Red Sea and thence by road to the Nile and so to Alexandria, a town which Strabo says had been founded to capture the Indian trade for Rome. We are concerned with this last route, as it was the usual one in the first century. Our information is fairly complete and comes from Strabo (63 B.C.–A.D. 24) and from recent excavation

[1] I Kings x. 22. See *Camb. Hist. India*, I, p. 594, note 2. Bishop Caldwell supported this hypothesis because of the affinity of certain Hebrew and Dravidian words, e.g. the word for peacock; but the same claim is made for Pegu and places in east and south-west Africa. See also Rawlinson, *Intercourse between India and the Western World*, pp. 12, 13.

in the Egyptian desert.[1] About 420 miles south of Cairo the town of Coptos had been founded at a place where the Nile bends to the east, and from this town the Romans constructed roads, supplied with fortified watering stations, eastwards across the desert to the Red Sea. Strabo says that the journey to the port of Myos Hormos took six or seven days; from there about 120 ships sailed to India in a year. It is evident that this trade was a regular and important feature of the Roman economy. At first (from about 90 B.C.) ships went from Aden and other Arabian ports direct to the mouth of the Indus, but later they began to use a port north of Bombay and finally discovered how to sail direct, diagonally across to Muziris, the port of Malabar, instead of tacking laboriously down the coast.[2] Malabar was in any case the end of the voyage, for it was from there that pepper, spices and precious stones were exported.

Pliny (A.D. 23–79), Ptolemy (A.D. 100–160) and the *Periplus of the Erythraean Sea* give a good deal of detailed information about the trading centres of Malabar, but the identification of the places that they mention cannot, except in the case of Muziris, be fixed with certainty. Some features of the country have remained unaltered, the red cliffs of Varkala are as much a landmark from the sea as they were when the *Periplus* was written. But the sea coast has receded since Ptolemy's time, and the area and shape of the backwaters and river estuaries have also changed considerably. The city of Neacyndi of Pliny ('Melkynde' of Ptolemy, 'Nelcynda' of the *Periplus* and 'Nincylda' of the Peutinger Tables) is identified with Niraṇam (reputed site of an apostolic church) or Mīnacil, both fairly near Kōṭṭayam and centres to which pepper could easily be brought. The 'Bacare' of Pliny and of the *Periplus* is either Kallaṭa or Purakkāṭ near Alleppey, both linked with Kōṭṭayam by water and both dispatching-centres of some importance centuries ago. It is not relevant to our purpose to record the identifications of the other places mentioned by these early writers; but the fact that the coast is described in such detail shows its more than local importance to trade in the first century.

Pliny mentions the name of the ruler of Muziris. Recent excava-

[1] Strabo, *Geography*, transl. Hamilton and Falconer, I, pp. 178ff.; 'How the Romans worked the world's sole source of porphyry', by D. O. Meredith in *Illus. London News*, 16 Dec. 1950.

[2] This information comes from Pliny. See Thomson, *History of Ancient Geography*, pp. 174ff., and Tarn, *The Greeks in Bactria and India*, pp. 373ff.

tions on this site have revealed sherds of first-century date similar to those found and dated at Arikamedu, a Roman trading station on the east coast.[1] Wheeler concludes that regular monsoon trade is now proved to have existed between the eastern Mediterranean and south-western India at least as early as A.D. 30 and possibly before the death of Augustus. The *Periplus* states that this use of the monsoon was discovered by a Greek named Hippalus about 50 B.C., but there can be no doubt that this wind was used for navigation long before it was known to Westerners, and the *Periplus* date is almost certainly too late.

We know something about the extent of this trade from references in Latin writers and from the coins discovered in south India. Arikamedu was an established Roman trading station and the Peutinger Tables show a temple of Augustus near Muziris, and it is said that two Roman cohorts were stationed there to guard the warehouses.[2] Pliny speaks with some dismay of a trade which cost the empire about one and a half million sesterces a year, chiefly for luxuries like pepper, ginger and precious stones, with no reciprocal export trade to compensate. Tiberius introduced various measures to curb the taste for oriental luxuries, but apparently with little success, and the disastrous drain of Roman gold went on.[3] Over a thousand coins of Tiberius have been found in south India, and 450 of Augustus, mostly in hoards uncovered by accident. Many of these have been in the Coimbatore district, not far from the ancient beryl mines but also on the line of a natural highway from west to east, along the valley of the Ponnani, between the western and eastern ghats. A hoard found recently at Eyyal, not far from Cranganore, contained forty-six silver coins of Augustus, fourteen of Tiberius (eight of them gold) and gold and silver coins of Claudius and Nero. There was also one gold coin of Trajan (d. 117). Very likely parties from the coastal trading stations went inland on trading trips, and probably Roman coins became recognized standard currency all over south India, as the south Indian kings do not appear to have had coinage of their own, thus setting a precedent for the later use of Venetian coins, and, until very recently, of the British gold sovereign. (The value of gold articles is still computed in sovereigns in Malabar.)

[1] 'Arikamedu', by R. C. M. Wheeler and others, *Ancient India* (July 1946), pp. 18ff.

[2] Warmington, *Commerce between the Roman Empire and India*, p. 58.

[3] Warmington, *ibid.* p. 41, quoting Dio Cassius, LVII, 15.

Some Tamil classics also speak of this trade.[1] One poem speaks of Muziris, where 'agitating the white foam of the Periyar river, the beautifully built ships of the *Yavanas* (Westerners) came with gold and returned with pepper, and Muziris resounded with the noise'; and in another poem we read of the Pandya king drinking 'the cool and fragrant wine brought by the *Yavanas* in their good ships'. We also read that some Indian rajas employed bodyguards of Western soldiers—'the valiant-eyed *Yavanas* whose bodies were strong and of terrible aspect'; who were 'excellent guardians of the gates of the fort walls'.

One further factor may be mentioned as not irrelevant to this inquiry. There is a Jewish colony settled in various places round the Periyar river and in Quilon, the very places which claim Christian churches founded by St Thomas. According to their own traditions they came originally in A.D. 68 and settled in Muziris, receiving a grant of privileges on copper plates just as the Christians did in the fourth century. There are Christian copper-plate grants associated with Quilon and generally thought to be of the ninth century which are witnessed by a number of Jews, subscribing their names in Hebrew. We cannot be certain of these traditional dates, but it looks as if Jewish immigrants, perhaps driven from the West or Arabia by persecution, settled in Kēraḷa and became respected trading communities in the first few centuries of our era. A Hebrew letter of 1768 records these traditions of the Jews and states that there were then six colonies of Jews, at Cochin (where the raja had received them and given them land on their expulsion from Cranganore (Muziris) by the Portuguese in 1566), Anjikaimal (near Cochin), Paṛavūr (where the synagogue is near the Syrian church), Cendamangaḷam (here also the synagogue adjoins the church), Maḷa, Tīrtūr and Maṛṛam. There were, however, other colonies besides, as we know from names like Judākkunnu, 'Jew's hill', near the church at Pālayūr and Judankuḷam, 'Jew's pool', near the village of Vadakkāṭ in Malabar. The spoken language of the first immigrants was undoubtedly Aramaic and much remains in the service books of the

[1] Iyengar, *History of the Tamils to A.D. 600*, p. 312, cited by Wheeler, *Ancient India* (July, 1946), p. 21. *Silappadikaram*, *Manituekkalai*, *Pattinippalai* and *Puranuru* are classics which contain descriptions of the ports of Malabar. See 'Roman trade centres in Malabar' by P. J. Thomas, *Kēraḷa Soc. Papers* (1932), series 10, pp. 259ff., who also says there were 'Yavana' soldiers in the service of the Cēra king.

Cochin Jews to this day. The later colony of 'White' or Spanish Jews arrived in the fifteenth century; they also went first to Cranganore and later settled in Cochin. The Jews, like the Christians, have songs about their origin describing their arrival by sea at Pālayūr and other places, and the building of the synagogues and the royal grants and privileges they received. If these colonies were in existence in the first century (which is not by any means certain), they would provide an obvious venue for an apostolic mission. But in any case they show how the trade route made it possible for foreigners to come, and their history demonstrates the tolerance and kindness of the Hindu rulers who allowed them to settle down and become a part of Indian society, making their own contribution to the life of the whole. In this way the coming of the Jewish community provides a close parallel to the Christian settlements, and like them, but to a much smaller extent, they struck roots in the country and added converts to their community.[1]

The evidence given above does not prove the apostolic mission of St Thomas in south India. It does show that there was no physical reason why Christian traders, or the Apostle himself, could not have come to Malabar in the first century. The existence of an old local tradition and of families whose ancestry seems ancient and indigenous, rather than of foreign immigrant trading stock, are factors which suggest the possibility of an early evangelist in the country, but the dependence of all traditions on the Edessene Church prevents us considering these factors conclusive proof that this early evangelist was St Thomas. In fact the Edessene dependence inclines most scholars to scepticism. It may be that scholars have dismissed too easily the story of Pantaenus's visit and his discovery of a Gospel brought by Bartholomew. (The memory of the Tatta sect may also point in this direction.) This tradition, known to Eusebius, has never been considered very seriously because it was overwhelmed by the later universal reference to St Thomas. It is not impossible that St Bartholomew was in fact India's Apostle, but his claim can no more be proved than can that of St Thomas.

[1] 'A Hebrew letter of 1768', by S. S. Koder, *Jour. Rama Varma Arch. Society*, xv (1949); 'Songs of the Jews of Cochin', by A. I. Simon, *Bulletin of Rama Varma Research Institute* (July 1946), pp. 25–37.

SOURCES

REFERENCES have been given in footnotes to various books and articles, but the literature on the subject of this chapter is immense. Fr H. Hosten, S.J., in his *Antiquities from San Thome and Mylapore*, gives an annotated bibliography of sources for a study of the St Thomas question, and therein lists 283 books and articles. Much material was brought together in two articles by W. R. Philipps in the *Indian Antiquary*, XXXIII, pp. 1 ff. and 145 ff. Bishop A. E. Medlycott collected the evidence in his *India and the Apostle Thomas, an Inquiry*. He was followed by L. M. Zaleski, *The Apostle St Thomas in India*, and J. Dahlmann, S.J., *Die Thomas-Legende*. R. Garbe tried to refute these books in *Indies und das Christentum*, but his book is not profound. An important contribution was *The Early Spread of Christianity in India* (Rylands Library Bulletin) by Mingana (mentioned above, p. 39), which explored Syriac writings for information about the earliest days of the Indian Church. This was followed by two Bulletins by Dr J. N. Farquhar, *The Apostle Thomas in North India* (1926) and *The Apostle Thomas in South India* (1927), which contain more conjecture than fact. Prof. Jarl Charpentier, in his small booklet *St Thomas the Apostle and India*, provides a useful short bibliography.

The record of the local traditions has been indicated in the footnotes. The number of Malayāḷam writings on the subject is very considerable, most of them having a polemical purpose. The *Kēraḷa Society Papers* contain various articles, among which 'Three St Thomas documents' (1932, series 9), and 'St Thomas and his feasts', by F. C. Burkitt (1930, series 6), repay attention. Two booklets have lately been published by local writers: in *The History of the Mar Thoma Church* K. K. Kuruvilla defends the tradition; T. K. Joseph, however, attacks it and him in *South India's St Thomas*.

CHAPTER III

THE MALABAR CHURCH COMES INTO HISTORY

THE only certain conclusion which can be drawn from an examination of the St Thomas tradition is that at any rate such a visit was physically possible. Malabar continued to be visited by traders from Alexandria by the Red Sea route until the fourth century. After that trade was again carried by the ships which came down the coast from south Arabia and the Persian Gulf. There were strong Christian and Jewish colonies in these places until the rise of Islam in the seventh century, and it is not unlikely that there would be Persian Christians settling on the Malabar coast for trade throughout the early centuries. The evidence available seems to confirm this probability, and whether or not the Apostle himself ever came to south India, it seems certain that other Christians from east Syria who claimed a connexion with him did come to reinforce, if not found, the Malabar Church in the first three centuries. We have seen that the sites associated in tradition with St Thomas are, with one apparent exception, on trade routes, and often associated with Jewish colonies. It is significant that Syrian Christians were, until this century, always reckoned as belonging to either Cranganore or Quilon, the main centres in turn of Portuguese, Dutch and British traders.[1] Each of these European powers left their mark behind, in persons claiming descent from them, and in church buildings erected for their religious needs. The occupation by East Syrian or Persian traders was of far longer duration, and while no monuments remain which can be attributed to them with certainty, the Syrian community forms their living memorial.[2] This is not to say that it was entirely a foreign community. Traders in those days of difficult transport probably often settled down for life in the country, marrying Indian wives, as the

[1] Cranganore was silted up in the seventeenth century, and the trade moved to the neighbouring factory of Cochin, where it remains.

[2] It is not improbable that the 'Moors' or Arab traders whom the Portuguese found enjoying the Malabar trade at the beginning of the sixteenth century were the lineal descendants of pre-Islamic traders, some of whom may have been Christian.

Armenians and Portuguese did, and we can also suppose that there were among the foreigners some who, faithful to the remarkable East Syrian genius for missionary work, preached the Gospel to the people of the country. If this were so it is easy to understand the devotion to St Thomas which has always been a characteristic of the Malabar Church, for apart from a possible local South Indian tradition the East Syrian Church also regarded the apostle as its founder, and at the beginning of the ninth century rested its claim to independence of Edessa on that ground.[1] Settlers in Malabar would have brought the proud claim to apostolic foundation with them; and the Malabar Church would also look back to St Thomas as its indirect, if not direct, founder.

The first probable reference to a Church in Malabar is contained in the story of Theophilus the Indian in the middle of the fourth century; the first certain reference is the account by Cosmas Indicopleustes in the early sixth century. Before the fourth century there are references to India, but the connotation of that name cannot be established, and the majority's opinion is that the India indicated was north-western India, which was closely associated with Parthia in early Christian times. Syriac writers of the second century do not mention an Indian Church, but they had no obvious cause to do so. In 196 Bardaisan contrasted the way of life of Christians among the Parthians, Kushans, Persians and Medes with that of their pagan neighbours, but he does not mention Christians in India.[2] The *Didascalia*,[3] of about mid third-century date, and the fourth-century *Acts* speak of the Indian labours of Judas Thomas, but these references are probably to the north-west. On the other hand there is evidence that Christian communities had been founded on the route from the Red Sea to India, and in Persia. There was a bishop at Basra and another inland in the Persian province of Fars by A.D. 225.[4] Before the end of the fourth century Bahrain had its bishop and there was a large monastery south of Baith Katraye. The first historical reference to the Indian Church may be the information in the *Chronique de Seert* that David (Dudi), Bishop of Basra, left his see in 295–300 to

[1] Asseman, III, pt. 2, p. 422; quoted by Heras, *The Two Apostles of India*, p. 18. The Edessene claim was not of direct but indirect apostolic foundation, Addai being sent by Thomas to Edessa.

[2] *Liber Legum* (Migne, *Patrologiae Cursus, series syriensis*, II, pp. 582–5, 600, 606).

[3] Cureton, *Ancient Syriac Documents*, p. 33.

[4] Migne, *Patrologiae Cursus, series orientalis*, IV, pp. 235, 292.

go to India where he evangelized many people.[1] It is not likely that any other place could be meant here by the term 'India' and in view of the trade connexions it is as likely that the bishop went to the south-west coast as to the north-west. The silence of existing literature about a South Indian Church in the first centuries is not surprising even if such a Church existed. The early stages of growth of any Christian community are usually unspectacular and apparently insignificant, and it is most unlikely that they would be widely noticed. We find little mention of any churches in Asia until they are so organized that their bishop has become a recognized figure.

John the Persian, 'Bishop of the churches of the whole of Persia and great India', was present at the Council of Nicea together with the bishops of Edessa and Nisibis, but it is plain that 'great India' refers not to the whole continent but to the area in north-western India which had been under the rule of Greek or Persian kings. Another reference to 'India' is the story of Meropius and Frumentius, told by several fourth- and fifth-century writers, but this 'India' was Abyssinia.[2] An echo of the story is to be found in the fact that in 356 the Emperor Constantius told Aeizanes, the Abyssinian king, to send Frumentius to him.[3]

Constantius is said to have sent a mission about the year 354 to south Arabia, Abyssinia, Ceylon and India,[4] and it is possible that we have here the first reference to a South Indian Church. Theophilus the Indian went to the Maldives and 'thence he sailed to other parts of India, and reformed many things which were not rightly done among them, for they heard the reading of the Gospel in a sitting posture and did other things which were repugnant to the divine law; and having reformed everything according to the holy usage, as was most acceptable to God, he also confirmed the dogma of the Church'. There is every likelihood that the part of India to which Theophilus first went was the Malabar coast, very near the Maldives, with good and well-known harbours. His

[1] Mingana, p. 18.

[2] Zaleski maintains that there were two bishops named Frumentius, and that the Indian one alone was canonized (the other Frumentius worked in Abyssinia). Zaleski translates Rufinus's account, derived, it is said, from Frumentius's brother, Edesius. *The Saints of India*, pp. 196, 205–36.

[3] *Encycl. Brit.* (14th ed.), art. 'Axumite kingdom', II, p. 819. In the sixth century this kingdom sent an expedition to wreck the Jewish state then existing in S. Arabia.

[4] Migne, *Pat. Cur. ser. gr.* LXV, pp. 481–9. Photius, *Bibliotheca*, quoted in Mingana, p. 26.

account assumes regular congregational worship, and a church life cut off from frequent contact with other countries, for standing to hear the Gospel is one of the oldest Christian ceremonies.[1] Mingana suggests that the Church which Theophilus found in India was very akin to the Church in Socotra, which used Syriac in its services. Socotra was a port of call on the regular trade to Malabar.

Syriac sources enable us to see the Indian Church in the fifth century sharing the life of the Syriac-speaking Church, but once more we cannot be sure to which part of India they refer. A colophon to Isho'dad's *Commentary on Romans*, of early fifth-century date, mentions that 'Daniel, the priest, the Indian' had assisted in the translation of the text from Greek to Syriac,[2] and we are told that Mana, Bishop of Riwarshir, wrote Pahlavi hymns and sermons and sent Syriac translations of Diodore and Theodore to Bahrain and India in the last quarter of that century.

The first unquestionable historical reference to the Church in south India is a passage in the *Christian Topography* of Cosmas Indicopleustes, who travelled widely between 520 and 525 and published his book about 535. Cosmas says: 'Even in the island of Taprobane in Inner India where the Indian Sea is, there is a church of Christians, with clergy and a congregation of believers, though I know not if there be any Christians farther in that direction. And such also is the case in the land called Male where the pepper grows. And in the place called Kalliana there is a bishop appointed from Persia, as well as in the island of Dioscoris [Socotra], in the same Indian sea. The inhabitants of that island speak Greek, having been originally settled there by the Ptolemies, who ruled after Alexander of Macedon.' Ceylon is described thus: 'This is the great island in the ocean, lying in the Indian Sea. By the Indians it is called Sielendibe but by the Greeks, Taprobane. In it is found the hyacinth stone. It lies on the other side of the pepper country. The island hath also a church of Persian Christians who have settled there, and a presbyter who is appointed from Persia, and all the apparatus of public worship. But the natives and their kings are quite another kind of people.'[3]

[1] *Apostolic Constitution*, book II, ch. 57 (*Ante-Nicene Christian Library*, vol. 17). See also Cureton, 'Doctrine of the Apostles, VII', in *Ancient Syriac Documents*, p. 27.

[2] Mingana, pp. 27, 28.

[3] *Christian Topography of Cosmas Indicopleustes*, ed. J. W. McCrindle, pp. 118–29.

Cosmas did not collect all his facts himself, but the description given above could not refer to anywhere except the west coast of India and Ceylon. Kalliana has been variously identified with Kalyani near Bombay or Quilon in Travancore. Fr Paul points out that, according to tradition, Quilon was not then founded. He thinks Kalliana was at the mouth of the Bakanur river, north of Calicut.[1] The reference to the pepper country must refer to Malabar. Cosmas was an East Syrian, and his evidence confirms the surmise that the early churches of Malabar were connected with colonies of foreign traders. The Portuguese found traces of other Christian colonies round Cape Comorin and the east coast, and they were probably remnants of the same connexion. Marco Polo in the thirteenth and Nicolo Conti in the fifteenth century speak of the Socotra Christians as having a Nestorian, or, as Cosmas called him, a Persian, bishop. There is other early evidence for the East Syrian or Persian connexion.

The Nestorian Patriarch Isho Yahb (650–60) rebuked Simeon, metropolitan of Riwarshir, for disobedience and for having refused to give the Indian Church the bishops it needed.[2] 'As far as your district is concerned, from the time you showed recalcitrance against ecclesiastical canons the episcopal succession has been interrupted in India, and this country has since sat in darkness, far from the light of the divine teaching by means of rightful bishops: not only India that extends from the borders of the Persian Empire, to the country which is called Kalah, which is a distance of 1200 parasangs, but even your own Fars.' Mingana thinks, with Reinaud, that Kalah is Galle in Ceylon, but Yule thinks it was Quilon, which Marco Polo called Coilum. The exact identification does not matter for the purpose of this argument. If Ceylon had a Church receiving regular episcopal visitations, or even possessing its own hierarchy, it is most improbable that this Church had no branches or connexions on the west coast of India, into whose good harbours any ship beating down the coast would certainly put for trade as well as revictualling. If this is correct, then the Persian Christians were a link in a long chain of mercantile traders, following the Romans,

[1] Paul, *India orientalis christiana*, p. 14.

[2] Under Patriarch Timothy I (779–823) the Christians of Fars based their claim to independence on the fact that they were 'Christians of St Thomas' and had nothing in common with the see of Mari. Mingana, p. 32; Asseman, III, p. 113; Yule, *Book of Ser Marco Polo*, II, p. 377; cf. Yule, *Cathay and the Way Thither*, II, footnote on pp. 129, 130.

and in turn followed by Muslims from their own country, Portuguese, Dutch and British, all of whom had trading stations down the west coast of India and round to Ceylon and the Coromandel coast.

It is important that we remember that the term 'Nestorian', often used of the East Syrian and Persian Church, at first may indicate a geographical factor rather than a theological conviction. Persian Christians had never been able to maintain close relations with the Church of the Eastern Roman Empire, because of the troubled political relations between the two countries. The Sassanian kings of Persia were tolerant so long as they believed their Christian subjects to be loyal, but savage persecutors when they suspected them of hankering after the protection of the Christian Empire. So the disputes of the Catholic Church were not known in Persia, and it was not until 410 that the Persian Church heard and accepted the decrees of Nicea. Fighting between Persia and the Eastern Empire in 420 brought bitter persecution to the Persian Christians: in 422 peace brought respite. The need for unequivocal independence of the Church of the Empire was probably the motive behind the Persian Church's declaration of independence of Antioch in 424, and her establishment of the Catholicos of Seleucia-Ctesiphon as Patriarch. This Patriarch of the East, or of Babylon, was acknowledged by the Malabar Christians when the Portuguese came. There is no reason to doubt the Indian assertion that he had ruled them for a thousand years. It is not necessary to follow the history of the Persian Church further at this point except to note that the definite adoption of Nestorian teaching and condemnation of Western doctrine dates from the patriarchate of Babai (597–602). From that date the connexion with the Church of the Persian Empire involved the Malabar Church in Nestorianism, though how far that doctrinal position was appreciated and understood is another question.

There are traditions of foreign immigration preserved among the Indian Christians and also a number of stone crosses with Pahlavi inscriptions which have been ascribed to the period under consideration. One tradition is associated with the name of Thomas of Cana, the other with the foundation of Quilon. In the latter case there is evidence of copper-plate records of grants to be considered, which refer to an already existing community of Māṇigrāmakkar, which may have been the remnant of a truly Indian Church evangelized by St Thomas or others in the first century. Unfortunately there is no certainty about the dating, either of the traditions or the grants.

The first tradition describes the strengthening of the Indian Church by immigrant Christians of East Syrian stock, but the various versions ascribe different dates to this event. Most of the local accounts of the story place it in 345 and this is accepted without question even by so careful a writer as P. Cheriyan.[1] The Syriac accounts of the history of the Malabar Church translated by Mingana, which he considers of doubtful value, agree in this date. One of these accounts, probably written by an Indian Jacobite at the beginning of the eighteenth century, says that the Catholicos of the East sent a merchant called Thomas of Jerusalem (Thomas of Cana) to inquire into the state of the Malabar Christians. He duly visited them, and returned to report their needs to the Catholicos, who was much moved. Then 'it happened by the power of our adorable God, and by order of the Catholicos, that after a very short time the merchant Thomas of Jerusalem left his country and accompanied by that very bishop who saw the vision,[2] and by priests and deacons, by men, women and children, from Jerusalem, Baghdad and Nineveh (Mosul). They went on board a ship and came to Malabar, and reached Malankara in the year three hundred and forty-fifth of our Lord. When the inhabitants of Malabar recognized them they assembled near them, and took advice from one another. They then went to Sharhun, the king of all Malabar, and brought him gifts and presents. The king was pleased with them and said to them: "I will gratify all your wishes" and he gave them land as long and broad as they desired. And he invested them also with royal honours inscribed on pieces of copper, which are preserved with us down to the present day. When they received all these from the king they returned to Malankara. Then they busied themselves with the building of the church and the town.'[3] Mingana shows that the Catholicate was vacant between 342 and 344 and that the Catholicos Baba Shemin was in prison from February 345 to 9 January 346, when he was martyred. He had no successor for twenty years. So he concludes that the whole

[1] P. Cheriyan, *The Malabar Syrians and the Church Missionary Society, 1816–1840*, p. 40.

[2] The Metropolitan of Edessa had had a vision of the needs of Malabar, which he reported to the Catholicos.

[3] Mingana, pp. 45–9.

story is absolutely unhistorical, as, in their short term of office during the persecution of Sapor, neither Catholicos could have attended to the business of a Jerusalem merchant. But the part of the Catholicos in the story is not at all essential, and even if he had nothing to do with the expedition it may still have occurred. The persecution of Sapor II, the Sassanian king of Persia, was very severe and may well have caused groups of Christians to flee his territory, just as in Islamic times the Zoroastrians left Persia and formed the present Parsi colonies in and around Bombay. Mingana refers to another account of the tradition, quoting Giamil, who speaks of a Bishop Joseph of Edessa, 'who in 345 was sent by the Catholicos of the East to the coast of Malabar'.[1]

The tradition of this early date is not confined to Christians: it is found in the Brahman history of Malabar called the *Kēraḷa Ulpaṭṭi*, but the date of this work is quite uncertain and the author may have used Christian sources. A manuscript in the Madras Museum reads as follows: 'At a late period in the Kāḷi Yuga the *bauddhas* came to Kēraḷadeśa and the king Cerumān Perumāḷ learned from them their system of religious belief. He was attracted and accepted their faith. He then told the Brahmans to unite with the *bauddhas* and follow their system, but they were very angry and arranged a public dispute. In this they were successful, the *bauddhas* had their tongues cut out and were banished from the country, while Cerumān Perumāḷ was dethroned and some lands were set aside for his support.'[2] This, says the *Ulpaṭṭi*, is not the Cerumān Perumāḷ who went to Mecca.[3] Another manuscript says that in 342 this Perumāḷ flourished at Tiruvanjikuḷam. A version of the *Ulpaṭṭi* belonging to the Nampūtiri house of Kapliṅāṭ gives the same story and says that the *bauddhas* came from Baghdad and were known as *paradēśis* or foreigners.

There is a tradition of a Hindu king who became a *bauddha* at Nilamperūr near Caṅanaśśēri. He is said to have built the Paḷḷiyil B-hagavati temple and a small one near it for *bauddhas*. He also instituted a mock fight to take place annually. This is continued and combatants always go first to ask permission of the king called Paḷḷivanavar, at his tomb outside the temple. About the year 1890

[1] S. Giamil, *Genuinae relationes*, pp. 578–9, quoted by Mingana, p. 64.

[2] The *Kēraḷōlpaṭṭi* was based on *Kēraḷa Mahālmyam*; no *Ulpaṭṭi* is more than 300–400 years old. See *Jour. Madras Literary Society*, VII (1838), pp. 41–74, translating Mackenzie MSS., book III, countermark 896, in the Madras Museum.

[3] T. K. Joseph, *Malabar Christians and their Ancient Documents*, pp. 8, 9.

a statue was unearthed in the tomb, of a person holding a staff in each hand and wearing a necklace of *tulasi* beads with a cross pendant. It is also said that a large stone slab with a sculptured cross was found, apparently covering a tomb. If the statue is of Paḷḷivanavar it seems to suggest that he had become a Christian, and the question arises whether he may be the converted Cerumān Perumāḷ of tradition. One furlong away from the place where the statue was found is a compound called Tiruvanjikuḷam (Cranganore where Cerumān ruled) which is still the property of the Cranganore temple.[1]

The dates in these various manuscripts are given in chronograms and these are not only inconsistent with one another but must be later than the period they describe, since this method of dating was not used in the Hindu period. The manuscript quoted above gives a chronogram *Rauravam Devarajyam*, literally, 'the kingdom of God is hell' which is taken to be equivalent to a date in 317.[2] It mentions Baghdad, which was not founded until the eighth century, a clear indication that this form of the tradition was much later than the events it described. Other versions give the date A.D. 745 for the arrival of the *bauddhas*, which agrees with the account given by the Nestorian bishop, Mar Gabriel, in 1705.[3] Early Portuguese visitors seem to have heard both versions of the tradition.[4] The copper plates themselves which conveyed the grants are no longer extant, and cannot be used to suggest a date. A Portuguese Jesuit report in the British Museum gives an account of the contents of the plates, in substantial agreement with do Couto's version, but this appears to be a seventeenth-century account of the local tradition rather than a translation from an authentic grant.[5] No secure conclusion about the date of Thomas of Cana's settlement can be reached, but the tradition is certainly dependent on an historical

[1] T. K. Joseph, *Malabar Christians and their Ancient Documents*, pp. 8, 9; Fr Placid in his unpublished history quotes R. N. Panikkar's *History of Kēraḷa Language and Literature*, which gives the tradition preserved in *Ulpaṭṭis*.

[2] H. H. Rama Varma and K. N. Daniel agree on this. The manuscript is described by T. K. Joseph, 'A Hindu date for Thomas in Malabar', *Powra Dhvani Annual*.

[3] Kaujiklettan Thamparan (of the Cranganore royal house) in *Kēraḷam*, p. 143. See Visscher, *Letters from Malabar*, p. 106.

[4] Do Couto, *Da Asia*, decada XII.

[5] Hosten published do Couto's version with a parallel English translation in *Kēraḷa Soc. Papers* (1930), series 4, pp. 180–2. The British Museum Add. MSS. 9853, pp. 525–37, contains an anonymous 'Relaçao da Christandade da Serra de 1604'; this is not in Roz's handwriting.

event. The Southist section of the Syrians trace their descent from Thomas and his Syrian wife, and claim that their blood is pure Syrian.[1]

We next turn to another tradition, that which claims the foundation of Quilon as the work of Christian immigrants in A.D. 825, the year from which the Malayāḷam era is reckoned. A Syriac document written in Malabar at the beginning of the eighteenth century recounts the tradition thus: 'In those days and in the days that followed, Syrian Fathers used to come to that town by order of the Catholicos of the East, and govern the diocese of India and Malabar, because it was from it that the Syrians used to go to other parts until they were dispersed. Then in the year 823, the Syrian Fathers, Mar Sapor and Mar Parut (Piruz) with the illustrious Sabr'isho came to India and reached Kullam. They went to the king Shakirbirti, and asked from him a piece of land in which they could build a church for themselves and erect a town. He gave them the amount of land they desired, and they built a church and erected a town in the district of Kullam, to which Syrian bishops and Metropolitans used to come by order of the Catholicos who sent them.'[2]

There has been a constant tradition about this settlement. The names of the bishops have been handed down in various forms—Xabro and Prodh, or Sapor and Aphroth.[3]

There are five copper plates still in existence which contain the record of grants made to the Christians and others of Quilon. The first set of plates is dated the fifth year of Sthanu Ravi.[4] This is reckoned by T. K. Joseph as *c.* A.D. 880. The donor was King Ayyan of Venāṭ, which corresponds to the southern portion of the present Travancore State, and he gave certain perquisites and

[1] See below, Part II, p. 175.

[2] Translated by Mingana, pp. 42ff.

[3] G. Curian in his Malayāḷam essay (Prize Essay on the Syrian Church) records this tradition. He says that the descendants of one of the colonists are the Kollakkaran Mutalāḷis of Cāttanūr, who probably moved from Quilon in the fifteenth century. Early Portuguese writers refer to colonies; Gaspar Correa, *Lendas da India*, III, p. 423; do Couto, *Da Asia*, decada XII, book III, ch. V. There are several Mutalāḷis in Quilon attached to the Kadisha Church who claim direct descent from Maruvan Sabr'isho mentioned in the Quilon copper plate. Mingana believes that the Mar Sapor of the tradition can be identified with Maruvan Sabr'isho—'our Lord Sabr'isho'. Sabr'isho is a common Syriac name meaning 'Jesus is our hope'. There are fifty families of Mutalāḷis at Cāttanūr and fifteen at Kallaṭa.

[4] T. K. Joseph says this king was a contemporary of the Cōḷa king, Aditya I, 877–907; *Malabar Miscellany*, p. 2. See V. A. Smith, *Early History of India* (1914), p. 463.

privileges to the Tarisa (now called Kadisha) Church built at Quilon by Sabr'isho. The king gave some low-caste people to be servants of the Church and exempted them from paying certain specified rates and taxes, and gave them the right of entry to the market (denied before because they were not caste Hindus). Any crime committed by these people was to be tried by the Christians. The Church was given also the administration of customs in Quilon, that is, the steelyard and weights and the *kappan*.[1] (We see an interesting parallel to some of these privileges in the arrangements made by the Portuguese in the sixteenth century with the Raja of Cochin, by which their fort was placed outside the king's jurisdiction and they had the right of trying cases connected with their own servants and also with the local Christians.) When Marignolli came in 1348 he found that the Christians were 'masters of the public weighing office'.[2] By Alfonso d'Alburquerque's time (A.D. 1504) they had lost the privilege of 'keeping the seal and the standard weight of the city'.[3] It is evident from these privileges that the Christian community had a reputation for integrity, as well as a recognized position in society. Even if the community consisted mostly of immigrants who had settled only some sixty years before, they had settled permanently and were recognized as playing a valuable part in the community life. Probably the slaves they were given would be baptized and absorbed into the community; we know that this practice was common until towards the end of last century.

The second set of plates were also given by King Ayyan and are of about the same date. The plates contain details of grants to the Tarisa Church, to the Jews, and to the Māṇigrāmmam. The Church was given land let out under certain conditions to four families of agriculturists and two of carpenters, so as to ensure a perpetual income to the Church. The boundaries of the land given to the Christian community were also marked out in the ancient way, by marking 'the course taken by a female elephant let free'. The Christians had the sole right of administering justice in this territory and of receiving the bride price, and were entitled to receive protection, if they needed it, from the Venāṭ militia called the Six Hundred, and the Jewish and Māṇigrāmmam leaders.

[1] Probably the official seal.

[2] Yule, *Cathay and the Way Thither*, III, p. 127.

[3] *Commentaries of the Great Affonso d' Albuquerque*, trans. by Birch, I, *Second Voyage to India*, p. 15.

Two other communities were given grants in the same charters. The Jews (Anjuvannam) had certain dues payable to the king remitted and the right to collect other dues, as well as assessing all dutiable articles coming by land or water on the king's behalf. They were to keep the customs income in safe custody and could withhold payment of this collection and the weighing fees until wrongs done to their community were redressed. They had the right of co-operating with government officials in the king's commercial transactions. They could try their own causes, live in the town of Quilon as tenants and they enjoyed seventy-two social privileges. The only one specified is that of bringing on the back of an elephant water for ablutions used in marriage ceremonies.

Similar privileges were given to the Māṇigrāmmam. The communities to which these grants were made exercised their authority after a well-known local pattern. Often the territory adjoining a temple was thought to be under the control of the god and was managed by the society or community who looked after the temple. Sometimes the local king might, for the sake of convenience, act as managing trustee of such a body.[1] At the head of all was the king drawing from the land a share of its produce. Another share went to the *paṭi* (overlord) or intermediary between the king and the landholder. The *paṭi* in these cases was not an individual but a corporation—the Jews in Anjuvannam, the Christians around their church, and the Māṇigrāmmakkar. In these plates the two *paṭis* of Jews and Māṇigrāmmakkar and the local Nāyars (possibly also organized in the same way) are given the responsibility of protecting the Christians and their church. It looks as if they had become really established in the country only recently and that the king was making sure of their continuance because of their usefulness.

The Māṇigrāmmakkar formed a separate community at the time of the grant, and there is reason to believe they were the descendants of lapsed Christians. It is possible that their existence is evidence that there was an ancient indigenous Christian community in south India, evangelized in very early, if not in apostolic, times, prior to the foreign Christian settlements.[2] In 1820 a Church Missionary Society missionary met a few families of

[1] K. P. Padmanabha Menon, *History of Kēraḷa*, IV, pp. 91, 92.

[2] K. M. Paṇikkar, in *Malabar and the Portuguese*, says that the only reason for thinking the Māṇigrāmmakkar had Christian connexions was Col. Macauley's action in handing over the plate to the Christians when he discovered it at Cochin. Paṇikkar thinks that Māṇigrāmmam was a Hindu trading guild. The

Māṇigrāmmakkar at Kaṭamaṟṟom. Whitehouse, in his book published in 1873,[1] gave some interesting details about the Māṇigrāmmakkar. He was of the opinion that these people were seeking continually to loosen the ties which still bound them to the Christians so that they might be accepted as Nāyars. Until about 1843 the Māṇigrāmmakkar at Kayamkuḷam paid a fee to the Church when they had a marriage, and received a new cloth for the bride from the Church. So also the Church gave a piece of cloth at a funeral, but the last priest they had had been cremated, contrary to previous custom, a further break with Christian practice. Whitehouse says that at Quilon there were thirty families who still had a priest, called Naimar, or Naimar Acan. He wore a long beard, lived alone, and at death was buried in a sitting position, like Syrian bishops. At the 1837 census these people tried to be classed as Nāyars, with whom they were intermarrying. They still in 1873 used some of their old privileges at weddings, such as using elephants and a palanquin for the bride. Now the process of separation from the Christians appears to be complete and they have achieved their ambition to be reckoned as Nāyars.

The local tradition about the origin of the Māṇigrāmmakkar as a separate community is handed down in at least two forms. One version says that in 293 there was a great persecution of Christians on the east coast, in the Cōḷa kingdom, and so the Christians fled to the west.[2] Seventy-two families reached Quilon in safety and entered into close and happy relations with the Christians they found there. In 315, however, a well-known Tamil preacher and magician of the Saivite sect, Mānikkavācakar, followed them up and tried to seduce them from the Christian faith by preaching and magic. Some Christians were attracted and learned *slokams* and Hindu stories and witnessed dramas in the temples. When the influence of Mānikkavācakar had been felt for some time the

same word occurs in inscriptions from Siam, Trichinopoly, Cranganore and Taḷekkad in Cochin, and in old Malayāḷam and Tamil (Commentary on 'Payannur', a song of north Malabar; and Gunavira Panditar's *Tamil Grammar*, 6, p. 63). The word does seem to indicate a trade guild, but no particular religious application is indicated. A. C. Burnell's guess that the word referred to a settlement of Manicheans has not been accepted. See *Indian Antiquary*, IV, pp. 153ff., 181ff., 361ff.; V, pp. 25ff.

[1] Whitehouse, p. 49.

[2] This is given on palm leaves preserved in an old Syrian family, Karuthodethu house, Mavelikkara. It is called the 'State of the Religion of the Way in Kēraḷa'; printed by T. K. Joseph in *Malabar Christians and their Ancient Documents*.

head-man of the Christian community died and a controversy arose between the 'indigenizers', who wanted to wrap the body in unbleached cloth and cremate it, and the majority of the immigrant families and the local Christians, who wished to bury their leader in the normal Christian manner, wrapped in a white cloth in his own compound. The dispute was very acute and 116 families said they would not give up the use of the five sacred products of the cow and left the Christian community. They have ever since been called Māṇigrāmmakkar, and the ones who would not apostasize D-hariyāykal, that is, 'those who would not wear the sacred ashes of Hinduism'.

The D-hariyāykal are now scattered, and only one family remained at Tiruvamkōt, their ancient headquarters, in 1952.[1] Their version of the tradition is as follows. When St Thomas preached at Mylapore a Vellāla community of sixty-four families dealing in gold, silver and precious stones accepted the faith. The local king ordered them to recant. On their refusal their property was confiscated and they were warned that death would follow. They accordingly went to Thomas and fled with him at night, making their way across south India and arriving eventually at Tiruvamkōt. The king there sent for them and offered the usual presents of *b-hasmam* (the five sacred products of the cow) and flowers, but they refused to accept them. The king was very surprised at this unusual behaviour of people who appeared caste Hindus and asked the reason for it. When told that they were Christians he gave them land for their own houses and for a church.

Both versions agree that in origin this divided community was an immigration from another part of India. If they had been of Vellāla caste formerly, or were engaged in that kind of trade, the use of the term Māṇigrāmmam is easily understood. It does mean precisely a trading community. T. K. Joseph does not accept the derivation of the word D-hariyāykal given in the two traditional accounts. He says that the modern equivalent, Taruthāykal, is a variant of 'Tarisa' found in the copper plates.[2] The meaning of this word is 'orthodox', and it is used in many ancient songs of groups of Christians at Kōṭṭayam and other places. It was also used of immigrant families supposed to have come with Thomas of Cana.

[1] These people are often called Tiruvankkōdanmar or D-haricacettikal. There are groups now at Kuṇdara, Pālā, Vāḻūr, Tumpamaṇ, Trivada and Piṛavam.

[2] Gundert, *Madras Jour. Literature and Science*, XIII (1844), pt. 2, says that 'Tarisa' simply means 'Christian' in Persian.

The dating of this tradition and the connexion of Māṇikkavācakar with the split are most uncertain.[1] The faithful D-hariyāykal were distinguished from all other Christians in language, in many cultural practices, and in dress until two generations ago. The men used to retain the *kuṭumi*, or single lock of hair on the crown of the head, and the sacred thread was put on their male babies after baptism. The women wore the *pandiada* and other Hindu ornaments. They have now assimilated themselves to the Jacobite community, and intermarried with them. As we have seen, the apostates were fully incorporated into Hindu society only in comparatively recent times.

There are other Christian monuments in Travancore generally thought to have been erected about the ninth century, but again the dating is uncertain. These monuments consist of four stone crosses and an incised slab at Taḷekkāṭ. A stone cross was dug up by the Portuguese in Madras in 1547, and quickly won a reputation for supernatural powers. The ancient Travancore crosses are replicas of the Mount Cross, as Gouvea points out in the *Jornada*: 'And all the ancient churches were made in the manner of Pagodas of the Gentios but full, all of them, of crosses after the manner of the cross of the miracle of St Thomas, which they call St Thomas' Cross; whence it is seen how much more ancient is the veneration of the cross, and affection for it, and manner thereof, than the time when the Portuguese found it, for the ancient churches of these Christians, built many years before the arrival of the Portuguese in

[1] Māṇikkavācakar is usually thought to have lived in the ninth century. On the basis of a synchronism with a Pandyan king, C. V. Narayana Iyer, in *Origin and Early History of Saivism in S. India*, says his date may be seventh century. P. Meile in *L'Inde classique*, p. 451, accepts this suggestion. Possibly this particular teacher was thought of because his name suggested a connexion with the Māṇigrāmmakkar, and, in any case, he was one of the best-known early Saivites. An extraordinary surmise was made by Thurston, *Castes and Tribes of Southern India*, v, p. 410, who accepted the story of the mission of Pantaenus to India in A.D. 190 and said that he was sent by Demetrius of Alexandria to combat the false teaching of Māṇikkavācakar, or of Manes. While it is true that Clement, the pupil of Pantaenus, does refer to Indians and gives some information about them (*Stromateis*, I, 15) his reference comes in the course of a discussion of the relation between Greek and pagan philosophies, in which other races, like the Scythians, are also mentioned. It is arbitrary to take this passage as a proof that Pantaenus had given Clement this information. Indians were common in Alexandria throughout the period of trade activity and their ideas and way of life were not unknown. The mission of Pantaenus (Eusebius, *Hist. Eccl.* v, 10) was very probably to N.W. India where there might well have been Christian communities with a Pahlavi translation of the Gospels in the Aramaic script. (We have portions of the Psalms in Pahlavi but at present no other parts of the Bible.) There is nothing in the story to indicate a South Indian milieu.

India, were all of them adorned with these, both in painting and sculpture.'[1] The cross found by the Portuguese was set behind the altar of the Mount Church in 1551 and began to sweat and change colour in 1557, and thereafter yearly. Gouvea mentions a shrine at Cranganore containing a cross of this type, before which a lamp burned always, and Hindus made their offerings as well as Christians.

The crosses are all cut in relief on slabs of granite. Their arms are of equal length, and there is floriated decoration, springing out of the base above the steps (or calvary) on which they all stand. All the crosses, except one, stand within a rounded arch cut from the granite, and on this arch is a Pahlavi inscription, almost identical in each case with that on the Mount Cross. The exception, the smaller Kōṭṭayam Cross, is similar except that it stands under an ogee arch. There is one cross in the Romo-Syrian Church at Muṟṟucira, one in the Jacobite Church at Kaṭamaṟṟam and two in the Knanaya Jacobite Church at Kōṭṭayam. Winckworth considered that the inscription on the smaller Kōṭṭayam Cross is original, and all the other crosses are copied from it.[2] T. K. Joseph, on the other hand, brings evidence which suggests that all the Travancore crosses are copies of the Mount Cross, executed after 1580 by a local craftsman who did not know Pahlavi.[3] The inscription has been variously interpreted, but Winckworth's translation is now generally accepted: 'My Lord Christ, have mercy on Afras, son of Chaharbukt the Syrian, who cut this' (or 'had this cut'). The crosses are usually thought by the palaeographers to date from the seventh to the eighth century. If Afras is the same man as Mar Aprod, mentioned in the Quilon tradition, the original cross, from which the present crosses take their pattern, would have been erected in the ninth century and would be another link with the Nestorian Church of east Syria and Persia. Any ecclesiastical fashion introduced by a socially prominent group finds its imitators, once conservative reaction to the introduction of a new thing has been overcome. It is probable, therefore, that this Nestorian cross came to be copied and regarded as the correct thing to have behind the altar of the church, or in other places where alms were offered. The veneration paid to the 'cross of St Thomas' by the Portuguese would be widely reported and lead to a reinvigoration of the cult.

[1] Gouvea, book II, ch. I, p. 391.
[2] C. P. T. Winckworth, *Jour. Theological Studies*, XXX (1929) no. 119, pp. 237–44.
[3] T. K. Joseph, *Malabar Christians and their Ancient Documents*, pp. 11–29.

PLATE II

THE SMALLER STONE CROSS IN THE VALIYAPPAḶḶI, KŌṬṬAYAM

The statements in the *Thoma Parvam* song that St Thomas everywhere established churches and planted crosses would then be aetiological, and reflect the sixteenth-century practice when many crosses were being made. By this time, however, large stone crosses outside the churches were probably a more usual gift as they were more prominent memorials of the donor's generosity, and attracted more alms from the passers-by![1]

The inscription outside the church at Taḷekkāṭ records a grant of land to merchants, presumably, but not certainly, Christians. The lettering, in old Vaṭṭēḷuttu Tamil, seems to be eighth–tenth century, coeval with the probable date of the grants and the cross.[2]

A tradition which recurs in several places in the north of Cochin speaks of the difficulties experienced by Christians and Jews as the Muslims gained strength. It says that in the ninth century there was a battle between Christians and Jews on the one hand, and Muslims on the other, over trading at Cranganore. The result of this was a scattering of Christians in other places. Ankamāli, the seat of the Metran (the Syrian bishop) when the Portuguese came, was settled at this time, and so were Kaṭuturutti and other Southist centres. This tradition may explain why Christian and Jewish colonies are found so close together in several places even now, and how it was that the Portuguese found the trading centres under Muslim control, with Christians still active in trade but settled in the hinterland.

We hear nothing more about the Church in India until European travellers first touched the Malabar coast in the thirteenth century, and mentioned the Christians there in the accounts of their journeys.[3] It is reasonable to suppose that during this time contact with the East Syrian Church was always maintained but that the proportion of foreigners to Indians among the St Thomas Christians gradually changed, and, as a result, the community

[1] The magnificent monolithic cross of Kaṭuturutti was hallowed by Archbishop Menezes in 1599. All churches have these crosses at the west end of the churchyard, and alms boxes are always attached to them or planted in front of them. See Plate I.

[2] T. K. Joseph, *Malabar Christians and their Ancient Documents*, p. 10.

[3] There is a legend recorded in one version of the Anglo-Saxon Chronicle and by William of Malmesbury, that in 883 two British bishops, Sijhelm and Aethelstan, took alms to Rome in consequence of a vow made by King Alfred, and also to India to St Thomas and St Bartholomew. This has been discussed in *Kērala Soc. Papers* (1932), series 10. It is generally agreed that the India mentioned could not have been southern India; B. Thorpe, *Anglo-Saxon Chronicle* (London, 1861), II, p. 66. See also R. Ker, *A General History and Collection of Voyages and Travels*, part 1, section 1.

gradually assimilated more and more of the outlook of the caste Hindus whose equals they had come to be, a status given formal sanction by the copper-plate grants. There are cases of intermarriage in comparatively modern times, when a Nāyar or Menon bride has been baptized on marriage, and also of slaves being bought and baptized. Such practices may well have been more common in the Middle Ages, but we have no record. We get a picture of conditions at the end of the sixteenth century through the decrees of Diamper, and we have seen that by then the custom was common.[1]

Marco Polo stayed on the Coromandel (south-east) coast of India at the end of the thirteenth century, probably in 1293. He described the place where St Thomas was said to be buried, after his accidental death at the hands of a pariah fowler. He said the place was unimportant from a commercial point of view, but was visited by both Christian and Muslim pilgrims. They took away red earth from the neighbourhood of the tomb and used it, mixed with water, as a specific for fever. The Christians in charge of the tomb supported themselves by the cultivation of coconut trees as tenants of the local raja. Marco Polo then went down the east coast and up the west to Quilon, where he found a few Christians and Jews.[2]

Forty years before Polo's visit Pope Innocent III had founded the Societas Peregrinantium pro Christo, a missionary society of Franciscan and Dominican friars, who were to evangelize the East. Many of the first western visitors to Malabar are known to have belonged to this society. The first was John of Monte Corvino, who stayed for about a year in 1291 on his way to China. He says that there were only a few Christians and Jews in Malabar then, and that they were people of little importance, often subjected to persecution.[3]

[1] See Fr Hosten's paper, 'Thomas Cana and his copper-plate grant', in *Indian Antiquary*, LVI (July 1927), p. 121, where he translates a document written in 1579 by A. Monserrate, S.J., 'Information about the Christians of St Thomas': 'who had but the name of Christians left [when Thomas Cana came] considering that they were intermarrying promiscuously with the Nāyars. However, at their doors and their windows they had as their emblems crosses and they gave the names of Christians to their children. And this Mar Thomas, they say, assembled them, and filling them with ideas of caste, which in that country is very strong, he caused to be baptised and himself baptised many of all those who were married with those Christians and were in any way descended from them.'

[2] Yule, ed., *Book of Ser Marco Polo*, II, ch. 18, pp. 353ff.

[3] Yule, ed., *Cathay and the Way Thither*, I, pp. 197, 214.

Jordanus was another friar who stayed in India on his way back to Rome from China. He gives the impression that the Christians in India were in a bad way, for he says: 'In this India there is a scattered people, one here, one there, who call themselves Christians but are not so, nor have they baptism nor do they know anything about the faith. Nay, they believe St Thomas the great to be Christ! There in the India I speak of, I baptized and brought into the faith about three hundred souls.'[1] But this was probably the east coast, as is evident from the fact that he says many of those he baptized were Muslims and that there was no pepper in that part of India. He says nothing about the church at Quilon, but he went there and in 1328 the Pope consecrated him in Avignon as Bishop of Quilon and sent him out with a letter to the head of the 'Nascarene' (*sic* for Nasrāni) Christians, commending him to them and inviting them to abjure their schism and enter the unity of the Catholic Church.[2] It is not known whether Jordanus ever reached his see.

In 1321 Odoric of Udine, also a member of the society, came to the west coast and collected the relics of some friars who had been put to death near Bombay by Muslims in 1302, and then came on to Quilon and Mylapore. He found fifteen Nestorian families there, whom he described as vile and pestilential heretics.[3]

The next friar to leave a record of his contact with Malabar was John de Marignolli. His account should be read in full: 'On Palm Sunday, 1348, we arrived at a very noble city of India called Quilon where the whole world's pepper is produced. Now this pepper grows on a kind of vines which are planted just as in our vineyards....These are things that I have seen with my eyes and handled with my hands during the fourteen months that I have stayed there. And there is no roasting of the pepper as authors have falsely asserted, nor does it grow in forests but in regular gardens, nor are the Saracens the proprietors but the St Thomas Christians. And these latter are the masters of the public weighing office (*qui habent stateram ponderis totius mundi*), from which I derived, as a perquisite of my office as Pope's legate, every month a hundred gold fanams, and a thousand when I left. There is a church of St George there, of the Latin communion, at which

[1] *Mirabilia Descripta*, p. 23.
[2] Bull of Pope John XXII of April 1330 addressed to Christians of Columbum, *Mirabilia Descripta*, p. vii.
[3] *Cathay and the Way Thither*, II, pp. 141–2.

I dwelt, and I adorned it with fine paintings and taught there the holy law. And after I had been there some time I went beyond the glory of Alexander the Great, when he set up his column. For I erected a stone as my landmark and memorial and anointed it with oil. In sooth, it was a marble pillar with a stone cross on it, intended to last until the world's end. And it had the Pope's arms and my own upon it, with inscriptions both in Indian and in Latin characters. I consecrated and blessed it in the presence of an infinite multitude of people and I was carried on the shoulders of the chiefs in a litter or palanquin like Solomon's. So after a year and four months I took leave of the brethren.'[1]

The church mentioned by Marignolli was probably erected by traders from Venice or Pisa, who had some connexions with Quilon at this time, just as, later, the English East India Company erected a church there for its garrison and employees.[2] It is hard to see why the Government paid Marignolli, unless it hoped to secure more favourable trade terms or other benefits through him.

The friars seem to have carried rumours to Europe of a Christian ruling house and Pope Eugenius IV sent envoys to the Indian Christian king with a letter which commenced: 'To my most beloved Son in Christ, Thomas, the illustrious Emperor of the Indians, health and the apostolic benediction. There often has reached us a constant rumour that your Serenity and also all who are subject of your kingdom are true Christians.'[3] It is said that these messengers never reached India.

The Italian trader, Nicolo de Conti, described conditions about 1440. He said that about 1000 Nestorians lived round the Church of St Thomas in Mylapore, where they venerated Thomas's tomb and added 'these Nestorians are scattered all over India, as the Jews are among us'.[4]

Another Italian traveller called Ludovico di Varthema spoke of the Christians at Kayamkuḷam (north of Quilon) in 1505. He said: 'In this city we found some Christians of those of St Thomas, some of whom are merchants and believe in Christ, as we do. These say

[1] *Cathay and the Way Thither*, II, pp. 342–5, or III, p. 217.

[2] This is Fr Placid's opinion. He quotes *Archivum Historicum Societatis Jesu* (Rome, 1932), pp. 35–46, for Roz's report of 1606 which mentions a pre-Portuguese Latin Church in Quilon. The pillar was seen by Baldeus in 1662. Howard (*Christians of St Thomas*, p. 9) says it was washed away a few years before 1864.

[3] G. Schurhammer in 'The Malabar Church and Rome', *Kēraḷa Soc. Papers* (1932), series 10, pp. 291–306.

[4] R. H. Major, *India in the Fifteenth Century*, II, p. 7.

that every three years a priest comes there to baptize and that he comes from Babylon. These Christians keep Lent longer than we do: but they keep Easter like ourselves and they all observe the same solemnities that we do. But they say Mass like the Greeks. They use four names, John, James, Matthew and Thomas.'[1]

References can be found in many other writers, western and eastern, to a considerable Nestorian dispersion all over India in the fifteenth and sixteenth centuries.[2]

NOTE ON THE COPPER-PLATE GRANTS

The grants of privileges, perquisites or land made by the South Indian rulers were usually recorded on copper plates, as much more durable and permanent records than the palm leaf strips which were in general use for literature or business transactions. At an exhibition in Madras in January 1947 the oldest plate shown was attributed to the fourth century A.D. and was in Prakrit. Sanskrit was used in later grants, but after the seventeenth century they were in the vernaculars.

The first plates with the alleged grant to Thomas of Cana are completely lost. Gouvea says that Mar Jacob was afraid that the plates, which were of immense value as safeguarding the privileges enjoyed by the community, might be lost, and he accordingly gave them to the factor of the Portuguese factory in Cochin, for safe custody. They were for many years in the factory, 'until from carelessness they disappeared. Whereof these Christians felt much concern, not having writings with which to defend themselves before the infidel kings, who keep violating these their privileges, which among other things ordered that the Christians alone, when they married, were allowed to wear the hair of their head tied with a golden flower, to ride on elephants, a privilege granted only to the heirs of kings, to sit on carpets, and other honours which no other caste had, and which are of great value and esteem among the Malavars; and the Christians esteem them so much that, because the king of Parur wished a very few years ago to grant one of these privileges to certain Moors of his kingdom for a great sum of money which they gave him, the Christians rose against the Moors, and there were many deaths and much bloodshed on both sides.'[3]

[1] *The Travels of Ludovico di Varthema*, ed. G. P. Badger, p. 180.
[2] Mingana, p. 54.
[3] Gouvea, book I, chapter I, pp. 17–18.

Do Couto says they were in the factory when he got to Cochin in 1599 but that of late they had disappeared (1603).[1] The later copper plates were recovered by the British Resident, Colonel Macauley, in 1806 from Dutch government archives in Cochin, but not the two with the grants to Thomas of Cana. According to Manuel y Faria de Sousa, Mar Jacob pawned the plates in 1554 for a sum of money.[2] Hosten says that do Couto gives the impression that the plates were taken to Portugal, but search in the Torre de Tombo in Lisbon has not been fruitful.[3] Panjikaran says that if the plates ever were in Portugal they were probably destroyed in the earthquake and fire which gutted the Indian Office.[4]

The basis of a version in the British Museum is a translation into the Malabar tongue alleged to have been made by a Jew with great difficulty from the original plates.[5] This version was in turn translated into Portuguese. The text starts with a prayer for the king's prosperity and long life and goes on as follows: 'During his reign the same king Cocurangon, being in Camellur, there landed Thomas Cananeo, a chief man, who arrived in a ship determined to see the farthest parts of the east. And some men seeing how he arrived, informed the king. The king himself came and saw and sent for the same chief man Thomas.' It goes on to say that the king gave Thomas his own name as a mark of honour and the city of Mogoderpatanam (usually read Mahādēvappaṭṭaṇam). Later the king gave Thomas an area of jungle land and built there a church and houses. The king not only gave Thomas this town but also 'seven kinds of musical instruments and all the honours, and to travel in a palanquin and that at weddings the women should whistle with the finger in the mouth as do the women of kings, and he conferred on him the duty and privilege of spreading carpets on the ground and to use sandals and to erect a pandal and to ride on elephants. And besides this he granted five taxes to Thomas and his posterity and to his associates both men and women, and for all his relations and to the followers of his faith for ever.'

It is difficult to resist the conclusion that the Jew was as ingenious as the Brahman who translated the inscription on the stone cross, found in Mylapore by the Portuguese in the sixteenth century, and that he was as fortunate in knowing the local tradition before he

[1] Ferroli, p. 80. [2] De Sousa, *Portuguese Asia*, II, p. 506.
[3] Hosten, *Kēraḷa Soc. Papers* (1930), series 4, p. 172.
[4] *Christianity in Malabar*, p. 100.
[5] See above, p. 73, n. 5.

PLATE III

THE COPPER PLATES IN THE POSSESSION OF THE MAR THOMA CHURCH AT TIRUVALLA

started his work. The Christians of St Thomas have kept many of their traditional privileges in practice, and they were also reminded of them by certain Hindu families who sang songs at weddings, recounting Syrian history and the royal grants. There is a tradition that a lithic copy of the grants was set up before the temple at Cranganore, but this has never been discovered.

The Quilon copper plates consist of two sets. The first consisted of three plates of which the first and second are preserved in the Syrian Christian Seminary, Tiruvalla. The second set had three plates of which the first is missing, the others being preserved in the Old Seminary, Kōṭṭayam. The plates were reproduced in the *Journal of the Royal Asiatic Society* in 1841,[1] and E. W. West translated them in 1870.[2] There is an article by V. Venkayya, 'The Kōṭṭayam Plate of Vira Raghava' in *Epigraphia Indica*,[3] of which Kielhorn approved.[4] In 1925 K. N. Daniel reprinted articles which had appeared in the *Indian Antiquary*, LIII (1924), under the title *Dissertations on the Copper Plates in the possession of the St Thomas Christians*. This booklet included photographs and diagrams of the Kōṭṭayam plates. In the same year T. K. Joseph published a booklet in Malayāḷam entitled *The Four Copper Plates of the Malankara Nasrānis* (Syrian Christians).

The copper plates are written in Old Tamil characters, mixed with Grantha letters. *Prima facie*, this suggests they are not contemporary plates but copies, as usually the vernacular is not found on plates until much later. The last plate of the Kōṭṭayam set has the signature of witnesses, in Pahlavi, Kufic Arabic and Hebrew characters. Unfortunately the plates are badly cut, and C. P. T. Winckworth considers they were copied by a local carver, ignorant of Pahlavi, Arabic and Hebrew.[5]

Professor H. W. Bailey has transliterated and translated the Pahlavi signatures as follows below. Missing letters are indicated by angle brackets 〈〉. Readings in Persian of Aramaic words are preceded by an accent ′. Dots below letters indicate uncertain readings. The stroke / indicates the final sign of Pahlavi words.

[1]hamgōnak ′man farraxv-. . .ṣ̌ạ̄ṣ ī   [2]dāt-m. . .gukās 〈′hom〉

hamgōnak 〈′man〉   [3]yōhanan ī. . .ī vēhzāt patiš   [4]gukās ′hom

[1] *Jour. Royal Asiatic Society*, VII (1841), p. 343.
[2] *Ibid.* IV (n.s.), pp. 79, 90, E. W. West, 'Sassanian inscriptions explained by the Pahlavi of the Parsis'.
[3] *Epigraphia Indica*, V (1899–1900), pp. 290–7.
[4] *Ibid.* VI (1900–1), p. 83.
[5] *Keraḷa Soc. Papers* (1930), series 6, p. 320.

hamgōnak ′man [5]. . .martōēh, ī farraxv-zātān [6]patiš gukās ′hom
hamgōnak ′man [7]. . .ī bagōēh patiš gukās [8]′hom
hamgōnak ′man [9]. . .ī yākōb patiš ⟨gukās⟩ [10]′hom
hamgōnak ′man ⟨ ⟩ [11]ī martōēh patiš guk⟨ās ′hom⟩
[12]hamgōnak ′man mārī ī yōhanan gukās ′hom
[13]′hač vēh-⟨dēn⟩ ān
hamgōnak ′man farr-bag ī [14]vindāt-ohrmazd patiš gukās ′hom
[15]hamgōnak ′man mart-farraxv ī bōršāt [16]patiš gukās ′hom
hamgōnak [17]′man āzāt-mart ī ahrāy patiš [18]gukās ′hom

Notes

1 hmgwnk / L plhw / ⟨. . .⟩ š’s y
2 d’t m. . .gwk’s HW⟨H̱m⟩ hmgwnk ⟨L⟩
3 ywhnn / ymš’s y wyhz’t / ptš
4 gwk’s HWH̱m hmgwnk / L
5 yzyhgn d’t / mltwyh y plhwz’t’n
6 ptš gwk’s HWH̱m hmgwnk / L
7 yylwmčyw y bkwyh ptš gwk’s
8 HWH̱m hmgwnk / L
9 yyhwy y y’kwp / ptš g⟨w⟩k ⟨’s⟩
10 HWH̱m hmgwnk / L ⟨ ⟩
11 y mltwyh ptš gwk⟨’s HWH̱m⟩
12 hmgwnk / L m’ly y ywhnn / gwk’s HWH̱m
13 MN wyh⟨dyn⟩’n hmgwnk / L plbg y
14 wnd’t ’whrmzd ptš gwk’s HWH̱m
15 hmgwnk / L mlt plhw / y bwr š’t /
16 ptš gwk’s HWH̱m hmgwnk /
17 L ’z’t mlt / y ’hry ptš
18 gwk’s HWH̱m

Translation

Likewise I Farrakhv. . .son of Dāt-m. . .am witness.
Likewise I Yōhanan son of. . .(of ?) Vēhzāt am witness to it.
Likewise I. . .Martōēh of Farrakhv-zātān am witness to it.
Likewise I. . .son of Bagōēh am witness to it.
Likewise I. . .son of Yākōb am witness to it.

Likewise I...son of Martōēh am witness to it.
Likewise I Mārī son of Yōhanan am witness.
From those of the Good Faith (=Zoroastrians):
Likewise I Farr-bag son of Vindāt-Ohrmazd am witness to it.
Likewise I Mart-farrakhv son of Bōršāt am witness to it.
...
Likewise I Āzāt-mart son of Ahrāy am witness to it.

Dr Burkitt deciphered the other signatures as follows:[1]

Arabic in Kufic characters:

> 'And witness to this Maimun son of Ibrahim, and Muhammed son of Mani, and...[?Sulk] son of Ali, and Uthman son of Al-Marziban, and Muhammed son of Yahyd, and 'Amr son of Ibrahim, and Ibrahim son of At-Tay and Bahr son of Mansur, and Al Kasim son of Hamid, and Mansur son of Isa and Isma'il son of Ya'kub.'

A kind of Persian in Hebrew characters:

> 'Hereby I hassan Ali Wit am witness. Hereby I Isaac ben Michael am witness. Hereby I Abraham ben am witness. Hereby I Y... am witness.'

There are several mistakes which suggest that the engraver did not understand what he was copying and which reinforce our suspicion that the present plates may not be the original record of the grants.

Mingana says that these signatures show that the witnesses were not Indians but had probably come as immigrants from Persia and Arabia.[2]

Another copper plate preserved in the Old Seminary, Kōṭṭayam, records a grant made by Vira Raghava Chakravarthi to Iravi Korttan of Cranganore, who is given the title of Māṇigrāmmam (which here seems to mean the headship of the Christian merchants), a number of social privileges, a position of authority over merchants and five classes of artisan, and brokerage and customs duty on various commodities levied at Cranganore and in the villages belonging to Cranganore. This grant is absolute and the enjoyment of it is also for his heirs so long as 'the sun and moon shall last'. The grant was made with the knowledge of all the ruling classes and the villages concerned and was written by the grand goldsmith of Kēraḷa. The date is disputed. It can only be decided by the

[1] Burkitt, quoted in *Malabar Christians and their Ancient Documents*, by T. K. Joseph.

[2] Mingana, p. 76.

astronomical data included in the document, computed by F. Kielhorn as A.D. 1320, but as A.D. 230 by K. N. Daniel.[1]

The Jews of Cochin also have a copper plate in their possession, given by the king, Bhaskara Ravi, to Joseph Rabban and his posterity granting him the land called Anjuvannam, the right of salutes from cannon (that is, *katina*, the local bombs), leave to have trumpets blown from the backs of animals, the use of cots with curtain frames, leave to use a cloth of five different colours, use of the lamp for ceremonies in daytime, use of beaded umbrellas, use of *d-hanam* (drum on an elephant), and of other instruments, of palanquins, of bouquets of flowers by bride and bridegroom, use of cloth spread on the ground for processions, use of a canopy on four supports (as for processions of sacrament), exemption from tax on lands, free grant of building land for seventy-two houses, exemption from various fees, the right to be head of the Jews everywhere in the king's territories. The date of this plate is disputed. K. N. Daniel claims to have fixed King Bhaskara (or Paskara) Iravi's date in the early sixth century and says that there is a local Jewish tradition of settlement in A.D. 490, which would agree well with that date.[2] T. K. Joseph believes the king reigned in the eleventh century.[3] The Jews to whom the grant was made could not be the present holders, the White Jews, as they settled in Cochin only after 1871. Malabar Jewish tradition says that Jews first came to Calicut in A.D. 69. The present Paṛavūr synagogue was finished in 1615 according to an inscription.[4]

If the early date of the Jewish plate could be established, it would be of great value in determining the date of the other grants.

[1] Kielhorn, *Epigraphia Indica*, IX, p. 234; Daniel, *Indian Antiquary*, LIII (1924), p. 251.

[2] Paṛavūr tradition, recorded in the Hebrew book *Masbith Milhamoth* (printed at Krahan, 1889). See also Buchanan's *Christian Researches* (8th ed.), pp. 243–4.

[3] K. G. Sanker in *Indian Antiquary*, LVI, pp. 141–3; T. K. Joseph, *ibid.* LVIII, pp. 21–7.

[4] A. de Costa, *Indian Church Quarterly Review*, April 1895.

SOURCES

FOR Syriac sources I have relied on A. Mingana, *Early Spread of Christianity in India*. Cureton's book, *Ancient Syriac Documents*, also prints one or two relevant documents.

The records of travellers were collected and published by the Hakluyt Society of London and I have used this series considerably, notably:

The Christian Topography of Cosmas Indicopleustes, ed. J. W. McCrindle, 1907.

The Book of Ser Marco Polo, I and II, ed. Yule, 1903.

Mirabilia Descripta of Jordanus, ed. Yule, 1863.

The Commentaries of the Great Affonso d'Albuquerque, trans. by Birch, I, *Second Voyage to India.*

Cathay and the Way Thither, ed. Yule, revised Cordier, I and II, 1866, and III, 1913.

I have used the work of two Travancore scholars on their own antiquities, especially:

T. K. Joseph, *The Malabar Christians and their Ancient Documents* (in Malayāḷam) and *The Four Copper Plates of the Malankara Nasrānis.*

K. N. Daniel's *Dissertations on the Copper Plates in the possession of the St Thomas Christians* is a useful study.

References to the other books used will be found in the notes in the text.

CHAPTER IV

THE JESUIT ARCHBISHOPS AND THE CARMELITE MISSION

IN 1600 Archbishop Menezes went back to Goa. He had secured the submission of the Malabar Church to Rome, but the life of the Church could not suddenly be transformed and assimilated to the Roman pattern. The task of building on the foundations laid at Diamper was entrusted to the Jesuits who had accompanied Menezes on his visitation. At first Menezes got reports from the Serra that all was going well there and that the archdeacon was loyally playing his part in carrying out the decisions of the synod, but there could be no security until a strong bishop was in power. This need of a bishop for the St Thomas Christians had not been overlooked at Rome, and various proposals had been made at intervals since 1593. In 1600 the Pope appointed the Jesuit Father Francis Roz to the see of Ankamāli, but at the same time he lessened its importance, making it a diocese suffragan to Goa and in the patronage of the King of Portugal. Roz was consecrated at Goa early in 1601, and at once returned to take charge of his diocese. He had a most difficult task, because the Indian Christians had never before been ruled by a bishop. The native archdeacons had always governed the St Thomas Christians in all matters except those liturgical functions which were reserved for bishops. Archbishop Menezes, and now Bishop Roz, came with a conception of the episcopal office radically different from that familiar in the Serra, and the consequent changes in administration were a greater annoyance to the Malabar Church than any liturgical or doctrinal reforms could have been. They were particularly galling to Archdeacon George who had, in fact, been nominated as bishop by a papal brief, but now found not only that promise unfulfilled but most of the authority he had traditionally enjoyed diverted into the hand of a bishop who was a foreigner.

An indication of the new order which aroused great discontent, as Roz himself well knew, was the reduction of the archdiocese to the rank of an ordinary diocese.[1] Another difficulty of a very

[1] Letter of Roz: printed in Ferroli, p. 294.

serious but different kind arose from the jealousy of the friars who were responsible for the diocese of Cochin. The bad feeling between the Jesuits and other orders was a factor which, perhaps more than any other, prevented the consolidation of the work. Menezes, himself an Augustinian and by that time Viceroy of Goa, was suspected by the Jesuits of working against them and favouring the Bishop of Cochin in the jurisdictional disputes which arose.[1] It must also be remembered that Menezes had been able to complete his task largely because he obtained, by persuasion, presents or threats, the support of the local kings, especially the Raja of Cochin. But soon after the turn of the century Dutch ships began to appear in Indian waters, and the kings began to realize that the Portuguese power was not so firmly established as they had thought, and that it was possible that they might not be in a position to carry out either their threats or their promises. All these factors combined to make the work of the Jesuit archbishops difficult.

Francis Roz was personally well qualified for his new work. He was pious and a hard worker. He knew Malayāḷam and Syriac well, and had already considerable first-hand knowledge of his diocese. He pressed on with the preparation and printing of Syriac translations of various service books of the Roman rite and as soon as he could he set out on a visitation of his diocese. He travelled, as Menezes had done, in considerable state, and everywhere celebrated the sacraments, settled quarrels, and persuaded people to give up heathen customs. At Quaringachare,[2] for example, he settled a dispute between the northist and southist parties among the Christians, which had led to fighting and arson, and at Kōlaṇcēri he persuaded four rich brothers, who were living like Nāyars, wearing the *kuṭumi* and sharing one wife, to reform and live like Christians.[3]

In Advent 1603 Roz dealt with matters affecting the welfare of the diocese in a synod at Ankamāli. Through this synod he secured money left behind by Mar Abraham, thus settling a matter which might easily have led to litigation and trouble. In this and in other matters he acted with full Portuguese support, as was evident three

[1] Ferroli, p. 328.

[2] This place is near Tiruppuṇittara. It is wrongly identified by Ferroli with Caṅanaśśēri.

[3] Letter of Fr J. M. Campari of January 1604; printed in Ferroli, pp. 295–301.

years later, when the Cochin fort sent a task force to land in the territory of the Raja of Paṛavūr, who had been oppressing some Christians and refused to listen to the bishop's remonstrances. The king was frightened by this display of force and at once did what the bishop asked, an event which increased the respect in which he was held by his flock.

One of Roz's difficulties was done away in 1608, when the Pope[1] re-established Ankamāli as an archdiocese. Later he removed Cranganore from the diocese of Cochin, making it the headquarters of the archdiocese of the Serra instead of Ankamāli.[2] It had been thought for some time that this place, a Portuguese settlement and under Portuguese law, would be much more convenient than inland Ankamāli. But apparently the disadvantages far outweighed the potential advantages. The Bishop of Cochin was annoyed that superior rank should be given to the Bishop of the St Thomas Christians and he was not at all willing to lose Cranganore. He resented bitterly the growing sphere of influence of the Jesuits, who had come into violent conflict with him in another mission field, the Coromandel coast. The struggle in this place need not be recounted here, but men were killed in the course of it, and at one point the Bishop of Cochin himself sailed in command of a fleet to expel the Jesuits from a certain island by force of arms. Bound up with the quarrel was the question of the extent of the authority of the King of Portugal in ecclesiastical matters in the East.

The bad relations between the Archbishop of the Serra and the Bishop of Cochin could not be hidden and it is not impossible that friars encouraged the archdeacon with the promise of support so that in 1608 he openly revolted against the archbishop. He succeeded in persuading local kings, especially the Raja of Cochin, that Jesuit influence was bad for their authority and he thus won their support for his own pretensions, probably with the knowledge of the Bishop of Cochin. When the archdeacon defied the archbishop, Roz excommunicated him and the few priests who had revolted with him, and denounced him to the Inquisition.[3] Unfortunately for him, Archbishop Roz and the Bishop of Cochin

[1] Bull of Paul V dated 22 December 1608; *Bullarium patronatus Portugalliae regum*.
[2] Bull of Paul V dated 3 December 1609; *ibid.*
[3] See his letter to Cardinal Bellarmine, 1609; quoted by Fr Heras, S.J., in *The Examiner* (Bombay, 1938), p. 171.

were reconciled about this time, and the archdeacon was not able to play off one against the other. So his sentence of excommunication was read also in the Cochin diocese, and the Cochin raja, as the price of Portuguese financial help in a war in which he was engaged, withdrew his support and drove the archdeacon from his territory. The fluctuations of local politics affected the archdeacon's position considerably and by 1615 he could find no kingdom where he could rely on protection and had to submit to the archbishop. He was released from his excommunication on Easter Sunday, on making profession of repentance. He wrote to the Superior General of the Jesuits in December of that year thanking him for the services of the Society to his people and asking that Fr de Brito, lately Rector of the Vaipikkoṭṭa College and then appointed to a cure in Cochin, who had been instrumental in bringing him to repentance and restoration, should be allowed to continue his work for the St Thomas Christians.[1]

But the reconciliation was very superficial. The archbishop had occasion to leave his diocese twice for business outside and both times he appointed the Rector of Vaipikkoṭṭa administrator in his absence, which the archdeacon regarded as a usurpation of his rightful authority and an indication of the true attitude of the Portuguese towards him. He revolted again, supported by a married Nestorian priest who had somehow reached him and was living with him. The archbishop acted at once, excommunicating him and trying to bring pressure to bear on the native kings to arrest and hand him over to the Portuguese. This stern treatment was approved by most of the archbishop's fellow missionaries but there were others of long experience who disagreed with his methods and thought that the archdeacon and his party could have been won by kindness and understanding.[2]

Two years later, in 1622, the revolt against the archbishop was still on, and about one-third of the Christians had joined the archdeacon. Ferroli has published letters written by the archbishop at this time, describing the character of the archdeacon and the treachery of the friars, to whose support his earlier defection was due. In these letters Francis Roz spoke of the sufferings he had to undergo in the Serra, and there is no doubt he spoke truly. He was unable to live either in Cranganore or Ankamāli, because of the

[1] Ferroli, pp. 310, 311.
[2] See letters of Fr Fenicio; Ferroli, pp. 304–9.

constant wars between the local kings, and in 1624 he died, a greatly disappointed man.[1]

Stephen de Brito, the next archbishop, was a man of very different type from Francis Roz. He had been working in the Serra for years, and for some time as rector of Vaipikkoṭṭa. He knew Malayāḷam but not Syriac, a lack which Roz considered a serious disqualification. But an even more serious one, in Roz's view, was his different attitude towards the archdeacon. He thought he could be won by kindness, which Roz considered showed an entirely wrong assessment of the archdeacon's character. De Brito had been consecrated as co-adjutor to Roz, with the right of succession, in 1620. He had a chance to test his ideas and try a different approach to the problems of the diocese when he succeeded in 1624. Apparently the archdeacon was at once reconciled and the Annual Letter of the Jesuits for 1626 reports him working in harmony with the archbishop, who was still living in the Vaipikkoṭṭa Seminary. The following year the two men, with several Jesuit missionaries, met to discuss the rapidly increasing number of clergy, of whom there were now more than the Church could support, over three hundred priests and deacons to serve seventy-five churches. It was agreed that admission to Vaipikkoṭṭa Seminary should be restricted and that only the best of the students there should proceed to ordination. The others, after five or six years' training, should go back to the world to live as good Christian laymen. De Brito started a religious order, or House of Recollects, at Vaipikkoṭṭa, hoping that this would be a great blessing to the Serra, but it did not fulfil his hopes and eventually was closed in 1634.

In spite of the appearance of peace and co-operation, fresh trouble was very near. Other Orders had long been jealous of the Jesuits' monopoly of the Serra and about this time Dominican missionaries entered without permission and started building a church at Kaṭutturutti. De Brito knew that this could result only in schism in the Serra, and wrote to the Jesuit Father-General asking him to get Rome to order them to withdraw. He said that Goa would take no action, as the Bishop of Cochin was there acting as Viceroy. In a letter to Propaganda (the Sacred Congregation for the Propagation of the Faith at Rome) written shortly after,

[1] He was buried in the church at Cranganore on 16 February 1624. A tablet in the old church at Paṛavūr records his death.

de Brito made serious charges against the friars. He said that they had told the people they were from the Patriarch of Babylon and so were rapidly attracting adherents, for the Christians of St Thomas 'are always on the alert to know if they are going to have a prelate like those who have governed them for centuries'.[1] He said that they were bribing native kings to support them, and even putting the portrait of the local king in the church to win his support, a proceeding which de Brito considered would lead direct to idolatry, considering the near-divinity which they already attributed to a king, and he stressed the difficulty which the political situation, with Christians living under the rule of different petty rajas, caused in any serious attempt to unify the life of the diocese. The archdeacon's affection for de Brito was not proof against the temptation of the obvious opportunity presented by the intrusion of the Dominicans. He wrote to the papal envoy in Lisbon against the Jesuits, complaining of oppression and unsympathetic treatment, and asked that other orders be allowed to work among the St Thomas Christians, suggesting that a Dominican be appointed co-adjutor to the archbishop.[2] The letter was sent to Rome and in 1630 the College of Cardinals accepted all the archdeacon's suggestions, ordering that other religious Orders should be admitted into Malabar, more native priests ordained, and the friar nominated in his letter consecrated as bishop *in partibus infidelium.* It is probable that the Dominicans did not realize what lay behind the archdeacon's friendliness towards them. He and the few priests working with them (who included the religious of Vaipikkoṭṭa) were still of the mind they had before Diamper. They did not want any Westerners ruling them, but a return to the old ways of their people. They had experienced the severity and efficiency of the Augustinian Menezes and the Jesuit Roz, and they thought they could achieve their ends more readily with an archbishop from another order, who was not Portuguese by nationality. It is plain that the jealousy between the friars and the Jesuits was often made more acute by national prejudice, Italian or Spanish against Portuguese.

Archbishop de Brito, however, was a very different type from

[1] Letter quoted in Ferroli, p. 364.

[2] He suggested Fr Francis Donato, O.P. According to the archbishop, the archdeacon had not been content with this, but had proceeded, on his own authority, to appoint another friar, Frey Manuel de Populo, O.P., as procurator of the diocese in his place. It seems an incredible story. Ferroli, pp. 365, 366.

his predecessors and did not change his treatment of the archdeacon in spite of this experience of his disloyalty. He attempted to win him from entanglement with the Dominicans and revolt against the archiepiscopal authority by trying to settle his grievances, the most serious of which was the loss of power and status he had experienced since the establishment of the Jesuit archbishops. De Brito at last went so far as to promise to consult the archdeacon in almost all administrative acts, so that nothing except the giving of orders remained in the sole power of the archbishop. He soon after realized, however, that he had made a grave mistake, and thrown away the sole means of consolidating the power Menezes and Roz had worked so hard to secure. The viceroy was passing through Cochin in 1636 and the archbishop went to him and explained the situation, with the result that the Raja of Cochin was persuaded to order the archdeacon to return the documents which restored to him his old powers. He returned some papers on the compulsion of the raja, but they were only copies, not the original patents. The attempted retraction only confirmed Archdeacon George in his rebellion, and in it the Dominicans constantly supported him. The following year George died but the archbishop did not use the opportunity to appoint in his place someone who would be favourable to the régime, nor did he leave the place unfilled. Apparently he still hoped to win the archdeacon's powerful family over and so appointed George's nephew, known as Thomas de Campo, as archdeacon. The new archdeacon was young, only thirty, and in possession of the document delegating many of the episcopal powers. Ferroli quotes a contemporary's remark about him—'De tal ovo nacque simil corvo'. From the Jesuit point of view the appointment proved a cardinal error. Events after de Brito's death in December 1641 were to show that his policy of kindness and compromise had failed completely.

Fr Francis Garcia, S.J., who had been consecrated as Archbishop de Brito's coadjutor in 1633, was the next archbishop of the Serra. He was not a young man and he probably did not know any Malayāḷam. He seems to have been conscientious but without any appreciation of, or sympathy with, the Indian point of view. He responded to the disloyalty and antipathy of the archdeacon's party with arbitrary and harsh action, probably in reaction from the fruitless forbearance and mildness of his predecessor.

Garcia began his rule under difficult conditions. He knew the Jesuits were hated and that most of the Christians in his jurisdiction were being subverted and urged to throw off the control of Roman missionaries. In the experience of his predecessors neither severity nor mildness had succeeded in winning the people to whole-hearted obedience. K. N. Daniel has a letter sent by Archdeacon Thomas in 1648 accusing the archbishop of ignoring the promises of protection and other benefits made by Menezes at Diamper, and speaks of a petition to Goa, representing the grievances of the community under Jesuit rule, which was to be signed by local kings and by the Christians.[1] There is extant also a document of the Raja of Kaṭuttu-rutti, ordering all to sign the petition (for some had refused) on pain of expulsion from the kingdom. Similar orders were given by the Raja of Cochin to the Christians living in his territory. We have a Portuguese view of these events which says that the archbishop had excommunicated formally only two priests, whom the archdeacon had immediately appointed vicars of churches.[2]

Fr Vincent Mary[3] of St Catherine of Siena says that the archdeacon and his friends wrote also to Rome for redress of their grievances and as they got no reply at last wrote to the Nestorian patriarch of Babylon, the Jacobite patriarch at Diabekr and the Coptic patriarch at Alexandria, asking for a bishop. La Croze says that this would seem incredible, as far as writing to the last two is concerned, if we had not other examples of similar action.[4] It was apparently in answer to these letters that a bishop named Ahattalla sailed for India. We know about him, as indeed about the events of this whole period, only from the accounts of the Roman missionaries, and their account of Ahattalla is not plausible. They say he was a Jacobite bishop from Palestine who was in disgrace and had taken refuge with the Coptic patriarch, who offered him this Indian office, on the way to which he is said to have called on the Nestorian patriarch at Mosul and obtained credentials from him also! Ahattalla is said to have arrived at Surat in 1652 and to have

[1] Recorded in his unpublished MS. History, chapter 40. He quotes a paper by Fr Heras, S.J., in the *Malabar Mail* of 6 July 1938.

[2] Letter of Conte d'Obidos of 21 Oct. 1653. Commented on by Fr Heras, *Malabar Mail*, 9 July 1938.

[3] *Viaggio all'Indie orientali*, p. 162. See La Croze, *Histoire du christianisme des Indes*, I, pp. 358–9.

[4] La Croze, *Histoire du christianisme des Indes*, II, p. 115. He refers to Renaudot, *Anciennes relations des Indes*, pp. 184, 188, for elucidation of this remark.

proceeded from there to Mylapore, where he was detained by the Jesuits. He is reported to have met some St Thomas Christians who had been on pilgrimage to the tomb of St Thomas, and sent a letter through them to the Church in Malabar, calling himself Ignatius, Patriarch of India.[1] The St Thomas Christians received the letter joyfully and called their archbishop to a conference. But he had already heard of Ahattalla, denounced him as an impostor, and refused to confer about him. The meeting was therefore one of malcontents alone and doubtless the anti-Portuguese case was put very strongly. Ahattalla had been taken on board a Portuguese ship at Mylapore, which put in at Cochin on its way to Goa. The St Thomas Christians heard of the ship's arrival and marched on Cochin, demanding their bishop. Most of the Portuguese are said to have been willing to negotiate, so that the Syrian clergy could see the falseness of Ahattalla's credentials, but a minority refused and arranged for the ship with the bishop to slip away at night and sail to Goa. Wild stories were circulated about the fate of Ahattalla, that he had been drowned in the sea at Cochin or killed by the Inquisition. The truth seems to be that he was found to be schismatic by the Inquisition at Goa and sent to Lisbon. From here he was sent to Rome, but died at Paris on the way.[2]

When the St Thomas Christians knew that Ahattalla was away and they had no chance of rescuing him they were very angry and meeting round the stone cross in the churchyard at Maṭṭancēri (the Koonen cross) they swore an oath to expel the Jesuits and to submit to no ecclesiastical authority except that of the archdeacon, until they should get a bishop from the Eastern Church. Two other assemblies were held, one at Vaipikkoṭṭa and the other at Maṅāṭ, and it is said that the archdeacon there received consecration as Metropolitan with the title of Mar Thoma I on 22 May 1653, the

[1] See also Mackenzie, note 64, pp. 75, 76. La Croze gives the letter (from Vincent Mary) thus: 'Atalla Patriarch, I have been sent to the Christians of St Thomas, for their consolation, by Pope Innocent X. At Calemini I have been taken prisoner by those whose profession is persecution. Soon they will make me leave for Cochin and then for Goa. Arm some of your people to save me.'

[2] Quoted in K. N. Daniel's MS., book v. A letter of the viceroy to Goa was sent to Portugal with Ahattalla on 28 January 1653. The King of Portugal acknowledged this on 7 October 1653. On 28 January 1656 he wrote to say that Ahattalla had died at Paris. See a periodical published under the authority of the Church of Goa, *Boletim of Goa*, 11 October 1872. Paul, *India orientalis christiana*, p. 92, says that Ahattalla was burned and buried in Goa. The Christians of Māvēlikkara still observe the third of the Malayāḷam month Makaram as a yearly day of mourning for the murder of Mar Ahattalla in Goa.

feast of Pentecost, at the hands of twelve priests.[1] Mar Thoma immediately proceeded to ordain a renegade Portuguese called Dias, who became his secretary, interpreter, confessor and counsellor, and he appointed four senior priests to form a council to assist him in the administration of the diocese.[2] Paul says that only four hundred Christians, out of two hundred thousand, remained loyal to Archbishop Garcia.[3] Apparently Mar Thoma performed all episcopal functions although he was warned repeatedly by the Inquisitors of India of the sin he was committing.

The new Pope (Alexander VII) heard of all these events and decided to send a mission of Discalced Carmelites to bring back the St Thomas Christians to the Roman obedience. He took this step in view of the hatred of the Jesuits expressed by the Indians in many petitions. He chose four men[4] to start the mission. Two of them, Fathers Joseph and Vincent Mary, arrived at Surat in 1656. They thought that the Portuguese would probably hinder them from reaching Malabar, for fear of displeasing the Jesuits, but their fears were unrealized and they were speeded on their journey. Indeed, a letter of the viceroy to Archbishop Garcia, who had asked that he should request the Raja of Cochin to take away the Christians' right of customs administration unless they expelled Mar Thoma, suggests that the authorities blamed the archbishop's conduct of affairs and were quite ready to see other orders taking up work in the Serra.[5] In any case Portuguese command of the sea had gone and in 1656 the Dutch took Colombo and with it control of the whole of Ceylon. So the new missionaries obtained passports from the Dutch, as well as from the Portuguese at Goa, and went to Calicut, eventually reaching the Serra in March 1657.

The archbishop had not been inactive during the four years which had elapsed since the archdeacon's 'consecration.' Portuguese pressure on the Raja of Cochin and the King of Purakkaṭ had resulted in orders that all Christians should submit to the archbishop. A number of the leaders of Mar Thoma's party submitted, among them three of the archdeacon's four counsellors. One of

[1] The archdeacon claimed that Ahattalla had sent authority for this.

[2] Kadavil Alexander Kaṭṭanar of Kadamaṭṭam, Abraham Thomas Kaṭṭanar (Itty Thommen) of Kalliceri, Gengoor George Kaṭṭanar of Ankamāli and Palliveetil Alexander Kaṭṭanar of Kuravilaṅaṭ.

[3] Paul, *India orientalis christiana*, p. 74.

[4] Hyacinth of St Vincent, Marcel of St Ives, Joseph of St Mary, Vincent Mary of St Catherine of Siena.

[5] Letter of 21 October 1653; quoted by Heras, *Malabar Mail*, 9 July 1938.

them was Alexander de Campo, who later became the first Indian bishop consecrated by the Roman Catholics. We are told that the archbishop received them back very graciously. 'The only penance imposed on them was to give them money instead of the revenue they were losing by their returning to the right path.'[1]

Fr Vincent has left a journal describing the adventures of the two Carmelite missionaries.[2] First, they called a conference at Vaipikkoṭṭa, and told the Christians of the Pope's concern at the complaints he had received and his eagerness to right their grievances. They had in fact been sent for just this reason. They also read a brief relating to Ahattalla and explained the consequence was that not only was the archdeacon's 'consecration' sacrilegious but that all his subsequent acts were null and void. Dias, the Portuguese secretary of Mar Thoma, replied at length to the missionaries and told them that the only way in which the Pope could set the whole matter right would be by arranging for the proper consecration of Mar Thoma, whom the whole community had chosen as their prelate. The missionaries had to reply that this was impossible, the archdeacon must repent and submit himself and could be sent to Rome for decision about his case. It is not surprising that Mar Thoma could not agree to this proposal. The Fathers heard that Mar Thoma was planning to arrest them, and so they left Vaipikkoṭṭa at night and in the next few days visited several churches, being received warmly at some of them. Meanwhile Fr Vincent had gone off to Cochin, to report progress there. He secured the rather half-hearted acquiescence of the civil authorities in the work the Carmelites had been sent to do, and then went to Cranganore and obtained Archbishop Garcia's blessing. The papal briefs did, in fact, charge the missionaries to hand back the Church to the archbishop when they had healed the schism. After this he joined Fr Joseph's party again.

Both sides were accusing each other of trying to gain their ends by bribery and in order to give the lie to these stories the Fathers in some places begged for alms, explaining their poverty and dependence. At the same time they recorded giving presents to the representatives of some native kings and others. They were able to influence many churches in favour of returning to Roman

[1] Heras, *The Examiner*, 14 May 1938, p. 242.

[2] *Viaggio all'Indie Orientali*. La Croze uses this a great deal, followed by Hough.

obedience, but none wanted the present archbishop to rule. The Carmelites did not disclose that part of their instructions bound them to restore the Church to the archbishop, but pretended to have nothing to do with him, except that they sent a number of priests ordained by Mar Thoma to Cranganore for re-ordination. The archbishop maintained that it was useless to try to restore the St Thomas Christians to the Holy See without bringing them at the same time under his direct jurisdiction. As the patronage of the see was in the hands of the King of Portugal a direct refusal of the archbishop's request could be represented at Goa as an infringement of Portuguese royal prerogatives by the Italian friars, so they told the archbishop that after the Church had been reconciled and Mar Thoma deposed they would try to bring the diocese back under his obedience.

This letter was intended to be very confidential but the archbishop showed it to enough people for the news of the undertaking to reach Mar Thoma. Vincent Mary said that people did not believe it, or it would have wrecked everything, because every discussion had been held on the understanding that there would be no question of the Christians returning to the rule of Archbishop Garcia. After this incident the archbishop sent a priest to visit the Fathers formally, to their great annoyance. The priest 'with imprudent zeal—I will not say with malicious imprudence' showed everywhere the archbishop's letters to the Fathers. They, however, refused to receive him and sent him back with the letters, which confirmed the archbishop in his suspicion that the Carmelites wanted to extrude him from his see, while restoring the Church to the papal fold. Chandy Kaṭṭanar and others were able to explain away these indications of collusion between the archbishop and the Carmelite Fathers and most of the churches in the south were won over. A synod was summoned for the fourth Sunday after Easter at Vaipikkoṭṭa and Mar Thoma, daily losing churches to the Fathers, promised to attend and accept its decisions. Then he and his friends worked hard and extensively, putting the case for freedom from Roman rule as strongly as they could, and their propaganda made a great impression, so that the Fathers, when they arrived for the synod, did not receive a warm welcome but were greeted with some suspicion, which was not allayed by their refusal to remain in the church while priests ordained by Mar Thoma were saying mass.

The synod was not held at once, but was put off from day to day. There is no record of a formal convocation, but negotiations were carried on without Mar Thoma coming face to face with the Fathers, who insisted on the abdication of his pretensions. Mar Thoma said that the Christians had made him bishop against his will and so were bound to support him now. He succeeded in confirming his own supporters by a reiteration of his uncle's claim that the supreme ruler of their Church was not the Pope but the Patriarch of Babylon, and, becoming more and more confident, at last received the Fathers dressed in his pontifical vestments. But this conference also was quite indecisive. The Fathers urged complete submission to the authority of the Pope, with the hope held out that the Pope would regularize Mar Thoma's position, but the other party insisted on that as a preliminary to settlement. They expressed great disappointment to find that the Fathers had no power to consecrate or ordain. They appointed four priests to negotiate the whole business, but three were staunch supporters of Mar Thoma, including his Portuguese secretary, Dias.

The result of these disputes was to divide the Christians of St Thomas sharply, some remaining loyal to the Holy See, others insisting that the Church must return to its former obedience. In many places the opposing parties resorted to violence, and Vincent says that at Kaṭutturutti the local raja had to pacify them by force. Priests whose ministrations were refused as invalid often went off to the archbishop and were ordained afresh. The Fathers, through the Portuguese Government at Cochin, persuaded some of the rajas to order their Christian subjects to obey them on pain of banishment and confiscation of goods, but this was probably more of a gesture than a real intention.

It seemed possible at last to bring together representatives of all the parishes at a meeting near Cochin on 23 September 1657. The first problem was whether or not to read the papal briefs in full. The Portuguese maintained that this was only proper, but the Fathers and their advisers among the St Thomas Christians were sure that if the first clause was read, commanding the Fathers to bring the Christians back to the obedience of Archbishop Garcia, the whole business would be without hope of success. The vicar of the archbishop and a party of his supporters chose this moment to arrive, which caused the Carmelites to come to an immediate decision. They read only the briefs appointing them to the work, and not those which defined their responsibilities. The deposition of Mar Thoma was not discussed, but it was agreed that Fr Joseph should assume the government of the Christians. Objection was made to this by the Portuguese, who said that the Christians must be told to obey the archbishop, but this was overruled, and the Christians accepted the Father as their prelate, embraced him and took him back to his house in procession.

After this meeting Fr Vincent and a Fr Matteo again visited some of the churches to try to win over the recalcitrant and if possible bring Mar Thoma to repentance. But this proved impossible and they decided they would have to deal only with churches which had come over to their side. They called the representatives of these parishes for a final meeting in Cochin in December. At this meeting, which was attended by representatives of forty-four churches, mostly southern ones, Fr Joseph told them that Fr Hyacinth, the leader of the mission, had arrived at Goa and that he would govern them until the Pope had taken further action. This he would go at once to Rome to secure. The St Thomas Christians at the meeting then declaring their adherence to Rome, executed a document for Fr Joseph to take with him, explaining why they could not submit themselves to the Jesuit archbishop. They begged the Pope to provide them with a pastor. Other churches later endorsed these petitions. So Fr Joseph and Fr Vincent left Fr Matteo to carry on until Fr Hyacinth's arrival and set out for Rome on 7 January 1658.

Fr Hyacinth arrived on 10 March 1658 and tried to govern the Church and to recover some of the churches which were still in rebellion. 'What he could not accomplish by persuasion he endeavoured to effect through the authority of the native princes; so that by imprisonments, sequestrations of property, and similar means, he managed to gain over many souls and to bring the whole country into the right way.'[1] He was an old man and not strong, and he died in 1660, but he was predeceased by Archbishop Garcia, who died on 3 September 1659, appointing a vicar general before his death. Meanwhile the deputation had reached Rome and presented their reports and petitions. It was decided to appoint a non-Portuguese bishop, but, as this would not please Lisbon, to do it secretly. Fr Joseph was accordingly selected and consecrated in the Vatican (as Bishop of Hierapolis i.p.i.) on 15 December 1659 (the news of Archbishop Garcia's death had not reached Rome by

[1] Joseph of St Mary, *Seconda Speditione*, p. 32; quoted by Hough, II, p. 349.

then) and appointed Commissary Apostolic for Malabar by a brief dated 24 December 1659, with power to consecrate two other bishops and appoint them as vicars-apostolic. He landed in Cochin on 14 May 1661, and started at once to exercise his powers.

Bishop Joseph found it harder to persuade the local rajas to enforce his wishes than his Jesuit predecessors had done. He could not expect that Portuguese pressure would be available whenever he asked for it, for he was an Italian[1] and the supersession of Portuguese ecclesiastical control in the Serra was not easily accepted by them, and in any case at that time they were more concerned with their own preservation than in supporting missionary endeavour. So he used presents and promises to persuade the princes, rather than threats of force.[2]

Gradually the bishop secured enough support to worry Mar Thoma and eventually the Raja of Cochin decided to arbitrate on the claims of both sides, and both sides agreed to submit their credentials before his court. The trial was held before the Cochin court at Tiruppuṇittara, thus setting a most important and regrettable precedent. This appeal to the secular courts has proved the first of a long series, continuing to this day. The bishop said it was necessary that the matter should be decided by the court because of the violence of his opponents. The bishop's deputies had no difficulty in producing full credentials, but Itty Thommen, the representative of Mar Thoma, had nothing to show except a copy of Ahattalla's letter, whose authenticity was notoriously disputed. The court decided that Bishop Joseph was lawful metran and made the two churches of Muḷanturutti and Kandanāṭ responsible for producing Mar Thoma when called upon. A certain Cochin prince was a partisan of Bishop Joseph and he surrounded Mar Thoma in Muḷanturutti with his men, to make sure of him, while a strong Portuguese force marched to Diamper. But Mar Thoma managed to escape, leaving behind his state palanquin and all the episcopal equipment he had been using. Most of this the bishop cere-

[1] Baldeus saw Bishop Joseph in Cochin in 1663 and says that he had two enemies to contend with, the Portuguese and the archdeacon 'who being a negro would neither submit himself or his flock to the Romish jurisdiction'; A. and J. Churchill's *Collection of Voyages and Travels*, III, ch. XIX, p. 635.

[2] K. N. Daniel in his unpublished MS. quotes a Malayāḷam proverb which says 'With a gun a stork can be caught, but *kallurkaṭ* with *koḷukkaṭṭa*', i.e. the native state with bribery. *Koḷukkaṭṭa* were biscuits baked with a gold piece inside each of them.

moniously burned in the presence of the Christians and the Portuguese. This, K. N. Daniel says, gave rise to the proverb, 'If so much to the palanquin how much more to the Metran!' Bishop Joseph was very angry at Mar Thoma's escape and the Christians of Muḷanturutti and Kandanāṭ now had to come and abjure the schism before the bishop in the presence of the Portuguese general and the Cochin prince, who saw to it that they really did vow in Malayāḷam what was dictated to them in Portuguese.

Bishop Joseph had come armed with a bull of plenary indulgence.[1] He made his headquarters at Varāppoḷi not far from Cranganore, took over Garcia's episcopal ornaments, asked the rajas of Cochin and Purakkāṭ to enforce his authority and everywhere he went he first made the clergy and church-people take an oath of obedience. He set out on a visitation on 22 August with great pomp. 'This display, which all the prelates of India have made, is absolutely necessary in a nation of barbarians, who can form no idea of God if they do not behold an exhibition of grandeur.'[2] He had little success in the north, although at Ankamāli the raja sold him the church for a thousand *fanams*! By such methods Bishop Joseph brought back eighty-four parishes to Roman obedience, only thirty-two remaining under Mar Thoma.

But the days of Portuguese power were ended and the Roman missionaries could no longer get the civil authorities to further their plans. The Dutch were pressing the Portuguese very hard. In 1661 they took Quilon, in 1662 they sailed past Cochin and captured Cranganore and in January 1663 took Cochin itself. The Dutch passed orders, immediately after the capture of Cochin, that all foreign priests and monks should leave the country.

Before Bishop Joseph left he consecrated Chandy Kaṭṭanar of Kuravilanāṭ,[3] who is generally called Alexander de Campo, as Bishop of Megara *in partibus infidelium*, with the approval of the raja, who made him a present of 2000 *fanams*. Bishop Joseph and Bishop Alexander went together to Cochin, where they had interviews with the Dutch authorities, and also with Baldeus, the chief

[1] Bull of 16 January 1660, Alexander VII, given in full by Baldeus in Churchill's *Voyages*, III, p. 636.

[2] *Mémoires de Joseph of Ste Marie*, p. 39, quoted by La Croze, *Histoire du christianisme des Indes*, II, p. 178.

[3] Two priests assisted Bishop Joseph at the consecration. This procedure was with the express permission of the Pope. Bishop Joseph's consecration had been secret but was similar. See Mackenzie, note 71, p. 77.

chaplain of the Dutch forces.[1] We are told[2] that Joseph told Baldeus that it was useless for the Dutch to try to convert the St Thomas Christians to Protestantism because they thought the essence of Christianity was the adoration of images and the crucifix, fastings and prayers and masses for the souls in purgatory, and that the priests depended on these things, abhorrent to Protestants, for their income. Mar Thoma also saw Baldeus but he told him that there had been no point in him visiting Cochin, as Bishop Joseph had been received with such honour.[3] He and his party had been solemnly excommunicated at the consecration of Bishop Alexander.

SOURCES

We have nothing from the Indian side to illuminate our knowledge of this period but there are fairly full records of the two opposed Roman Catholic points of view. Most of the relevant books have already been quoted.

The Jesuit material is collected in *The Jesuits in Malabar*, vol. I, by Fr D. Ferroli. Ferroli had access to all the archives and his compilation is most valuable.

Contemporary Carmelite accounts are contained in the *Speditione* of Fr Joseph of St Mary (books I and II; book I being published in Rome in 1666) and the book of Fr Hyacinth of St Vincent. These are extensively used by La Croze in *Histoire du christianisme des Indes*, and references are taken from him by Hough, *History of Christianity in India*, vol. II, who also uses the *Viaggio all' Indie Orientali* of Fr Vincent Mary of St Catherine.

The Carmelite vicar-general in Travancore from 1776–89, Fr Paul of St Bartholomew, was able to use all the papers of the vicariate-general. His most important book is *India orientalis christiana*. Neither Jesuit nor Carmelite writes with impartiality. The collection of documents called *Bullarium patronatus Portugalliae regum* contain some of the papal briefs and records of councils (vol. I, appendix).

Baldeus recorded his experiences as chaplain of the Dutch occupying forces in 1663. His account is translated into English in Churchill's *Voyages*, III, pp. 561 ff.

[1] Baldeus, in Churchill's *Voyages*, III, ch. XIX.

[2] *Mémoires de Joseph Ste Marie*, p. 86, quoted by La Croze, *Histoire des christianisme des Indes*, II, pp. 416, 417. Bishop Joseph went to Rome in 1665 as he saw no hope of return to Malabar, even after the peace between Portugal and Holland, 1664.

[3] Baldeus, in Churchill's *Voyages*, p. 642.

CHAPTER V

THE CONFUSIONS OF THE EIGHTEENTH CENTURY

THE coming of the Dutch was welcomed by the Christians of St Thomas as the end of Portuguese control. The protection for which they had petitioned the King of Portugal through Vasco da Gama had proved to be as oppressive to freedom in spiritual things as the demands and injustices of the local kings to security in social and economic life. One of the first acts of the Dutch was, as we have seen, to order all foreign priests and missionaries to leave Malabar at once. Bishop Joseph was given ten days in which to put his affairs in order and go. In that time he consecrated Parampil Chandy Kaṭṭanar (latinized as Alexander de Campo) as bishop for the St Thomas Christians. The Indian Church thus had its first native bishop and it is very probable that had competent Indian bishops succeeded him the St Thomas Christians would have been united in the Roman obedience, but this was not to be. In fact the next hundred years was a period of the greatest confusion in the affairs of the Church, and led to its disintegration, and to the sadly divided state in which it finds itself today. There were two reasons for this. The first was the nature of the community itself. For centuries the parishes had been more or less independent of each other, each jealous of its own standing and prestige. There was very little church, as opposed to parochial, organization. The bishop, a foreigner, stayed in each parish church to perform his liturgical functions and perhaps settle quarrels which might be disturbing the parish, and then moved on to the next church. He, in his own person, was the centre of the Church's unity. He had very little administrative authority. But the Jesuit archbishops and Carmelite bishops had a different conception of their offices and Bishop Chandy had accepted the newer idea. But he belonged to the ancient priestly Pakalomaṟṟam family and knew the old ways and so could speak in a way people understood in commending his ideas. He was successful in bringing many churches over to his side. Personal rivalry with Mar Thoma had been a factor in his desertion to the Roman camp, and with his consecration it became more bitter. It seems that this spirit, throughout the years, has been the most potent factor in perpetuating and extending division in the Malabar Church. The second reason for the break-up of the Church was that foreigners were fishing in troubled waters. They had their own objectives, but they could be used by the Indian parties to strengthen their position, even while the foreigners thought they were consolidating their own.

For some time the Malabar Christians were left alone, the two rival parties each headed by a native of the country. Bishop Chandy was visibly gaining ground, as he exploited the doubtful validity of Mar Thoma's consecration and more and more churches submitted to him. In the Serra in his family nephew had always succeeded uncle in high ecclesiastical office, as was customary also in the mother see of Babylon. He naturally wanted his nephew to succeed him as Bishop of the Serra but here he came into conflict with the Carmelites, who were allowed to return after the Concordat between Portugal and Holland of 1698 but had in fact come to neighbouring territories long before that. Rome had already repudiated any idea of entail in ecclesiastical office in Malabar when Bishop Joseph was consecrated. She now refused to appoint Bishop Chandy's nephew and instead a commission of four Carmelites in 1676 appointed a Eurasian called Raphael. This was a most unwise move, as it directly offended the strong community pride of the Syrians, and in the event, Raphael proved incapable of the work. An Indian view of the matter describes it thus: 'Towards the end of Alexander's life the Carmelites found a plan to extinguish the rank and honour of our Church altogether, they consecrated a half-caste Portuguese, Raphael by name, over the Malabar churches. Our people, however, insisted they would not submit to a half-caste bishop.'[1]

We shall not follow the progress, under Bishop Chandy's rule,

[1] A document of 1787 quoted in Whitehouse, p. 308. Paul commenting on Bishop Raphael says: 'Ex paucis his lineis patet Indorum ambitionem in sectandis honoribus et dignitatibus infinitam esse, cui publicam pacem et religionem facile sacrificant', *India orientalis christiana*, pp. 78, 79. From Raphael's time until 1896 all the vicars apostolic of Malabar were foreigners. The first bishop appointed for the oversight of the St Thomas Romo-Syrians alone (other provision being made for converts of the Latin rite living in the same area) in 1868 was also a foreigner. In 1896 the request of the Romo-Syrians for a bishop of their own race was at last granted and three bishops were consecrated to rule from Trichur, Ernakulam and Caṅanaśśeri.

of that part of the Syrian Church commonly called the Romo-Syrians or Paḻayankkūr (Old Believers), but shall turn to study the fortunes of Mar Thoma's party, still looking for a bishop from the East but using, like the Romo-Syrians, the Nestorian liturgy as corrected at Diamper, without substituting mention of the Pope for the Patriarch. Yet the same national characteristics are evident in the history of both Churches—there is a willingness to use the foreigner, but a strong (and natural) antipathy to being controlled by him. There was a great agitation in both Churches in 1704 when the Carmelites were preparing to hand the Romo-Syrians back to the rule of a Jesuit archbishop of Cranganore and the project had to be dropped. Both sides knew from experience that the Jesuits were harder to influence than the Carmelites.

We shall have occasion to refer to the Romo-Syrians from time to time, because their proximity and never abandoned hope of bringing all Syrians within their fold have had a very powerful influence on the other Church.

The letters sent by Mar Thoma and his friends to the Eastern Patriarch were answered in 1665, when Mar Gregorios, a bishop sent by the Jacobite Patriarch at Diabekr, arrived in Malabar. No one apparently knew enough theology to be worried by the possibility of doctrinal revolution and the bishop was willing to conform to local custom as far as he could. He was received at first as a bishop of their old tradition and created the first doubts in the minds of the faithful when he celebrated mass in a way they had not seen before.[1] Mar Thoma persuaded him to use the local rite, which he did, refusing only to use unleavened bread and Roman vestments. He also apparently insisted on anathematizing the Pope as well as Nestorius, and professing the single procession of the Holy Ghost in the Creed. Fr Paul's view was that 'the schismatic followers of Thomas de Campo were professing the orthodox faith established in the Synod at Diamper until the year 1665, when Gregorios the Patriarch of the Jacobites introduced heresy in Malabar, and they were not disagreeing in anything from the

[1] Letter of Fr Azevado of 28 July 1666 sent from Ambalakāṭ (the Jesuit headquarters in the Samorin's territory after their expulsion from Cochin). K. N. Daniel has a liturgy in the Chaldean script, as reformed at Diamper but with Jacobite additions. This is one of the interim liturgies used until the Jacobites were securely established and could use their own rite.

Catholics except that...they were not willing to abide by the Roman decrees respecting Thomas'.[1]

It is claimed that Mar Gregorios gave Mar Thoma valid consecration but this has not been established from contemporary evidence.[2] Paul quotes a letter to the effect that Mar Thoma opposed the Jacobite bishops who arrived in 1678, in order that he might not be deprived of his dignity, which seems to imply that he had not received episcopal ordination from Mar Gregorios.[3] In any case, however, it seems that Mar Thoma was left in control of the administration of the Church while Gregorios performed his proper liturgical and teaching functions.

Mar Gregorios died in 1672 and was buried in north Paṛavūr. A special feast has been celebrated every year since, on the anniversary of his death.

Another foreigner, Mar Andrew, arrived in 1676 and said he had been appointed bishop of the Syrian Christians by the Pope. He was disowned by the Carmelites and was not accepted widely by the other Church, as he was addicted to drink, and is said to have been drowned in the Kallaṭa river in 1682. Whether he was a bishop or not his memory is still preserved and he is referred to as Valiyappan of Kallaṭa or Puthenkāvu. An annual festival, with an offering of fowls was still being held in 1782.[4] He is of no importance for the history, except to show that foreign priests and bishops were in circulation in those days and that the St Thomas Christians were not unknown to the Churches of Asia Minor.

'In 1678 Mar Baselios, patriarch and Mar Ivanios, bishop, arrived. Mar Baselios died within thirteen days of his arrival and was buried in Kōtamamgalam church.[5] Mar Ivanios afterwards governed our Church. He consecrated a bishop, re-established our former Church services and taught that Christ has one nature and that the Holy Ghost is equal with the Father and the Son. Thus he laid aside some of the Roman tenets and caused us to walk according to the Church of Antioch. He died at Molandmatta [Muḷanturutti] and is buried in the church of that place.'[6] We have

[1] Paul, *India orientalis christiana*, pp. 98, 99.

[2] See an 'account of the Church written in 1770', quoted by Whitehouse p. 307.

[3] Paul, *India orientalis christiana*, pp. 96, 104.

[4] Paul, *India orientalis christiana*, p. 105. P. M. Patrose has written a Malayāḷam pamphlet on the traditions concerning Mar Andrew.

[5] His anniversary is still kept there.

[6] The 1770 MS. by Whitehouse, p. 307.

letters to Propaganda[1] describing the activity of Mar John (Ivanios) and how he was spreading the Jacobite heresy everywhere. We gather that his teaching included not only technical monophysitism but also had an iconoclastic turn, though he did not mind painting on the wall or on crucifixes. He also allowed the marriage of priests and taught people to pray standing. The Council of Chalcedon was, of course, rejected.

It is possible that on Mar Thoma I's death, which seems to have taken place in 1685, there was dispute about his successor, and that one or two candidates tried to secure the office, though without episcopal consecration. This would account for the story of two bishops, both 'laics', whom Fr Paul mentions when dealing with this time. Mar Thoma II, who seems to have been a brother of the late Metran, was bishop in name (probably he had no consecration) only for a year, dying in 1686.

There is considerable uncertainty about the succession of bishops who governed the non-Roman Malabar Church (referred to hereafter as the Jacobite Church) at this time. We are not sure how many bishops there were, or how many of them were consecrated. Our information comes from two main sources. Mackenzie prints a list compiled by Mar Dionysios in 1900. The other source is a list compiled by Fr Paul in 1794. Whitehouse usually follows Fr Paul but takes into consideration also the Indian Syriac account of 1770. Hough and Rae follow Whitehouse. The two lists do not agree in the number of bishops or the dates of their rule. They often agree in the number of years in particular reigns. The succession described in this book is not established with accuracy, but it can claim probability.

Mar Thoma III reigned for two years, from 1686–8. He, like his predecessors, was a member of the Pakalomaṟṟam family. He was succeeded by Mar Thoma IV, the first of this line who begins to appear in established history. There is a letter of 1720 extant in which this prelate describes himself as the fifth Mar Thoma, but it is likely he is reckoning St Thomas himself as the first bishop of the name in Malabar.

In 1698 a political arrangement of some importance to the Syrians was the concordat between the Dutch and the Portuguese,

[1] Letter of Fr Bartholomew Hanna of 4 November 1685; Paul, *India orientalis christiana*, pp. 105, 106. Ivanios was opposed by Fr Hanna.

which permitted twelve priests and one bishop to live in Malabar.[1] This seemed an occasion for the Archbishop of Cranganore to come once more into his own, and the Carmelites were prepared to recognize his jurisdiction. In 1701 the King of Portugal appointed a Jesuit, John Ribeiro, to the post. But in the same year a successor was consecrated to Bishop Raphael, for the oversight of the Romo-Syrians, namely Fr Angelus Francis, Carmelite. Apparently the Portuguese were against this appointment, as both the Archbishop of Goa and the Bishop of Cochin refused to consecrate Angelus, but he was consecrated by a certain Mar Simon,[2] who was a Chaldean bishop (that is, sent by the Patriarch of Babylon in communion with Rome) but not allowed by the Portuguese to minister in the Serra. Mar Joseph and Mar Abraham had not been forgotten. Bishop Angelus and his successors sent their bulls of appointment to the Dutch at Cochin and got permission to reside in the Serra. The account of 1770 states that Bishop Angelus 'on arrival said he was not of the Roman Catholics, and wished to join himself to us. He used flattering language and offered bribes and endeavoured to deceive us.' Perhaps as a part of the alleged deception he is said also to have worn a long beard!

The appointment of Ribeiro brought prompt reaction among the Indian Christians and nearly led to a fusion of the two Churches. Both had emergency meetings to consider the situation. Mar Thoma called his people together in Iṭappaḷḷi Church and forwarded a petition to the Pope, through Bishop Angelus, representing the difficulties which had come to them before through the Jesuits, praising the Carmelites, asking for the Pope to command the use of Syriac rites and customs in all Malabar and suggesting that the pastoral care of the St Thomas Christians be divided between Bishop Angelus and Mar Thoma.[3]

At the same time representatives of the churches south of Paṛavūr are said to have met under the presidency of the Romo-Syrian archdeacon and complained of the delays in answering petitions sent to the Pope, and of the small support and encourage-

[1] Resolution of Dutch East India Company, 1 April 1698. The Pope in exchange granted toleration for Protestants in Hungary.

[2] At Alāngaṭ on 22 May 1701. Simon was Chaldean Bishop of Aden sent by Patriarch Joseph II. He died at Pondicherry in 1720. Mackenzie, p. 79.

[3] J. F. Raulin, *Historia ecclesiae Malabaricae*, p. 447. The petition was sent to Rome in 1704 by Fr Augustine, O.C.D., and asked that Mar Angelus Francis and Mar Thoma should be allowed to govern the Syrians and use leavened bread in the Eucharist. The petition was refused.

ment they had received from the Carmelites. Their object was apparently to indicate their desire for an eastern bishop, or a native one. They describe the document as 'An agreement and oath drawn up by the Christians of St Thomas on account of the coming of the Archbishop'.[1] Paul, commenting on the former petition, says that Mar Thoma's one desire was to have a bishop of Malabar appointed formally either by the Pope or the Patriarch, so that foreign control, whether by Catholic or Jacobite, might be ended. It appears that the Romo-Syrians felt the same way. Visscher, Dutch chaplain at Cochin from 1717–20, speaks of the close relations between the two parties, and says that they shared some churches, like the Ceriya Paḷḷi at Kōṭṭayam, but that the images used by the Romo-Syrians were a continual scandal to the others.[2] It is likely that doctrinal differences and ecclesiastical affiliations often concealed quarrels of a more personal nature between the Indian leaders of each side.

The Dutch noted the disturbance caused by the prospect of another Jesuit archbishop, and they forbade him to reside in their territory, and the Christians to recognize him.[3] So Angelus moved to Varāppoḷi and ruled from there, with full Dutch recognition, as bishop of the Romo-Syrians.

A further complication was caused by the arrival in Malabar in 1708 of Mar Gabriel, a bishop sent by the Nestorian Patriarch to reclaim his flock.[4] He seems to have caused a good deal of trouble to both Romo-Syrians and to Mar Thoma. The latter wrote a letter to the Jacobite Patriarch in 1709 telling of Gabriel's arrival, and saying he confessed two natures in Christ and two persons,

[1] Whitehouse, p. 205. They met at Kaṭuturutti in June 1704.

[2] Visscher, *Letters from Malabar* (1743); English transl. (1862), p. 102.

[3] Whitehouse, p. 206; edict of 9 July 1704. Archbishop Ribeiro went to live in the Samorin's territory and administered the northern churches which recognized him from there.

[4] So the 1770 MS. quoted by Whitehouse; and Paul, *India orientalis christiana*, p. 107. He reached Quilon in an English ship from Madras. Moens says he came in 1705. Mackenzie, p. 86, says Gabriel had in 1704 sent to Rome a profession of faith which was rejected as insufficient. Elias X, Nestorian Patriarch from 1700–22, sent Gabriel to India, and Rome sent orders to him to leave the country, which he disobeyed. In the confession of faith which he made to the Carmelites in Caṅanaśśēri in 1712 he called himself Archbishop of Jerusalem; Paul, *ibid.* p. 107. He said he had come to convert dissidents to the Catholic faith and would not do anything against the Carmelite bishop and Fathers. But he began to govern twenty-two churches of Catholics and dissidents from 1715. In 1722 Rome prohibited Catholics from following him; *Analecta ordinis carmelitarum discalceatorum* (1937), p. 154. It is possible he was sent by the Uniat, and not the Nestorian, Patriarch of Babylon.

and that he denied to Mary the title Mother of God. Mar Thoma asked urgently for bishops to be sent to rescue the flock from this heresy.[1] He wrote a similar letter in 1720, saying that since the death of Mar Baselios and his party the Indian Church was drifting like a ship without a rudder. The Indians were not following Mar Gabriel except for one Jacobite priest and a few of the Romo-Syrians, but they could not answer him. He asked, as in his previous letter, for bishops and learned priests, and asked the Patriarch also to write to the Dutch commander of Cochin, requesting him to use his influence on behalf of the St Thomas Christians.[2] This letter also was intercepted by Rome.

It seems that Mar Gabriel had gone to Bishop Angelus after his arrival and made a profession of faith but that in 1714 his insincerity had become apparent and that Bishop Angelus then tried to expel him from his territory, without success. A Syriac history says that Gabriel won over forty-two Romo-Syrian parishes, but the Carmelites and Jesuits got ten of them back.[3]

Several Protestant writers mention the sad state of the Syrians, divided into three factions, the Romo-Syrians, and the followers of Mar Thoma and of Mar Gabriel.[4] Mar Thoma himself wrote to the Danish Lutheran missionaries of Tranquebar in 1727 deploring the divisions of the Christians and asking for their help in establishing his own position. Visscher, the Dutch chaplain of Cochin, visited Mar Gabriel in his quarters in Kōṭṭayam and has given the following description. 'Besides their priests, the St Thomas Christians have bishops, who exercise supreme jurisdiction over their churches. At present there are two, Mar Gabriel and Mar Thomas, who do not agree well together, as each of them, especially the latter, claims authority over the other. Mar Gabriel, a white man, and sent hither from Baghdad, is aged and venerable in appearance, and dresses nearly in the same fashion as the Jewish priests of old, wearing a cap fashioned like a turban, and a long

[1] Mar Thoma sent this letter through the Dutch viceroy, but when it reached Leiden they did not send it on but gave it to Dr Schaaf, of Leiden University. He published the letter in *Relatio historica* (Leiden, 1714) with the result that Rome saw it and was prepared to stop the Jacobite bishops reaching Malabar. Dr Schaaf entered into a correspondence with Mar Thoma.

[2] Asseman, IV, 466, quoted in full by Mackenzie, pp. 86, 87. In this letter Mar Thoma calls himself 'fifth Bishop of the Syrians in India'.

[3] *Oriens christianus* by Le Quien, II, pp. 553, 589.

[4] In *Quatorzième continuation des missionnaires danois de Tranquebar*, pp. 71, 72, it is stated that Mar Thoma had only twenty-five churches in the south left under his jurisdiction.

white beard. He is courteous and God-fearing, and not at all addicted to extravagant pomp. Round his neck he wears a gold crucifix. He lives with the utmost sobriety, abstaining from all animal food. He holds the Nestorian doctrine respecting the union of the two natures in our Saviour's person.'[1] Mar Gabriel seems to have impressed the Dutch, who presumably found it easier to feel sympathy for a white man. Moens says that he died in 1730, having suffered much at the hands of Mar Thoma.[2] He seems to have kept in touch with the Dutch, for we find him asking the Commandant of Cochin to order the local rajas to allow his priests to marry.[3] He seems also to have ordained a number of priests.

Mar Thoma IV did not impress Visscher so favourably. He says: 'Mar Thoma, the other bishop, is a native of Malabar. He is a black man, dull and slow of understanding. He lives in great state, and when he came into the city to visit the Commandant, he was attended by a number of soldiers bearing swords and shields, in imitation of the princes of Malabar. He wears on his head a silken cowl, embroidered with crosses, in form much resembling that of the Carmelites. He is a weak-minded rhodomontador, and boasted greatly to us of being an Eutychian in his creed, accusing the rival bishop of heresy.'[4]

Mar Thoma IV is believed to have died in 1728,[5] and was succeeded by his nephew. There is no record of his consecration, which is impugned by Roman writers, who imply, as with several other bishops, that the rite was limited to the imposition of the mitre and handing over of staff and ring at the hour of his predecessor's death. Mar Thoma V wrote in 1729 to the Dutch governor, trying to win his support against Mar Gabriel and against the Roman missionaries. His great object seems to have been that of his predecessors, to unite again the Christians of St Thomas under his own authority, and he could not do this without the

[1] *Letters from Malabar*, p. 103.

[2] K. M. Paṇikkar, *Malabar and the Dutch*, pp. 176, 177. Paul says that he died in 1731 (*India orientalis christiana*, p. 108).

[3] Selections from the Records of the Madras Government, Dutch Records, No. 13. Press List of 7 May 1719; Gabriel said Romo-Syrians bribed rajas to interfere to prevent this.

[4] Visscher, *Letters from Malabar*, p. 104.

[5] Paul says Mar Thoma IV died in 1717. Ittoop says he died on 13 March 1728. Moens says 1735. Paul says Mar Thoma V wrote to the Patriarch in 1720 from Paṛavūr asking for a bishop to consecrate him. Placid agrees the year was 1728 but says he was wrong in calling himself the fifth bishop in his letter of 1720 as he was the fourth Mar Thoma.

support of the secular power.[1] In the course of his letter he said: 'We acknowledge the Church of Antioch for our head, that the Messias has but one nature and one person, and that the Holy Ghost goes out only from the Father: and in the Holy Sacrament, we distribute fresh bread which is baked that same day. Also in fasting there is difference between us and them.' Mar Gabriel, with the Christians in the south, kept the fasts and holy days according to the rule of Antioch, 'but the mass and the Lord's Supper with wafers, he causes to be administered after the Romish way'.[2] The chaplain of Cochin, Valerius Nicolai, was instructed to try to deal with the matter. He did so by pointing out that both Gabriel and Thoma were heretics, each in his own way, and that the only solution was for them both to return to the orthodox faith. But efforts to convince them of this were useless, as had been realized before by the Danes at Tranquebar, with whom he corresponded about the matter.[3] It appears from the correspondence that two of the matters in dispute which caused great irritation were the use of leavened or unleavened bread in the Eucharist and the marriage or celibacy of the clergy.

During this period the Raja of Travancore had been extending his State by conquest and one by one the local rajas, in whose territories the Christians were scattered, lost their power and saw their States absorbed. Raja Martanda Varma had a Belgian Catholic general, de Lanoy, and perhaps because of his influence he was not unfavourable to the Christians. Fr Paul, Vicar General of the Carmelites, had frequently to represent his flock in cases before the raja, and sometimes received him at the house at Varāppoḷi. But the State was suspicious of Christian proselytization and the Raja of Cochin used to send a letter annually to Varāppoḷi, forbidding the Carmelites to receive any catechumens from Cochin into their house and the Raja of Travancore 'threatened all the high-caste men about his court with imprisonment and death should they dare to turn Christians'. Paul had to go to court in 1787 to answer a charge, brought by some Jacobites, that the Carmelites had made converts. The case was not pro-

[1] Hough, II, pp. 393–6. He wrote again in the same strain in 1737.

[2] Hough, II, pp. 391, 392.

[3] The S.P.C.K. had asked the Danes, whom they supported, to do anything they could to help the Syrians, and this led to the correspondence. The Society were already thinking in terms of using the Syrian clergy to evangelize the non-Christians, but Kohloff and Horst sent a memorandum showing reasons why they considered this impossible; Whitehouse, p. 210.

ceeded with when the Diwan pointed out that the difference between Christianity and Hinduism was so slight that it really did not matter very much if there were converts. Such cases show, if nothing else, that the Jacobites were no more ready for evangelism than their forefathers whom Menezes had tried to stir up to take the Gospel to their fellow countrymen.

Mar Gabriel's death did not end the difficulties caused to Mar Thoma and his followers by the presence of a foreign bishop who wished to reform customs and take over administrative functions among the Indian Christians. In fact such a situation is a constant feature of their history from the time of Mar Joseph and Mar Abraham. We do not know of serious disputes between them and the Indian Christians but if there were not it was probably because they did not know Malayāḷam and did not interfere in the administration and government of the Church, leaving this to the native archdeacons. From the coming of Menezes almost every foreign ecclesiastic who came, unless he confined himself to liturgical and teaching duties, as some of them like Mar Gregorios seem to have done, made the Church situation more confused by attracting a body of personal adherents and arousing the opposition of others.

Anquetil du Perron, a French traveller who visited Malabar in 1758, says that the Syrians had grown tired of obeying Mar Thoma, because he was only an archdeacon, and had asked the Dutch to get them a bishop from Syria. They obtained a Jacobite bishop, another Mar Ivanios, and received him with a salute of guns in 1747. But he was profoundly unsatisfactory; he embezzled church money and was a drunkard. He quarrelled constantly with Mar Thoma, whom he did not consecrate, or re-consecrate, and was eventually deported to Bassorah in 1751. Ivanios burned images that he found in some Syrian churches, even figures of Christ and crosses, and gave wives to priests.[1]

According to Carmelite sources Mar Thoma submitted a petition to Rome in 1748 asking for union and stipulating only that they might continue to use leavened bread in the Eucharist. He said that if the Portuguese bishop was removed and the Carmelites encouraged the schism could be ended. He signed the petition 'Thomas, Head of India'. Propaganda told the Vicar apostolic to

[1] Mackenzie (note 95) gives extracts from Paul and du Perron about Mar Ivanios. As du Perron got his facts so soon after the event his account is to be preferred. Paul thought that he was a Jew, not a Christian at all.

work for Mar Thoma's conversion but gave no hope that he would be given any ecclesiastical dignity.[1]

Another party of foreign bishops of a much more respectable character arrived in 1751. They too had been brought by the Dutch at the request of the Syrians,[2] who had promised to pay their passage money. The party consisted of Mar Baselios (1751–3), Mar Gregorios (1751–73) and Mar Ivanios (1751–94), two clerics and a chorepiscopus named George Nameattalah, who was a clever man of business from Alleppo. They first met the Mar Ivanios who had come four years before; they disapproved of him and at once sent him back with ready Dutch consent to the place he came from. Although the Indian Church had asked the Patriarch to send bishops, Mar Thoma V was apparently unwilling to receive them graciously when they arrived, and a very protracted dispute at once started about responsibility for the travelling expenses of the party, and other matters.[3] The 1770 manuscript[4] says that these disputes continued for nineteen years. Apparently the Dutch Government tried to reconcile the foreign bishops with Mar Thoma and succeeded to the extent of an agreement executed in 1754 by which no ordinations or appointments to cures were to be made by Mar Baselios without the approval of Mar Thoma. The customs and rituals existing in the Syrian Churches would not be changed.[5] Moens tells us that Mar Thoma kept the agreement for some time but he was continually irritated at the way the foreign bishops tried to reform the Church, refusing to consent to the ordination or appointment of men they considered unworthy through youth or bad character, reforming Roman and Hindu customs which had persisted unquestioned since Diamper, and attracting to them both Jacobite and Romo-Syrians.[6] But Raja Marthanda Varma of

[1] *Travancore State Manual* (1st ed.), II, pp. 206, 207. *Analecta ordinis carmelitarum discalceatorum* (1938), pp. 32, 33.

[2] Governor Moens, memo. of 18 April 1781. Baselios brought with him a copy of the liturgy of St James, written at Mardin. The number of episcopal names used by Jacobites is very limited, hence the number of bishops concerned in this history called Mar Ivanios.

[3] Madras Government Records, Dutch Records, no. 13. E. M. Philip gives a long description of their journey and expenses in his Malayāḷam history (*The Indian Church of the Apostle St Thomas*, pp. 169–73), but gives no indication where he got it from.

[4] See above, p. 115 n. 4.

[5] E.g. the Roman custom of shaving the beard had been adopted and some priests wore small caps; Court of Final Appeal, Case III of 1061, III, pp. 258, 259. The legal records are not published in any one series of volumes. See the note on Sources at the end of Ch. VI.

[6] Letter of Bishop of Cochin, 1755, quoted by Whitehouse, p. 210.

Travancore and the Dutch Company were both concerned for the harmony of the Christians and it was unwise to displease them by open agitation. After the raja's death in 1758, Mar Thoma was able to unsettle the position of the foreign bishops by creating mistrust between them. He consecrated his nephew in 1760, to succeed him as bishop.[1] He took the name of Mar Thoma VI and succeeded his uncle in 1765.

South India was far from peaceful during the latter half of the eighteenth century. Tippu Sultan, the Tiger of Mysore, was invading and subjugating State after State and forcing great numbers of conversions to Islam. He devastated the north of Malabar but was recalled to his own country by the march of Lord Cornwallis with British troops on Seringapatam, as he was about to invade Travancore. He had tried to buy Cochin from the Dutch but had been refused. Paul says that about ten thousand Syrian Christians lost their lives through Tippu's invasion and that a number of churches were destroyed, all in the north. Three Jacobite churches were among them, including the old see-church of Ankamāli.[2]

The difficulties of Mar Thoma came from the foreign bishops with whom he shared the government of the Church, his own sense of insecurity and his consequent flirtation with Rome, and from the unsettled state of the Romo-Syrians who wanted to shake off foreign control and would have accepted Mar Thoma as their Metropolitan if he could have been recognized by Rome. He also had a good deal of difficulty with the Travancore Government, particularly during the time when Mathu Tarakan, a leading Romo-Syrian layman, was one of the three men at the head of affairs (1799).

On the other hand his own Jacobite flock was quiet and peaceful. Paul says that after 1770, when Mar Thoma had been universally acknowledged and a sufficient maintenance had been allotted to the sole survivor of the foreign bishops, Mar Ivanios, 'the terrible tumults which had long agitated the schismatics were appeased'.[3] The Dutch authorities too were consistently working for peace. Although Mar Thoma had frequent differences with Mar Ivanios

[1] Moens, quoted by K. M. Panikkar in *Malabar and the Dutch*, pp. 177, 178.

[2] Paul gives the number of Romo-Syrians as 90,000 with sixty-four churches, and of Jacobites as 50,000 with thirty-two churches; see Whitehouse, pp. 234, 235. The Christians of Ārttātt were hanged on trees round their churches.

[3] Whitehouse, p. 229.

and Mar Gregorios, they were not allowed to develop but were settled through the good offices of Governor Moens, for instance in 1773. The religious policy of the Dutch was not one of interference but of toleration. They were sorry to see that most Dutch-Portuguese marriages in Cochin resulted in children who became Roman Catholics and realized that their chaplains could do little to convert either Roman Catholics or Hindus to the reformed faith without a knowledge of Portuguese. Moens tried to train an Indian priest for missionary work among the non-Christians, but he was found unsuitable, even after his training, and became a school-master.[1] The Pope heard of the generous treatment accorded to the Carmelites and in 1772 sent a special message of thanks to Moens.[2]

Mar Thoma VI knew that his consecration at the hands of his uncle was not considered sufficient and in 1770 (or 1772) he received all the holy orders again, from the first tonsure to episcopal consecration, from the hands of Mar Gregorios in the presence of Mar Ivanios.[3] He was given the name of Mar Dionysios,[4] and will hereafter be described as Mar Dionysios I in this book.

Mar Dionysios had a clear objective. He wished to re-unite all the Christians of St Thomas and he was determined to be their Metropolitan.[5] The first step seemed to be submission to the Pope, because without recognition from Rome it was certain the Romo-Syrians would never come under his jurisdiction, so firmly had belief in the authority of the Holy See been fixed during nearly two hundred years of obedience. He must have made definite proposals to Rome for Propaganda formally discussed his case on 22 July 1774 and sent to the Vicar apostolic at Varāppoḷi instructions empowering him to offer to Mar Dionysios the temporal, but not the spiritual, superintendence of his subjects and to succour his poverty by an annual allowance of a hundred rupees or more. Propaganda added that the Vicar apostolic would be well advised to

[1] Dutch Records, No. 13, pp. 171–9.

[2] K. M. Paṇikkar, *Malabar and the Dutch*, pp. 122, 123.

[3] Gregorios died in 1772.

[4] The name of Mar Thoma was not a traditional episcopal name in the Jacobite Church; *statikon* (document of appointment) in case III, III, pp. 55, 56 in 1826. Bishop Heber said that Mar Dionysios was the last Metropolitan appointed by a Jacobite Patriarch of Antioch.

[5] See Mackenzie, note 98, p. 104. A letter of the Carmelite Vicar apostolic of 1787 says that Mar Dionysios was willing to make his submission on condition that he be recognized as Metropolitan of all Syrian Christians in Malabar, not only his own flock but also the Syrians in communion with Rome.

admit no discussion 'concerning the desire which this nation has to have a bishop or head of their own rite'.[1]

The relations between the Romo-Syrians themselves and their bishop were very bad at this time, and Mar Dionysios was naturally in close touch with the dissident elements. A priest of that party, Fr Kariaṭṭil, educated at Rome, was sent back there in 1777 or 1779 with petitions from the Romo-Syrians[2] and a letter from Mar Dionysios.[3] In this letter he said that neither Jesuits nor Carmelites had taken notice of his repeated requests to be received, and that they had not forwarded his representations to Rome. He swore with his people 'to embrace and believe with our whole strength what the Catholic embraces and believes'. We do not know what Rome thought of Dionysios's renewed entreaties but after a long delay Kariaṭṭil was consecrated as Archbishop of Cranganore[4] and reached Goa in 1786. Here he died, and the Archbishop of Goa then appointed Thomas Pareamakkal Kaṭṭanar, who had gone to Rome with Kariaṭṭil, as Vicar General. The Romo-Syrians came together in large numbers at Ankamāli at the beginning of 1787, to consider the situation and to discuss union with the Jacobites. They drew up a memorial in which they said that Archbishop Kariaṭṭil met his death at Goa through treachery, and that 'as nothing but strife and grievance must continue to arise if we have our Metrans from a race which oppresses us, we have sent information to Rome and Portugal, to the effect that our Church should have Metrans from among its own body...and that our mind is made up that in future we will have no bishop but from among ourselves; and until we obtain such a one, we will only receive ordination and holy oil according to the command of our honourable Governor'[5] (the Vicar General, Fr Thomas Pareamakkal).

They also wrote petitions to the same effect to place before the rajas of Travancore and Cochin. The Carmelite Vicar General (Paul) was swift to act. He went to Trivandrum with a Dutch official and secured a judgment from the court fining the Christians and forbidding the rebellion. A record of the judgment was sent to the Dutch Governor of Cochin and the Raja of Cochin was induced to give a similar decision. The Travancore court was

[1] *Travancore State Manual*, II, p. 209.
[2] See document of 1787 in Whitehouse, p. 309.
[3] Printed in Mackenzie, note 116, pp. 93, 94.
[4] The King of Portugal nominated him in 1782, the see being vacant.
[5] Whitehouse, pp. 308–10.

involved again later, when Mar Dionysios met the Romo-Syrians near Alleppey in June 1799 and said that he accepted the decrees of Diamper. As a proof of his sincerity he was asked to say mass with unleavened bread, which he apparently did, though most of his supporters left. He went back on his submission in December, however, and was fined 20,000 rupees for his conduct. The court realized 5,000 rupees by distraint and sale of Mar Dionysios's possessions and the balance was eventually paid. This fine was apparently imposed through the influence of Mathu Tarakan, who had been the foremost Romo-Syrian in the union negotiations and wished to punish Dionysios for their breakdown.

This seems to have been the end of Mar Dionysios's efforts to be recognized by Rome. The motive of the Romo-Syrians is clear from a book by Fr Thomas Pareamakkal, the Vicar General whom they themselves nominated as their Metropolitan in place of Archbishop Kariaṭṭil. 'If Mar Thoma is admitted into the Catholic Church the Vicar apostolic will have no place in Malabar, and so the authority of Propaganda over Malabar will come to an end. Thus the Christians of Malabar will be liberated from the thraldom of Propaganda. We could see clearly that it was owing to this fear that the Secretary of Propaganda was opposing the admission of Mar Thoma into the Church. More, when once he was thwarted by the Malpan [a representative of the Romo-Syrians] in argument, he openly asked "Who can rule there, if an indigenous bishop is made in Malabar?"'[1]

In 1796 Mar Dionysios consecrated his nephew Mathan, who had already been ordained ramban (monk) by the aged Mar Ivanios,[2] and who became known as Mar Thoma VII. Mar Dionysios had been visited eleven years before by Fr Paul, who left the following description: 'When I entered his chamber, I saw an old man seated among his kaṭṭanars, with a long white beard, holding in his hand a silver crozier curved at the top in Greek style, wearing a pontifical cope, on his head a round mitre, such as oriental bishops wear, bearing a cross worked on it Phrygian fashion, from which a white veil flowed from head to shoulders. I tried him in a long discourse. I found him shrewd enough,

[1] *Journey of the Archbishop Kariyaṭṭil* by Administrator Pareamakkal, p. 244. The King of Portugal had promised Propaganda he would not nominate Pareamakkal (Mackenzie, note 84). Pareamakkal was Vicar apostolic till his death in 1799.

[2] He died in 1794 and was buried in Cenanūr.

talking grandly of his house and dignity, the matter of his conversion putting by for some other occasion, and striving that his nephew may succeed him. I knew the beast by its horns, and having left it, hastened on my journey.'[1]

Political factors were once more to have an influence on the Christians of St Thomas and create a changed situation. In 1795 Cochin was taken from the Dutch by the English and in 1800 a British Resident was appointed at the courts of Travancore and Cochin. He exercised a much closer control over the affairs of the States than had ever been attempted by Portugal or Holland, and the first two Residents, Macaulay and Munro, were virtually rulers of the country. Munro was for a time both Resident and Diwan of Travancore and thus responsible for the whole administration of that State as well as for the oversight of Cochin. The first two Residents were also men of strong Christian and Protestant convictions who, while being just to the Roman Catholics, were anxious to encourage the Jacobites by every means in their power.

Probably at the Resident's suggestion, the Madras Government of the East India Company sent their senior chaplain, Dr Kerr, to visit the Syrian Church. He was very impressed by the moral quality of the St Thomas Christians and by the honour and obedience they gave to their clergy. He says that they were much respected by the raja and the Nāyars. The same year, 1806, Dr Claudius Buchanan, Provost of Fort William College, came to Travancore and toured the Syrian Churches, with the raja's full co-operation and help. In his *Christian Researches in Asia* he describes his journey. Many of the Christians deplored the state of their community, impoverished both in money and influence, and some ascribed this to Portuguese oppression, which had driven them to the native rajas for protection and put them under their power. Few copies of the Scriptures existed among them, and there was little preaching. The priests, many of whom knew Syriac well, were accustomed to translate into Malayāḷam lections read in Syriac during the public services. There were fifty-five churches belonging to the Jacobites.

At Kandanāṭ, Buchanan was received by Mar Dionysios with great courtesy, and spoke about the need for translation of the Scriptures from Syriac into Malayāḷam. The Metropolitan expressed great interest in this project and presented Buchanan with

[1] Paul, quoted by Mackenzie, note 98.

a copy of the Scriptures which he said they had preserved for a thousand years.[1] He gladly accepted Buchanan's offer to send printed Syriac Bibles to them. These they had never seen. Mar Dionysios's interest was genuine. He set to work on the translation himself and in 1807 completed the Gospels in Malayāḷam and gave his book to Buchanan for printing. The Gospels were printed in Bombay in 1811 and we read of some copies being given to Mar Thoma VIII by Colonel Munro.

The other important matter discussed was the possibility of a union between the Syrian Church and the Church of England. Buchanan made it clear that he had no authority to speak for the Church of England but he said such a scheme would be of great benefit. It would enable the Syrians to receive the help of English missionaries (which would stem the advance of the Roman party and raise the cultural and spiritual level of the Church) and might enable Syrian priests to minister in English churches outside Travancore to other Indian Christians. The Syrians were anxious for assurance of the validity of English ordinations and stipulated that in any official negotiations the antiquity and purity of Syrian ordinations should be expressly admitted. Buchanan assured the Metropolitan that the dignity and purity of his Church would in no way be compromised but rather protected and defended. After these conversations Mar Dionysios gave a written statement 'that a union with the English Church, or, at least, such a connexion as should appear to both churches practicable and expedient, would be a happy event, and favourable to the advancement of religion in India'.[2] It is not unimportant, when meeting such statements, to remember the background of frustrated petitions to the Roman Church against which they were made. Buchanan offered to take two young kaṭṭanars to England for training. He returned to England in 1808, and by sermons and, in 1811, by the publication of his *Christian Researches*, brought the Christians of St Thomas to the attention of the Christians of England, especially pressing their claims for help upon the recently formed Church Missionary Society.

In 1807 a Jacobite bishop named Mar Dioscoros arrived from Syria, and at first lived with Dionysios at Kandanāṭ. But he is said to have extorted money from the kaṭṭanars and quarrelled with the

[1] This is now in the Buchanan Collection in Cambridge University Library. F. C. Burkitt says this book had been kept in India only for about 150 years; 'The Buchanan MSS. at Cambridge' in *Kēraḷa Society Papers*, Series 1, p. 44.

[2] Buchanan, *Christian Researches in Asia*, pp. 164–7.

Metran. He was deported by the company in April 1807 at the instance of the Resident.

Mar Dionysios died on 13 May 1808 and was succeeded by his nephew Mathan, who had been consecrated in 1796, with the title of Mar Thoma VII. There is nothing to record about this Metran's short reign (he was a sick man and died in 1809), except that the Resident invested three thousand star pagodas in the East India Company, 'for the expenses of benevolence' in the churches under Mar Thoma.[1] A Church Missionary Society report in 1835 said that this trust fund represented compensation obtained by Colonel Macaulay for injustices suffered by the Syrians in the past.[2] These 'star pagodas' were to figure prominently in the protracted litigation of later days.

There is great dispute about the successor of Mar Dionysios. In 1809 he was dying. Ittoop says that one party wished to have his cousin Thomas Kaṭṭanar appointed archdeacon, and later consecrated by a bishop from Antioch, but the other party clothed another relative also called Thomas in episcopal vestments and laid the sick Metran's hand on his head, and invested him with episcopal ornaments.[3] The following day they reported to Col. Macaulay that this Thoma was the successor to his uncle.[4]

As a result of a quarrel between the bishop and two rambans whom he had himself ordained, the consecration of Mar Thoma VIII was later called in question. The rambans maintained that the late Metropolitan was opposed to his consecration, that his hands were laid on his successor's head after he was unconscious, and that no mass was celebrated, which made all the proceedings invalid. They explained the fact that they had not protested before, or refused to obey the Metran, as the result of an order from Col. Macaulay enforcing obedience.[5] The quarrel went on till Mar Thoma's death on 10 January 1816, and although the Resident tried to mediate between the parties, his efforts seem to have been inconclusive.

Soon after Mar Thoma VIII's appointment a meeting of the St Thomas Christians was held at Kandanāṭ and an agreement was executed accepting certain rules and regulations for the conduct of

[1] Bond dated 1 December 1808; Syrian Church Records, Travancore. Romo-Syrians have a similar bond dated 17 November 1808.

[2] P. Cheriyan, *The Malabar Syrians and the Church Missionary Society, 1816–1840*, p. 59. See Mackenzie, note 100, for other theories of the source of this fund.

[3] Ittoop, pp. 174–5.

[4] Ittoop, p. 157.

[5] Ittoop, pp. 167, 168.

Church life.[1] The assembly acknowledged Mar Thoma as Metropolitan and resolved that Pulikoṭ Ittoop Kaṭṭanar should be ordained as ramban and that he and Philipose Ramban should be the Metropolitan's advisers. They worked happily together for eighteen months and then quarrelled.

In 1810 a new Resident, Col. Munro, took office and was at once presented with a petition by Ittoop Ramban denying that Mar Thoma's consecration was valid and making a further point that the bishops must be from the Pakalomaṟṟam family, in which he had no rights, since his father had been adopted into another family, and so, they said, lost all rights in his own.[2]

Col. Munro was anxious only for peace and arranged for representatives of the parishes to meet at Mavelikkara in June 1811 to discuss the situation and make peace. The two rambans were asked to be present, but they did not come to the meeting but sent a letter stating their grievances. No settlement was reached at the meeting. An important document is said to have been executed by responsible kaṭṭanars before the Government in which they acknowledged themselves bound by the results of a Government inquiry into the validity of Mar Thoma's orders. The decision was apparently to have been made by learned Hindus.[3] If this was really the case a very grave precedent had been established, and we shall see later cases in which the courts were called upon to decide similar questions of validity of orders.

We are told by Ittoop that in consequence of this Col. Munro in 1814 gave a judgment that Mar Thoma had no right to the properties and office of the previous bishops and was not to perform episcopal functions.[4] Mar Thoma, however, refused to surrender the *statikon* (document of appointment) from Antioch which he apparently had, or the episcopal ornaments. There seems good reason to doubt Ittoop's statement, for, as K. N. Daniel has pointed out, Munro seems to have remained on good terms with the bishop and to have sought his help in Bible translations.[5]

While it seems probable that the Resident did not commit himself to any definite decision or action about the orders of Mar Thoma VIII it is clear that he got to know his chief opponent,

[1] Ittoop, pp. 154–7.
[2] See below, pp. 178, 184, on adoption. The present custom is that adoption makes no difference to a man's rights in his own family.
[3] 13 December 1811; Ittoop, pp. 174, 175.
[4] Ittoop, pp. 185–7. [5] *C.M.S. Missionary Register* for 1816, p. 387.

Ittoop Ramban, well and placed considerable reliance on him. The interest on the 'star pagodas' endowment had not been paid by the Government because of the troubles in the Church; but in 1814 Ittoop Ramban received the interest for the past five years, to be used in building a seminary. Later in the same year the rani gave a plot of land at Kōṭṭayam to the ramban for the purpose.[1] The seminary was duly built, and began its work in 1815, with Ittoop Ramban in charge.[2]

In 1815 Ittoop Ramban took the further step of receiving consecration with the title of Mar Dionysios II (Pulikoṭ Mar Dionysios) at the hands of Mar Philoxenos.[3] Mar Thoma naturally complained to the Resident, but no action was taken; he died on 10 January 1816.

Before he died he is said to have consecrated as his successor Mar Thoma IX his uncle Ipe Kassisa, who was an old man lacking force and decision. But before he could act at all Mar Dionysios went to Kaṭamaṟṟam, where Thoma IX was living, and took away all the episcopal ornaments of the late Metran. The old man continued thereafter to minister as a priest. Soon afterwards a royal proclamation was issued, ordering the Christians to obey Mar Dionysios. This was also a precedent, though perhaps the action of local kings in the days of Menezes, Roz and Archdeacon George was not really dissimilar. Mar Dionysios II ruled the Church only for a very short time, as he died on 24 November 1816.

NOTE ON THE TOḶIYŪR DIOCESE

The foundation of an independent small diocese must be recorded here, as it has proved to be of importance in the later story of the Syrian Church, in both its Jacobite and Reformed branches. The foreign bishop, Mar Gregorios, was not satisfied with the way Mar Dionysios looked after him in his old age, and he consecrated a certain ramban Kāṭṭumanyaṭṭ Kurien, in Muḷantturutti Church on

[1] Gouree Lakshmi Bai on 19 November 1814. Case II of 1061, p. 62.

[2] Ittoop, p. 188, says that the ramban wanted Mar Philoxenos of Toḷiyūr to run it, but Mar Thoma suspected a plot to supersede him, and so this project was abandoned.

[3] Ittoop says on 21 March 1816. E. M. Philip agrees, but the royal proclamation gives the date of Mar Thoma's death as 10 January 1816. Dionysios's consecration was before that. Munro speaks of differences between Ittoop and Mar Thoma in a letter dated 7 August 1815: so his consecration must have taken place between these two dates. See the note on Toḷiyūr for information about Mar Philoxenos.

28 November 1772, with the title Mar Kurilos. (Kurien was a descendant of Mar Andrew's brother, who had come to Malabar with him, married, and been ordained priest by Mar Ivanios.) Gregorios died in 1773 and left Kurilos all his property. Kurilos obtained from the Cochin raja recognition of his consecration and of his consequent authority over the churches in Cochin State; but this was later withdrawn (2 July 1774) when Mar Dionysios and Mar Ivanios protested at the clandestine consecration, performed without the consent of the Church. Mar Kurilos was ordered to submit to Dionysios, but sooner than revert to the rank of ramban he escaped outside the jurisdiction of the raja and of the Dutch and established himself at Āññūr or Toḷiyūr, in British Malabar. In 1794 he consecrated his brother, who became Mar Kurilos II and succeeded him on his death in 1802. Mar Kurilos II consecrated Mar Philoxenos I and died in 1807, and Philoxenos I consecrated Philoxenos II before his death in 1811.

SOURCES

In this chapter we come to a period which has been recorded by many writers. So much of the writing, however, is polemical in intention, without any evidence of submission to historical methods and discipline, that it is very difficult to be sure of the truth. The assessment of the relative reliability of contradictory statements is almost impossible because no records seem to have been kept in the Jacobite Church at the time.

The only records contemporary with the period are the books of Fr Paul, especially *India orientalis christiana*, Buchanan's *Christian Researches in Asia*, and various official Dutch Government documents and royal proclamations. These are available in Madras University Library. Some are used in T. I. Poonnen's book *The Rise of Dutch Power in Malabar*; others in K. N. Daniel's 'History of the Syrian Church in South India', as yet unpublished. Paul is not consistently reliable and, while he depends sometimes on records, he appears to accept many statements on hearsay.

Documents of the period have been collected by G. T. Mackenzie, British Resident in Travancore, and printed in full in the notes to *State of Christianity in Travancore*. A Church Missionary Society missionary at Cochin, T. Whitehouse, in *Lingerings of Light in a Dark Land*, translates documents he has collected, particularly statements of history written in 1770 and 1787 by Indian Christians, but these are somewhat tendentious and are not historically dependable. J. Hough, in his *History of Christianity in India* uses various similar sources. G. M. Rae, *The Syrian Church in India*, depends largely on Hough. His work is not based on independent research.

There remain a number of Malayāḷam church histories, all of them written to prove a particular case, and none of them giving satisfactory authority for their statements. Many doubtful statements in these writers are exposed by Mr K. N. Daniel in his unpublished 'History of the Syrian Church in South India'. *Suriāni Kristyānikaluṭe Sabhacaritram* (Church History of the Syrian Christians) by Pukadiyil Ittoop, G. Curian's *Prize Essay on the Syrian Church*, *Keralaṭṭile Satyamarggatinṭe Caritram* (History of the True Religion in Kerala) by Fr Marcellinus, and E. M. Philip's *Indian Church of St Thomas* are the most important of these books.

CHAPTER VI

THE MODERN PERIOD

COL. MUNRO, Diwan and Resident of Travancore and Cochin, was a devout Christian of the evangelical school. He was particularly interested in the ancient non-Roman Church he found in Malabar and he thought it his duty to do all he could for the Christians. He decided that three needs of the Church were paramount: the clergy must be given an adequate and efficient education, the Scriptures must be translated and distributed in the vernacular, and discipline within the Church must be strictly enforced.[1] It was obvious that these needs could not be met from Indian resources, so he got into touch with the corresponding committee of the Church Missionary Society in Madras and asked for the help of English missionaries. At his request Thomas Norton, the first English missionary of the Society in Asia, was diverted from Ceylon to Travancore, where his services were placed at Munro's disposal. Munro acknowledged this action in an important letter in which he states his reasons for wishing to raise the Syrian community to a stronger position, and the means he proposes to that end. There is no hint of any idea to change Church polity, liturgy or customs. He considers that missionaries in Travancore must be ready to take his advice generally, as the support of the Resident 'will indeed be essential to the success of their exertions', but that they should be under the control of the Society as regards their detailed proceedings. Munro thinks that English education will be of importance in promoting the Protestant faith, as Portuguese has been useful to the Catholics. He has already released the Christians of the country from civil oppression, from all compulsion to perform duties in, or pay taxes to, the temples, and secured the appointment of Christian judges in the reformed judiciary. The Syrian bishop has promised to make a Malayāḷam translation of the Scriptures and Munro is insistent on the need for it. At the same time he has arranged that deacons studying in the newly founded college should transcribe the Syriac Scriptures, so that no church should be without a copy. He regards

[1] Letter no. 7, *Proceedings of C.M.S.* (1819–20), p. 168, cited by P. Cheriyan, p. 344. See 'Sources' at the end of this chapter.

'the diffusion of genuine Christianity in India as a measure equally important to the interests of humanity and to the stability of our [British] power'.[1]

In this letter Munro mentioned the college or seminary which had been founded at Kōṭṭayam for the education of the Syrian deacons in Malayāḷam and Syriac. The land had been given by the rani, the first of a series of benefactions for the same object.[2] It seems likely that most of these gifts were given in gratitude for Munro's services to the Sirkar, or State Government, rather than with the immediate motive of assisting the Christians. The bishop lived in the seminary, which in June 1816 was about half finished but had already enrolled twenty-five pupils.

Norton arrived in Alleppey on 8 May 1816 and was followed in November by the Rev. Benjamin Bailey, who worked in the country till 1850. Two other missionaries—the Rev. Joseph Fenn and the Rev. Henry Baker—arrived in 1818 and 1819 respectively. These men are mentioned by name as they worked in co-operation with the St Thomas Christians, and for some time had their confidence. But it is not surprising that some of the St Thomas Christians were apprehensive about this new foreign contact, and a few actually left the Syrian Church for Rome, believing that their bishop was going to betray his position. At the first interview he had with the Metropolitan Norton tried to make clear that the Church Missionary Society had not come to proselytize but to help the Syrian Church to become itself the great missionary Church of India. In subsequent talks Norton discussed various problems, including the marriage of the clergy. The Metropolitan was not opposed to this in principle, but said that the income of the clergy (derived largely from funeral feasts and weddings, when certain dues had to be paid to the priest) was insufficient to allow them to bring up families. Munro's reaction when he heard of this was immediate and characteristic. He offered (and soon after paid) a present of 400 rupees to the first priest to marry.[3] Apparently at these meetings Norton

[1] Letter of Col. Munro, *C.M.S. Missionary Register* for 1816, pp. 452–4, reprinted in appendix 1 A, Cheriyan, pp. 340–1.

[2] Cheriyan, pp. 88–90.

[3] By the following year forty-one kaṭṭanars were engaged to be married and the Resident wanted to give them 150–200 rupees a head. The bishop suggested that monthly payment of a small sum like 10 rupees would be more helpful, but Norton expressed his doubts as to the wisdom of the State assuming responsibility for part maintenance of the Syrian clergy. His point of view was accepted, which was a good thing. Had Syrian clergy relied on this regular subvention they would have been in difficulties when Munro left, for many of his measures to assist the Syrian community were stopped.

and other missionaries of the Church Missionary Society were given permission to preach in the Syrian churches.

Although the Metropolitan's fears of English interference in the affairs of his Church may have been relieved by Norton, it is evident there were good grounds for them. Even though the Church Missionary Society had made its policy of non-interference clear, its missionaries were there at the invitation of Col. Munro, who took a keen interest in all the affairs of the Church and seemed to consider he had a right to exercise paternal powers, and to use the missionaries as his agents. Thus when Dionysios died in 1816 Norton, at the Resident's request, met Mar Philoxenos and asked him 'whether he was willing to take on himself the office of Metropolitan and, if so, whether he would unite with us in adopting whatever measures might be deemed necessary for the prosperity of the Church'.[1] The bishop agreed, on condition that the missionaries and Resident would help him as they had the late Metropolitan. He was then proclaimed by the Sirkar—the formal recognition by the State which had lately become customary. Later in the same year we find Munro writing at length to Bailey concerning the management of the College and other matters. He approved the suggestion that Archdeacon George be consecrated Metropolitan, as Philoxenos was not strong enough to carry out the duties of his office. He reaffirmed his conviction that the Syrian language, liturgy and forms of church government should be preserved, but asked Bailey to tighten up discipline in the Church. 'I again request that you will assume a control and direction over the whole system of the discipline and church government of the Syrians, employing, of course, the Metropolitan as your coadjutor. The first point to be attained is to establish invariable obedience to your commands: and I request that you will in conjunction with the Metropolitan address a circular letter to all the churches enjoining strict, uniform and implicit obedience to all your orders on pain of such penalties as you may think proper to establish. If any contumacy or neglect should be manifested by the kaṭṭanars you will suspend them from office, and may report the case to the Resident who will adopt measures for their trial and punishment. All candidates for Priests' Orders should be carefully examined by you before their ordination by the Metropolitan, and should be invariably rejected if found to be unqualified. All matters of

[1] Letter of 28 February 1817; Cheriyan, pp. 106, 107.

internal church government such as fines for crimes etc. should be reported to you, and subjected to your consideration and decision.'[1]

The action Munro requested of Bailey was directly against Church Missionary Society policy. Not only had the Home Board of the Society already cautioned the missionaries against any such action, but the Madras Committee warned them strongly 'against any interference with the Syrians and their Church except in perfect understanding with the Metran'.[2] Although Munro was insistent that the deacons must be taught Syriac and certainly did not contemplate the absorption of the Syrian Church into the Church of England, his advocacy of such drastic interference with the life of the Church could not but give a different impression.[3]

The choice of the new Metropolitan was apparently acceptable to Philoxenos, who was only too happy to retire from active work. He consecrated his archdeacon, Punnathra George Kaṭṭanar, as Dionysios III in October 1817,[4] and himself went back to Toḻiyūr. The new bishop and the missionaries seem to have worked together very happily, the latter assisting the bishop in every way possible but not usurping episcopal authority. Hough speaks of a report to the contrary in 1820 and the Bishop of Calcutta on his second visit inquired particularly of the Metropolitan if he had any complaint to make on this account.[5] Dionysios III stated in reply that he was perfectly satisfied as to the correctness of the missionaries' attitude towards him and his Church.[6] Even though the Metran was satisfied with the missionaries, they do seem to have accepted, as of right, a position of considerable authority. At a synod convened

[1] Letter of 6 August 1817, no. 24, in appendix A, Cheriyan, pp. 361 ff.

[2] Quoted by Cheriyan, p. 131, from Madras Committee's circular letter commenting on report for 1819.

[3] Cheriyan, pp. 131, 132.

[4] The Sirkar proclamation ordering obedience was dated 30 December 1817.

[5] He had visited Mar Dionysios and Philoxenos in October 1816 in Kōṭṭayam.

[6] *Life of Bishop Middleton*, by Le Bas, II, pp. 205, 206; Hough, IV, pp. 71–3. See also Cheriyan, pp. 150–1. Principal Mills visited Travancore and wrote as follows on 29 July 1821: 'They do nothing but by the express sanction of the Metropolitan consulting and employing them; their use of the Anglican Service for themselves and their families at one of his chapels is agreeable to the catholic practice of these Christians (who allowed the same 250 years ago to the Portuguese priests, as to persons rightly and canonically ordained, even while they were resisting their usurpations) and is totally unconnected with any purpose of obtruding even that liturgy upon the Syrian Church; while their conduct with respect to those parts of the Syrian ritual and practice, which all Protestants must condemn, is that of silence; which, without the appearance of approval, will tend to undermine, and at length by regular authority to remove them.' Quoted in *Church Missionary Register* for 1823.

at Māvēlikkara in 1818, for instance, we find Fenn and Bailey seated on either side of the Metran in front of the gathering and proposing that a commission of kaṭṭanars should sit with the Metran to test all ceremonies and rites by the Holy Scriptures and reform the Church by that rule.[1] The Malpān at the time, Konāṭṭu Malpān, was a man of forceful personality and conservative disposition and he probably performed a useful service in not allowing reforms to be carried through faster than people were ready to accept. Already great changes were taking place: clergy were marrying, images were being removed from the churches, Scripture was read every Sunday in the vernacular, and schools were opened in most parishes.

Mar Dionysios III died in 1825 and Philipose Malpān was elected in his place by a synod in which, according to custom, clergy and laity voted together. Mar Philoxenos again came out of his retirement and consecrated Philipose as Mar Dionysios IV. Dionysios did not, however, take over the Metran's authority, but acted as coadjutor to Philoxenos until the old man's death. The strong hand and keen interest of Col. Munro were withdrawn in 1819, when he retired, and from that time difficulties increased for the Syrians. Some of the privileges and exemptions granted them by Government were at once withdrawn and the Jacobites no longer enjoyed special favour. In 1825 a clash took place between the Indian bishop and a representative of his foreign Patriarch, the start of the troubles which have continued until now. Perhaps it may be true to say that the quarrel has been between parties in the Indian Church rather than between Malankara[2] and Antioch, and that the Antiochene connexion has been kept largely because one party or another has always found it useful to claim the Patriarch's authority in its own support. A third difficulty was the tension between the party which stood firm by the old ways, and disliked the attitude of the English missionaries, doctrinal as well as practical, as much as their ancestors had resented the interference of the Portuguese in their affairs, and those who had accepted the new ideas and wished to reform their Church in line with what they now came to recognize as Biblical standards.

[1] Fenn's address is published in the *Twentieth Annual Proceedings of the C.M.S.*; appendix B in Cheriyan, pp. 370–4.

[2] The Malabar Church is often called the Church of Malankara, after the place where St Thomas is believed to have landed on his arrival in India.

In 1825 a bishop named Mar Athanasios arrived in Bombay from the Patriarch and was received by Heber, Bishop of Calcutta, who happened to be there at the time and sent him on his way with letters to the Governor of Madras and the Travancore authorities.[1] Athanasios arrived in Travancore and at once demanded recognition as lawful Metran of Malabar, in supersession of the local bishops. The Resident refused to support Athanasios's claim but gave him permission to visit the churches. This gave the opportunity for a party in the Church which was antagonistic to Dionysios and suspicious of the influence of the missionaries upon the Church, to make contact with Athanasios.[2] He listened to their story and excommunicated both Dionysios and Philoxenos, calling them children of Belial. Confident in the support of his party he went further and condemned the appointment of the previous four Metrans as invalid, holding that only the Patriarch could appoint Metrans for Malabar. He then tried to take possession of the College by force, whereupon he was restrained by the local magistrate and soon after deported. The missionaries said they had no hand at all in the deportation in 1826, though they did on at least one occasion prevent Athanasios from meeting Philoxenos, as they were convinced he intended to coerce the old bishop.[3] Philoxenos rebuked those who had supported Athanasios, and they were outwardly reconciled for the time. Philoxenos died in 1829, leaving a fragrant memory of patient kindliness and piety behind him.

In place of Philoxenos his coadjutor Dionysios IV was proclaimed Metran by the Government, and from this time the situation inside the Indian Church worsened, the antagonism of the conservative party having always been more against him than against Philoxenos. He has been accused of avarice and other faults; whether he had those faults or not it is clear he was not a strong enough man to hold together the reforming and reactionary wings of the Church. The publication of the Malayāḷam New Testament in 1830[4] did not improve the feelings between the parties. On the one hand it was warmly welcomed and studied, on the other the whole weight of conservatism was against the Bible

[1] Athanasios received Holy Communion from Heber in Bombay.
[2] The leaders were Konāṭṭ Malpān and Idavalikkal Philipose Kaṭṭanar.
[3] *C.M.S. Proceedings* (1827–8), pp. 96–7, 600–1.
[4] The translation of the Gospels produced by Dionysios I had been found quite inadequate, and the version of the Peshitto done at the College little better. Bailey's New Testament of 1830 was more or less a new translation.

being read in the common tongue or in private houses. Matters came to a head when Bishop Wilson of Calcutta came on a visitation in 1835. He must have been aware that the missionaries, on their side, were profoundly dissatisfied with the results of nearly twenty years' work. They had taught in the College and preached in the churches, but had not publicly exposed Syrian errors, as they saw them. They had not attempted to form any congregations who would follow a reformed rite more in line with their own convictions. But they had, of course, influenced many inside the College and outside it, by their privately expressed opinions. Some of the missionaries, but not veterans like Bailey, felt that the indirect influence which was all they had so far been allowed to exert was fruitless. Stronger measures were required; and if the Syrian Church deliberately refused to consider any reformation by the Word of God, her errors should be publicly denounced. Some missionaries, indeed, had already begun to take up a more uncompromising position. Joseph Peet, for example, felt that to tolerate some practices was to deny the Gospel. Accordingly he went one day to a church where great crowds had assembled to celebrate a feast in honour of St Mary, and had purified themselves for the feast by washing. Deliberately touching them, to defile this ritual purity, he proceeded to preach violently against their superstitions in the church. It is certain that only his white skin protected him from violence, but the resentment of the crowd did not stop his fulminations. There were many such incidents, and while they may be deplored as discourteous and unwise, it has to be recognized that the missionaries had become convinced that silence on their part would be, in fact, a denial of fundamental Christian truth. So, indeed, had Menezes been convinced two hundred and fifty years before. While Bishop Wilson was not a Church Missionary Society missionary he sympathized to a great extent with the missionaries' feelings, but still hoped that the English Church would help the Syrian Church to reform itself, without any breach in such fellowship as there was already between them. He accordingly met the Metran and his advisers and suggested certain reforms, mainly in administrative and financial matters. Wilson tried to make clear that he put forward these suggestions as a brother in Christ, and not as one who claimed any jurisdiction or authority in a sister Church. The Syrians promised to consider his proposals and they parted with a show of amity.

In 1836 a synod met at Māvēlikkara in the presence of Mar Dionysios IV and Mar Kurilos (the new Bishop of Toḻiyūr, consecrated by Dionysios to fill the see vacant by the death of Philoxenos). All the proposals made by Bishop Wilson were rejected and a resolution was passed reaffirming the adherence of the Church to the Jacobite Patriarch (in spite of the way his last envoy had been received by the Metran) and the customs received from him.[1]

This synod marks the end of the official connexion of the Church Missionary Society with the Syrian Church in India, and the triumph of the reactionary party within the Church. An immediate result was the necessity to settle the administration of property previously controlled by the Metran and the missionaries together. The Resident suggested that arbitrators should decide the question and so three were appointed, representing the three interested parties, the Metran, the missionaries and the Travancore Government.[2] They announced their award in 1840 dividing the property into two lots, one to be administered by the missionaries and Resident for the sole benefit of the Syrian community according to the intentions of the original donors, and the other to be handed over to the Syrians absolutely and used at their discretion. The Madras Government, when appealed to by the Metran, confirmed the arrangement. The interest on the star pagodas was to be paid to trustees, the Metran with two others, a priest and a layman, to be selected by the Syrian community.[3]

The conservative party had won a great victory but the problems of the Church were far from settled. Relations with the Patriarch were still undefined, and no agreement had been made as to the limits and nature of his authority in the Indian Church. Those who had come under the influence of the missionaries were not willing to throw away the teaching which had come to some of them with the force of a revelation.

It will be convenient at this stage to see the effect of the synod decisions on this latter group. A number of Syrians who had worked closely with the missionaries left their Church altogether

[1] The resolutions of the Māvēlikkara Synod are printed in Cheriyan, appendix H, pp. 390–1.

[2] Baron d'Albedhyll, Messrs Vernede and Horsley. Their decision is given in Seminary Case Exhibits, III, pp. 223–9 (see 'Sources' at the end of this chapter).

[3] Judgment A.S. 68 of 1096, p. 5. Throughout Travancore the case has always been called the Vaṭṭipaṇam Case, i.e. the case of the star pagodas.

and accepted the liturgy of the English Church, which had by then been turned into Malayāḷam. Some of this group were later ordained; they provided the leadership for the Anglican diocese which later came into being and now forms part of the Church of South India. But the official policy of the Society was against proselytization. The Madras Committee at once said it was their 'decided conviction that we ought to preserve their [i.e. Syrians in sympathy with the missionaries] identity and not attempt to amalgamate them with the Church of England'.[1] The Parent Committee of the Church Missionary Society gave their decision about the future of the work in 1838. The Travancore Mission was to continue but must direct its efforts to the evangelization of non-Christians rather than the uplift and reform of the Syrians. At this point we must leave the English missionaries and their contact with the Syrian Church. Their official connexion was finished, but friendly contact with the community has gone on until now, particularly through the Church Missionary Society College and High School in Kōṭṭayam, at which many thousands of Syrians have received their education. We shall have occasion to refer later to these institutions.

The Syrians who left their Church to join the missionaries were a relatively small group, many more who desired reform stayed inside the Church, and there were others whose antagonism to Mar Dionysios had personal, rather than doctrinal, grounds. These groups presented a memorial to the Resident in September 1836 complaining of the Metran's misdeeds, but the petition was ignored. The Metran replied with an order, read in all the churches, prohibiting the faithful from inviting missionaries to preach and excommunicating any who joined them.[2] But the order had no effect on the reforming group. They had a most able leader in Abraham Malpān, professor of Syriac in the College and vicar of Marāmon, who had already prepared a revised version of the liturgy, omitting everything for which he could find no Scriptural warrant.[3] This liturgy was being used in three churches and the

[1] Resolution of 14 March 1836; recorded in Cheriyan, p. 243.

[2] The order was published in March 1837; Cheriyan, p. 285.

[3] He omitted prayers for dead and prayers to saints: 'Thee am I holding who holdest' prayer, 'We offer to thee this unbloody sacrifice', 'Thou art the hard rock' prayer to chalice, the rubric saying the Holy Spirit will bless the incense; he ordered Communion in both kinds; no celebration if no communicants; no auricular confession; service to be read in Malayāḷam. See the third part of this book.

priests there were in difficulties because they were no longer celebrating masses for the dead and living on the fees paid for these services.[1] Abraham Malpān next broke a statue kept in the church at Marāmon, which was venerated at an annual festival, but which he declared idolatrous.[2] A little later he abolished the festival itself. This act has given definition to the beginning of the reform movement within the Syrian Church, which is often called the Reform of 1012 (1837).

It was clear to Abraham Malpān that there was no prospect of widespread acceptance in the Church of the reformed ideas he had accepted from the missionaries and yet he had no desire to separate himself from the Church of his fathers. He seems to have concluded that the only hope lay in contriving that Mar Dionysios's successor should be a man brought up in the atmosphere of the new ideas and inclined to the reformation of the Church. He therefore arranged for his nephew, deacon Mathew, who had been studying in a Church Missionary Society school in Madras, to go to Mardin and seek consecration from the Patriarch himself. Mathew arrived there in July 1841 and stayed for two years as a member of the Patriarch's household. At last he was consecrated bishop as Mar Athanasios, in spite of many letters from Dionysios warning the Patriarch against him.[3] This was, of course, an arbitrary act on the part of the Patriarch, for no Indian bishop had been hitherto consecrated without the election and approval of the people.

Mathew Athanasios arrived in Malabar in May 1843 and was met by Konāṭṭ Malpān, who had been a strong supporter of the foreign Mar Athanasios against Dionysios IV, but had joined with him when he supported their campaign against the influence of missionaries in the Church, which culminated in the resolutions of the Māvēlikkara Synod. It is, however, clear that Dionysios had never won Konāṭṭ Malpān's full confidence. Abraham Malpān was anxious that his nephew should take no steps to secure Government recognition as Metran, but others advised him to do so, and he went to Trivandrum to influence the Maharaja and the Resident on his behalf. Any such recognition would mean the supersession of

[1] Marāmon, Kōḷaṇcēri and Ayrūr.

[2] Commonly called Muṭṭappan, but probably of Mar Baselios, who had died at Kōtamamgalam.

[3] 14 February 1842; *statikon* shown in Court of Appeal, case III of 1061, III, pp. 31, 34.

Dionysios. Mar Dionysios summoned a synod to hear the *statikon* (mandate) the Patriarch had given Athanasios, but asked for it to be entrusted to him so that he might first study it privately. This Athanasios refused to do. Dionysios's synod did not meet, but in September the supporters of Athanasios met near Kōṭṭayam and issued a statement rejecting the orders of Dionysios and his predecessors, accepting Athanasios as lawful Metran and stating that everything ought to be done in the Church in accordance with the Scriptures and the decisions of the first three Councils.[1] They created a precedent in claiming that the *statikon* of the Patriarch was essential to the exercise of any lawful jurisdiction in the Malabar Church. On these grounds they decided to ask the Government to withdraw their recognition of Mar Dionysios and recognize Athanasios in his place.

Dionysios had, of course, taken the matter up with the Patriarch. He accused Athanasios of altering the faith of the Church, a charge based more on apprehension about the future than on any violation of tradition actually observed. It seems possible that the Patriarch believed these reports and excommunicated Athanasios; but, if he did, the document was never at Dionysios's disposal in Malabar or he would certainly have produced it. In 1846 another foreign bishop, Yoyakin Mar Kurilos, arrived from the Patriarch to investigate the whole position. Dionysios was sick and getting tired of continual strife and so resigned his charge to Kurilos, petitioning the Resident to have him proclaimed as his lawful successor. The Travancore Government and the Resident were not willing to do this without investigation. A special committee accepted Athanasios's *statikon*, but dismissed Kurilos's credentials and letter of condemnation of Athanasios as forgeries.[2] Before any further action was taken, however, another bishop, Mar Stephanos, arrived from the Patriarch. He had come to supersede Kurilos, and at once sent a petition to the Resident, putting forth his claims, and also asking that all money due from the Syrian Church to the Patriarch should be handed over at once. Stephanos was told that the Patriarch had been misinformed and that there were no funds in the Malabar Church at his disposal.[3]

The Governments of Travancore and Cochin soon after decided

[1] Exhibit 206, Court of Appeal, case III, III, pp. 39–41.
[2] Ittoop, pp. 245 ff.
[3] Exhibit Book of Seminary Case, pp. 208, 246–8.

that Athanasios was lawful Metran of the Malankara Church.[1] Dionysios retired to a country church and died there not long afterwards, receiving the last sacraments from Athanasios, who stayed with him and did all he could to help him. Kurilos was banished from the two States and lived in British Cochin. For a year or two he acted as suffragan to Athanasios but this attitude of co-operation did not last. Stephanos went to Calcutta and to London seeking more favourable treatment, but did not succeed, and on his return to Mardin was apparently removed from his office by the Patriarch. The Madras Government expressed the view that the Syrian Church itself alone could determine who should be Metran, and that the civil Government should not be concerned at all, apart from the preservation of peace and order.

Athanasios was now sole Metran but his position was not really secure. He was suspected of too much sympathy towards the English missionaries, although he had not carried out any reforms, or been in a position to do so. There was also a good deal of jealousy, and Mar Kurilos was active to encourage doubts of the Patriarch's attitude towards the Metran.[2] Athanasios carried much weight with the Government and it is certain that he tried to carry out his duties conscientiously, and all parties recognized that in knowledge of the Scriptures and theology he was perhaps the most able Metran the Christians of St Thomas had ever had. But latent jealousy and mistrust became open whenever opportunity presented itself. Thus when in 1856 the old Mar Kurilos of Toḷiyūr died, Mar Yoyakin Kurilos at once presented a plea in the Calicut court that he was the only lawful Metran of the Syrian Church appointed by the Patriarch and had been directing the affairs of Toḷiyūr. The local court decided, and the Madras court confirmed, that the recognition or repudiation of any ecclesiastic sent from Antioch was a matter which rested with the members of the Syrian Church alone.[3] They said that Athanasios was so recognized, and Joseph Mar Kurilos, consecrated in 1856 to fill the Toḷiyūr see by Athanasios, had also been accepted by the Church. The property therefore was left in their hands.

Involved in this litigation was a priest called Pulikkoṭ Joseph who

[1] He was proclaimed by Travancore on 28 July 1852, and by Cochin on 4 October 1853.

[2] It is interesting that a foreign bishop, Mar Gregorios of Jerusalem, came in 1855 and lived peaceably with Athanasios.

[3] On 28 May 1863. See Court of Appeal, case III, III, pp. 259–63.

had led a secession in Kunnamkuḷam in 1852 and built a new church for his followers.[1] This secession church was the first of eighteen new churches, which were built and placed under the jurisdiction of the foreign Mar Kurilos. Then Joseph went to Mardin and was consecrated as Mar Dionysios (V) in 1865, coming straight back to Malabar.[2] He presented a petition for recognition to the Government, but they refused to judge between Athanasios and the new Dionysios. They said that they had acted throughout the whole affair with no partiality to either side and they strongly advised the parties to compromise, or failing that to take the case to the courts, to decide the ownership of the property, a decision which would involve judgment as to the standing of the two rival Metropolitans.

This was the point of view taken by the judge of the Alleppey court, who heard a case about some property attached to the Valiappaḷḷi Church in Kōṭṭayam, claimed by adherents of Athanasios but held by Dionysios's party. The judge said that it was clear that the real question at issue was whether Mar Athanasios or Mar Dionysios was legitimate Metropolitan of Malabar. He continued: 'The whole of the property belonging to the Syrian Church must be taken to vest in the Patriarch as its supreme head. If a portion of the Church do not choose to recognise the delegate sent by him, the portion who do not choose so to recognise him ought to be considered schismatic, but not those who adhere to their ancient allegiance.'[3]

The appeal court ordered the case to be re-tried. They gave their opinion that the statement of the lower court that all property vested in the Patriarch was a serious error and denied that the question at issue was a decision about the rightful Metropolitan. They said: 'Indeed we may go further and say that inasmuch as the Syrian Church in Travancore is altogether local no Metropolitan claiming to be such can be recognised by the Courts unless he has been so recognised by the State.' On this principle Mar Athanasios was, in law as well as in fact, Metropolitan.

But Mar Dionysios was encouraged by the disagreement between the courts and in the same year (1869) he applied for the accumu-

[1] He had been ordained priest on 19 August 1852 by Kurilos. He was a grand-nephew of Pulikkoṭ Mar Dionysios.

[2] 7 May 1865. His *statikon* is no. 194; case III, III, pp. 9ff.

[3] The whole judgment is quoted in the judgment of the Court of Appeal in 1869, case III, III, no. 230, pp. 175–8.

lated interest on the star pagodas and the 14,000 rupees allotted in 1840 to the Metran and his co-trustees. He lost the case and this money was awarded to Athanasios and most of it invested by him in land.[1] The interest on the star pagodas was paid to him until his death in 1877.

Other cases were brought to the courts and decided in favour of Athanasios as legal Metropolitan. One concerning property left in Paḷḷikkara church was, however, lost on the ground that the previous connexion of the Metran with that particular church, which had formerly been adhering to Kurilos and Dionysios, was not proved.[2] On the whole it seemed that the position of Athanasios was well established, though a number of churches rejected his authority and adhered to Dionysios. In 1868 he had consecrated his cousin as coadjutor, with the title of Mar Thomas Athanasios, and a religious revival which started in his churches in 1873 also tended to unite his people and strengthen their bishop. Under the influence of the revival quarrels were made up and Hindu customs abandoned, but there was naturally a reaction of suspicion among the more conservative people. They wondered whether the Syrian Church was once more in danger of going over to the missionaries' point of view.

Mar Yoyakin Kurilos died in 1874 and with him Dionysios's main support had gone. But the following year the uneasy peace of the Church was shattered by the arrival of the Patriarch Peter himself, come at the request of Dionysios.[3] Everywhere he was greeted with profound respect, and the whole church was deeply divided, one party saying that the only proper course was complete and immediate submission to the Patriarch, the other, that, while due respect must be paid, the St Thomas Christians ought not to come completely under foreign control. All the parishes in the north went over to him, but some in the south remained faithful to Athanasios. Whatever the Patriarch's previous attitude to Athanasios may have been there was now no doubt about it. He moved the Government to withdraw its recognition of Athanasios and

[1] A total of 36,899 rupees awarded on 29 December 1869. The money had not been paid out since the dispute about the lawful Metropolitan had started.

[2] Case III, III, pp. 58, 59.

[3] The Patriarch had gone first to London and got permits for his journey and saw the Governor of Madras on his way to Travancore. This gave many the impression that he had the full support of the British Government for his position.

publicly anathematized him. The Government did not know how to act. It is probable that its sympathies were on the side of Athanasios, a subject of the State and a man held in great respect by all sections of the community. For some months they considered the matter, occasionally having to inhibit the Patriarch's activities to preserve the peace. In March 1876 a proclamation referred the whole matter to the decision of the courts. The Government stated that they had no interest in the alleged deposition of one metran or the appointment of another, and were concerned only with the maintenance of peace and good order. 'Any apparent connection with appointments relating to the Syrian Church which Proclamations issued under times and circumstances now altered may seem to indicate will henceforth be avoided.'[1] So the State Government returned to its ancient attitude towards the Christians of St Thomas, an attitude which had been changed through the interest of British Residents in the affairs of the Church, and their influence on Government policy on its behalf. The Cochin raja followed the lead of Travancore in this matter.

The Patriarch was thus free to act against Athanasios without incurring legal penalties or extradition, provided he kept the peace. He summoned a synod at Muḷanturutti in 1876[2] which passed resolutions settling the relation of the Indian Church to the patriarchal see. The Malankara see was to be in the same relation to the Patriarch as a diocese in Syria, and each parish was to execute a registered deed of complete submission to the Patriarch. A fund was to be raised to fight Athanasios in the courts for the ownership of all property. The Syrian Christian Association was founded 'to manage and control all the religious and social concerns of the whole of the people in general'. It had a managing committee of eight priests and sixteen laymen, with a paid secretary and treasurer. The ruling Metran was to be president, but he had no other special powers, and thus all effective authority in the Church was taken from him.[3] That the decisions of the synod did

[1] Proclamation in case III, III, no. 205, pp. 38, 39.

[2] 27 to 29 June. Mr Justice Ormsby in his judgment throws doubt on the method and extent of representation of the whole church at this synod. No deeds of consent (of congregations to the proceedings of the synod) were produced before the royal court; see pp. 70–8. 'The synod at Mulanturuṭṭi in no sense whatever represented the Syrian Churches in Malankara' and 'the resolutions passed thereat are not binding on that Church' (p. 82).

[3] The Patriarch Peter III's letter and the decisions of the synod; case III, III, pp. 81–96.

not reflect the mind of the people is evident from the resolutions of the Parumala seminary synod of 1878, which refers to a want of agreement between the Patriarch's commands and the will and determination of the people.[1] The funds which the Muḷanturutti synod had agreed should be raised to institute a civil suit against Mar Athanasios for the property had not been collected, nor had the *rasissa* or tax due to the Patriarch. It had also been decided that the canons ought to be printed and a sealed book kept in each parish. Many of the canons were explained in the bull issued by the Patriarch in 1877, which sought to regulate the life of the Church and even included rules enjoining men to wear beards and women trousers. Peter apparently wished to conform the social life of the community to the pattern familiar to him in Syria.

In 1876 the Patriarch also consecrated four new bishops, apparently without any election by the Church as a whole.[2] He divided the see of Malankara into seven dioceses and made each bishop responsible directly to the Patriarchal throne and to the Association. There was no single bishop left in Malabar in exercise of metropolitical powers. The Patriarch clearly did not intend to allow Mar Dionysios to gain the same authority as Athanasios had been enjoying and he assigned him Quilon, the smallest of all the new dioceses.[3]

Mar Athanasios had lost many of his followers as a result of the Patriarch's excommunication but he had carried on his ministry without bitterness until his death on 15 July 1877. His last letter was an exhortation to faith in Christ, and his only reference to his own affairs is the claim that all he had taught could be proved by the Scriptures. An English missionary writing at the time of his death speaks of the Metran's later years as exemplary, though he is critical of him for his temporizing policy towards the conservative and reforming wings in his Church. It must be remembered that

[1] Case III, III, p. 97.

[2] Geevarghese Mar Julios said in court: 'The Patriarch alone gave me the dignity.' (Contrast this with Bishop Middleton's account of the method of election of bishops at Kōṭṭayam in 1816.) The bishops were Paulos Mar Athanasios for Kōṭṭayam, Geevarghese Mar Julios for Tumpamon, G. Mar Kurilos for Ankamāli, G. Mar Gregorios for Niraṇam. A little later Mar Ivanios was consecrated for Kōḻancēri and Simon Mar Dionysios for Cochin.

[3] The intention of Peter III in creating seven dioceses was to make each independent of the others, subject only to Antioch. The common link was to be the properties, and for that the Malankara Association was to function: Dist. Court, Kōṭṭayam, Judgment O.S. 111 of 1113, Kōṭṭayam, 1943, p. 63.

this Church claimed to be the original Syrian Church. It had not at this time received any significant alterations in its way of life or worship. Mar Thomas Athanasios succeeded as Metran on the death of Mathew Mar Athanasios.

In the same year that the Patriarch left Malabar and Mathew Athanasios died Mar Dionysios applied to the Resident for the interest of the star pagodas, saying he was the lawful Metropolitan. He failed in this application and the money was paid to Mar Thomas Athanasios.[1] Two years after (1879), Mar Dionysios V filed a suit against Mar Thomas Athanasios to recover all the property in his possession, chiefly the right to the interest of the star pagodas and the seminary, on the ground that the Malankara Church had always been under the supremacy of Antioch. In the local court and the High Court, to which appeal was made, judgment was given in favour of the plaintiff. The case was then taken to the Royal Court of Final Appeal and the majority judgment upheld that of the lower courts, saying that the Patriarch of Antioch was head of the Church in Malabar and that consecration or at least authorization by him was essential to the Metropolitan. As the consecration of Mar Thomas Athanasios was, by that standard, imperfect, the court declared in 1889 that he was not competent to hold the position and dignity of spiritual head of that Church.[2] The court also ruled that the Patriarch had no control over the temporalities of the Malabar Church.

This decision was the signal for many other cases to be filed for the possession of property, and all these were decided against Mar Thomas Athanasios. One by one the churches were taken by Mar Dionysios's party, until only two or three remained.

Here we take our leave of the reforming party in the Syrian Church. They had been driven out of almost all the churches and their Metropolitan was no longer recognized as the legal head of

[1] 28 December 1877, pp. 235, 236, III, judgment, Royal Court of Final Appeal.

[2] Paragraph 224 of majority judgment, Zilla Court, 28 June 1884; High Court, 13 November 1885; Royal Court, 12 July 1889. The third judge, a European, dissented from the majority, taking the view that Mar Mathew Athanasios had been in possession of the property until his death and therefore Metropolitan. He showed, in his judgment, that the Muḷanturutti synod was not representative of the whole Church, that the question of Dionysios's election or ratification as metran did not come up, and that he was not accepted in the Church nearly as widely as he claimed to be.

the Syrian Church. In the light of later history it is evident that this set-back proved the greatest possible blessing, except that no separation of members in the body of Christ can ever be unequivocally described as a blessing. The separated body became known as the Mar Thoma Syrian Church. A revival movement had been gaining strength for some years, and it was stabilized through the formation of the Mar Thoma Evangelistic Association in 1889, a society with very small beginnings which steadily permeated the whole Church with a sense of responsibility for evangelism, and is now a big organization, with several missionary colonies or ashrams in other parts of India. The Mar Thomites, as they are generally called, had to build new churches, which was by no means an easy undertaking, both because of the material cost and because of the opposition usually encountered from Dionysios's party and the Hindus. A strong link was formed with the Toḻiyūr diocese,[1] whose bishops in 1894 consecrated the younger brother, Titus, of Mar Thomas Athanasios, who died in 1893. The spiritual revival we have already noticed gained in influence and in 1895 the great annual Marāmon Convention was founded, at which some thirty to fifty thousand people now meet annually for religious addresses. One result of the revival was a powerful impetus to the reform movement, and, with no material goods to lose, the Church did not hesitate to reform its liturgy in the light of an evangelical interpretation of the Scriptures. The Church today is still active in every way and has just established two degree colleges. There are five bishops and about two hundred thousand members. The Church was in communion with the Anglican diocese of Travancore and Cochin and continued this connexion after the formation of the Church of South India. As we have already ignored the Romo-Syrians and Anglican Syrians as continuing bodies so now we leave the Mar Thoma Church and return to the conservative party, under Mar Dionysios, in communion with the Jacobite Patriarch and in triumphant possession of all the ecclesiastical property of the community.

The acts of the Muḷanturutti synod in 1876 had not been the outcome of general discussion and agreement. They were proposed

[1] Mar Kurilos had assisted at the consecration of Mar Thomas Athanasios. On 13 March 1883 he consecrated Joseph Mar Athanasios as his assistant bishop (with Mar Thomas Athanasios assisting). Mar Kurilos died on 1 February 1888. Mar Thomas Athanasios and Joseph Mar Athanasios then consecrated Geevarghese Mar Kurilos as assistant of Toḻiyūr (Joseph Mar Athanasios becoming diocesan) on 13 September 1893. The present bishop of Toḻiyūr was consecrated by the Mar Thoma Metropolitan and his suffragan (1951).

by the Patriarch to stabilize his own position and they were accepted by the Indians because the support of the Patriarch against Mathew Athanasios and his party was at that time essential. As we have seen, the Church made no effort to implement many of the resolutions, and the plan to divide the Church into seven more or less autonomous dioceses was against its continuous tradition, and bound to fail, the more certainly because it was directed against the powerful personality of a metran standing squarely on that tradition. Dionysios's letter to the Resident claiming the interest due to the trustees of the Syrian Church stated that he was the Metropolitan of the Syrian Church in Malabar, and this was no empty claim. The other six bishops were speedily reduced to the status of suffragans. One bishop, Simon of Cochin, challenged Dionysios's authority and won a case against him in the courts. Dionysios had pleaded that Simon's consecration was invalid, as the consent of the people had not been obtained. Such an appeal to the local tradition involved flouting patriarchal authority, and brought an immediate rejoinder from the Patriarch that he had full authority to consecrate anyone he liked, at his sole discretion. The Patriarch also wrote to the committee of the Association reminding them that no bishop could be its president, but he was protesting against an inbred attitude to the metran, which had behind it pride in the antiquity of the community and in their honoured position in local society. The Malabar Church wanted to have its native metropolitan, and it had been unlikely, from the outset, that the influence of a foreign Patriarch, living thousands of miles away, would have been sufficient to change their old system of church government for rule by a college of bishops, particularly when, side by side with themselves, the Syrians saw the Mar Thoma church administered wisely and well by a local metropolitan and gaining rapidly in prestige and influence. The Patriarch Peter died in 1894 but the powers he had claimed have remained the subject of bitter dispute in Malabar.

At first there was no open controversy with the Patriarch. Dionysios did not consecrate any bishops[1] and when two rambans were elected to the episcopate in 1908 they were sent to the Patriarch for their consecration. Dionysios and the Association

[1] This statement is not wholly accurate as two bishops were consecrated, but not for Malabar, and at the express command of the Patriarch. The first was Mar Julios Alvarez. He was a Goanese priest who had left the Roman Catholic Church consequent on a quarrel, at the same time as a number of Roman

had asked that one of them, Fr Geevarghese, might be given the right of succession to the Metropolitan. Although Patriarch Abdalla[1] consecrated the Indians as Mar Dionysios and Mar Kurilos he did not mention the right of succession on Dionysios's *statikon*, and he also consecrated a Syrian monk as Mar Eusthathios, and sent him to India as his delegate and personal representative.

In 1909 Dionysios V died, and the Association at once communicated with the Patriarch asking that Geevarghese Dionysios VI should be appointed Metropolitan in his place. The Patriarch made no reply until he received a formal request through his delegate, Mar Eusthathios. Then at last he made the appointment. Patriarch Abdalla knew the temper of the Malabar Church, and must have realized that his position was by no means assured.

In the autumn of the same year Abdalla came to India himself, and called a synod at Kōṭṭayam, to implement the decisions of Muḷanturutti. His coming led, however, not to consolidation but to schism. The Travancore High Court complained in 1928 that the two parties formed as a result of the synod gave wholly discrepant accounts of its proceedings. It seems that the synod met and at once plunged into hot debate about the extent of the Patriarch's jurisdiction and other matters arising from the last synod. Apparently the synod did not allow the Patriarch to take any part in its proceedings, but regarded these questions as ones which the Indian Church had to settle for itself. Possibly Abdalla's previous connexion with the Church had left a party inimical to

Catholics in Ceylon, Goa, South Kanara and Tinnevelly and Cape Comorin. Julios died in Goa in 1926 and his followers have mostly been reconciled to their Mother Church. In 1892 an American called Rene Vilatte was consecrated as Mar Timotheos by Mar Athanasios and Mar Julios. Vilatte was first a Presbyterian and then had been ordained priest in the Protestant Episcopal Church of America. He was deposed from the priesthood in March 1892. He was consecrated at Colombo in August 1892, in spite of his American bishop's letter and telegram. He returned to America as archbishop of the Latin Syrians, converts from Anglicanism. These numbered about two hundred and fifty. See *A Statement for the Anglican Episcopate* (facts and original documents showing proselytizing by the Jacobite Metropolitans of Malabar, and disorderly consecrations by order of the Jacobite Patriarch of Antioch), by W. J. Richards and Archdeacon Caley (Kōṭṭayam, 1904). A number of *episcopi vagantes* owe their orders to Vilatte.

[1] It seems that Abdalla had not immediately succeeded Peter. Abdul Massih was enthroned as Patriarch in July 1895 but was deposed by the Sultan of Turkey in 1905. The reasons for this action have been disputed in the Travancore courts. Abdalla was enthroned in 1906. As Mar Gregorios Abdalla of Jerusalem he had accompanied Peter to Malabar but is said to have quarrelled with him and been excommunicated. At all events he stayed on in India for some time after the Patriarch left, visiting the churches and collecting money. He is said to have become a Roman Catholic after his return to Syria, but later came back to the Jacobite Church.

him on personal grounds which persisted in that attitude even though he was now Patriarch; perhaps the Indian Church was determined to allow no more than spiritual authority to the foreign Patriarch.[1] The synod passed resolutions in September 1910 confirming the powers of the throne of Antioch over the Church of Malabar but defining those powers by reference to the canons of the Church, local custom in Malabar, the decisions of Muḷanturutti and the judgment of the Royal Court of Final Appeal in 1889. The majority of the synod seems to have been with Mar Dionysios in these resolutions, but not all. He was a man of autocratic temperament who had already had sharp differences of opinion with his co-trustees, Konāṭṭ Malpān and Mr C. J. Kurien, about the management of property. They had, in fact, declined to act with him in drawing the interest on the star pagodas from 1909. Dionysios's position was also morally weak, as he had executed a document at his consecration, promising implicit obedience to the Patriarch.

Patriarch Abdalla was very angry, both at the decisions of the synod and the treatment he had received. His anger was naturally focused on Mar Dionysios. All attempts to bring about an understanding between the two men failed, and in June 1911 Abdalla excommunicated the Metran, making charges of misconduct and insubordination, and saying that a tremor of the hands made it impossible for him to celebrate the Kurbāna, and thus to function as a bishop. He appointed Mar Kurilos president of the Association and Malankara Metropolitan. Abdalla had been taking what steps he could to strengthen his supporters. He had consecrated two bishops, Paulos Mar Athanasios in June 1910 and Mar Severios in August. By the latter move he gained the support of a prominent lawyer who had been one of Dionysios's closest advisers[2] but gave recognition to a division among the Syrians which Menezes had tried to heal.[3] The co-trustees of Dionysios had both gone over to the Patriarch's side, and were appointed to continue in that capacity with Mar Kurilos.

[1] The view of the majority judgment in the seminary case was that foreign bishops had authority only over spiritualities in the Malabar Church.

[2] Judgment, Dist. Court, Kōṭṭayam, p. 69.

[3] Severios was a Southist and his community was constituted as a separate Knānaya diocese. In 1926 Severios consecrated Dioscoros as his suffragan. He succeeded on Severios's death in 1928 but joined the Roman Church in 1941 and died soon after. Mar Clemens was consecrated in 1951 by the Patriarch and has taken charge of his see. A Southist Roman Catholic diocese was erected in 1911 under a bishop of their own section, Dr Mathew Makil.

As soon as the Patriarch's order excommunicating Dionysios was published, the Association committee met, with Dionysios in the chair, and declared the excommunication inoperative. They also removed the co-trustees from office and appointed two others. These actions were confirmed by a general meeting of the Association and amounted to a deliberate rejection of the Patriarch's authority. Once more there were two bishops in Malabar, each claiming to be lawful Metropolitan, one pointing to the adherence of the majority of the churches as his credentials, the other showing the Patriarchal order. From the State's point of view, only the courts could decide between the two, and award the enjoyment of the trusts to the party it considered the true continuing Church.

For some time, however, no appeal to the courts was made. Each party tried to justify its own position. The Dionysian party contended that the Patriarch could not annul orders (though they had treated the orders of Mar Athanasios as annulled as a result of the Patriarch's excommunication and insisted on the re-ordination of any priests who came over to them from that section), and that his approval was not necessary for the appointment of a Malankara Metropolitan. Further, Dionysios claimed that a metropolitan has power to consecrate muron (holy oil), though in the Royal Court of Appeal it had been explicitly stated that only the Patriarch has that power.

In spite of the vigour of these affirmations Dionysios's party wished to regularize their position in relation to the Patriarchate for which, in their opposition to the Mar Thoma Church, they had previously made such a strong claim. They therefore arranged for Mar Abdul Massih, the ex-Patriarch, to come from Mardin to Malabar. He arrived in June 1912. There is still dispute about his status. Some claim that he was rightful Patriarch, unlawfully deposed by the intrigues of Abdalla and losing only jurisdiction by the withdrawal of Turkish recognition, not spiritual powers; others say that he had been deprived of office by a synod, on account of lunacy, and that the Turkish authorities had confirmed this action and recognized Abdalla.[1] The arrival of Abdul Massih exacerbated

[1] See Exhibit Ek. in O.X. 111 of 1113. Tewfick Pasha is said to have warned Sir Edward Grey that Abdul Massih had no authority in the Syrian Church; A.S. 68 of 1096, judgment, pp. 76, 77. The conclusion one draws depends partly on the likelihood of the Turkish action, which all admit, being based on the previous decision of a synod of the Church.

the high feelings between the two sections, and the Maharaja of Travancore refused to receive him. The district magistrate of Kōṭṭayam prohibited him from entering that division, as he feared a breach of the peace. Abdul Massih went therefore to the ancient church of Niraṇam and there, on 14 July 1912, he consecrated, whether willingly or under duress is a matter still disputed, Paulose Mar Ivanios as Catholicos, that is to say as local Patriarch for Malankara, recognizing the spiritual supremacy of the Patriarch of Antioch but not under his jurisdiction in any way. It is perhaps curious that this title should have been chosen, as the Jacobites in Syria called a similar officer 'Maphrian', avoiding the title Catholicos, because of its use by the Nestorians,[1] but the office itself, if duly created, would have satisfied all the aspirations of the Malankara Church. It would have given them autonomy and at the same time avoided a breach with Antioch.[2] The difficulty has been that the status of Abdul Massih and his authority to take such action was doubtful and is still disputed.

In September Abdul Massih consecrated three more bishops, Geevarghese Mar Philoxenos, Geevarghese Mar Gregorios and Yoyakin Mar Ivanios, and the following year signed a document which gave the bishops of the Malankara Church authority to consecrate a new Catholicos whenever the holder of that office should die. It happened that the first Catholicos died shortly afterwards, but his office was not filled immediately. Mar Dionysios was still the real ruler of the Church, ruling as Malankara Metropolitan.[3]

An inter-pleader suit had been instituted in 1913 to decide which of the parties was entitled to enjoy the trust funds of the Syrian Church. This case was decided in the court in favour of Mar Dionysios. They said Abdalla's excommunication was void, as it was

[1] Paul, p. 92, quotes Renaudot, *Anciennes Relations des Indes*, p. 239, to this effect.

[2] It was pointed out in the High Court appeal of 1928 that the Patriarch would have had no practical place in the Malankara Church at all as a result of this action. The attitude of the Catholicos party was shown in two editions of the Church catechism: in 1909 the head of the Church was said to be the Patriarch, in the 1914 edition the Catholicos. It was contended that thus a new Church had been created; judgment, p. 73. According to the Kōṭṭayam District Court judgment, p. 86, an agitation for a maphrianate started in the time of Joseph Dionysios in 1900, and Konāṭṭ Malpān was its great protagonist.

[3] The practice of calling the ruling metran 'Metropolitan' dates from Mar Thoma VI; District Court judgment, Kōṭṭayam (1938), p. 120.

caused only by Dionysios's refusal to grant temporal authority to the Patriarch and that in any case it was not promulgated with the consent of a synod, as was customary. Further, Dionysios's action in respect of Abdul Massih had not weakened his position, since all that bishop had lost by withdrawal of recognition by the Turkish Government was jurisdiction, not the power to perform purely spiritual functions. The court made its judgment about the powers of Metropolitans from a printed version of the Hudaya canons, rejecting a manuscript version produced by the Patriarch's party. On appeal, the High Court in 1923 reversed most of the decisions of the district court, preferring the manuscript canons and deciding for the patriarchal party. Its leader in Travancore was Mar Athanasios who had succeeded as Metropolitan in 1917, on the death of Mar Kurilos. This decision of the High Court was reviewed in 1928 and judgment given that the excommunication of Mar Dionysios was contrary to natural justice, and void. The findings of the district court were accordingly confirmed.

In 1923 Mar Dionysios went to Syria to see the Patriarch Elias, who had succeeded Abdalla. He carried petitions from his suffragans that the excommunications which lay upon him and his adherents should be removed. The Patriarch sent him back with a Syrian bishop, Mar Julios, who was to investigate the whole affair on the spot and report back to the Patriarch. At first Dionysios seems to have given people to understand that the excommunication had been lifted, but this is unlikely, as later we find him asserting that it was not possible for the Malabar Church to recognize the authority of the Patriarch, as it had had no part in his election. Mar Julios's reports seem to have been wholly unfavourable to Dionysios.

Both parties were trying to strengthen their position. The Patriarch consecrated a number of new bishops, Michael Mar Dionysios and Thomas Mar Dioscoros in 1926 and Augen Mar Timotheos in 1927. All these bishops are said to have executed registered documents binding themselves to implicit obedience to the Patriarch, and pledging themselves to reject all ordained by Abdul Massih, and never to unite with them.[1] On the other side Mar Philoxenos was made second Catholicos in 1925. He died in 1928 and was succeeded by Geevarghese Mar Gregorios, who took the title of Mar Baselios. He consecrated Mar Gregorios the day

[1] District Court, Kōṭṭayam (1938), III, I; exhibits C.R., C.Q.

after his own elevation and in 1930 consecrated Geevarghese Mar Philoxenos.

An attempt to bring peace to the Malabar Church was made in 1931 by the Viceroy, Lord Irwin, who invited the Patriarch Elias III to India. On arrival in Malabar he seems to have cancelled the excommunication of Mar Dionysios, but a little later he declared that Abdul Massih had been deposed from office and so all he did in India was wholly invalid and void. The Patriarch died while touring the Malabar churches, and was buried in 1932 in Manjanikkara, without any reconciliation between the two parties having been effected. Two years later Mar Dionysios also died.

Both sides tried to convene meetings of the Malankara association but failed, and many efforts were made by Bishop Gore and others to bring them together. Soon after the death of Mar Dionysios the third Catholicos set out for Homs with Mar Julios to see the new Patriarch Ephraim I. Neither side was able to modify its position sufficiently for any compromise to be possible, and the Catholicos and his party returned to Malabar after a fruitless journey. Later in the year the Catholicos was anathematized by the Patriarch and the faithful forbidden to have any contact with him. In 1935 Mar Ephraim gave a *statikon* to Paulos Mar Athanasios as Metropolitan after he had been elected at a meeting of his party.

After he had got back from Homs in 1934 the Catholicos's supporters met and elected him Metropolitan of the Malabar Church. They also approved a written constitution for the Church, an entirely new departure. It was later held in the High Court that this act in fact erected a new Church, holding forms inconsistent with the Jacobite Church of Antioch. It was pointed out that in all the 127 articles of the Constitution there was no reference at all to the Patriarch, though four articles contemplate recognizing him if he will accept the Catholicate as a *fait accompli*.[1] There were now once again two Metropolitans of Malabar and two sets of trustees, and once more appeal was made to the courts for a decision between them.

The judge in the district court at Kōṭṭayam, where the case was heard, gave his judgment in 1936 (published in 1938). The case had turned on the authority of Mar Abdul Massih, affirmed by the

[1] Nokes, J., judgment of the High Court of Travancore 1948: articles 92, 93, 109, 113.

PLATE IV

HIS HOLINESS THE CATHOLICOS,
MAR BASELIOS GEEVARGHESE II

Catholicos party and denied by Mar Athanasios.[1] The judge ruled that no satisfactory evidence had been produced of Abdul Massih's canonical removal (though all agreed that his mandate had been withdrawn by the Turkish Government), and that he was fully competent to act as Patriarch. He held that the Patriarch or his authorized representative is the only authority competent to consecrate a Metropolitan for Malankara, and that he acts in his own right and does not need synodical approval for his actions. He accordingly gave judgment in favour of the Catholicos, as lawful Malankara Metropolitan.

An appeal was lodged against this decision and the case argued before the High Court. There two judges agreed that the Catholicos's party, with their new Constitution, had in effect formed a new Church to which the Patriarch was an alien. As the trust envisaged the supremacy of the Patriarch it was clear that judgment must be given in favour of Mar Athanasios. The case was fought for the ownership of the old seminary and other central church property, as well as the trust funds, but a stay order was served on Mar Athanasios and appeal lodged against the High Court decision. In 1951 the Court of Appeal confirmed the previous judgment and ordered that no appeal could be made to the Supreme Court of India.[2] The Supreme Court, however, quashed this provision and heard the appeal. In their judgment of 1954 the judges expressed dissatisfaction with many of the findings of the High Court and ordered a re-trial.

Public opinion in the two Churches was very weary of this interminable legislation, and pressure was brought on the authorities so that their representatives met and reached agreement on many points. The Patriarch was to be recognized as Supreme Spiritual Head of the Universal Syrian Orthodox Church of which

[1] The Catholicos party took up the following position: they denied the deposition of Abdul Massih and the existence of any contemporary document witnessing to it. They admitted that his firman had been withdrawn, but said that this alone could not affect the validity of his spiritual ministrations. They had not been consulted in the election of Mar Abdalla and hence this election could not be regular. They had agreed to the ordination of Geevarghese Mar Dionysios and Mar Kurilos by Abdalla because they recognized he was competent to perform spiritual functions, but this did not involve recognition as Patriarch. On this point canons were quoted to show that if two men, for any reason, filled metropolitical or patriarchal thrones at the same time, one should function and the other 'sit quiet'. They sought support for their attitude to Abdul Massih in the admitted fact that he was buried in the patriarchal monastery.

[2] In 1952 the Catholicos moved to a new house near Kōṭṭayam, and Mar Athanasios moved into the old seminary, as a result of the High Court judgment.

the Malankara Syrian Orthodox Church forms a part, and was in turn, after an exchange of letters, to recognize the Catholicos. Provision was made for the consecration of future occupants of the Catholicate, for the consecration of holy oil and the payment of tax to the Patriarch. But further meetings have defined outstanding differences; the Orthodox party want the establishment of the Catholicate by Abdul Massih to be recognized and accepted, and the Catholicos's consecration or installation to be done by the Malankara synod. The Jacobite party refuses both these conditions. It seems that the matter will again go to the High Court (October 1954).

Although this protracted litigation is the melancholy background of the life of the Syrian Church for the last half century it must not be supposed that the two parties have been rigidly separated from each other. In social life the division was not strictly observed and inter-group marriages were often arranged. In the north the majority of the people supported the Patriarch, with Mar Athanasios living in the Āluvā Seminary, as their centre. The south, on the whole, was for the Catholicos, centred in the old seminary at Kōṭṭayam. Several bishops have been consecrated by the Catholicos, Alexios Mar Theodosios in 1938 and Thomas Mar Dionysios the following year, and five more in 1953. This party was also immensely heartened and strengthened by the coming-over of Augen Mar Timotheos from the patriarchal party, with the majority of his Kandanāṭ diocese, soon after the judgment of the district court was given. There were, however, secessions also. Mar Ivanios, the founder of Bethany Ashram with Mar Theodosios, went over to Rome, and was granted a special rite and jurisdiction and the dignity of Archbishop of Trivandrum. (He died in 1953.) Another bishop, Mar Severios, went with him. Mar Dioscoros, of the Patriarch's Knānaya diocese, also went over to Rome in his old age.

All through the last quarter of a century efforts have been made to bring the two parties together. After Lord Irwin and Bishop Gore had tried without success, certain local laymen persuaded the Catholicos to go to Homs in 1934, as we have seen. This visit was abortive. Then Bishop Pakenham Walsh, a former Anglican Bishop of Assam and Principal of Bishop's College, Calcutta, went to see the Patriarch. The bishop, supported by local people, brought the two sides together in conference in 1938. Resolutions were accepted by the Patriarch's section but rejected by the Catholicos. The situation was deteriorating rapidly. Vast sums were being raised and spent on legislation, and the youth of the Church grew impatient. In 1950 they persuaded all the bishops to meet in conference in Ciṅa-vānam, and they then cordoned off the house in which the meeting was held, telling the bishops they must stay there until they had reached agreement. These rather high-handed tactics at first seemed successful, for almost unanimous agreement was said to have been reached, and terms of peace and a constitution for the Malabar Church were sent to the Patriarch for his approval. The most important point was the granting of a maphrianate for Malabar by the Patriarch, making the Church autonomous but acknowledging the Patriarch as its spiritual head. The Patriarch accepted the proposals, except the provision that the episcopal synod of Malabar might consecrate a bishop for a vacant diocese without reference to the Patriarch if the maphrianate should be vacant. The maphrian was to be appointed by the Patriarch. On this point the whole thing broke down, and the decision of the Court of Appeal at the end of 1951 was regarded as final, shutting the door to any hope of reconciliation.

The official reaction of the Catholicos's party, who saw that they would soon lose a large portion of their property, as the reformed party had done sixty years before, was that they now had complete freedom from foreign control, were recognized as an independent Orthodox Church, and should collect large funds to build churches and rally the faithful. A new house was bought for the Catholicos, and a good deal of patriotism shown. When the judgment was given the Catholicos was in Bombay; but he was met at the railway station when he re-entered the State by a long procession of cars, which escorted him back to Kōṭṭayam, to demonstrate both the strength of his party, and the fact that they were not dismayed by the decision against them. It was disappointing, in view of the publicity given to this attitude, to find that a further appeal had been made to the Supreme Court.

The ordinary life of the mass of church members has changed considerably since the turn of the century. The coming of buses even into remote country districts has profoundly affected the habits of the people and broken down, to an ever-increasing degree, the conservatism which had for centuries been a mark of the community. Together with this go the rapid increase of educational facilities, and the wide scatter of educated men and women in trade and the professions all over India, in East Africa, Ceylon and Malaya. The produce of coconut estates, pepper and other country crops has become more and more valuable, and the prosperity of the community has been greatly increased. The Church Missionary Society College and High School at Kōṭṭayam were the pioneers of Syrian education and have had the largest share in this task. The funds awarded to the missionaries by the arbitrators in 1838 have ever since been spent solely on the education of members of the Syrian community, of all persuasions, Jacobite, Orthodox, Mar Thomite and Anglican. The two institutions have lately been separated, and the college raised to degree status, with a governing board drawn from all sections of the Syrian community. In 1892 Mar Dionysios and others started a high school for boys in Kōṭṭayam. This institution continues as the Mar Dionysios Seminary and has now a theological seminary attached to it. Mar Gregorios started a girls' high school at Tiruvalla at this time, with the help of English women who came out to help in an honorary capacity. In recent years very many schools, primary and high, have been started by the Church. They include a residential high school at Sāstamkōṭṭa, and the Mahilalayam for girls at Āluvā, run by a fellowship in which all the different groups are represented. At Āluvā, too, is the Union Christian College, started thirty years ago by a group of brilliant young Syrian graduates. The College has given a superb example of Christian service and fellowship and it has always been the hope of its leaders that it would make a contribution towards the unity of the Syrian Churches in Malabar. The Kēraḷa Council of Christian Union was founded by Mr K. C. Chacko, a very saintly professor at the College, who had a formative influence on the lives of hundreds of young men in his Church. The Council received little support from the Churches and appears now to be extinct. The most recent foundation is the Catholicate College at Pattanamtiṭṭa (1951). The community is probably completely literate, and many of its members have proceeded to high academic honours in the universities of Europe and America, and have filled with distinction important posts. The Finance Minister in India's first free Government, and the Chief Secretaries at one time in Mysore and Travancore were all Syrian Christians.

The disputes within the Church are one of the factors which have prevented any wide recognition of its evangelical duty. But some advances have been made. Ramban Patrose started the Servants of the Cross Society in 1924, for work among the depressed classes. They now have one hundred centres of work and twenty missionaries. Ramban Patrose was one of the Catholicos's party. The Evangelistic Association of the east started in 1925, under the patronage of the Patriarch. It also works among people of the depressed classes in Travancore–Cochin and has about fifty mission stations.

List of bishops serving in 1954

Orthodox Syrian Church	Diocese	Date of Consecration
His Holiness Moran Mar Baselios Geevarghese II	Catholicos of the East	Bishop, 1912; Catholicos, 1929
His Grace Augen Mar Timotheos, Metropolitan	Kandanāṭ and Ankamāli	1927
His Grace Kuriakose Mar Gregorios, Metropolitan	Kōṭṭayam	1929
His Grace Alexios Mar Theodosios, Metropolitan	Quilon	1938
His Grace Mar Thoma Dionysios, Metropolitan	Niraṇam	1940
His Lordship Petros Mar Eusthathios, Episcopa	Malabar	1953
His Lordship Mathew Mar Ivanios, Episcopa	Kōṭṭayam	1953
His Lordship Mathew Mar Athanasios, Episcopa	Principal, Orthodox Theological Seminary	1953
His Lordship Daniel Mar Philoxenos, Episcopa	Tumpamon	1953
His Lordship Mathew Mar Kūrilos, Episcopa	Quilon	1953
Jacobite Church—Patriarch Section		
His Grace Michael Mar Dionysios, Metropolitan	Kōṭṭayam	1926
His Grace Geevarghese Mar Gregorios, Metropolitan	Ankamāli	1946
His Grace Paulose Mar Severios, Metropolitan	Cochin	1946
His Grace Abraham Mar Clemis, Metropolitan	Knānaya Diocese	1952
His Grace Paulose Mar Philoxenos, Metropolitan	Kandanāṭ	1953

Mar Thoma Syrian Church	Diocese	Date of Consecration
Most Rev. Juhanon Mar Thoma	Metropolitan	1937
Right Rev. Dr Mathew Mar Athanasios	Missionary Bishop outside Travancore-Cochin	1937
Right Rev. Dr Alexander Mar Theophilos	Central Diocese	1953
Right Rev. Thomas Mar Athanasios	Southern Diocese	1953
Right Rev. Philipose Mar Chrysostom	Northern Diocese	1953

SOURCES

THE early period is splendidly documented in a book by the late Judge P. Cheriyan, *The Malabar Syrians and the Church Missionary Society, 1816–1840*. Many relevant documents are printed in full as appendices. The book is a model of its kind.

Much of the material in this chapter is drawn from the printed judgments and volumes of exhibits prepared in the court cases. The most important are the following:

(i) Judgment of the Huzur Court in case 54 of 991 M.E. (A.D. 1816).

(ii) Exhibits in case III of 1061 in the Royal Court of Final Appeal (A.D. 1886) (vols. I, II, III, IV, judgments of Chief Justice Krishnaswamy Rao and Justice Sitarama Iyer and minority judgment of Justice Ormsby).

(iii) Judgment in case 253 of 1081 in the High Court of Travancore (A.D. 1906).

(iv) Judgment in case 94 of 1088 in the District Court of Travancore (A.D. 1913).

(v) Judgment in case 68 of 1096 (Syrian Church Fund Case) *Travancore Law Times*, III (A.D. 1921).

(vi) Judgment First Appeal 471 and 506 of 1100 *Travancore Law Times*, VI (A.D. 1925).

(vii) Judgment of the District Court of Kōṭṭayam in Case III of 1113 (A.D. 1938).

(viii) Judgments of the High Court, Trivandrum (1948).

(ix) Judgments of the Appeal Court, Trivandrum (1951).

Many of these Judgments are to be found in the Syrian Church Collection in the Library of Kēraḷa United Theological Seminary at Trivandrum. They are also probably all available in the Library of the Law College, Trivandrum. The documents listed above are all printed in English and were published, but not in any continuous series of Law Reports.

There is a considerable Malayāḷam literature about the period, most of it controversial in character. The most generally useful book of this type is *Suriāni Kristyānikaḷuṭe Sabhācaritram* (The Church History of the Syrian Christians) by P. Ittoop.

Many of these judgements are to be found in the Syrian Church Collection in the Library of Kerala United Theological Seminary at Trivandrum. They are also probably all available in the Library of the Law College, Trivandrum. The documents listed above are all printed in English and were published, but not in any continuous series of Law Reports.

There is a considerable Malayalam literature about the period, most of it controversial in character. The most generally useful book of this type is *Suriani Kristianikalude Sabhacaritram* (The Church History of the Syrian Christians) by P. Ittoop.

PART II

CHAPTER VII

THE SOCIAL LIFE OF THE ST THOMAS CHRISTIANS

At the beginning of this century life in Travancore and Cochin was still very simple, based on the land and the cycle of agricultural duties. Crops were raised for home consumption, except for pepper and similar cash crops which had been exported for centuries. Families remained on the land on which they had lived for generations. The St Thomas Christians had a recognized place in this rural economy and their way of life was deeply influenced by that of the society in which they lived. This chapter attempts to describe that way of life, although it is now to be found only in the remotest country districts, and even there is modified by the many influences which are shaping India's new culture, Western education, easy transport, a money economy and increasing industrialization. The purpose of this description is not merely to record a way of life which is passing away, it is to supply data for the inquiry how the Syrian Christian community, foreign in origin, put down such deep roots in Indian soil that it became accepted without question as indigenous, a position hardly yet attained by the Christian Churches which are the fruit of the European Christian missionary movement of the nineteenth century.

The position of the St Thomas Christians in relation to the Hindu and outcaste communities is indicated in the first section. The second section attempts to describe the social organization of the Christian community, and is followed by a third which sketches the ordinary life of Syrian Christians at the beginning of this century.

I

There is no uniform pattern for Indian society. While the four great caste divisions can be recognized in most parts of the country, the extensive ramifications and subdivisions of each show a different picture in every geographical or linguistic area. In Kēraḷa, the Malayāḷam-speaking area of Malabar and Travancore–Cochin, the pattern of society is distinctive, owing no doubt to the virtual isolation imposed on the country for centuries by the sea on the west and the Western Ghats on the east. There were no large towns until modern times, and very few groupings of people sufficiently concentrated to be called villages. There were Brahmans of a group peculiar to the country, called *Nampūtiris*, and a *Śudra* caste of Nāyars, farmers and fighters. But there were no *Kshatriyas* except the Cochin ruling family and no *Vaisyas*, the trading caste. The rest of the population consisted of the many divisions and subdivisions of the outcaste, labouring community. The Brahmans were naturally associated with the temples, and held land derived from them. The Nāyars, from which community the rajas of Travancore were elevated, farmed land which was granted by the rajas or was the perquisite of certain State or temple duties. In course of time the land became more and more divided up, but originally large tracts must have belonged to the Hindu joint families.

It has been suggested that the first Christian groups in Kēraḷa were foreign traders who settled permanently in the land, and increased their community by marriage and by the baptism of slaves, as well as by indirect evangelism. It seems unlikely that there was ever direct evangelistic preaching. If this account of the origin of the community is correct, it is easy to see that the coming of the Christians filled a gap in society and that the foreign connexions of the immigrants would be of great value in providing a market for produce. Many traditions of origin support this view. For example, there was an ancient group of Christians at Tiruvamkkōṭ in South Travancore, who said that they were *Ceṭṭi* converts who came from the east coast because of persecution there, and were granted land and trading facilities by the local raja. The other immigrant traditions refer to foreigners, as in the case of Jewish immigrants. It is to be noticed that the traditional sites of St Thomas's evangelism were all, with one possible exception, on trading routes. As we have seen, until the beginning of the century all Christians were described in official documents as belonging to either Cranganore or Quilon, two places which are still the chief centres of trade on India's south-west coast.[1]

The Christian groups lived in villages, on land granted by the

[1] This statement is simplified for the sake of clarity. But Cranganore silted up in the sixteenth century and was replaced by Cochin, a few miles seaward.

raja.[1] They erected a church and had a street of houses to the north of it, often called *aṅāṭi* or *cānta* (that is, bazaar). It is sometimes possible to find old settlements by the persistence of these names long after the buildings have vanished, as at Ārttāṭ in Cochin. There is evidence to suggest that this arrangement fitted well into an existing practice, whereby the land belonging to a temple was considered the property of the god of that temple, administered by the Brahmans as the god's agents, and constituted a *yōgam* or company for this purpose. Often the raja acted as managing trustee. The *yōgam* had the duty of protecting certain groups of employees and enjoyed rights of service in return. This picture of a recognized privileged group matches the picture given by the evidence we have of the early Christian settlements, and can be paralleled by the conditions of subsequent Portuguese, Dutch and British trading stations. The Dutch, for example, had jurisdiction over all Christians living in Cochin, and half-caste Christians living near the fort. It is recorded that many Hindus crossed into Dutch territory and were baptized, in order to enjoy Dutch protection and escape certain duties and taxes for which they would otherwise be liable to the raja.[2]

The ability and usefulness of the first Christian groups were recognized not only by the grant of land by local rajas but by the grant of concessions and privileges recorded on copper plates. They were given charge of the collection of revenue for the rajas in certain places and in the fourteenth century Marignolli found that they were in charge of the public weighing office in the Quilon customs. Associated with concessions in the pepper and other trades was the grant of service from certain castes and the responsibility of protecting them. A seventeenth-century writer says that the carpenters, metal smelters, blacksmiths and goldsmiths recognized no superiors except the priests of the Thomas Christians, and that the barbers were also under Christian protection.[3] This relationship was in force only in the neighbourhood of the Christian centres, not over the whole country.

[1] A Vaṭṭaleluttu inscription at Cochin, probably eighth–tenth century, records a grant from the raja giving certain privileges, and the right to put up shops. The merchants concerned were probably Christians; T. K. Joseph, *Indian Antiquary*, LVII (1928), p. 29.

[2] K. P. P. Menon, *Hist. of Kerala*, IV, pp. 91, 92.

[3] T. K. Joseph, *The Four Copper Plates of the Malankara Nasrāṇis* (in Malayāḷam), pp. 41–4. The MS. referred to is Sloane MS. 2743 A in the British Museum.

The other privileges granted by the rajas were of use in establishing the position of the Christians in society and as such were most jealously guarded. In the sixteenth century the raja of Paṛavūr tried to give similar privileges to the Nāyars of his State but the Christians rose in armed revolt and forced him to change his mind.[1] One reason the Christians gave for adhering to the Portuguese at the beginning of that century was that the rajas were letting their privileges fall into desuetude whenever they could; but even at that time any Christian who was injured or insulted by a Nayar would soon have the whole community roused to get satisfaction and 'they were not appeased before either the person who had insulted them or the raja himself presented the model of a silver arm or some other gift to the church by way of satisfaction for the admitted offence'. In Iravi Korṭṭan's plate sixteen privileges are mentioned but seventy-two are said to have been granted by Cerumān Perumāḷ. At the time of marriage the *pantal* (pavilion) may be supported by a pillar holding up the ridge pole, as with Brahmans. In the procession silk umbrellas and other special poles may be carried, men may walk with wooden swords and shields covered with leopard skins, triumphal arches may be erected on the route and lamps lit outside the houses, the bridegroom may ride on an elephant, or, if the bridal party walk, a canopy may be carried over them and they may be preceded by a band. At the house the chief guests may sit on black and white cloths, and two plantain leaves may be supplied as plates.[2] Many of these processional ornaments could be used also by bishops, and are still used, as they were also by the rajas until their supersession in 1947.

The enjoyment of these privileges was not the only mark of distinction given to the Christians, they were also given certain honorific titles, most of which they shared with the Nāyars. *Taragan* is a word derived from the word for tariff; it is used by some Christians and Nāyars and is now hereditary. *Mutalāḷi* is the

[1] Gouvea, p. 18. There were professional champions of the Christians called *amouques* who bound themselves to get satisfaction on these occasions. This attitude has not entirely disappeared: in fairly recent times a Latin Christian at Karunāgappaḷḷi was prosecuted for daring to use silk umbrellas in a wedding procession and for spreading cloths on the path; *Kēraḷa Society Papers* (1931), series 8.

[2] Rufinus relates that a Hindu courtier gave Bishop Frumentius only one leaf in place of the two ordinarily used by princes. Frumentius ignored the insult, bent under the tip of his leaf, and went on with his meal. This was the origin of the present Christian custom of bending under the tip of one's leaf. Zaleski, *The Saints of India*, p. 225.

title of a group of families near Quilon who claim direct descent from eighth-century immigrants. The name is also used by some Moslems. The title *paṇikkar* denotes proficiency in military training; it is found among Brahmans, Nāyars and a few Moslems and Christians. The commonest name of the Christians was *Nasrāṇi Māppiḷa*. The first word is self-explanatory. There is much dispute about the origin of the second; it is certainly a title of honour and was probably originally granted by the rajas. It is the commonest cognomen of Nāyars.

The Christians shared many other things beside names with the Nāyars. They occasionally took wives from that community, and their children often went to school with Nāyar children.[1] They joined in many of the ordinary celebrations of the country such as Ōṇam and Vīshu or New Year's Day. At Nilampērūr they engaged in temple celebrations which took the form of a sham fight with the Hindus, first asking permission to play this game at the tomb of Paḷḷivānavar who may have been a Christian chief or king.

Christians were accustomed to give offerings to the temples. An example quoted by Whitehouse is that of a respectable Syrian named Eapen in Mallappaḷḷi in 1833.[2] He was attacked by a bad cancer in the breast which his friends thought was caused by the Kaudiar god who was angry with him because he had fallen into arrears with a yearly payment he had promised for the protection of himself and his family. He was urged to pay up this money, not only by Nāyars but also by his Christian friends, one of whom ascribed the sudden death of two relatives to the same cause and said that he had presented a buffalo to the temple when his own son was ill. Whitehouse says that in his day there was an image of B-hagavati in the bazaar in Māvēlikkara at which many Syrians used to make offerings. Many families still have certain privileges in the temples which are believed to have been granted in recognition of some service given or some present made in former times. For example, at the Aṛaṭ festival in Pāṛappāṭattu temple the oldest member of the Puḷikkamaṛṛattil family of Syrians (who bore the title Paṇikkar or Mēnōn) had the right to go before the image of the deity and received rice and other presents. Some Christians still give gifts to temples although this custom has almost entirely died out with the growth of communal feeling. This giving was reciprocal. For example, at Putupaḷḷi Hindus used to come for the

[1] Synod of Diamper, session VIII, decrees 1–4. [2] Whitehouse, p. 250.

Peruṇāḷ or annual feast of St George with offerings of fowls and cows. Miraculous cures were said to be effected in this church and many presented small models in silver of legs and arms which had been cured. This festival was still being held in 1853 and the reformer Abraham Malpan suspended all his people who attended it. In the church at Kōtamamgalam where Mar Baselios was buried, there is a celebration on the anniversary of his death in September, and Whitehouse reports that in his time some Hindus as well as Christians rolled blindfold round the church in fulfilment of vows. Gouvea mentions the offering made by Hindus to the cross of St Thomas in Cranganore. 'The heathen there made their vows, brought their offerings of oil and wax to replenish the lamp that burnt before the cross and went thence, recovering their lost health or property but not becoming converts to the faith.' The churches were often situated very near temples, as in Pālayūr, Paṛavūr, Niraṇam, Kallūppāṛa, Kaṭutturutti, Iriṅālakkuṭa and Piṛavam. It often happened in such places that Christians were trustees[1] of the temple and Hindus of the church. They often shared things used in festivals. All the paraphernalia of Hindu religious processions were used also by Syrians—various kinds of ceremonial umbrellas, drums, musical instruments, fly whisks, and bombs. A flagstaff was a prominent feature of both church and temple. The Kuṛavilaṅāṭ church formerly had elephants for its festivals which were lent to the Ēṭṭumanūr temple. The Christians at Pālayūr still follow the Brahman custom of bathing in the sea on their chief festival day and some of the old Christian families there share house names with the Brahmans or Nāyars, Śankurikkal, Malayikkal, Pakalamaṛṛam. Many Hindus join them in the festival and bring offerings.

Horoscopes were cast for new-born babies, the *tāḷi* is the sign of a married woman, and pollution is observed after births and deaths. I am told by a man who was a boy in 1890 that he was often asked by temple servants to touch provisions for the Cāttāyakuḷanara temple which had become polluted by the approach of an outcaste or in some other way.[2]

[1] Thurston, *Castes and Tribes of Southern India*, VI, p. 445; e.g. one of the trustees of the Anaprampal B-hagavati temple was a Syrian Christian called Valleḷattu Paṇikkar. At Aranula four Brahman families are said to have been converted, but one family continued to serve the temple, the head of the family raising the flag at the beginning of festivals. The custom was only discontinued when the headship of the family devolved on a priest.

[2] Fr Placid says this happened with all families living near temples and quotes a Malayāḷam proverb, 'Flies, cats, dogs and Nasrāṇis have no pollution.'

(*a*) FONT AT KAṬUTTURUTTI CHURCH, SHOWING HINDU INFLUENCE IN DECORATION

(*b*) STONE LAMPS OF HINDU TYPE IN THE CHURCHYARD AT CEṄANNŪR

Some of the assimilations to Hindu society have completely died out; for example, at Koḷencēri Roz found four brothers who were landowners living entirely as Hindus, wearing the tuft of hair and sharing one wife. Even then it is clear this was most unusual and such things have not been known for centuries.

Christians observed many of the ceremonies connected with birth, adolescence and marriage and death like Hindus. At the time of the first feeding of rice (*annaprāśanam*), celebrated generally in the sixth month after birth, the parents of the child often vowed to perform this ceremony in a particular church just as Hindus vow to perform it in a particular temple. In many ceremonies the senior woman of the house would bring a lighted lamp which was a relic of *agni* worship, and there is a special word, *tavikkuga*, used by Christians, which means to extinguish a lamp with a small ladle. Christians, like Nāyars, would never blow out a flame with their breath, as this would be an insult to the fire goddess. For centuries the popular belief in the power of omens to determine good or ill fortune and the belief in auspicious days, prevailed among the Christians too, and is not extinct. The acceptance of Hindu beliefs led to Christians adopting many conventions, such as sleeping with the head to the east and the feet to the west, and never north-south.

The result of the honourable place given by the rajas to the Christians, and of their assimilation in social custom to their Hindu neighbours, was that they were accepted as a caste, and often thought of their community in this way. They ranked after the Brahmans and as equals of the Nāyars. Many Christians would claim that there was Brahman convert blood in the community and that for this reason they were superior to Nāyars.

It was in consequence of this position that the St Thomas Christians, so far as our evidence goes, never attempted to bring their non-Christian neighbours to a knowledge of Christ, and so into the Christian Church. The Portuguese Archbishop Menezes did his best to create a sense of evangelistic responsibility among the Indian Christians by preaching to the Hindus whenever he could, and the eighteenth-century Carmelites had a number of baptisms from the heathen every year, so much so that they had to defend their action before the Raja of Travancore, but the Indian Church itself was not aroused to share this work.

A further consequence of acceptance as a caste was that untouchability was observed by Christians as by Hindus. Their tradition required that some functions at a wedding be performed by converts (menial offices like bringing the large pan required for preparing certain foods) and it seems that outcaste people were baptized for this purpose, but not incorporated in the community. Gouvea explains the Christian attitude as follows: they followed the custom of the rest of the people of Malabar; if they touched any low-caste person they immediately bathed themselves; not that they thought, as the heathen do, that they were polluted by such contact, but because the Nāyars, who are forbidden by the Brahmans to touch the lower castes, would not have any communication with them unless they purified themselves.[1] The reason given for Christian observance of untouchability is thus pure expediency, so that the caste people would trade with and give or rent land to the Christians. Other evidence suggests that the attitude was more fundamental. Christians thought that the value of a fast was lost if they happened to touch an outcaste. Respectable landowners used to change their clothes and bathe in a special shed on returning from the fields, where they had inevitably had contact with outcaste labour, before entering the house.[2]

II

The most obvious divisions among the Syrians are those caused by ecclesiastical obedience. We have seen in the first part of this book how the divisions came into being and why today Syrians owe allegiance to Rome, under the Chaldean or Antiochene rites, to the Patriarch of Antioch or the Catholicos of the East, to the Mar Thoma Church, or to the Church of South India (that is, former Anglicans). These divisions are not an unbridgable obstacle either to ordinary social intercourse or to marriage. There is not very much intermarriage between Roman and non-Roman, but there are occasions when the opportunity of uniting wealth to wealth provides a motive strong enough to overcome *odium theologicum*.

[1] Gouvea, p. 315.

[2] This was told by the late Mar Ivanios of his father. This attitude is now profoundly modified but has not disappeared. The writer was once strongly rebuked by Syrian Christians for having outcaste Christian parishioners in his house, on the ground that it made it hard for the Syrians to have social contact with him afterwards. It is right to add that the Jacobites have had a mission to the outcastes since the 'twenties, the Servants of the Cross Society, and the Mar Thoma Evangelistic Association has worked among them with great success. I do not think that the converts are fully integrated into the life of the Church as yet. Certainly there are no clergy from among their number.

Marriages between Jacobite and Orthodox, Mar Thoma and Church of South India are common. The bride always conforms to her husband's Church.

There is another division within the St Thomas Christians which runs through all ecclesiastical differences. Every Christian is either a Northist or a Southist, no matter what his ecclesiastical allegiance may be. Usually both groups are endogamous; they differ from each other in customs and to some extent in physiognomy, the Southists being fairer. Archbishop Menezes found the two groups in the otherwise undivided Malabar Church of his day and did all he could to persuade them of the wickedness of their mutually exclusive attitude. He tried, with little success, to persuade them to worship in each other's churches, for in some places churches belonging to both groups were built almost side by side. Bishop Roz also tried to deal with the problem and on one occasion was successful in stopping a fight between the two sections at Caṅanaśśēri, but not before a street of houses had been burned down. The cleavage was unfortunately given ecclesiastical recognition in 1910 when the Patriarch Abdalla consecrated Mar Severios and set up a separate Knānaya diocese in the Jacobite Church for the Southists. Rome had to follow suit, and in 1911 a separate diocese was established for Southist Romo-Syrians.

The story told to explain the division is that Thomas of Cana, the fourth- or eighth-century settler, had two wives. One was his lawful wedded Syrian wife, the other a woman of the country. His lawful wife lived with him in the south street of Cranganore, the other woman was kept in the north street. The offspring of these families are the ancestors of the Southists and Northists respectively. The story is sometimes told by the Northists the other way round, the Southists being the illegitimate children.[1] The Southists claim that their ancestors married with Syrian immigrants and deny that they have ever married Indians. They use special songs at their weddings describing the colonization of Cranganore and their subsequent history, and are said to use still some purely Syrian names.[2]

[1] Sloane MS. 2743 British Museum. Several controversial books have been written in Malayāḷam on this subject: *The Southists and the Northists* by J. Kurmanakan (1941) is a Northist answer to *The History of the Southists* by J. Chazhikan (1940). It will be noticed that both these are written from within the Roman Church.

[2] Thurston, *Castes and Tribes of Southern India*, VI, p. 414, gives the names Baji, Kojah, Kujalih and Mayanuth, but the Northists say these are of recent importation.

It seems likely that Fr Montserrate, S.J., was on the right track when he wrote in 1579 from Cochin, trying to explain the difference: 'Among Christians there are many petty quarrels about birth and caste, those that are descended from the slave woman being less considered. And that both [wives] were noble, at least Nayre women, is proved by the custom existing in this Malavar, that there is no pollution between the Christians of St Thomas and the Nayres, nor penalty of death, if there are between them marriages or friendship, all of which arises, according to the custom of the country, for castes higher or lower than these two. What is more likely is that they originated from both, that is from the glorious St Thomas and from Mar Thoma [Thomas of Cana] and from many Nayres who are daily converted. They are a Christianity of 72,000 souls and they are reduced to these two clans by the lie of the land, and not only because they are descended from them [the two wives] for some live on the south side, others on the north side.'[1]

Fr Montserrate suggests two theories, that each group had its origin at a different time and that part of the reason may be geographical. It is true that there are also Northists and Southists among the Nampūtiri Brahmans and that those who live on opposite sides of a certain river neither intermarry nor come together on socio-religious occasions. It is said that in a similar way Iḻavas from the north do not intermarry with those from the south.[2] This geographical factor certainly influences the Christians, but geographically northern and southern sections are distinguished in both the Northist and Southist communities, and intermarriage between the two is not common in either group. So this geographical factor does not explain the whole difference. The theory that the Northists are the descendants of converts, of St Thomas or later evangelists, while the Southists are the more or less pure descendants of immigrants, is attractive.

The Northists were described as belonging either to Mahadevappaṭṭaṇam (Cranganore) or to Kollam (Quilon) in all legal documents until the introduction of Government registraries.[3] They include a number of families who claim descent from the thirty-two Brahman families which tradition says St Thomas converted. Each of the seven places traditionally associated with

[1] Quoted in 'Thomas of Cana and his copper plate grant', by H. Hosten, S. J., in *Indian Antiquary*, LVI (July 1927), p. 121.
[2] E. A. Ravi Varma, *Kēraḷa Society Papers* (1932), series 9, p. 177.
[3] *Cochin State Manual* (1911), note on p. 218.

St Thomas's work has a number of families claiming to be Thomas's Brahman converts connected with it, although these have now moved to other places. Precedence is given in Syrian society to the descendants of these families, and the episcopate and priesthood were for many centuries confined to two of them, Pakalamaṟṟam and Sānkarapuri.[1] The tenacity with which these family traditions have been held and the fact that they certainly existed before the coming of the Portuguese makes it impossible to discount them completely, even though the connexion with the Apostle cannot be proved. As will be shown when we examine the life-cycle of Syrians, there are some customs which the Christians alone share with the Nampūtiri Brahmans. The small group of Tarisa Christians from Tiruvamkōṭ, whose tradition of origin is conversion by St Thomas on the east coast and subsequent flight from persecution, also claims Brahman origin and had a number of customs like the tying of a *pūnūl*, or Brahman thread, on male children after baptism, which were not shared by the Syrian Christian community.

Thus the Northists and Southists form endogamous clans among the Syrians, their internal cohesion somewhat impaired by the complicating factor of ecclesiastical division. But the clan spirit is stronger than church distinctions and marriages take place across these lines, more rarely between Roman and non-Roman, commonly among the different parties not of Roman obedience.

Within the clans various factors determine the choice of a bride or bridegroom. Today the most important factor is usually the amount of money possessed by the prospective bridegroom, or the amount which can be obtained as a dowry with the bride. This is a development which has come with the growth of a money economy. The degree of education possessed by a bride will affect her value now more than the old criteria of fairness, health, and ability to manage a household well and do household tasks. Premarital chastity on the part of the bride is taken for granted. This emphasis on money is a new thing, formerly the amount was fixed at a very moderate sum (10,000 cakrams or 350 rupees), and was supplemented by the jewels given at the time of marriage and the

[1] The most important families are: Pakalamaṟṟam, Sānkarapuri, Kaḷikkāvunkal, Kōyikkam, Maḍeippūr, Muṭṭōdal, Vīyacchaḷḷi, Kōṭṭakkara. Four families, Pakalamaṟṟam, Kalli, Kaḷikkāvunkal and Śānkarikkal, are believed to have become Christians at Pālayūr and then emigrated to Kuraviḷaṅaṭ. At Pālayūr there are still compounds with these names.

household equipment and cattle sent back with the bride after the birth of her first child in her mother's house. In those days, until 1900 or so, parents would always try to marry their daughter into one of the old families, and the parents of a boy would similarly hope to get a bride for their son from one of the respected families of the locality, or another parish with which they were in some way connected. Marriage between close relations, including first and second cousins, was forbidden, and children who shared the same godparents at baptism could never marry.

The wife normally becomes part of her husband's family, and their children heirs of that family. It is thus clear that the loose use of *taṛavāṭ* for a Syrian Christian family is wrong. It is the term used by Nāyars for their joint family system in which a man's children are members of his wife's *taṛavāṭ* but his sister's of his. (This is the *marumakkattayam* system of matrilineal inheritance which obtained, for instance, in the ruling family of Travancore until their ancestral rights were abolished in 1947.) If there was no male heir in the wife's family her husband might be adopted into her family, and become the legal heir. This system often led to disputes between husband and wife over the real ownership of property.

The dowry is given to compensate the daughters of the family for the loss they sustain in marrying out of the family; it used to be roughly equivalent to the share of property a son would receive on his father's death. The amount of dowry was fixed by the girl's parents but in practice certain factors modified the amount. The older families might expect a fixed amount of dowry and if the bridegroom's family was more important than the girl's, the dowry would be greater. Any physical blemish in the girl or any lack of education would also affect the amount to be given, and so would the colour of the girl's skin. Formerly the customs among the Northists and Southists were different. Among the Northists the dowry was not given until two or three children had been born but the girl's family would provide everything for her confinements and in the end they might pay more than a Southist family which paid the dowry at the time of the wedding. If a young wife were to die at her first confinement, a quarter of the marriage expenses and the dowry must be given back to the bride's family. Naturally this often led to difficulties between the two families. Nowadays a marriage is sometimes thought of as much as a business deal to increase capital as anything else, and the same system is beginning to affect the Nāyars, among whom dowries were formerly unknown.

Within the family very great reverence was always paid to the old men and women, and when anything affecting the welfare of the whole family was in question, like the choice of a bride for a son of the house, all members must do their best to attend the deliberations. Nothing was ever done without consulting the grandfather or grandmother of a house, and often the life of the household revolved round them. The situation was a little different when the grandfather was living in retirement, with prayer and fasting; but even then he had an important, usually the final, voice in all important decisions. The executive head of a family, or *karnnavan*, was the eldest brother. It is he who still has to carry a good deal of responsibility in the marriage ceremonies of his younger brothers' children, and it is he who is responsible for the arrangements when his father dies. The paternal grandfather's name is given to the first son of a marriage, the paternal grandmother's to the first daughter. The maternal grandfather's name is borne by the second son, and the maternal grandmother's by the second daughter. After that there is freedom of choice of names. It was usual never to sit in the presence of old people, but to stand slightly away when speaking to them. Within a family the members are called either by a 'pet name' carried over from their childhood (it is common to hear very old men called 'Baby') or by the title of relationship in which they stand to the speaker. It is said by old men that, until the twenties of this century, it was more usual to address members of the family by their baptismal name.

The following is a list of the most common kinship terms:

Table of Kinship Terms

I. FAMILY CIRCLE	TERM OF REFERENCE	TERM OF ADDRESS
Great-great-grandfather	Valiyavaliyavaliyappan	
Great-grandfather	Valiyavaliyappan	Valiyappaccā
Grandfather	Valiyappan	
Great-great-grandmother		
Great-grandmother		Valiyammacci
Grandmother		
Father	appan	appaccā
Mother	amma	ammacci
Stepmother	raṇḍānamma	kōccammē
Brother	sahōdaran	*none*

I. FAMILY CIRCLE	TERM OF REFERENCE	TERM OF ADDRESS
Sister	sahōdari	*none*
Eldest brother	valyaccāyan	valyaccāyā
Eldest sister	*name and* pēṅṅaḷ	*name and* pēṅṅaḷē
Elder brother	*name and* accāyan	*name and* accāyā
Elder sister	*name and* pēṅṅaḷ	*name and* pēṅṅaḷē
Younger brother	anujan	*name*
Younger sister	pēṅṅaḷ	*name*
Youngest brother	anujan	*name*
Youngest sister	pēṅṅaḷ	*name*
Infants (both sexes)	kuññā	kuññē
Son	makan	mōnē
Daughter	makaḷ	mōḷē

(There are no special terms for eldest son, etc., but children are called by a 'pet' name, which is usually different from the baptismal name.)

Grandson (son of son or daughter)	koccumakan	mōnē
Granddaughter (daughter of son or daughter)	koccumakaḷ	mōḷē
Great-grandson or daughter	same as above	
Spouse	*no word*	
Husband	b-hartāva	*none*
Wife	b-harya	*none*

II. COLLATERALS		
Grandfather's brother	valiyappan	*house name and* valiyappaccā
Grandfather's sister	valiyamma	*house name and* valiyammacci
Grandmother's brother	valiyappan	*house name and* valiyapacca
Grandmother's sister	valiyamma	*house name and* valiyamacci
Father's brother (elder)	appan	appaccā
Father's brother (younger)	uppāppan	uppāppa
Mother's brother (elder or younger)	ammāccan	accāyan
Mother's sister (elder)	amma	ammacci
Mother's sister (younger)	koccamma	koccamma
Cousins, male	sahōdaran, elder	*name and* accāyan
	sahōdaran, younger	*name*
Cousins, female	sahōdari *or* pēṅṅaḷ, elder	*name and* pēṅṅaḷē
	sahōdari *or* pēṅṅaḷ, younger	*name*

No distinction is made between first and other cousins in reference or address.

First cousins once removed or children of other cousins are addressed and referred to as one's own children, even if they are older than the speaker. Nephews and nieces are treated as one's own children, and their children also.

III. AFFINES	TERM OF REFERENCE	TERM OF ADDRESS
Grandfather's brother's wife		*same as grandmother*
Grandfather's sister's husband		*same as grandfather*
Grandmother's brother's wife		*same as grandmother*
Grandmother's sister's husband		*same as grandfather*
Father's elder brother's wife		*same as mother*
Father's younger brother's wife	ciṟṟamma	ciṟṟamma
Father's sister's husband	māvan	māvan
Mother's brother's wife	ammayi	ammayi
Mother's elder sister's husband		*same as father*
Mother's younger sister's husband		*same as father's younger brother*
Father-in-law		*same as father*
Mother-in-law		*same as mother*
Spouse's grandparent		*same as grandparent*
Son-in-law		*same as son*
Daughter-in-law		*same as daughter*
Father and mother of son- or daughter-in-law		*by name*

Husband's and wife's brothers and sisters are addressed and referred to in each case as one's own. It is insulting if this is not done.

There are no terms used to refer to or address siblings among the Syrian Christians. The 'name' used in some cases is usually the 'pet' name (as they always describe it in English), rarely the baptismal name. The 'house name' is carried by a family over several generations, even though the family moves from the original house which supplied the name in the first place.

The clergy are treated with even more respect than old men, and it seems appropriate at this point to deal briefly with their position, while we are discussing the social structure of the community. The fact that the clergy had no income other than the fees received for celebrating the *kurbāna*, baptism and marriage, and gifts made at the time of confession and whenever the various feasts were performed in the houses greatly worried the reforming Archbishop Menezes. The Portuguese considered this practice simony and tried to make other arrangements for a regular income for the clergy, but they failed to alter the old custom. Marriages and funerals still produce the main income for the church and half the income at church festivals belongs to the clergy. The clergy were and are greatly respected. They always walk in front of others; they are given chief places at feasts and always sit on a cot as a special place of honour. It is for them to decide when a feast must start. All Christians still stand at the sight of a priest and remove the cloth from their heads if they are wearing one, or put down their umbrella. The priests would normally not go out without attendants, although this has changed in the towns. It used to be the custom to ordain one boy in a generation from each family. It was thought that it was not only useful spiritually but brought honour to the family and provided a useful man to represent them in court cases and so forth. Unfortunately the deacons, who often lived with a senior priest or *malpān* or with the bishop, usually had very little training beyond learning their services in Syriac. It was not unusual for a church to be served by one family, the senior priest acting as vicar and succeeded in due course by his nephew. The clergy were allowed to marry before they were ordained priests and their wives were treated with special honour. They had a special title of respect and were distinguished in Portuguese days by a small gold or silver cross worn round the neck. The clergy now are being trained in a church seminary, and a number are university graduates. The age of ordination is rising, though there are still deacons ordained at the age of twelve or fourteen.

The way the St Thomas Christians ordered questions of inheritance was not clear to the Government of Travancore and so they appointed a committee to compile a definitive code. It issued its report in 1912. Certain arrangements were clear and universal among Christians but the committee stated that in many matters there was no definite and settled custom. The Syrian Christians of Roman obedience also had slightly different customs from the others. Mar Mathew Athanasios had written down the observances of his own day and published them in a Malayāḷam canon in 1857, but it was noted that in some respects this did not follow the Hudaya canon which is claimed to be normal for the Jacobite Syrian Church. The committee gave evidence to show that the customs of the community in this respect also had changed with time. In ancient days a Syrian Christian would not sell any ancestral property without the consent of his heirs, and the eldest son would therefore usually be a party to the sale deed, following the Hindu custom.

The committee[1] reported that the following are generally recognized as laws of inheritance: (i) there is no difference between movable and immovable property; (ii) there is no difference between the property of a male and a female; (iii) there is no difference between a living heir and one begotten by the testator, but born after his death; (iv) the heirs in the descending line always exclude the heirs in ascending or collateral line; (v) collaterals of any degree and their descendants have priority over ascendants of the same degree; (vi) subject to other rules, heirs of equal proximity to the last holder divide property equally among themselves whenever of the same sex; (vii) the heirs of any degree and their descendants generally exclude heirs of more remote degree; (viii) among heirs of same degree and related to proprietor on same side and related in the same way (full or half blood), male heirs always exclude female heirs except when heirs are in descending line; (ix) paternal heirs are preferred to maternal; (x) if a son, daughter, brother, sister, uncle, aunt, dies before an intestate his or her descendants will, on the intestate's death, get that share in the property which he or she would have got if alive when the intestate died; (xi) when an intestate dies with no children but only grandchildren, by sons or daughters, they take among themselves what their fathers or mothers would have taken if alive at the time of intestate's death. An intestate's property is divided among heirs *per stirpes* and not *per capita*.

Two differences from Hindu custom may be noted which show the different attitude to women prevailing in the Christian community. If a man dies without sons, a daughter can inherit the estate of the Syrians and if he dies without children or brothers, his sister can succeed to the property. Neither of these provisions obtained among Hindus. The heir of a minor child of a man is the child's mother. If a man has only a daughter by a first

[1] *Report of the Christian Committee on Inheritance* (1912), pp. 18ff.

marriage and then sons by a second marriage, the daughter is entitled to the share of a son.[1]

Mar Athanasios said that a man cannot will his ancestral property to anyone but his natural heirs. Against this is a statement of the committee that Syrians can dispose of their property by will. The Hudaya canon allowed a man to dispose of one third of his property in this manner. It is probably more common for property to be divided according to the old custom. It has been said that wills are only necessary when the sons are likely to quarrel. If they will agree to divide the property equally, a will is not necessary. Some property would be set apart for women who are married away from the family and some would be set apart also for the Church. Sometimes adoption was practised among Syrian families, as we have already seen, a daughter's husband being adopted into her family if there was no male heir.

III

Any attempt to describe the life cycle of the St Thomas Christians is bound to be superficial and to fail to convey the inner attitude to life which conventions and customs both convey and cultivate. The customs which are described below are those which generally obtained among Northist Jacobite Syrians fifty or sixty years ago. There were variations caused by local differences and also by ecclesiastical allegiance, though through all variations a common pattern can be discerned. Many of those old customs have now been dropped; they presuppose a rural economy and a social life centred in the parish church, with most members of the family accessible and able to spend a considerable time away from their cultivation in family celebrations. These conditions no longer obtain.

It will make for clarity if the contents of this section are summarized. First, the customs of birth and childhood are described, followed by the ceremonies of betrothal and marriage. Then there are notes on the occupations of Syrians, their food, dress, attitude to omens and witchcraft, their art forms, buildings and furniture. A mention of the use of vows is followed by a description of the customs connected with death. There is a note on language. No description is given here of the liturgical services appropriate to each stage of life, as these will be found in the third part of this book.

[1] Synod of Diamper, session IX, decree 20.

The first child of a couple is always delivered at the mother's house; a bride who had been pregnant five or seven months would be taken to her home from her husband's house where she had been living since marriage. In the old days seven women, including her mother, had to go to fetch her home.[1] The child would be delivered with the help of the women of the house and possibly of a village mid-wife—a woman trained only by experience. If the child was a boy, the birth was greeted with tremendous joy and with great noise. Women would slam the wooden bolts of the doors backwards and forwards and grind coconut shells in a mortar to make a noise, as well as making the *kurava* sound (a shrill sound made with fingers moved up and down in the mouth). Anyone within ear-shot would know at once that a boy had been born. Immediately after the child was born it was washed, and then a priest or a male relative would shout in the child's ear 'Maron Yesu Maśiha' ('Jesus Christ is Lord'), and the child would be fed with three drops of honey in which a little gold had been rubbed. This custom, shared with Brahmans, was intended to ensure prosperity. The mother of the child would be considered under pollution until the tenth or fourteenth day after the birth when she would bathe and be cleansed. Immediately after the birth a messenger had to be sent to the father's house to tell him of the happy event, and it was an old custom that for this office a 'new Christian' had to be found. It is a matter of speculation what this means. It probably indicates that servants, either local people or those bought as slaves, were baptized and given a place in the community life. The messenger would receive certain traditional presents of cloth and food, and the following morning the father would go to see his first child.

Eight or ten days after the birth the husband's family would go together to see the baby but they had to see that they were an odd number as an even number is considered always to bring bad luck. On seeing the child the women who had come would put a gift in kind (or, more recently, of money) into the palm of the baby held in its mother's hand. It is considered a very essential thing to give these presents. The baptism might take place at this time or later, but after baptism the mother would bring her child back to her husband's house with all the household equipment and livestock

[1] When seven months pregnant she would be given a drink of tamarind and water. Nampūtiris do this. Apparently it was formerly a ceremony at first menses, i.e. *after* marriage.

promised at the time of the wedding. In former times the bride usually wore nothing over her breasts until after the birth of the first child when she would wear a cloth called *yēttāppa* which was worn from the left shoulder, hanging down in front. She would also start wearing bracelets. Her mother had to accompany her on her return and she and the servants who came with her would be given presents of cloth before they went home again.[1]

Six months after the birth of the child came the ceremony of *annaprāśanam* (now disused by Christians but kept up by Hindus). The correct procedure was for the mother's grandmother to bring the child to church wrapped in a piece of silk. The father would then sit on a very low stool and take the child into his lap. A priest came and placed a plantain leaf with sweet rice and plantain and jaggery before the father[2] and then three times he took a pinch of the mixture and placed it in the child's mouth. Among Southists the child sat on his mother's lap. The unused food was taken by the grandmother and given as a special perquisite to the dhobi. After the child had been taken home the grandfather would take out the family ornaments one by one and place them on the child. Guests were expected to give ornaments as presents to the baby. The ceremony finished with a feast for all.

At three or four years of age the education of the child started. The teacher of the local village school (*Kaḷari*), who might be a Christian but was probably a Hindu, was called and sat down beside the child with a large brass plate full of paddy in front of them. A lamp was lit and the members of the family stood round while the teacher took the child's forefinger and traced with it in the rice the words 'Hari śrī Gaṇapatē Namā', the name of the Hindu god Ganapathi who was believed to guide education and remove obstacles to success. The teacher was, of course, given a present before he left. From this time he was considered to be in a special relation to the child and had to come to bless him on special occasions such as marriage. In modern times a Christian priest is often called to perform this ceremony and the name of Jesus substituted for that of the Hindu deity. From this time the child was more or less entered in the village school where children were taught writing in sand and on strips of palm leaf. Boys also learned

[1] Formerly a mother was considered unclean for forty days after the birth of a son and fifty days after the birth of a daughter. In some places the period of pollution was only fifteen days (as with Nampūtiris).

[2] As Nampūtiris. Among Nāyars the maternal uncle does this.

the use of weapons from eight years of age and the teacher or *paṇikkar* was held in great honour, whether Hindu or Christian. It was the custom that when the child began to use an iron pen, after learning his letters, a present should be given to his teacher and light refreshments to all his fellow-pupils. Gouvea testifies to the great reverence and loyalty felt towards the teachers and says that they could call to arms all their pupils, whoever they might be. The Syriac prayers used in the home in the morning and at night were also taught to the children in these village schools. The children had first to write them on palm leaves and then learn them by heart.

For girls a definite stage was reached when their ears were pierced for ornaments in their sixth year and some kind of pluck inserted to enlarge their lobes in preparation for the heavy ornaments which were then worn by Syrian women.

Girls were usually married before reaching puberty and it was considered a disgrace if this was not done. The Romo-Syrians have never observed any period of pollution for menses but the Jacobites used to keep their girls in seclusion for three days like the Hindus. Up till 1890 or so it was still common among Jacobites for a boy to be married at the age of ten or twelve and for the girl to be six or seven.[1] With the coming of Western influence the marriage age was gradually raised until now a Syrian man doing agricultural work will marry in his early twenties and his bride will be three or four years younger. Members of the community engaged in commerce have gone all over India and to many other places and they very often marry even later than that. The novel *Pariśkkārapāti* well shows the state of tension about 1870 between the newer ideas and the old. In the story the father wishes to keep his daughter at home until she is fourteen but the mother wants to make the marriage arrangement when she is nine years of age. A marriage could only be celebrated when the girl's ears had been pierced and the lobes extended to take the ear-rings worn by married women, and the hair must have grown sufficiently to make a bun at the back. In these child marriages the girl went to live with the groom's family and had to work hard in the house. The marriage was not consummated for some years. There were local differences in this as in all other customs. In the north the girl had far less freedom than in the

[1] Patriarch Peter III (1877) says that the girls are married at eight or ten; according to the canons the boy must be at least fourteen and the girl twelve. After 1600 the Catholics kept to the ages of fourteen and twelve.

south, and she even had to hide her face from strange men in the house with a leaf umbrella and might not speak to them.

It was usual for the boy's family to search for a suitable bride rather than for the girl's family to look for a groom. The father would not undertake this duty himself but would usually entrust it to his elder brother. Often the boy's mother's younger brother or servants like dhobies would suggest eligible girls first. When the uncle had been to see the girl a family council would be held at which all the relatives possible had to be present because the reception of a new member into a family was felt to be a matter concerning all. At the meeting of the groom's family questions would be asked about the complexion of the girl, her accomplishments, her family and their financial position, especially with regard to the dowry they would be prepared to pay.

If the bridegroom's family approved of the choice, a representative would go the following day to fix everything with the bride's family. They would naturally have satisfied themselves beforehand that the bride's family would approve of the match. After all these matters had been settled, the announcement of the wedding had to be made in church by the calling of banns immediately after the *kurbāna*. The priest would come to the altar step and send for the church treasurer who would stand with his *ōla* or strip of palm leaf prepared for writing and his iron stylus at the bottom of the step. An uncle of the boy would come forward with one of the girl's uncles and they would tell the priest the girl's name and the amount of the dowry. Then they would state the boy's name. The priest would then announce the marriage and give an opportunity for impediments to be alleged. This calling of the banns took place in front of the lamp which hangs in front of the altar step, signifying the presence of Christ. After this the two parties would go to the bride's house with the priest and sit down. Water would be given to the guests to wash their mouths, preparatory to a meal. At this point the priest simulated surprise and asked the reason for the meal. In reply the father of the girl would tie his second cloth (normally worn over the shoulders) round his waist and announce the marriage of his daughter. In answer to the priest's questions all the arrangements for the marriage would be announced, the amount of dowry, the church in which it was to be celebrated and the day. The marriage was usually celebrated very soon after the betrothal. When all details had thus been settled everyone washed their hands and took part in the betrothal feast. This feast was considered of very great importance and specially good plantain leaves would be chosen for serving the food. Among the Northists only people immediately concerned with the wedding were invited for this feast, but among the Southists others were invited and those who received no invitation to this feast could not attend the wedding.

A betrothal feast started with salt, sweet rice and jaggery, served in that order. Then the priest said grace and gave permission to start eating. (There is a similar custom among Brahmans and Nāyars in that something sweet must always be served first on all occasions of joy.) When the sweet was eaten, rice and curries would be served. The last item at Syrian feasts is always rice with curd, a kind of plantain and sweet palm juice. When all had washed their hands and mouth after the meal, they went back to the room where they had first met, for the payment of the dowry (if they were Southists). It was usual for the bride's father to hand this over or if a senior member of his own family was present he would be given this honour provided that he was not disqualified by having a barren wife or by a second marriage. The bride's mother would stand to watch the proceedings with a lighted lamp in her hand and make the remark that *agni*, the fire, would be a permanent witness of what they were doing. The representative of the bride's family then stood on the verandah facing east and the bridegroom's representative faced him. First they had to ask permission of the assembly to give and receive the money. It was thus made clear that the marriage arrangement was not a matter of individual decision but was essentially an affair with which the whole family was concerned. When permission had been given the girl's representative handed over the money on a palm leaf wrapped in a white cloth. The dowry money must always be an odd number of units (formerly *cakrams* or *fanams*; now rupees), a Hindu convention, like the orientation of the principals in the transaction. The giver handed over the money with both his hands joined and the receiver took it similarly and they embraced each other. This finished the ceremony, but the host was always particular to walk to the gate of his compound with his guests of the bridegroom's party. Failure to do so, as with Hindus, was considered an insult.

The days that followed the betrothal saw intense activity in the two houses. Relations had to be summoned, special foods prepared, the dress for the bride and bridegroom obtained and the customary presents prepared for all those who were entitled to them. Apparently in the early days there was no special dress for the wedding but special ornaments were certainly used. Gouvea mentions that Christians were allowed to wear a golden flower in their hair which was tied in a knot.[1] The Patriarch Peter tried to reform the marriage dress of the Syrians in 1877 according to his own ideas. It is likely that the dress ordered by the Patriarch, a long velvet coat trimmed with gold, trousers and a gold lace turban for the bridegroom and a dress made of silk for the bride, was usually the property of the local churches and lent for the occasion. A coat kept at Cūngam has six-pointed stars on each sleeve. A very important item was the jewellery. The bride wore a special headdress which covered the forehead (but not like the crowns used in the Orthodox Church) and a large number of necklaces, some of them made of Venetian gold coins which were highly valued. It is said that the bridegroom formerly wore a crown but for many years his most imposing ornament has been a gold chain and cross round his neck. These crosses are still treasured as family heirlooms and used at weddings. Wedding invitations were formerly sent on *ōlas* or strips of palm leaf. The length varied; in the south it was the length of the elbow to the fingertips but among the Northists much shorter ones were used. When all these were prepared, a servant went off to distribute them, usually carrying them for convenience in an umbrella made of palm leaves which served as a tray. It is to be noted that the wedding had also to be announced to the chief women in the houses of all men invited and failure to give this direct invitation was an insult. The invitation was to the bathing of the young man and the marriage of the girl. The special ornaments to be given to the bride by the bridegroom's party consisted of a cloth which had to be of a quality that would last for the rest of her life (and indeed would be used as her shroud) and the *minnu* or *tāḷi*. This is a small pear-shaped ornament of gold worn on a thread round the neck; those used by Hindus are decorated by a tiny image of a goddess, those used by the Christians with a cross made of twenty-one tiny gold beads. A very big under-

[1] A photograph of such a flower belonging to the church at Cūngam was published in the article by Fr Hosten, *Indian Antiquary*, LVII (1928), pp. 117ff., which also contains photographs of Syrian Christian couples.

taking would be started on the Thursday before the wedding, when close relatives would erect the end posts of a large palm-thatched shed or *pandal* in front of the house, where most of the ceremonies would take place. The privilege of using pillars at the end was an ancient one shared with the Brahmans. Most of the work was done voluntarily by the neighbours. The girls of the house would be learning the special songs to be sung[1] and helping with the cooking; and the men folk would see that the house and its approach road were in good order. Most of the neighbours would have a special function to perform at the wedding. *Pulayars* would bring fire-wood, *Iḻavas* chickens, plaintains, and other supplies, and the local Nāyars would all look in. In old days the women made the *kurava* sound while preparing certain foods and while drenching unboiled paddy. There would be considerable competition among the women for such pleasant jobs as drawing a design on the ground in front of the *pandal* by making lines with rice paste. This is an accomplishment of young Hindu women and is now unknown among Christians.

On the Saturday night when all these preparations were finished or nearing completion, the boy's brother-in-law brought him to the place where the designs had been drawn on the floor, and where a new cloth had been placed on a stool. As soon as he reached the stool barbers came outside the *pandal* which was by this time full of people listening to music. As soon as the music stopped they asked permission to cut the boy's hair, and shave him. This custom probably dates from the time when boys were married young and this would be their first ceremonial shave. It is probable that several centuries ago the betrothal took place about a year before the marriage and that the growing of the beard was a symbol of a pure and ascetic life. The barber received the new cloth as his fee. After this, permission was asked to give the bridegroom his bath and he was led to the well followed by a crowd singing songs. As he went bombs were often exploded, presumably to scare off evil spirits, as well as to express joy. The bath seems to have had a symbolic purificatory intention, as formerly the bridegroom had to fast from this time until the marriage feast. When the bathing was finished, his married sister would bring a new cloth, his coat, and the

[1] These songs were taught to all young Syrian girls in their first school. The songs are translated into English and printed in Ananta Krishna Iyyer's *Anthropology of the Syrian Christians*.

cross on its chain for him to put on. The songs sung by the women were special ones dealing with the early history of the Church.[1]

From his bath the bridegroom went to the *pandal* and stood there facing east. His sister would put a half-sari or shawl over her blouse, take a lighted lamp, a small vessel of water and a cup of paddy and water and stand in front of him facing west. Three times she had to put her right index finger in the cup, transfer the water to her thumb and touch him with the thumb between the eyebrows in the middle of the forehead. Her husband, who acted as 'best man' throughout the ceremonies, then took the boy away to a specially prepared room and sat him on a low wooden seat, to which his mother brought a dish of rice on which jaggery and plantains were placed on a cross-shaped arrangement of coconut leaves and gave it to him. At each stage of these marriage ceremonies, as at other formal feasts, permission had to be asked from the people in the *pandal* before the next stage. Every stage in the ceremonies was performed after permission had been asked to proceed to that stage and it was a recognized thing that the old men would be very critical of the way in which questions were asked or of the dress of the person asking them or of the fact that the young man asking permission had not a moustache (which was a symbol of the angels keeping the door of the mouth). A nervous man whose duty it was, because of his relationship to the bridegroom, to undertake this, could be held up for a long time by insistence on the correct form being used without hesitation, and sometimes a penalty in the way of a fine to the church was imposed on people who did not perform their tasks adequately. Permission being granted, a priest or an elderly relative would wash his right hand, place his index finger in the food and touch the boy's lips three times. After the priest, four or five old women did the same thing. This was the last ceremony on Saturday night and after it at about midnight everyone went to bed.

The custom of having weddings on Sundays continues, though occasionally they may be celebrated on Mondays. Patriarch Peter objected to all the noise of drums and bombs and dancing at wedding processions which he thought hardly appropriate for Sundays, and the early missionaries of the Church Missionary Society were even more scandalized by it. (Mar Thomite Syrians

[1] P. J. Thomas, *Marriage Customs and Songs of the Christians of Malabar*.

allow marriages now only on Thursdays or Mondays.) On Sunday morning, as soon as it was light, a goldsmith would come to the *pandal* and the oldest male member of the family would go to him to buy the *minnu* to be used in the wedding ceremony. The goldsmith had to place the small ornament on a special tray prepared with one and a half measures of paddy and coconuts and a bunch of plantains on it. A lit lamp was there as a witness of the transaction. The *minnu* was taken and exchanged for the tray with its food and twenty-one *cakrams*. At about eight o'clock all who were going to the church service were given refreshments. (This was possibly connected with the custom of feeding Brahmans before they offer worship.) Before the bridegroom could set out for the church he had to go to the *pandal* where his *āśān*, the man who had given him his first formal lesson, was waiting. The groom made him the customary present of nuts for chewing, money and cloth, and his teacher laid his right hand on the boy's head and blessed him. This formality was thought to be of great importance, whether the teacher were Hindu or Christian. After this the party set out for church in a kind of very loose procession, not organized as such except that royal umbrellas were carried and a band played in front of the groom. Possibly a lit lamp was also carried in front of him. It was considered important that on leaving the house the party should first set out in an easterly direction. When they arrived at the church the bridegroom must enter the building before the bride, even if she and her party had arrived some time before. The bride came in after the groom and had to stand just inside the west door. In the old days she would be very young and so heavily loaded with jewellery that she would find it hard to move, and very tiring to stand through the long service, with her eyes cast down to the ground. Thus they would attend the *kurbāna*, the bride and bridegroom not looking at each other. (They would probably never have seen each other, and even now this is true of a decreasing number of marriages.) Immediately after the *kurbāna* the churchwardens would collect the *passāram* (the 10 per cent tax of the dowry which had to come to the church). The settling of accounts would take some time and was done in the north porch of the church with the help of the usual chewing materials. It was necessary also to produce a banns certificate from the groom's parish and to arrange for the payment of that percentage of *passāram* which was their right. There were also other amounts payable to the church. In all these payments it was usual for the bride's party to pay a half share plus one money unit. The bridegroom paid the other half share. When this business had been satisfactorily settled the bride and bridegroom would go to the priest to make their confession and receive absolution.

While this was going on one or two old people used to go outside the church and take a number of threads from the wedding cloth to be given to the bride. Three threads were twisted together and seven of such composite threads were then spun together to form the thread for the *minnu*. (Brahmans wear a thread made in exactly the same way and for the same purpose.) Syrian women like Brahmans never take their thread off while the husband is alive. If the thread wears out a new one is placed through the ornament and secured round the neck before the old one is removed. It is considered a very bad sign indeed by both Brahmans and Syrian women if the thread breaks or they lose their *minnu*.

By the time the thread was made for the wedding and the *minnu* threaded, the couple's confession would be finished in church and they would be taken to the chancel step. The couple would not go forward together but the bride would come slowly after her future husband, partly out of modesty and apprehension and partly because of the great weight of the jewels she was wearing. She had to stand at the right side of the groom. The *kappiar* (sexton) of the church then took the cross from the bridegroom's neck and the ring from his hand and placed them on the table in the centre of the *katastroma*, so that they might be blessed. During the service the groom tied the *minnu* on the neck of his bride and the priest threw the marriage cloth over her head. This tying of the *minnu* is commonly considered the moment of marriage (which is called 'the tying').

After the service the couple were taken to a room at the side of the church and fed by the priest with *curuṭṭu*, a kind of cake made of rice flour and plantains. Then the relations gave money presents to all the priests attending the wedding and to the sextons. When well-to-do families were uniting in marriage priests would attend from all the neighbouring parishes and each had to be given something, as is done by Brahmans on similar occasions. The special cake used for the feeding would have been brought to the church by the bridegroom's married sister, or by some other relation if he had no sister. She would receive a ring from the groom's party in return for this service. Twenty-one pieces of cake had to be brought; any left over was the special perquisite of the priests and church officers. In olden days at this point the women would produce more jewellery to adorn the already over-burdened bride and bridegroom, but this is no longer done. The whole party in former days after giving a final alms to the church would walk to the bridegroom's home with bands and ornaments, or perhaps ride in a palanquin or on an elephant, accompanied with cries of joy, like the Brahmans. On arrival at the house it was important that the couple saw a favourable omen, such as a woman with a pot of water, so when the sound of the returning procession was heard his mother would take a lit lamp in her hand and a brass pouring pot of water and stand ready at the entrance gate to greet them. When they arrived in the *pandal* they at once turned to face east until the groom's mother had come with her lamp and placed paddy and water in their hands. Then his father took the bridegroom to a portion of the house verandah and sat him on a bench, covered with a cloth in readiness. The bride had to accompany her husband and both must be careful to step across the threshold of the house with the right foot. The bride sat at the right hand of the bride-groom on the bench but as far away from him as she possibly could.

The guests by this time had taken their seats in the *pandal.* The priests had beds to sit on, the old men had white and black cloths spread on benches or on the floor, and all others sat on palm mats on the ground, arranged according to the precedence of their families, in long rows along the sides of the *pandal.* The women did not sit with their husbands but were given their food in the verandah and rooms of the house. Young men with rose water in silver bottles stood at the doors of the *pandal* and sprinkled the guests as they came in, and gave sandalwood paste to be smeared on the forehead as a sign of joy. Meanwhile the women of the house would be singing the old marriage songs. Chewing materials were given and then the feast started with a plantain leaf plate placed before each guest, with sweet rice. At this stage a member of the family would ask permission to take the couple to a special room prepared for them to eat in. The feast over, everyone washed and returned to their places. At this stage it was the custom for a *paṇam* or low caste tailor to arrive and sing songs about Mar Thoma the Apostle, after greeting the people. He was rewarded

13-2

with a special fee of money and cloth and a double portion of food.[1] This was the end of the marriage feast. The bride's party would start their journey home, after collecting the jewellery they had lent her, and would leave the young girl alone in a strange house where she knew no one and was forbidden by convention even to speak to her husband.

On Monday there was another feast at the bridegroom's house called *maṇavāḷan taḻuka*, that is, the embracing of the bridegroom. The bride's mother had to come back with her relatives as she was responsible for providing the food and taking a leading part in the proceedings. The bridegroom and ten or twelve friends would be settled inside the wedding room singing and the bride's mother had to tie her second cloth round her shoulders as a servant and ask their permission to give them chewing materials. Whatever they asked had to be given. At about ten o'clock the groom was taken to the *pandal* and seated on a special stool facing east. All the men then rose from their seats and in turn embraced the bridegroom and all the women embraced the bride in a similar manner. Then the groom was seated in the place of honour in the *pandal* on a cot and for forty-one days was the most important man in the district, taking precedence of everyone else. Then the women from the bride's house served the cake, jaggery and plantains which they had brought with them while singing the special wedding songs about the bridegroom and the bride.

On the Wednesday night there was a somewhat similar ceremony. A party from the bride's house would arrive just after dark bringing oil for their lamps which were immediately lit. As soon as she arrived the bride's mother would go to the wedding chamber to put everything in order, bringing in fresh chewing materials and so forth. Then she went off to bring the bride and a girl attendant and seat them in a corner of the room. The bridegroom and his friends would be there already. The mother-in-law had to do all the young men asked of her and then she sang the Mar Thoma song and made the *kurava* noise three times. During the singing of another song the door was shut at a particular line, with the mother-in-law outside. She had a lit lamp in her left hand and had to call out seven times the names of all kinds of objects which she intended

[1] A song called 'Vēradian Pāṭṭu' was kept by this caste of Hindus, called Vēradian or Pupandaram or Kalikkulam Nāyars, as ordered by Cerumān Perumāḷ. Fr Placid knew one family in Vaḻappaḷḷi near Carianaśśēri.

to give the bridegroom, ending up with the promise of a cow and a calf. (This promise was usually fulfilled when the bride came back to the husband's house after the delivery of her first child.) Then she called the bridegroom her own son. The party inside listened with apparent disrespect and often made the mother repeat her speech because of alleged errors and demanded songs from her. At last she was allowed to ask the groom to open the door. Then she would go in again, with a lamp and a vessel of water. (The Nāyars have a somewhat similar custom to this and a service called 'shutting and opening' is provided in the Chaldean rite.)

When all this was finished the couple were ceremoniously taken to the well and bathed while the girls sang songs, after which there was an exchange of presents of new clothes. Wearing the new clothes they all then went to the *pandal* where there followed a very interesting ceremony. The bridegroom and other men stood round a lamp, placed a ring on it, and sang one of the traditional songs. They then moved round the lamp three times, touched it, signed themselves with the cross and stood a little way away from it, in a circle. Then a party with the bride did the same thing singing other songs. This ceremony was called the *marggam kaḷi*; it was the wedding dance of the Syrians and told the story of how St Thomas had preached the Gospel in Malabar. All Syrians used to learn this story in their early childhood. The lamp represented Jesus Christ.[1] The husband then sat down with his wife on his right hand and presented a cloth to the bride's uncle, who in turn put a ring on the groom's finger and embraced him. He then gave a cloth to the bride, received it from her again, and embraced her. A third piece of cloth was given to the head of the bridegroom's house and fourth and fifth pieces to the bride's maternal and paternal grandmothers.

As soon as it was light on Thursday morning the wedding party prepared to leave for the bride's house. This came as a great relief to the bridegroom because ever since the wedding, except for the ceremonies in the *pandal*, he had had to stay in the special wedding chamber with his friends and his clothes had not been changed until the ceremonial bath the night before. Before leaving the

[1] The dance is rarely performed now; I think only by Southist Roman Catholics. The Nampūtiris have a similar song called 'Yātra kaḷi'. A *Kēraḷalolppatti* says this was invented by foreign Brahmans who argued against the *bauddhas* who came by ship to Vana Perumāḷ. But the language of the song is modern.

house the bridegroom and his friends touched the lamp which represented Christ at the dance the previous night and then they set off followed at a little distance by the bride and the women who were with her. Arrived at the bride's house they found a *pandal* erected in the yard and the bride's mother waiting to receive them with a vessel of paddy and water, and the pair had to step over the threshold of the house before the others. After a meal the bridegroom's friends went away, leaving him with his wife's family. In order to show their acceptance of him the bride's mother was expected to show him great attention and to feed him with a different kind of sweet preparation every day for four days.

On the following Monday the party returned to the bridegroom's house and the bride's father had to give the customary presents to the servants who had come with the party. On setting out the bride's mother gave the groom a ring and he in reply called her 'Mother'; it was taken as a very happy omen of future good relations with the family. During all this time the married couple had not spoken a word to each other, but the groom had begun to leave food on his plate as his wife's portion which she duly ate. This is still a Hindu custom, but I think never done now among Syrians. For some time after the marriage there would be no contact of any kind between the couple. They would begin to sleep together after a time which varied with their age at the time of marriage. The end or beginning of Lent was reckoned as a propitious time for the first cohabitation.

Many marriages were held just before Lent and during Lent there would be no further observances but as soon as this season was over two or three months would be spent in visiting all the relations of both sides. During the first years of marriage all fasts and feasts must be kept by the groom in the bride's house and thus the whole family would soon get to know him well. At *Ōṇam*, the national festival, the bridegroom had to give presents of cloth to the near relations of the bride and received rings from them in exchange.

It will be apparent that much time was required for all this elaborate system of feasting and visiting; nowadays the ceremonial is much simplified and usually compressed within a fortnight's annual holiday.

There is nothing peculiar about the food of the Syrians. They use the ordinary food of the country, rice and various kinds of curries. These have not changed in composition down the centuries. There are some dishes used on special occasions as at weddings, funerals, on Good Friday and so forth, most of which are used also by Brahmans. Gouvea remarked that Christians had not a horror of meat like Hindus but they had no taste for it and did not use it much. It is commonly used nowadays. Gouvea also notes that drink—toddy arrack made from palm juice—was commonly used and a good many crimes of violence were committed under the influence. The spread of Prohibition is likely to remove this evil entirely and for a long time more puritan notions have had much influence among the non-Roman Catholic Syrians. Generally speaking, Hindu food restrictions are not observed, although in some places the eating of beef was strictly forbidden, on pain of excommunication, probably because of the offence it would cause to Hindus.

Fasting was very rigorously observed among the St Thomas Christians. The Great Lent started on Quinquagesima Sunday. No fish, milk products or wine were allowed during Lent and there was no sexual intercourse. Only one meal was eaten after sunset. Old people, however, were allowed to eat what they liked.

When the Portuguese came to Malabar they found it easy to distinguish Christians from Nāyars, although their dress was the same. In those days they were naked to the waist and from the waist to the knees wore a fine cloth often ornamented with gold bands woven in. They also wore gold ornaments on their arms. The hair of older men was worn long, tied at the side with a piece of coloured silk and often had a cross of gold or silver attached to it. On occasion, when going away from their own districts, the men would wear a long white or blue coat which Gouvea calls a *cabayac*. The men always carried arms with them—a short sword and a round shield. These arms were generally left outside the house or the church when their owner entered. In the sixteenth century all men, as we have seen, were trained in the use of arms and were considered very good warriors.

The women kept themselves mostly to the house. They wore a cloth from the waist to the ankles, the ends of which in front and behind were pleated to form a small fan of cloth which became, and still is, a community characteristic. Married women, especially out of the house, wore another cloth over their breasts. If women had to go out of the house they often kept their faces covered with a fan or palm leaf umbrella, just like Hindu women, and this custom still persists in Kunnamkuḷam and other places in the north among old women. Dr P. J. Thomas says that the women wore a veil over the face made of embroidery. This, however, was not a local product but came from Venice. It was known to Malabar because even before the coming of the Portuguese Venetian goods came through the Arab traders. The necklace worn at weddings and treasured as a family heirloom was made of Venetian gold coins. This influence affected particularly Christians living in the ports of Cranganore, Paravūr, Purakkāṭ and Quilon. Christian girls used certain ornaments on certain special days. These varied according to the locality and were kept as family possessions. It seems that the use of flowers in the women's hair was never allowed because this custom was characteristic of Nāyar women. At first sight this appears odd when so many other Hindu customs were accepted. It is possible that Nāyar women were permitted a degree of sexual licence strictly forbidden to Christians and hence it was desirable that the women should be immediately distinguishable.

Old men shaved their head and grew their beard. In this they were joined by those who had renounced marriage and those who had undertaken a pilgrimage to the shrine of St Thomas in Mylapore. After a death in the house one young man in the family was also expected to grow his beard for a year. During the time in which he had a beard, the mark of asceticism, he was not allowed to marry.

A community which shared the general presupposition of the society of which it formed a part was naturally influenced by some of the ideas of supernatural influences commonly held. We have seen that the Syrian Christians were believers in omens (*śakunam*) like their Hindu neighbours. They thought it important to see the right objects when setting out for a journey or for any important business. Thus to see a cow or a person with a lighted lamp was fortunate, but if a priest or a Brahman was seen, or a woman without ornaments, the traveller would be well advised to turn back at once. In the old days no one would set out on an important journey, for instance, a young wife returning to her home for her first pregnancy, unless the omens were favourable. Widows were not allowed to retain the *minnu* and in the old days, to avoid being constant bearers of ill fortune, they often wore a rosary instead.

Astrology was firmly believed in and it was very common to consult local experts (*kanniyān*) before fixing the day for a marriage, building a new house, or any important business matter.

The Christians had in their possession a number of books of charms which were condemned by the Synod of Diamper and a book called *Parisman* which was said to be full of sorcery.[1] Other books condemned are the Book of Lots or *Vāpustakam*. It was opened anywhere and the kind of passage or picture that met the eye decided whether a course of action about to be undertaken would be wise or not. A book kept in the churches and consulted when arranging marriages was called *Pālpustakam*.[2] The priests would make the sign of the cross, recite the Pater and Ave and the Creed and then get someone to say any number up to forty-nine. In the book, written in Syriac, were forty-nine statements of a rather general and moralizing character and it was believed that guidance would be given through the statement with the number thus selected. On wedding days Christians used to perform certain rites inside the circles they had drawn and also performed other similar superstitious ceremonies. Some men achieved a reputation for skill in magic which became legendary. One of the most famous was a priest called Kaṭamaṟṟom Kaṭṭanar, many of whose spells were in the name of Christ or of the Virgin or the Apostles. It is related that when the Patriarch Peter came to Malabar and tried to prepare holy oil in the Kaṭamaṟṟom church on Maundy Thursday he could not get the mixture to boil, and eventually it was found to be due to a hand of the deceased kaṭṭanar which had been buried in the wall of the church after his death. Even today in country parts many of the less educated people are convinced of the power of magic.

Another superstition condemned by the synod of Diamper was the practice of proving the truth of a statement by an ordeal. Such ordeals were handling bars of hot iron, thrusting the hands into boiling oil, or swimming through rivers full of crocodiles. Baldeus found it was a common ordeal in Malabar to swim across the river between Cochin and Cranganore which was full of crocodiles.[3] Gouvea does not at all approve of this practice, but he tells the

[1] Session III, decree 14. It seems to be connected with a *Book of Protection*, Hermann Gollancz (London, 1912); see review in *J. Theolog. Studies* (January 1914), p. 288, by R. H. Connolly. Connolly thinks that some of these charms have Indian features and have derived from Malabar. The word *Parisman* probably comes from *praśnam*, 'astrological calculations'. Fos. 63–71 in the Buchanan Collection in the University Library, Cambridge, is a quire of writing belonging probably to the sixteenth century. It was marked 'Liber Prohibitus' by a former owner and contains astrological data, lists of unlucky days, etc.

[2] A Malayāḷam and English version of this is given in Ananta Krishna Ayyar's *Anthropology of the Syrian Christians*, pp. 137–46.

[3] Whitehouse, p. 26.

story of an ordeal with burning oil successfully undergone by a Christian wife falsely accused of adultery. It is obvious that he was very impressed by this story.

The religious dances and songs held mostly at weddings were the chief Indian Christian art form. Gouvea and other Portuguese saw these dances and marvelled at the complete modesty and religious earnestness of the proceedings. Menezes on his tour after the synod was greeted by Christians at Ankamāli and Kuraviḷaṅāṭ, singing songs composed in his honour, praising his exploits and blaming the Patriarch of Babylon who had deceived them. Although tired, the archbishop attended a dance at night which started at eight o'clock and finished at one in the morning. Before the men danced, they first signed themselves with the cross and recited the Lord's Prayer, followed by a song in honour of St Thomas. They kept up certain dances for a long time, singing songs concerning the life of Christ or the doings of the saints as they did so. A party of men armed like their ancestors with round shields and swords came to meet the bishop. Then they danced round a big brass lamp with twelve wicks, a twelve-petal lotus which stood for Christ, and the dance went on for two hours with endless clapping of the hands, gesticulations and prostrations, all in strict time. They sang of Christ, of the life of St Thomas, of Thomas Cana and the Perumāḷ. These dances are now very rarely performed and there are probably few who still know them. Fr Hosten saw the dances at Kōṭṭayam in 1924. The songs which accompanied these dances, which were usually performed on the occasion of marriages, have been collected and published.[1]

The old houses are decorated with beautiful carving on some of the beams and this is also to be seen in many of the older churches. This work, however, is characteristic of the country as a whole and is not a Christian production. The west wall of the churches is usually built in a Portuguese style with a number of pinnacles and crosses. Sometimes there are figures in relief on the plaster, also a result of Portuguese influence. The Virgin and Child are sometimes enthroned in a niche on the wall and there are often crosses of various floriated designs and angels, sometimes a pair adoring the chalice and host, clearly Portuguese in inspiration. Fr Hosten has drawn attention to images of male and female beings, half man

[1] P. V. Lucas, *Sūriyāni purātanapāṭṭa* (The Ancient Songs of the Christians of Malabar).

and half fish, holding a ship above their heads, as at Kallupāra, and he wonders whether this may not depict a tradition of origin. He says: 'We may imagine that a strong Parthian infiltration had set in, before the Christian era, from Sindh all along the west coast as far as Mylapore, that in fact the best part of the commerce in the first century of our era was in the hands of the forbears of our Syrian Christians.'[1] Some of these plaster decorations depict hunting scenes, such as a man shooting a tiger, and have no religious significance.

Some old churches, such as Ceṅannūr and Tiruvamkōṭ, have well-designed lintels of granite carved with floral designs, the lotus frequently appearing; and almost always the cross is a central feature, often with a peacock on either side. It has been surmised that this very common use of the peacock points back to some ancient connexion with the Yezidis of Iraq who worshipped the peacock but associated the symbol with the devil. It is thought that they are probably a lapsed Christian sect and it may be that they were also once St Thomas Christians.

I do not think that there is any painting in houses or churches which is definitely pre-Portuguese; most of it seems of foreign inspiration, as are the paintings in the Ceriyapaḷḷi and Valiyapaḷḷi at Kōṭṭayam and the church at Cēppāṭ.

Christian buildings were anciently conformed to the Malabar style of architecture, which was different from that of any other part of India and quite unlike the Dravidian style found on the east coast and in the extreme southern part of Travancore. The style depends on the fact that the early buildings, whether temples, mosques, churches or private houses, were built entirely of wood. Teakwood buildings are said to last for four hundred years, as was remarked by Fr Paul. The Syrian house of good class was built of wood very much on the plan of a Nāyar house, and the situation of the house and the method of construction were in accordance with the Hindu rules *Manuśyālayā* and *Mahācandrikā*. The front of the house always faced east and often there was a small porch over the gate in the compound wall exactly opposite the front door of the house. This is called *paṭippura* and in old and wealthy houses was sometimes an elaborate gate house with a room over the gate. In small houses it was often just a thatched lych gate. Exactly the same feature can be seen in temples and churches, although in their case

[1] *Indian Antiquary*, LVI (July 1927), p. 121.

PLATE VI

A TYPICAL SYRIAN CHRISTIAN HOUSE

four churches, being disgusted at the Hindu style of those he found. The structure of old stone churches like Cūngam, Kayamkuḷam and Tiruvamkōṭ suggests that they were adapting stone to the old design. The Portuguese and other foreign missionaries, however, introduced a new style which has become standard for all church buildings and is quite different from that used in domestic architecture. Church architecture will be described in Part III.

The third stage of life for an orthodox Hindu is to retire from the world and to give himself entirely to religious meditation. In popular Indian history there are many stories of kings and great men who renounced their thrones or high office and ended life either in this kind of meditation or as wandering pilgrims living only for God. The Cochin rajas were always accustomed to abdicate some time after the age of sixty and spend the rest of their lives concentrating on spiritual matters while the next heir ruled the country. Formerly male Syrian Christians followed the same custom from the age of sixty-four. After that time they would live in a small detached room by themselves, spending their time in prayer and concentration on religious affairs and growing their beards as a sign they had renounced the world.

When death was near, the last unction would be given and the sacrament received and then if the old man could be raised he laid his hands on the heads of all his children, sons and male grandchildren first and then daughters and granddaughters, saying, 'May the blessing which Abraham gave to Isaac, the blessing which Isaac gave to Jacob and the blessing which Jacob gave to the Heads of the twelve Tribes and the blessing which they gave to my fathers and my blessing be now given to you my children.' When death was very near the relations would crowd round the bed to see from which organ—mouth, ears, eyes or nose—life went out. The priest and sexton from the church would chant prayers and as soon as the man had died a *kauma* would be sung to give his soul an easy journey. Then the women present at once began to wail and beat their breasts. After a short time servants would come and wash the body and dress it in special clothes, as no relative would help or touch the corpse. Low-caste people would come to share in the mourning and to sing special songs. When the body was ready they would place it on a bed facing east with lighted candles on the bed posts and a cross at the head. Usually a dish of embers was placed underneath the bed with incense to keep the atmosphere sweet. The family would sit round on mats on the floor and as the mourners arrived the old custom was to place a piece of cloth on the corpse. As soon as all the mourners had arrived the body was taken to the church for burial accompanied by the men folk. Women did not attend the funeral service but they assisted in the various services held by the priest in the house before the body was taken to the church. As the body left the house the women raised a great cry. No one took food from the time of death until after the funeral. It is now common for the relatives to kiss the face of the corpse just before it is removed from the house, but this, and the custom of relatives acting as coffin bearers, are very recent in origin.

The family was considered under pollution until a special feast called *pulakkuḷi* was given, which took place a few days after the funeral, usually ten days, as with the Nampūtiris, but among the Southists eight days. During this time the family would attend church daily and abstain from all animal food. Among the Southists there was a custom that tender coconuts should be taken to church and the priest would bless one, drink a little of the water and give to the relatives of the deceased to drink in turn. (In 1939 the Southist Romo-Syrians decided to abolish the whole observance of death pollution.) On the third and ninth days after death special services were held and preparations were made for the *pulakkuḷi* feast by erecting a *pandal* in the courtyard of the house.

On the morning of the feast everyone would bathe in the river and about midday priests would arrive from various churches with their sextons. (Similar feasts among Hindus are attended by Brahmans from various places.) Everyone could come to the feast including all the poor of the neighbourhood, but no flesh or fish could be used. The priests would first of all conduct a service of prayers and chants for a considerable time and the sextons would go round with incense, offering everyone the smoke. All attending the feast would place a coin in a vessel before the priests and receive the Peace from them (*kaiyyasūri*). Women were not given the kiss of peace but they joined their hands and said 'Praise be to Jesus Christ.' After making this offering and receiving the kiss, the people would take two or three grains of cummin from a plate placed before the priests and eat it, and then return to their places. After this the food was eaten and the priests departed after dividing the collection among themselves and their sextons. After the priests had gone, Hindus would come to be fed and last of all outcastes.

Requiem *kurbānas* were said daily for forty days (the old fee for which was five cakrams). On the fortieth day another big feast was given which would start with sweet rice like a marriage feast, and at which fish and flesh were served. After the meal the priests would conduct worship and again the Peace would be given with fees and alms for the priests. Special sweetmeats were made for this feast. It was usual to arrange for a *kurbāna* to be said for the deceased man's soul every month on the day of his death but sometimes this was done even weekly.

Every year the day of the death was marked by a *cāttam* or feast, just as among the Hindus who believe that the soul comes back for this yearly occasion. Many special dishes had to be prepared and the married daughters of the house were expected to come home the night before bringing *neyyappam*, a kind of cake, with them. Early in the morning there would be a *kurbāna* in the church, a candle would be lit on the grave and the son would bow as a mark of respect. The priests would come to the house some time after noon for the feast. Afterwards a *kauma* would be said and all would receive incense. It is interesting to note that the word used for some of the prayers in Malayāḷam was *mantram*,[1] the Hindu word for prayer. This worship was followed as on previous occasions by everyone offering money to the priests and receiving from him the Peace. People older than the deceased in whose memory the feast was held and his executors were not allowed to join in. After the Christians had had their food, certain Hindus and outcastes were given food outside. Those non-Christians entitled to come on these occasions seem to be the members of the castes traditionally placed under the protection of the Christians. The custom of a yearly feast on the anniversary of the death has mostly been given up now, but very often special prayers are offered in the house as well as a *kurbāna* in the church attended by the priests and near relations.

In some places, for instance Ārttāṭ and Niraṇam, the bones were disinterred from old graves after a lapse of years and thrown into a well in the corner of the cemetery, the ground being used again for fresh graves.

[1] Some think the use of the word *mantram* is incorrect; it may be a corruption of the Syriac word *madrasa*, a special form of prayer.

The Malayāḷam spoken by the Christians does not differ from that used by Nāyars of the localities in which they live. There may be some local peculiarities but these have nothing to do with community difference. There is, however, a very important distinctive element in the language of the St Thomas Christians. A very large number of technical words concerning Christian worship and life in the Christian Church are used in speech, and written in Malayāḷam characters though they are really Syriac words. Such are *māmmōdīsa* (baptism), *kurbāna* (Eucharist), *ślīhanmar* (Apostles), *slībā* (Cross), etc. There are many such words in everyday use, forming a distinctive Christian vocabulary. No Syrians bear Indian names, except as honorific surnames. The only names used are Biblical ones. There are many names which are Syriac in origin but have been Indianized. Such names are:

Jacob: (Chakko, Chakkappan, Iyakku)
Job: (Iyyu)
Peter: (Patros, Pathe or Pathappan)
Paul: (Piley, Pailoth, Pailo)
Zachariah: (Cheriyan)
Matthew: (Mathai, Mathen)
Ephraim: (Aippuru)
George: (Vergese, Varied, Varkey)
Titus: (Itty)
Alexander: (Chandy)
Isaac: (Ittack)

SOURCES

THERE are very few written sources. The most important is a novel by Kochuthommen Apothecary which describes the everyday life of a typical, fairly prosperous, Syrian family and gives an accurate account of the customs as still observed in the last quarter of the nineteenth century. The novel is called *Pariśkkarapati* (The Half of Civilization). Dr P. J. Thomas has written on the subject, notably in *Kēraḷaṭṭile Kristīya Sāhityam* and in *The Marriage Customs and Songs of the Christians of Malabar*. The songs are dealt with also in *Sūriyāni purātanapāṭṭa* (The Ancient Songs of the Syrian Christians of Malabar) by P. V. Lucas. All the above are in Malayāḷam and are difficult to obtain now.

to give the bridegroom, ending up with the promise of a cow and a calf. (This promise was usually fulfilled when the bride came back to the husband's house after the delivery of her first child.) Then she called the bridegroom her own son. The party inside listened with apparent disrespect and often made the mother repeat her speech because of alleged errors and demanded songs from her. At last she was allowed to ask the groom to open the door. Then she would go in again, with a lamp and a vessel of water. (The Nāyars have a somewhat similar custom to this and a service called 'shutting and opening' is provided in the Chaldean rite.)

When all this was finished the couple were ceremoniously taken to the well and bathed while the girls sang songs, after which there was an exchange of presents of new clothes. Wearing the new clothes they all then went to the *pandal* where there followed a very interesting ceremony. The bridegroom and other men stood round a lamp, placed a ring on it, and sang one of the traditional songs. They then moved round the lamp three times, touched it, signed themselves with the cross and stood a little way away from it, in a circle. Then a party with the bride did the same thing singing other songs. This ceremony was called the *marggam kaḷi*; it was the wedding dance of the Syrians and told the story of how St Thomas had preached the Gospel in Malabar. All Syrians used to learn this story in their early childhood. The lamp represented Jesus Christ.[1] The husband then sat down with his wife on his right hand and presented a cloth to the bride's uncle, who in turn put a ring on the groom's finger and embraced him. He then gave a cloth to the bride, received it from her again, and embraced her. A third piece of cloth was given to the head of the bridegroom's house and fourth and fifth pieces to the bride's maternal and paternal grandmothers.

As soon as it was light on Thursday morning the wedding party prepared to leave for the bride's house. This came as a great relief to the bridegroom because ever since the wedding, except for the ceremonies in the *pandal*, he had had to stay in the special wedding chamber with his friends and his clothes had not been changed until the ceremonial bath the night before. Before leaving the

[1] The dance is rarely performed now; I think only by Southist Roman Catholics. The Nampūtiris have a similar song called 'Yātra kaḷi'. A *Kēraḷa-lolppatti* says this was invented by foreign Brahmans who argued against the *bauddhas* who came by ship to Vana Perumāḷ. But the language of the song is modern.

PART III

is enriched with wood or stone carving—often there are seats by either wall, and open lattice work above them. This construction is not unlike that found in Malabar Hindu temples.

The great west door, often of heavy carved wood studded with brass nails, opens on to the *haikkala* or nave. There are never any seats provided in the nave, and in the old churches it was badly lit, with a few small windows high up in thick walls built of squared granite blocks (as at Tiruvāmkoṭ or Ceṅannūr), or of laterite bonded with mud and plastered. In the centre of the north and south walls are smaller doors, usually with a porch outside. The eastern quarter of the nave is used as the choir or *katastroma*; it is separated from the rest by strong wooden rails, or a stone wall, about four feet high (the *aḷi*). On the nave side of the rail is usually a treasury, or wooden alms box cemented in the floor.

Inside the *katastroma* on the south side is the font, large enough to immerse infants, and always covered with a cloth when not in use. Just inside the entrance to the *katastroma*, between it and the steps of the sanctuary, is a large hanging, or standing, lamp of brass, with a number of small cotton wicks resting in a reservoir of coconut oil, which is replenished by the offerings of the worshippers. This lamp is kept burning continuously in most churches. Just behind it or in front of it stands a small rather high table, with a wooden cross, candles, a small hand-bell and books needed for the service. The daily office is said before this table, and sermons are preached from behind it. It takes the place of the prayer desk in Anglican churches.

The nave ends with three or four steps into the sanctuary, joined to the nave by an arch, and with higher walls and roof than the nave. On either side of the arch, inside the *katastroma*, may be two small altars. These are used only for concelebration at requiems and on other occasions. They may be up the steps inside the sanctuary on either side of the high altar. The whole of the sanctuary space is called *madbaha* or altar. It is screened from the nave by a curtain (*tiraśila*) which runs on a rod across the arch, and can be drawn by cords. Stone or wood screens are not found in Malabar. The main feature of the sanctuary is what I have called the 'high altar', known as the 'table of life', or 'altar of sacrifice' or 'throne'. This is a stone structure about six feet by three feet, with a number of steps going up at the back, and some kind of ornamental stone or lacquer or wood carving as a reredos. In the centre of the

PLATE VII

THE CHURCH AT CEṄANNŪR

gradines, on the highest one, is always a cross, usually of wood with the figure of Christ painted on it. There may be many other crosses also in front or at the sides of this altar cross. There will be many candles in wooden or brass sticks, and ornaments of carved and gilded wood representing conventional flowers in a vase. Fresh flowers are never used in Jacobite churches, nor are images or crucifixes. There may be some pictures, usually Roman Catholic prints of the Sacred Heart or the Blessed Virgin. The throne is built away from the east wall so that the ministers can walk round it. In the back is a cupboard in which the cross is 'buried' on Good Friday, and holy water is kept in memory of Christ's baptism. The throne is always provided with a silk frontal, and there is a very narrow foot-pace in the middle for the priest.

Other furniture of the sanctuary includes a small lectern which is brought forward to the steps when the Gospel is read, a *golgotha* or stand for the cross and two candles, a censer usually kept hanging on a nail by a side window, and the fans (*marwah'tho*), metal discs on long handles, ornamented with angels' faces and with small silver bells fastened all round. They are held over the priest's head at the most solemn parts in the *kurbāna*.

The *kurbāna* is not celebrated directly on the throne, but on a *tablitho*, or small stone or wooden slab consecrated by the bishop and given to a priest at his ordination. This stone is covered with seven layers of silk; the *kurbāna* cannot be celebrated except on it.

If there are any bishops buried in the church their tombs may be in the nave or just outside it, with doors giving access to the chapels in which the tombs are placed.

The ordinary dress[1] of priests in Malabar is a white cassock with wide sleeves and a 'sailor-collar' at the back, so that the whole garment is shaped like a cross. Jacobite priests always wear this *kamissa*, with a round black cap about an inch high. In church a black cassock is worn, and over it an alb (*kuthino*). The stole is a broad strip of silk of the same material as the *kāppa* or cope; at the top a slit permits the head to be passed through. It is held in position by a belt of the same material. Cuffs are also worn over the alb, of the same material as the stole. The *kāppa* or cope is really the ancient form of chasuble, or *phaino*. It is tied on the chest with tapes, no amice being worn. Deacons and readers wear

[1] Vestments are fully described in Codrington, *Syrian Liturgies*, pp. 8–10.

deacons, or only one or two, it is he who often acts as master of ceremonies, who is thurifer, and who starts the hymns of the people. He has responsibilities similar to those of the parish clerk of an English church in the eighteenth century. There are usually several men in minor orders (below the diaconate) in a parish, and they come to help, putting on the *kuthino* or alb for their ministry.

When the people enter the church the veil hides the sanctuary and the secret prayers which are being said there. The public celebration starts when the veil is drawn back. Twice more during the service the veil is drawn and the sanctuary hidden, while the congregation sing hymns. The three periods when the veil is withdrawn and the whole church joins in worship together can first be considered. Afterwards the secret prayers and actions will be explained. These three periods of worship may be conveniently described as the Pre-anaphora and the Anaphora proper from the Pax to the Great Intercession which immediately follows the Consecration; the Eucharistic Adoration; and the Communion of the people and Thanksgiving. These three parts each have a blessing (or 'seal') attached to them, first in the name of the Trinity, then in the name of God the Mighty One and our Saviour Christ, and lastly again in the name of the Trinity. The three withdrawals of the veil are said to signify the Incarnation, the Rending of the Veil at the moment of our Lord's death, and the Second Coming of the Lord.

When the veil is first drawn aside the liturgy of the catechumens commences, with the priest saying 'Mary that brought thee forth and John that baptized thee shall intercede for us, have mercy on us'. This is not really as abrupt as it appears, for the congregation have been singing hymns and also listening to the readings of the prophets by the deacon in the preparatory prayers. At the beginning of the rite proper all are recalled to the Incarnation as the miracle through which alone true worship is possible. The congregation's response emphasizes this, and speaks also of Christ's death by which he trampled under foot our death and destroyed it. The note of praise is struck here at the outset, the church and altar bells have rung and the priest censes the altar while the people are singing. Then the *trisagion*, the constant praise of the Jacobite Church, is sung, without prostrations[1] but with signing at the threefold repetition of 'O thou who wast crucified for us, have mercy upon

[1] See p. 234.

us'. The Lord's Prayer, which in the offices always follows the *trisagion*, is not used here but instead the people join in a threefold *Kyrie* (in Greek). This praise is preparatory to the reading of the Epistle and Gospel. The Epistle is preceded by a hymn commending the teaching of St Paul, and is read from the north side of the sanctuary. After this a small lectern or table is brought to the sanctuary step and the priest places on it the Syriac book of the Gospels, with lights and incense. The following dialogue ensues:

Deacon (*Barekmore*). Let us stand in silence and awe and modesty, and listen to the proclamation of the living words of God from the Gospel of our Lord Jesus the Messiah.

Priest (*facing the congregation*). Peace be unto you all.

Congregation. May the Lord make us also worthy, with thy spirit.

Priest. The life-giving preaching of the holy Gospel of our Lord Jesus the Messiah, from the [*names the Evangelist*] who is the evangelist that preacheth life and salvation to the world.

Congregation. Blessed is he that hath come and is to come in the name of the Lord. Praise be to him who sent him for our salvation, and may his blessings be on us all.

Priest. In the time of the dispensation of our God and our Saviour Jesus the Messiah, who is God, the Word of life, that was incarnate of the holy Virgin Mary, did these things happen so.

Congregation. Thus we believe and confess.

Priest reads the Gospel (*St Mark iii. 31–5, or the lesson of the day*) *and then says*: Peace be with you all.

Congregation (*singing*).

Blessed are those good servants
Who when their Lord cometh are found
Awake and working in his Vineyard.
He will gird himself and serve them
Who worked with him from morning till evening.
The Father will place them round the table,
The Son will minister unto them,
And the Holy Ghost, the Comforter,
Will make crowns;
Hallelujah,
And put them on the head of each.

Deacon. Stoumen kalōs.

Congregation. Kyrie eleison.

the altar, and waves it above them, reciting secret prayers while the deacon again summons the congregation to attention:

Deacon. Brethren, let us stand well with awe, reverence, purity, holiness, love and true faith, and watch this holy *kurbāna* which is offered before us by this reverend priest. For he offers this living sacrifice to God the Father in unity and peace on behalf of us all.

Congregation. This *kurbāna* is blessing, peace, sacrifice and thanksgiving.

The first of the three blessings is now given, the priest turning to the people. The *Sursum corda* and call to praise follow, and the preface, *Sanctus* and *Benedictus.* The act of Institution follows immediately, with no introduction, said aloud;[1] the blessing of the Bread and Wine is in two separate acts, each with its *Amen* from the congregation. The Bread is not broken here, but at the appropriate words it is bent in the priest's hands and cracked across. The *Anamnesis* and *Epiclesis* follow at once, in the following form:

Priest. Do this as the memorial of me, as oft as ye partake of this holy mystery, and commemorate my death and my resurrection, until I come.

Congregation. Our Lord, thy death we commemorate and thy resurrection we confess, and we look for thy second coming. May thy blessings be upon us all.

Priest. We commemorate, O Lord, thy death, and thy resurrection on the third day, and thy ascension into heaven and thy session at the right hand of God the Father, and also thy second coming when thou shalt judge the world righteously and render to every man according to his deeds. Therefore we offer unto thee this bloodless sacrifice. Deal not with us according to our debts nor requite us according to our sins. But according to thine abundant mercies blot out the sins of thy servants; for thy people and thine inheritance beseech thee, and through thee, thy father, saying, Have mercy upon us, O God the Father Almighty.

Congregation. Have mercy upon us, O God the Father Almighty: O Lord, God, we glorify thee, we bless thee, we worship thee, and we beseech thee, O thou who art good, have mercy upon us and bless us.

The priest waves his hands to signify the descent of the Holy Spirit.

[1] See secret prayers, pp. 230, 231.

Deacon (*Barekmore*). My beloved, how fearful is this moment and how dreadful is this time when the Holy Spirit descends from heaven, from the heights above, and dwells upon this holy *kurbāna*, and sanctifies it. Stand ye in silence and pray.

Congregation. May peace be with us all and good will to us all.

Priest (*after a secret prayer*). Give answer to me O Lord, Give answer to me O Lord, Give answer to me O Lord, and have mercy upon us.

Congregation. *Kyrie eleison*, *Kyrie eleison*, *Kyrie eleison.*

Priest (*waving his right hand over the paten*). May the Holy Spirit abide and transmute this bread into the life-giving body, the redeeming body, and the very body of our God, the Messiah.

Congregation. Amen.

Priest (*waving his right hand over the chalice*). And perfect this chalice into the blood of the new covenant, the redeeming blood, and the very blood of our God the Messiah.

Congregation. Amen.

Priest (*lifting up both hands*). That they may be to all who receive of them the hallowing of soul and body, for the bearing of the fruits of good works, for the confirmation of thy holy Church which is founded on the rock of invincible faith, against which the gates of hell cannot prevail. Deliver her unto the end from the stumbling-blocks of heresy; that she may offer up glory and praise to thee, and to thine only-begotten Son, and to thy Holy Spirit, all holy and good and adorable and life-giving and consubstantial with thee, now and for ever.

Congregation. Amen.

At the *Epiclesis* the priest waves his hands, shaking them from the wrists and bringing them up and down with a motion like the flight of a bird, rising and falling over the Bread and Wine.

The deacon, standing in the middle of the sanctuary, facing east, now begins to chant the Great Intercession, and the people sit on the floor if they wish, the only time they can rest during the whole service, unless there happens to be a sermon. The Intercession is divided into six parts, each called a *tubdon*, and ends with supplication for the worshippers themselves and the second blessing or seal of the liturgy. In each *tubdon* the deacon first calls '*Barekmore*' and then bids prayer for certain people, to which the congregation respond with a *Kyrie.* The priest meanwhile has been reciting a

the *paṭippura* was often massive and impressive (compare Kayamkuḷam, Ceṅannūr, etc.). The house itself stood in a sanded yard and was built on a plinth of laterite stone, sometimes only six inches or so high but often eighteen inches, with steps leading up to it from the yard. This plinth formed a verandah at the front of the house. The wooden house itself was built round an open court behind this front verandah and consisted of four large rooms and four small. The front verandah was enclosed by wooden lattice work which gave privacy while not excluding air. Somewhere in the house was the *aṟa* or strong room, also made of heavy teak, in which paddy and household utensils not in use were kept. The woodwork in old houses was decorated by carving and sometimes by brass studs.

The furniture of these houses was very simple; cots of wood were used and the Christians like Hindus took care to sleep with their head to the east and feet to the west. Hindus used to think that this position brought them the protection of certain forces without which they would be taken by tigers or molested by spirits. In the old days people mostly sat on the floor on finely woven palm-leaf mats. Floors were smeared with cow dung and swept regularly, except on Maundy Thursday and Good Friday. Domestic articles like mirrors were made of polished metal and the fine brass vessels, cleaned every day with ashes, reflected the prosperity of the family. Cooking was done largely in earthen or copper vessels or for frying in a large iron bowl called *cīnacaṭṭi* (Chinese vessel). Other indispensable objects included brass lamps of various designs, hanging or standing, and a brass box for chewing materials.

In Travancore all buildings approximated to the same design and in most of them the ridge of the roof rose at the ends, providing a gable enriched with pierced carving and providing ventilation in the roof. The ancient church of Pālayūr was of wood. Thus we find Fr Fenicio, S.J., writing between 1600 and 1607 that he was building a stone church outside the ancient teakwood church of Pālayūr. The wooden structure was not demolished until the Christians had overcome their superstitious dread that any who attempted to meddle with God's house would be struck down with sudden death; but when it was at last removed 'the new building stood out in such fine proportions that the Hindus, Mohammadans and Jews flocked to see it'.[1] Fenicio obtained permission to build

[1] Du Jarric, *Thesaurus rerum indicarum*, III, lib. 2, cap. 5, pp. 50–1; quoted by Medlycott, *India and the Apostle Thomas*, p. 30, note.

hymns as well at this time, and the deacon and the congregation have a colloquy together, leading up to the second withdrawal of the veil and the recitation of the Catholic—the Our Father with an embolism said by the priest. Prayer for worthy reception of 'the life-giving mysteries of our Saviour the Messiah' is made and the third blessing given.

The elevation which now takes place at the altar is marked with the fullest possible expressions of joy—bells ring out and if the day is a festival bombs may be exploded in the churchyard. The ceremonial accompanies words of great beauty and power:

Deacon (*Barekmore*). Let us watch with fear and trembling.
Congregation. Lord, have compassion and bless us.
Priest (*lifting up the paten*). These holy mysteries are given to the holy and to the pure alone.
Congregation. There is none other holy save the Holy Father, the Holy Son, and the Holy Spirit. Amen.
Priest replaces the paten and lifts up the chalice.
Congregation. Praise be to the one Father, to the Son, and to the living and Holy Spirit, for ever and ever. Amen.
Priest (*holding the chalice and paten in his hands*). The one Holy Father, who by his mercy created the world, be with us.
Congregation. Amen.
Priest. The one Holy Son, who by his own precious sufferings redeemed us, be with us.
Congregation. Amen.
Priest. The one living Holy Spirit, the perfecter and fulfiller of all that is, and all that hath been, be with us. May the name of the Lord be blessed as it was in the beginning for ever and ever.
Congregation. Amen.

This is followed by hymns of adoration of God which remind the congregation that they worship in company with the saints and ask for their help in prayer. A number of hymns may be used here, the most common being hymns with the Blessed Virgin Mary, with the saints in heaven, and with St Thomas, patron of the Indian Church. The priest and ministers join in these hymns and then the priest again turns to the people, asking humbly for their prayers, and the veil is drawn for the second time. Inside the sanctuary the priest communicates and gives to those who are with him. Outside, the people join in more hymns, the priest from within leading the *Gloria* at the end of a hymn, after which the deacon starts another, which is taken up by the people.

The veil is drawn aside for the third time and the priest comes down from the altar, carrying the sacrament in his hands for the Communion of the people. Unfortunately the custom has arisen of giving Communion only after the service, as ordered by Patriarch Peter in 1877. It seems from his language that until his visit the people used to receive the sacrament at this place, the proper place, in the service. The effect of this change has been to make the ceremonies here another kind of elevation and to rob the prayers of their meaning. The priest comes down from the step with prayers and congregational response bearing the paten in his right hand, and the chalice in his left, both vessels covered with tight fitting embroidered silken covers. Then he lifts the elements up, crossing his hands and saying:

Praise be to thee, O Lord our God, for ever.
Praise be to thee. Praise be to thee.

Our Lord Jesus the Messiah, may thy holy body which we have eaten and thy sanctifying blood which we have drunk, be not for punishment and condemnation, but for life and salvation to us all. And have mercy on us. (*The priest then turns east.*)

Congregation. All the earth shall bow down before thee, and adore thee. Every tongue shall praise thy holy name. For thou art the raiser of the dead and the good hope of those who are enclosed in the grave. And chiefly we thank thee, O Lord, and give thanks for thy mercy towards us.

Then are said short prayers of thanksgiving and the congregation is dismissed with the following blessing:

My brethren and beloved, with the blessings and provisions for the way which ye have received from the sanctifying altar of the Lord, at this time when I commend you to the grace and blessings of the holy and glorious Trinity, depart ye in peace.

Congregation. Amen.

Priest. For ye who are afar off and ye who are nigh, and the living with the departed who are saved by the victorious cross of Our Lord and sealed with the seal of holy baptism, this blessed

Trinity will remit your debts, and forgive your offences, and grant rest to the souls of your faithful departed.

Congregation. Amen.

Priest. I am a weak and sinful servant. May I receive mercy and be helped by your prayers. Depart ye in peace, glad and rejoicing, and pray for me always.

Congregation. May the Lord accept thy *kurbāna* and help us by thy prayers.

The veil is drawn for the last time but the congregation do not leave the church immediately. For some time they stand in their places, everyone saying his own private prayers aloud, with a noise like the sea beating on the shore. One by one the people go out, as they entered, unless a bishop is present, in which case they file past him, bowing their heads and receiving a touch of his hand-cross on their foreheads, in token of blessing. To priests the bishop offers his cross held flat, for them to kiss. If any have made their confession and so prepared for Communion the priest will come out from the sanctuary and place the Bread dipped into the Wine directly in their mouths, as they stand to receive it. There is no ceremony connected with this, in marked contrast to the procession of the mysteries within the liturgy, but a deacon pours a little water into the communicant's mouth, from a long spouted brass vessel, immediately after reception. Even babies are given Communion in this way.

The Preparation Service said behind the veil consists of prayers said while the elements are being prepared and placed on the altar, a service of penitence with the offering of incense, the vesting of the priest, an oblation of the elements with a prayer affirming the intention of the *kurbāna* which is to be offered, and another solemn offering of incense.

At the end of the obligatory night office the priest, wearing his black cassock over his ordinary clothes (the white *kamissa* and black cap), stands before the sanctuary and prays that the worship the Church is about to offer may be accepted by God. All recite Psalm LI and then the priest turns to the congregation and, with arms outstretched and palms extended to the people, asks for their prayers, that he may be made worthy to celebrate the holy and living sacrifice for the whole Church.

Then he enters the sanctuary and the veil is drawn. The priest bows, kisses the altar, lights the candles and sets on bread and wine as follows.

The priest (*holding the 'seal' over the paten and saying*):

He was led as a lamb to the slaughter and he was dumb as a sheep before the shearer. He opened not his mouth in his humiliation. Thou hast set up thine abode, O Lord. Establish thy sanctuary with thine own hands. The Lord shall reign for ever. (*As the 'first-born' is placed in the paten*) O thou first-begotten of the heavenly Father, accept this oblation from the hands of thy weak and sinful servant.

(*Pouring the wine into the chalice*) Our Lord Jesus Christ was crucified on the tree between two thieves in Jerusalem and was pierced in his side with the spear and there flowed out from him blood and water, the remission of sins of all creation. He that saw it bare witness and we believe his witness is true. What reward shall I give unto the Lord for all his benefits towards me? I will receive the cup of salvation and call upon the name of the Lord. I will give my offerings unto the Lord in the presence of all his people. (*Mixing water in the chalice*) O Lord God, as thy divinity was united with our humanity unite this water with this wine.

The *sēdra* in the penitential service seems to define the sacrifice of the *kurbāna* in terms of self-oblation of the Church, but this is not an exhaustive definition.

O God, lover of men, meek and lowly, gracious and loving, who delightest not in sacrifices but in mercy, who lovest a broken heart more than burnt offerings and who acceptest a humble heart more than the blood of fat oxen and lambs and peace-offerings, accept now our spiritual sacrifice, well-pleasing to thee. Vouchsafe unto us to offer on thy heavenly altar spiritual and reasonable sacrifices with broken hearts and humble spirits. Grant that we, being transformed in newness of life by the knowledge and wisdom of the truth in our souls, may become a noble flock without blemish, worthy to enter into the new life, holding the bright torch of the true faith. Make us all worthy to sing praises in thy house to the Father, Son and Holy Ghost, now and ever, world without end. Amen.

The priest then takes off his *kamissa* and puts on the eucharistic vestments, the shoes, the alb (*kuthino*), stole (*uroro*), the cincture (*zunoro*), the cuffs (*epimanikia*), and the chasuble (*phaino*). Then he unveils the elements, and taking the paten in his right hand and the chalice in his left he crosses his arms and lifting them above the altar slab (*tablitho*) he says the prayer of intention:

The memorial of our Lord and our God and our Saviour Jesus Christ and of all his saving dispensation on our behalf; especially the message of the watcher; his glorious conception and his birth in the flesh; his baptism in the Jordan and his fast of forty days; his saving passion, his raising on the cross, his quickening death, and his honourable burial; his glorious resurrection and ascension into heaven and his session on the right hand of God the Father; according to his own command we commemorate these at this time by the eucharist that is set before us. First, we remember our father Adam and our mother Eve and the holy Mother of God, Mary, and the prophets and apostles, preachers and evangelists and martyrs and confessors, righteous men and priests and holy fathers and true shepherds and orthodox doctors, solitaries and cenobites and those who are standing and praying with us, with all those who beginning from Adam and Eve have been well-pleasing unto thee even to this day. Again, we remember our fathers and our brethren and our teachers, who have taught us the word of truth; our own departed and all the faithful departed, particularly (*by name*) them that are of our blood and them that had part and are still taking part in the support of this place and all that take part with us whether in word or deed in little or much, especially him (her) for whom and in whose behalf this *kurbāna* is offered. (*Here he mentions those for whom the* kurbāna *is offered.*) Pardon his offences and sins by thy mercy.

If he is offering for the Mother of God the following is said:

We commemorate then the holy Mother of God, Mary, in whose honour and for whom this *kurbāna* is offered today particularly and distinctly that she, O Lord, may intercede unto thee on behalf of thy servants who have taken refuge in her prayers. O gracious and merciful God, by her prayers which thou hast heard and accepted, answer in thy goodness the petitions of those who hold her in honoured remembrance. Remove from them temptations and chastisements and the rod of thy wrath and forgive their offences in thy mercy by the prayers of thy Mother and of all thy saints. Amen.

The above prayer, with necessary alternatives, is also used when the *kurbāna* is offered for a saint.

After another prayer praying for many people by name, and beginning with the words: 'O God, thou art the *kurbāna* and to thee the *kurbāna* is offered', the priest replaces the vessels on the stone; he veils them with the *sosafa*, singing: 'The heavens are covered with the splendour of the glorious one. All creation is full of his glory.' The priest then censes the altar[1] and says a final short intercession, the *kauma* and the creed, and then the veil is drawn aside and the public celebration of the mysteries commences.

We have seen that in the *kurbāna* service the people sing many hymns while the priest is employed in secret prayers, which may be accompanied by action necessary to the proper performance of the rite. Similarly, during the Great Intercession, the priest offers secret prayers while the deacon is bidding the prayers of the people. Most of the secret prayers affirm in other words the petitions of the people, or else are supplications that the priest may be made worthy of his ministry. The first secret prayer of special interest is that said while the priest waves the *sosafa* or veil over the mysteries, saying:

> Thou art the rock of flint, which sent forth twelve streams of water for the twelve tribes of Israel. Thou art the hard rock, which was set against the tomb of our Redeemer.[2]

During the *Sanctus* the priest says the first strophe of the Eucharistic Prayer secretly, commemorating the creation and fall of man and his redemption:

> Holy art thou, King of the ages and giver of all holiness, Holy is thy Son, Jesus Christ our Lord, Holy also is thy Holy Spirit, who searchest all things, even thy deep things. Thou madest man out of dust and bestowed upon him the delight of paradise; And when he transgressed thy command and fell, thou didst not despise nor forsake him, but didst call him by the law, and instruct him by the prophets, And in the fullness of time thou

[1] See p. 296.

[2] The prayer used is that of Dionysios Barsalibi. It is given, with the action of the rite, in Codrington, *Syrian Liturgies*, p. 27.

didst send into the world thy only-begotten Son, who being incarnate of the Holy Ghost and the Virgin Mary renewed thy image in mankind.

Another secret prayer is said before the *Epiclesis*, praying that God will 'send forth upon us and upon these gifts before thee' the Holy Spirit.

The secret prayers offered during the deacon's biddings during the Great Intercession are in effect collects offering up the petitions of the biddings.

The fraction, consignation and commixture is a most complicated ceremony, performed behind the drawn veil of the sanctuary. There are three ways of arranging the broken Bread, said to represent a cross, an angel or a man, respectively.

During the Catholic the priest prays for himself with the prayer of Mar Jacob the Doctor.

The priest's prayers at the time of Communion are worthy of notice.

(*He kneels before the 'table of life' and prays*) Vouchsafe us, O Lord God, to eat thy holy Body and to drink thy propitiatory Blood and may we be heirs in thy heavenly kingdom with all who have been well-pleasing to thee, O our Lord and our God for ever. Amen.

(*He ascends the step and when he takes the host from the chalice with the spoon he says*) Thee I hold, who holdest the bounds, thee I grasp, who orderest the depths, thee, O God, do I place in my mouth; by thee may I be delivered from the fire unquenchable and be accounted worthy of the remission of sins like the sinful woman and the thief, O our Lord and our God for ever. Amen.

(*When he communicates he says*) The propitiatory live-coal of the Body and Blood of Christ our God is given to me, a sinful servant, for the pardon of offences and for the remission of sins in both worlds for ever and ever. Amen.

(*When he drinks from the chalice he says*) By thy living and life-giving Blood which was poured forth on the cross may my offences be pardoned and my sins remitted, O Jesus, Word of God, who camest for our salvation, for ever and ever. Amen.

(*Then he communicates the priests, deacons, and other persons in the sanctuary who are prepared to receive the sacrament, saying*) The propitiatory live-coal of the Body and Blood of Christ our God is given to an illustrious priest [*or* a modest deacon, *or* a monk, the steward of God, *or* a true believer] for the pardon of his offences and the remission of his sins in both worlds for ever. Amen.

There are no more secret prayers said during the service. The consecrated elements remaining are consumed and the vessels cleansed with appropriate prayers. While he washes his hands he recites Psalms XXIV and XXIX, and then says a prayer for the faithful departed, especially for those for whom the *kurbāna* has been offered, and who have been mentioned by name whenever the sign of the cross has been made. Then he says the Our Father and bows before the 'table of life' saying:

Into thy house, O God, have I entered.
Before thy throne, O heavenly King, have I worshipped.
Pardon all wherein I have sinned against thee.

(*He kisses the 'table of life' and says secretly*) Remain in peace, O holy and divine altar of the Lord. Henceforth I know not whether I shall return to thee or not. May the Lord grant me to see thee in the church of the first-born which is in heaven and in this covenant do I trust.

Remain in peace, O holy and propitiatory altar. May the holy Body and propitiatory Blood which I have received from off thee be to me for the pardon of debts and for the remission of sins and for boldness before the fearful judgment seat of our Lord and our God, for ever.

Remain in peace, O holy altar, table of life, and entrust our Lord Jesus Christ that I may never cease to be remembered on thee, henceforth and for ever, world without end. Amen.

Bread which has not been consecrated (*burksa*) is often blessed and distributed at the end of the *kurbāna*, as follows:

May the grace of the holy Trinity come from heaven and abide upon this bread ✠✠✠, and upon them that give it, and them that minister it. May the mercies of God be upon all who have partaken and are partaking from it, in both worlds for ever. Amen.

SOURCES

THERE are a few English translations of the Syriac Liturgies used in Malabar which may be consulted. J. Hough, *History of Christianity in India*, includes some translations as an appendix to vol. IV. G. B. Howard in *The Christians of St Thomas and their Liturgies* includes the anaphoras of St Peter, the Twelve Apostles, Mar Dionysios, Mar Xystus and Mar John, all of which he obtained in Malabar. The best recent translation of St James, the liturgy in common use, is *The Order of the Holy Qurbana of the Orthodox Syrian Church of Malabar*, by Mar Ivanios. There is also a translation of St James, with notes of Indian Christian usage, by K. N. Daniel, in *A Critical Study of Primitive Liturgies*. This, though polemical in tone, is a valuable source book. A reliable account of the different Syrian traditions is *Studies of the Syrian Liturgies*, by H. W. Codrington, being a reprint of articles which appeared in the *Eastern Churches Quarterly* (1936–7). I have cut out a good deal that I had already written, as the facts are now available in Mr Codrington's book.

The text of the liturgy of St James, as well as of twelve other anaphoras,[1] is given in the *Kurbāna Taksā* (Eucharistic Order) published by Malpān Maṭṭaykkal Alexander. There is another collection (published by the Mar Julios Press, Pampakuda, 1931) which contains eighteen anaphoras. The *Kūdāśakramangaḷum anīdāyum*, translated by Fr Punūs, gives all the occasional offices. The special offices for the seasons are contained in the *Āṇdutaksā* (Order for the year), also prepared by Fr Punūs. The daily office is published by the Pampakuda Press in Syriac; a Malayāḷam version is *Nitya Prartana Kramam*, translated by Konāṭṭ Mathan Malpān.

[1] The other anaphoras given in Fr Alexander's book are Mar Dionysios Barsliba, Mar John Chrysostom, Mar John, Mar Matthai, Mar Eustathios, Mar Julius of Rome, Mar Xystus of Rome, Mar Peter, the Twelve Apostles, Mar Isaac, Mar Abraham, the Patriarch Mar John. Fr Punūs adds the anaphoras of Mar Lazarus bar Sabhetha, Patriarch Peter, Mar Cyril the Great, Mar Ignatios Nurono, Mar Thoma.

CHAPTER IX

THE DAILY PRAYERS AND SPECIAL OFFICES

THE *kauma* is the Common Prayer of the Jacobite Church and is ordered by the Hudaya Canon and the Ēthikon to be recited by all believers. It is as follows:

Preface.

Holy, Holy, Holy is the Lord God Almighty.
Heaven and earth are full of his glory.
Hosanna in the highest.
Blessed is he that hath come and is yet to come in the name of the Lord. Hosanna in the highest.

Kauma.

Holy art thou, O God,
Holy art thou, Almighty Lord,
Holy art thou, Immortal Lord,
O thou that wast crucified for us, have mercy upon us.

(At this point the worshipper prostrates himself, kneeling down and bowing until his forehead touches the ground. The *kauma* with its prostration is repeated three times.)

Lord, have mercy upon us,
Lord, have compassion and mercy upon us,
Lord, hearken unto our prayers and have mercy upon us.
Glory be to thee, O Lord,
Glory be to thee, O Lord,
Glory be to thee, O Lord, our hope, for ever and ever.

If a priest is present the petitions of the *kauma* are slightly different:

Lord, have mercy upon us,
Lord, have compassion and mercy upon us,
Lord, accept our worship and our prayers and have mercy upon us.
Glory be to thee, O God,
Glory be to thee, Maker of all,
Glory be to thee, O Christ the King, who hast compassion on thy sinful servants. *Barekmore.*

In either Common Prayer or the canonical hours the Lord's Prayer is said immediately after the *kauma.*

All priests have to say the offices of the seven hours every day, but in practice these are generally read in two groups.[1] The early morning prayer includes matins (*lilīyō*), prime (*saprō*) and terce (*tlōsāśāyin*). In the evening, about sunset, the other four offices are said, sext (*pelgitiyouda*), none (*irupattiraṇdara*), vespers (*rāmiśō*) and compline (*sūttāṛa*). Priests usually say the offices now in Malayāḷam, but until recently they were always read in Syriac.[2] They still are read in Syriac by older priests and in the monasteries, where the offices are said at their proper hours. At the beginning of the office a hand-bell is rung and the clergy receive the Peace from the senior priest. In Malabar the Jacobites do not sing the offices in choir. The Malayāḷam version of the office book is used a good deal by the laity; it contains all the offices but does not provide as great a variety of prayers as the Syriac version.

The canonical structure of each office is the same: first is the *Sanctus* and *kauma* with the Our Father. On Sundays and great festivals Psalm LI is then chanted, and then the proper psalms for the office. Then *ekbo*, a short collect leading to *Stoumen kalōs, Kyrie eleison*, and introducing the prayer of incense, is said. After this there must be at least five prayers, to the Mother of God, the saints, the saint who is being commemorated that day, a prayer of contrition and one for the dead. Not all the prayers need to be read, but the order in which they are given must be followed, and at least one of each group used. The office finishes as it began, with a *kauma*, and the Creed. When offices are said grouped together the Creed is said only once, at the end of the group, but each office must begin and end with the *kauma*, so that in the evening prayer there will be eight *kaumas* and twenty-four prostrations. There are variants of the *kauma* given in the special offices for the festivals, and used there alone (not even in the *kaumas* of the *kurbāna* on these days), which indicate very clearly that the *kauma* is addressed to Christ, and not to the Father, and which are worthy of a wider use than they at present enjoy. Instead of 'thou who wast crucified for us', at Christmas the Church says 'thou who wast born for us'; at the Epiphany, 'thou who wast baptized for us';

[1] A more thorough description is in Codrington, *Syrian Liturgies*, pp. 34–44.

[2] 'Our prayers are in the Syriac or Chaldean language which was given us by our Lord St Thomas'; Giamil, *Genuinae relationes*, doc. 22.

during Lent, 'thou who fasted for us'; during Holy Week, 'thou who suffered for us'; at Easter, 'thou who rose again for us'; and at Pentecost, 'thou who sent the Paraclete to be with us for ever'.[1]

Special prayers and hymns are provided for the different days of the week in every season: the seasons have their special variations in the office and particularly in the *prūmion*. These prayers are never read in a speaking voice but chanted in the Indian recitative manner. There are only eight tunes used for the singing in the Syrian Church and these are used in order. For example, on Advent Sunday the first tune may be used; on Monday the fifth tune will be used, and these two, the first and the fifth, on alternate days for the rest of the week; for the second Sunday the second tune and on Monday the sixth; for the third Sunday the third tune and on Monday the seventh, and so on. One tune will be used for the Sunday, Tuesday, Thursday and Saturday and the other for the Monday, Wednesday and Friday in each week. The following Sunday the change will be made.

Throughout the services the tune to be used for special chants and hymns is indicated.

The Church's Year

The special ceremonies for Christmas Day come at the end of matins which is said at about three o'clock in the morning. About an hour afterwards the whole congregation follows the priest out of the door of the church, receiving a handful of incense as they go, to a space in front of the churchyard cross. A cross-shaped hole has been dug, the arms all of equal length, and in it a large pile of palm leaves, preserved for the purpose since the previous Hosanna Sunday, has been placed in readiness. The Epistle and Gospel are sung by the light of candles held by deacons and immediately after the Gospel the fire is lit by the priest. All start singing the *Gloria in excelsis* as the flames dart up and the congregation moves round the fire led by the priest twice from left to right and then once from right to left. The first time round all the worshippers cast incense on the fire. This is the only time in the year when the

[1] It is well known that the phrase 'thou who wast crucified for us' assumed great controversial significance. It is said to have been inserted by Peter Fuller, Patriarch of Antioch, 471–5. A later Patriarch amended it to 'O Christ the King who wast crucified for us', but it is said that the Monophysites would not accept this change. A. Fortescue, *Lesser Eastern Churches*, pp. 190–2.

people offer incense. All carry candles in their hands. After this threefold procession, a procession is usually made round the church building with lights and crosses and umbrellas to show joy at our redemption. Then all re-enter the church through the southern door for prime and the *kurbāna* starts. At Christmas and Easter the floor of the church is covered with aromatic leaves brought the night before.

Various explanations are given of the fire. This is said to be a symbol showing the destruction of the unclean and the purification of the clean, or it may represent the fire from which God spoke to Moses. It is also explained as a commemoration of the shepherds' fire, or the star of the Nativity. The incense offered is said to commemorate the gifts of the Magi. On festival days the hymn after the Gospel, in this case the *Gloria*, celebrates the event of the day, and the last part of the liturgy and the seraphic hymn also refer to the events commemorated.

The feast of the Epiphany is celebrated on 6 *Makaram* (the Malayāḷam month) and is marked by the blessing of water, commemorating the baptism of Christ. When morning prayers are finished the ministers put on their albs and the priest his cope. Then he takes an earthen or metal vessel of water, places on it a cross and covers it with a cross-embroidered veil. The Gospels, the cross, the censer, state umbrellas, candles and all other apparatus of a procession are taken up and all go out through the north door and proceed round the church to the south door, singing as they go, the priest going first and carrying the water in its vessel. They enter the church and the water is placed on the table inside the rail with lighted candles on either side. The people sing:

> The glorious voice of John at the river Jordan proclaimed aloud: Behold the Lamb of God. He who begot him is well pleased in him. The Holy Spirit was seen coming upon him in the form of a dove. O all ye languages of peoples near and far, praise him, thank him, honour him and laud him for ever.

They also sing other chants describing the baptism of Christ.

The proper service takes about an hour to perform; after preliminary prayers and chants explaining the importance of Christ's baptism in Jordan, it proceeds to the *Magnificat*, with praise of the Blessed Virgin and recollection of John the Baptist's part in the events of the day. A feature of these Syrian prayers is the way in which the Bible record is expanded in the interests of doctrinal exposition as:

> O God without beginning and without end, thou didst raise from destruction the old man hidden with thee in the water. By thy voice incomprehensible to man thou didst grant him renewal. The Father proclaimed: 'This is my beloved Son; He is one with me in essence and equal with me in divinity.'

The *prūmion* which follows with its *sēdra* is concerned with praising the Creator for his power and work, with an emphasis on the place of water in God's purpose, and the new birth through baptism. A *kukkoyo* is then sung. In it, as in many other places in this service, illustrations of God's use and blessing of water are drawn from the Old Testament:

> King David stood near the river until the woman with the marriage lock [of hair] had finished bathing and come up out of the water. Then he took his *vīna*[1] and began to play and sing, O holy Church, who hast been blessed with prosperity, go forth, leave thy people and thy father's house so that the king may see and desire thy beauty. Behold thou art become the Queen. Hallelujah.

We are told that when Christ descended into the waters of Jordan they became hot, though there was neither fire nor fuel, and John, acting as the blessed *ācārya* (bishop), laid his hands on his head, while the Holy Spirit as a dove hovered over the water. There are references in other prayers to Mara, to Elijah's purifying of the water in Jericho with salt (*sic*), to Cana, to Noah, to the crossing of the Red Sea, and to the water which Elijah poured over his sacrifice on Carmel. Whenever water is mentioned in the Bible it is taken here as a type of baptism.

Then incense is offered and a *summōrō* introduces the readings.[2] These are followed by Hallelujahs and the Gospel.[3] The Gospel is followed by a long litany led by the senior deacon facing west, the people responding with Kyries to each petition. Then another *prūmion* and a long *sēdra*. The first part recalls God's use of water and goes on to pray for heavenly power to be added to the water which is now to be blessed. Incense is again put on, the Creed is recited and the priest, raising his hands as at the *kurbāna*, prays that

[1] Indian musical instrument.

[2] Num. xx. 1–11; II Kings ii. 19–25; Isa. xii. 1–6; Acts viii. 35–40; Heb. x. 15–25.

[3] John iv. 4–42.

the Holy Spirit be sent upon the water. Then he takes the veil from the vessel of water and waves it, while the deacon calls everyone to reverent attention, the people replying 'This water is mercy and peace and blessing'. The priest puts the cross laid upon the vessel to one side, and then blesses the people in the name of the Trinity. Another prayer of blessing is said, referring to Christ's baptism in Jordan, where he bruised the serpent's head, and including the petition: 'Fill this water with divine power that it may bring healing to the sick, help to the weak and a defence against the spiritual enemy.'

Then the priest waves his right hand over the cup and blesses the water three times, saying: 'This water is blessed in the name of the Eternal, Father, Son and Holy Spirit.'

There follows an act of adoration for the water. The priest replaces the cross on the mouth of the vessel and turns east, saying:

Thou who art served by angels,
O God, thou art holy.
Praised be the glory of the Lord for ever from his place to whom the cherubims sing.
O God, thou art holy.
Holy, holy, holy art thou O Lord, to whom the seraphim cry aloud.
O immortal one, thou art holy.
We sinners pray to thee with penitence.
O thou who wast baptized for us, bless us.
(*Then he turns west*)
Thou who art praised by the fiery ones,
O God, thou art holy.
Thou by whom spirits are strengthened,
O God, thou art holy.
Thou who art adored by the sons of earth,
O immortal one, thou art holy.
The children of holy Church pray to thee,
O thou who wast baptized for us, bless us.
(*He turns north*)
Thou who art praised by those above,
O God, thou art holy.
Thou who art praised by those in the middle world,
O God, thou art holy.
Thou who art extolled by those below,
O immortal one, thou art holy.

We sinners pray to thee with penitence,
O thou who wast baptized for us, bless us.
(*He turns south*)
Our Lord, bless us.
Our Lord, graciously bless us.
Our Lord, receive our worship and prayers and have mercy on us.
Praise be to thee, O Lord.
Praise be to thee, O Creator.
O Lord the king, who has mercy on his sinful servants,
Praise be to thee. *Barekmore.*
Our Father....

Then the priest goes to the font and sprinkles it in the form of a cross with the blessed water, east to west, north to south. After another short prayer the priest proceeds with the *kurbāna*. When it is over, all drink of the blessed water before going home. Thereafter it is kept in the Easter Sepulchre behind the throne and used for the sick, or those in other kinds of trouble.

The first day of the great Lent is Monday, and a special service is appointed for use after the noon prayers have been said. The purpose is to ask God's forgiveness for sin and to ask for grace to keep a holy Lent. As a preliminary all the people in the parish are called to forgive one another any wrongs committed in the past year, and it is the priest's duty to go specially to ask forgiveness of any parishioners whom he knows he has offended. The service is called *śubkkōnō*. Most of the prayers and chants praise God's love and the reconciliation He has accomplished in Christ, and pray that we may forgive one another and be forgiven, and all be reconciled with each other.

The first part of the *sēdra* gives an idea of the tone of the whole service:

O Lord the Messiah, who art the eternal reconciliation of all creatures and the true peace of all the quarters and districts of the earth, thou art love. Thou art called love. Thou dost rejoice in the name love more than in all other names. Because of this thou art known as the lover of men. Thou dost honour those who have received love. For love's sake thou didst become for us an acceptable sacrifice and a holy saviour. On thy cross thou didst break down the might of the enemy. Thou hast reconciled in thine own blood all that is in heaven and earth. Through the union of thy Godhead which cannot be changed, which is thine own self-existence, thou didst make the two one. Through thy manhood which was for a time thou didst call and bring in those who were far off and those who were nigh. In the unity of thy holy love and by receiving them into thy kingdom without beginning or end thou hast bound them together. Thou didst preach peace and reconciliation to the world. Through the peace greeting of the archangel thou didst make thy Virgin Mother to understand thy birth. In peace thy mother met Elizabeth the mother of the preacher, John. She, joyful at thy greeting, bowed down with joy in thy holy presence like a servant before his master. On the day of thy birth the angels caused the shepherds to know thy peace.

So this prayer continues, with many Biblical references to peace and to reconciliation.[1] The 'reconciling incense' is offered and prayers lead to the reading. More songs, and prayers by the priest, lead to a prayer of blessing:

O God, give answer to me. Give answer to me and bless me. Do thou turn men's hearts to repentance.

A short sermon is preached about love and forgiveness (the only time a sermon is ordered in the Jacobite liturgy, as far as I know); then the priest kneels before the other priests and people and says:

My brethren and dearly beloved, I have sinned against you. As a pastor put in an honourable place, I yet bid you forgive me, out of your affection and oneness of spirit and filial love. I bow down before you.

After this the other priests and the people bow themselves down before him and say: 'Bless us with forgiveness.' Then the priest says:

I beg and beseech your true love, my beloved brethren, come forward. In order that God may reconcile us to himself let us be reconciled one with another. (*Bowing, he continues*) I bow for the honour of the most holy Trinity.

Again all bow and say: Bless us with forgiveness. With a repentant heart and integrity of conscience I beseech your love and with a loud voice cry aloud and say: Beloved brethren, come, if you

[1] I John iv. 11–21; I Cor. xiii. 4–10; Matt. xviii. 19–35.

forgive one another, your sins and trespasses also will be forgiven; each one of us must forgive the sins and faults which we have committed one against another, if we are to be reconciled to God. (*Bowing*) May the Lord God forgive and do away with your sins and mine.

After a prayer, the Creed and various songs are recited, and all prostrate themselves forty times. Incense is then again offered and a prayer of intercession said, after which the priests, standing in order of seniority, give each other the Peace. The deacons and people then kiss the priests' hands and give the Peace to each other. Women kiss the priests' hands and then give the Peace among themselves. As all give this outward sign of reconciliation they are expected and instructed to forgive each other from the heart. Then all join together in the Our Father, and leave the church.

On the Wednesday which marks mid Lent, the *kurbāna* is always said; but after the praise of the Virgin it is interrupted by a ceremony of elevation of the altar cross, which is intended to bring to mind the words of Christ, when he used the brazen serpent lifted up in the wilderness as a type of his own saving power, shown forth on the cross. At the night office the cross had been placed on a *golgotha*, or special stand for the cross and two candles, placed in the middle of the nave. Now it is removed, and taken, with the book of the gospels and the customary umbrellas, candles, flags and so forth, out of the north door of the church in procession to the south door. After the procession is over the proper office of the day is said, during which the cross is lifted up towards the four quarters of the earth, and solemnly waved up and down, with prayer, and the people's Kyries in response. After this ceremony the cross is replaced on the *golgotha* and the *kurbāna* continues. At the end all kiss the cross before they leave the church.

The special feature of Hosanna Sunday (Palm Sunday) is the blessing of palm leaves (which are, however, called 'olive branches' throughout the Malayāḷam translation of this rite). The special service starts with a procession round the church, which halts halfway down the nave on its return, for the proper service of the day. There is nothing remarkable about the structure of the first part of the service; the prayers and chants naturally refer to the events of Palm Sunday, and ask that God who accepted the praises of his children will enable this congregation also to offer acceptable worship. Jerusalem is apostrophized, and bidden to glorify the Lord. The *sēdra* contains an interesting metaphor to make plain the Church's real position before God. As Christ chose a despised ass to carry him, so also he chose us from the outcasts (that is, the Gentiles), and rescued us from the deceptions of the devil. Some of the Biblical illustrations are traditional rather than literal, as is usual in these services.[1] The *kukkoyo* starts thus:

> The old man said to the children: Pick up stones and go out to oppose the man who comes to enter Jerusalem. They took stones and went out to meet him. But when they saw him come on the Mount of Olives they threw away the stones which were in their hands, took branches of the olive trees, and welcomed him as the King of Israel, and shouted aloud: O God, blessed be thy coming.

The *etro* prays that by the incense our prayers may be fully answered, and that all the faithful may be kept in God's mercy and all the departed cleansed from sin and stain. The Hallelujahs, between the lections and the Gospel,[2] proclaim of the Church: 'I am like a glorious olive tree in the house of the Lord.'

After the litany the priest waves his hands over the branches to be blessed and prays that the trees from which they are taken and those who carry them may also be blessed. Then there is a salutation and a reverent inclination, with a special prayer. This is followed by a longer prayer of blessing, during which the branches are 'sealed' many times. This prayer is fairly general in character:

> Bless us all, our paddy fields, our vegetable gardens and such like, and these branches. Make them a blessing to the districts of the parish, a guard to the households, an obstacle to Satan and a remover of temptation. Make them to avert wars, do away with all evils, and banish anxieties.

After the long prayer is ended he waves his right hand over the branches and says:

> These branches are blessed for eternal life in the name of the Father and of the Son and of the Holy Ghost.

[1] Gen. xlix. 8–12; Zech. ix. 9–12; Isa. li. 9–11; I John ii. 7–15; Rom. xi. 13–24.
[2] Mark xi. 1–18.

The people take the blessed branches away to their houses, and any remaining are carefully kept in the church until the next Christmas morning, when they are burned in the holy fire of that day.

There is a special procession on the Monday of Holy Week, with the people carrying candles and chanting Ps. cxvii. They go out of the south door as usual, but stop at the west door, which has been shut. Special prayers are said and the Gospel[1] is read, and then the priest opens the door saying an *ekba*, and concludes the special office of the day.

On Maundy Thursday the *kurbāna* must be celebrated and it is customary to make one's communion on that day. In churches where a bishop is present the special office of the day, including a feet-washing ceremony, is used.

A special form of worship for Good Friday is held at the end of the nine o'clock or noon office. It is a very solemn occasion and for it the church is always packed with worshippers. The priest and his deacons wearing black cassocks go to the chancel and take the cross from the altar. Preceded by bell and incense the priest carries the cross slowly and mournfully out of the south door of the church. The procession then goes towards the west showing the cross to the people as it goes, and entering the church again by the north door. Then the Gospel is read and the cross is placed on the *golgotha* in the middle of the church with a candle placed on either side. When the cross is placed in this position and shown to the people all join in lamenting Christ's suffering. The cross is later taken from the stand and placed on a table fittingly arranged. The service of the veneration of the cross then commences. Many of the prayers are in litany form and during the whole of this service the people prostrate themselves from time to time, going down on both knees at once and touching the floor with the forehead and the palms of the hands. There seems to be no particular number of prostrations prescribed; some people are performing them the whole time of the service, and the packed church with about half the congregation prostrate before the cross at any given moment is a very impressive sight. A number of readings give the

[1] Matt. xxv. 1–3.

history of Christ's sufferings and their Biblical interpretation.[1] These readings are commonly chanted from the body of the church by deacons and others, except for those from the Gospels. After the readings a sermon is preached. Incense is then offered before the cross and the people say: 'Hail, O Cross, saving our souls. We say to thee what the thief said, "O Lord when thou comest to thy kingdom remember me".' Then the priest holds the cross and turns, from north to south, then east to west, and then to the north and south again, finally turning east and carrying the cross to the chancel. There is a strong element of drama at this point of the service. For the story is recited of Joseph and Nicodemus asking for Christ's body to bury it. Then someone brings a vessel of aloes and bitter water in which rice has been boiled, and the priest puts the extremities of the cross into this bitter water. Then, in memory of the way Joseph and Nicodemus bathed the Lord's body, he washes the cross by pouring rose-water or ordinary water from a vessel over it, taking care to catch all the water that falls in a dish set underneath. Then the cross is carefully wrapped up in a special white cloth, and another cloth is wrapped round it, representing the napkin tied around Christ's head. A girdle is tied round the shaft of the cross, and it is then buried in a special place 'under' the altar, in the recess at the back of the throne. The Jacobites celebrate the *kurbāna* on Holy Saturday but not on the altar under which the cross is buried. The cross is placed in the recess with the 'head' to the south and the foot to the north, and the 'face' turned east. The right side must be placed towards the ground and supported in that position so that the wound in the side is hidden. After the burial of the cross the bitter water is drunk by the faithful as a means of receiving blessing from Christ's death and burial. The service finishes with *prūmion* and *sēdra* describing the benefits brought to men through burial and resurrection and with Mar Jacob's prayer which speaks of all the different classes of people in hell coming to Christ as he visits them for their salvation. It finishes: 'O Jews, behold your house is left unto you desolate. You have nothing left, no king, no leader and no vision for your life.' Before the people go home to break their fast the angelic song, the *kauma* and the Creed are recited near the 'tomb'.

[1] Gen. xxii. 1–14; Exod. xvii. 8–16; Isa. lii. 13–liii. 8; I Pet. ii. 19–25; Gal. ii. 21–3, 24; Luke xxii. 63–xxiii. 12; Matt. xxvii. 3–10, 19; Luke xxiii. 13–23; Matt. xxvii. 24–5; Luke xxiii. 24–44; Matt. xxvii. 51–4; John xix. 23–42; Matt. xxvii. 60.

The mournful service of Good Friday is followed by the joyful celebration of Christ's resurrection on Easter Day. At the end of the night prayers the senior priest dressed in his vestments and accompanied by the other priests and deacons goes to the tomb at the back of the altar and amidst the smoke of incense takes out the cross, removes the grave clothes and places round the arms a small red stole fastened by a red girdle round the stem of the cross. The stole must be red in colour, in reference to Isa. lxiii. 1, which is regarded as a prophecy of the triumphant risen Messiah. The cross is then brought and set before the altar with lights and 'angels' on each side. While this is done, a triumphant song of praise celebrates Christ's victory over his enemies. In the prayers the joy of the Church is several times contrasted with the discomfiture of her enemies at Christ's resurrection. In the intercession which follows the praise, the *sēdra*, and the *prūmion*, there are references to the peace which is given when we receive Christ's risen power. 'Sow, we beseech thee, thy reconciling power within our churches and thy peace in our monasteries. Abolish from our midst quarrels and destructive anger. Help us to give the Peace to one another with holy embracing. May we be children of peace and lovers of reconciliation.'

Half way through the service a procession is formed. A three-horned mitre is sometimes put on by the officiant with his vestments and the cross is lifted up as he walks, accompanied by the other priests, out of the west door and round the church in procession, with deacons swinging censers and the whole congregation following with lighted candles. As they go they sing a song addressed to Mary Magdalene, reminding her of her encounter with the Lord in the garden and of his words to her. At intervals the priest calls out 'Kyrie', the last syllable long drawn out, and the people at once respond 'Ele-eison'. This procession takes place at about four in the morning and in country parts there is deep silence, broken only by the shouts of praise, and the whitewashed church shines white against the heavy plumes of coconut palms outlined against the sky round the churchyard wall. The candle flames and heavy scent of incense in the air add to the solemn and deep appeal of the ceremony. Then the cross is carried into church again and placed on the step of the throne and there are readings from Lev. xxiii. 26–32; Micah vii. 8–13; Isa. lvii. 19–21, lx. 17–22; I Peter v. 5–14; and Rom. xvi. After this the congregation breaks into a response typical of this day: 'Hallelujah, Hallelujah, the heavens rejoice and the earth exults at the resurrection of our King the Messiah.' The Gospel is then read, John xiii. 34–5, xiv. 27, xv. 11–15, 17–19. The Gospel is followed by an act of praise called the 'celebration' of the cross. It starts with the *Gloria*, and then the priest goes on: 'O Lord who by thy brutal death effected that reconciliation which has reconciled those above and by thy sacrifice that peace which has joined together those below, thou by thy cross hast become the saviour of the Gentiles and by thy resurrection hast shed abroad the love which has gathered in those who were scattered abroad; on this thy day of resurrection forgive the foolish rebellion of earth and by thy cross keep us from all oppression. Make us now and at all times and for ever to praise thee and thy Father and thy Holy Spirit.' This prayer of the priest is followed by a response of the people ending in a threefold *Kyrie*.

There are four such sets of prayer and praise in this worship of the cross. The angelic praises are sung and the priest blesses the people with the cross in his hands. Then going to the sanctuary he gives the kiss of peace to the table of life, to the cross, to the Gospel book, to the holy tomb, and to the relics of the saints. Then a hymn is sung during which the people give each other the kiss of peace with mutual forgiveness. They sing: 'Peace to the sanctuary and the cross, peace to the holy tomb, peace to the Gospel, to the communion of saints, to the priests and deacons and all members of the Church. Our Saviour and Lord Jesus Messiah, may thy reconciliation and peace dwell with us and in our midst; make us to embrace one another with a holy kiss, and may peace reign in the four corners of the earth until the end of all things.' (Two stanzas of the hymn are quoted.) When all the clergy have given the Peace to each other they go to the west door with the cross, the gospels and the relics of the saints. The people file out and the clergy standing at the door touch them on the forehead with the various holy things mentioned. While they go the deacons sing a song reciting the various events of Easter Day and the reactions of the disciples to the news of their risen Master.

Pentecost is marked by three services said in the middle of the *kurbāna*, after the praise of Mary (*basmalka*). A cup of water is placed on the step below the throne, and in it a sprig of hyssop. The three services are almost identical in form; at their end the priest sprinkles both the altar and the people, using each time a different cup of water.

The form of the services is briefly this. Prayers of preparation are said by the priest, including in the first service Ps. li with a litany to Christ, and in the third the *Magnificat* with praise of the Blessed Virgin and prayer that she will send the Holy Spirit through her Son.[1] In the first two services the preparation is followed by chants of praise which celebrate the work of the Spirit, and *prūmion* and *sēdra*, addressed in the first service to the Holy Trinity, extremely theological in its expression, in the second to Christ and in the third to the Spirit. After the *sēdra* each service has another statement about the Spirit and his work, drawn from Scripture. Then incense is put on with an *etro*, to the Spirit in the first and third services, to Christ in the second, and a brief act of praise. In each service, lections follow from the Old and New Testaments, then a threefold Hallelujah and the Gospel.[2]

The services all finish in the same way. The deacon says a litany, the people responding to each suffrage with the *Kyrie*. Then the whole congregation falls on its knees and cries aloud 'Kyrie eleison' continually, while the priest says a secret prayer asking for the Spirit, or addressed to him. At the end of the prayer the priest calls them to rise in God's strength. He sprinkles both the table of life and the congregation with water and declares once more the mystery of redemption, as follows:

> Our Lord the Messiah suffered in the flesh, for our sakes, that passion which was according to God's will. He rose from the dead with glory and made us to rise with him. But we are perishing in sin and dwell in the midst of death. He has shattered and utterly removed from us the rule and authority of the devil. (First service.)
>
> This is the reason why we do not kneel on the ground to pray until the day of Pentecost. We sing with David, the divine singer

[1] 'A maiden given immaculate conception by God received her innocency from him. Through the Son who sits at his Father's right hand may she who delivered him without pain that he might bring new life to our earthly race [lit. that he might become the medicine of new life to our earthly family], send and give to us the grace of the Holy Ghost the Comforter.'

[2] In the first service: Gen. xi. 1–9; Judg. xiii. 24, xiv. 7; Acts xix. 1–6; I Cor. xiv. 20–5; John xiv. 1–17. In the second service: II Kings ii. 14–17; Joel ii. 25–32; Acts xix. 8–12; I Cor. xiv. 26–33; John iv. 13–24. In the third service: Num. xi. 16–35; I Sam. x. 10–13; Acts ii. 1–21; I Cor. xii. 1–25; John xiv. 25–7, xv. 26–xvi. 15.

and prophet against our enemies. They are bowed down and fallen, but we are risen and stand upright; but when the Holy Spirit rose upon us and manifested himself with tongues of flame we were not able to bear the sight, therefore we kneel and recognize that God is worthy to receive all glory. (Second service.)

The descriptions of the Spirit's work which form the substance of the praises and prayers of these services are almost all drawn from the Scriptures. There are several references to the deliverance of the Church from idolatry: 'We had to worship a lifeless image made of gold, with songs and music. But now the grace of the Paraclete Spirit inspires us to praise and worship the One in Three.' (First service.) This note recurs.

The *prūmion* and *sēdra* in the first service contain a theological description of the Trinity, as in the third they describe the Spirit and his work. 'He is God the Comforter who purifies the churches and perfects all godly worship. He bestows offices of leadership [lit. the bishop's place, *ācārya sthanam*], he makes baptism effective and sanctifies the sacraments. He does away with sins. He searches the deep things, he speaks secret things, he makes known things which are to come, he works wonders.' The Holy Spirit is 'he who is taken'; he does not take anything for his perfection, for 'he is perfect, he is not to be perfected'. So the *sēdra* starts; it goes on to give a long theological description. At the end he is addressed as 'Thou who hast been taken from the holy Son'.

CHAPTER X

THE OCCASIONAL OFFICES

The Baptismal Service

THE baptismal office has a very simple structure, though the ceremonies used are many and complicated.[1] The first part of the service may perhaps be called a general preparation, containing prayer for the candidates and the reading of the Scripture. Then there is a more immediate preparation, including the exorcism, the baptismal promises and the blessing of the font. The third part of the service contains the actual baptism and the anointing and crowning of the newly baptized in joyful recognition of his place in God's Kingdom.

The parents bring the child outside the rail, near the font, which is usually on the south side, inside the sanctuary but below the altar steps. The godmother holds the baby during the service, which starts with a prayer, for the salvation of those who come to the washing of regeneration, and a hymn (a different one being used according to the sex of the candidate). The priest continues:

Glory be to the Father and the Son and the Holy Ghost.

Let us hearken to what David says as he stands here in spirit by those who have come to receive baptism: O all ye that thirst, come to God the Lord. Be strengthened and put on strength. Wretched Adam when he had fallen called sadly upon the Lord God and he answered him. When he came to the waters of the river Jordan God renewed him who before had fallen into destruction.

All. As it was in the beginning....

May the seal of grace be a protection to us who believe. As by the blood sprinkled on the door-posts the Hebrews were saved from the destroyer, by the grace of this living and divine washing of renewal may we who take refuge in it be saved. So by this unquenchable light within us shall we behold the Trinity.

The prayers and verses which follow all teach the new birth of

[1] The service is printed in Malayāḷam in *Kūdāśakramangaḷum Anīdāyum* (The Sacraments and Observance of the Syrian Christians), translated from Syriac by Fr Punūs; and in English in Hough, IV, appendix, pp. 645–50.

man through water and the Holy Spirit, associated together in holy baptism. The *etro* follows a *prūmion* and *sēdra*, and with it incense is offered before the reading of Scripture.

> O Lord we offer to thee this incense for the abundance of thy mercy that this thy servant who is prepared for holy baptism may be sealed by thee to everlasting life, may become an heir of thy house, and may keep thy holy commandments. And thee shall we praise with....

The Epistle is Rom. v. 20–vi. 7. The Hallelujah rejoices in the cleansing God gives, and leads to the Gospel, Luke iii. 15–16 and John iii. 5.

After this general preparation, in which the purpose and meaning of baptism has been declared, part of Ps. li, the *Kyrie* and the priest's secret prayer for the enlightenment and purification of the candidate lead to the entering of his name and the names of his sponsors in the baptismal register. Then the priest prays in a manner which clearly points to the time when the candidates were usually adult converts from heathenism.

> Do thou give to him that holy breath which thine only Son breathed upon his holy disciples. Do thou prepare him to receive thy holy spirit and banish from his mind all vestiges of idol worship.

He breathes on the faces of the candidates in the form of the cross, praying that they may be made worthy of the new birth and of remission of sins. Then the priest signs their foreheads without oil three times, sealing them in the name of the Trinity. The outer garment of the candidates is removed and their faces are turned to the east, while the deacon calls 'Kyrie eleison' and the priest inclines his head and prays secretly that God will enable the soul who comes to him to renounce all evil spirits and that he will confirm his own promise of life to the candidates. Then he stands face to face with them, and prays aloud a prayer of exorcism, commanding all evil spirits to depart and affirming union with God. During this prayer the candidate is 'sealed' nine times. Then the candidate turns to the west, and the priest moves round to face him while the sponsor takes his left hand in his own and says this vow on his behalf:

> I who receive baptism renounce thee, Satan, and all thy angels and all fear of thee and of thy deceits.

The candidate turns east and the priest again goes to face him, while the sponsor ('mediator') takes the candidate's right hand in his own and says in his name:

> I who receive baptism believe in thee, O Lord Christ, and in all the holy teaching which has been delivered by thee through the prophets, apostles and holy fathers.

Then all join in the Creed.

The service has been conducted up to this point at the entrance to the space below the sanctuary steps. Now the priest goes to the font and prepares to bless the water. The child's clothes are removed and the priest prays secretly that the candidates may be accepted and planted in holy Church. Then he dips his forefinger in the holy oil and signs the child saying:

> This child is sealed with the oil of gladness for eternal life, that he may be worthy of the adoption of sonship through being born again, in the holy name of the Father and of the Son and of the Holy Spirit.

Then the priest prepares the font. He takes a vessel of warm water in his right hand and one of cold in his left, and crossing his right hand over his left pours the water into the font and prays that God through the Holy Spirit will mix the water that it may become a spiritual womb and a furnace to burn off the doors of mortality. Then he covers the font with a cloth while the congregation sing of the mystery of baptism and describe baptism and the holy Church as sisters, one bringing forth and the other bringing up children; presenting them to the Lord as spiritual offspring. It is a joyful song, punctuated by Hallelujahs. The song continues as the priest removes the cover from the font, praying secretly for the Spirit to descend on the water. Then he blows three times upon the water in the form of a cross, from west to east, and from south to north, praying secretly:

> O Lord, may the head of the great serpent which kills the children of men be bruised under the sign of thy cross. May the formless ones who because of him cannot appear but belong to the firmament flee away. We pray thee, O Lord, that the spirit of darkness may not be able to hide in this water and may not be able to enter into him who received baptism, in anger and evil thoughts. May no evil influence have power over him.

He passes to a colloquy of praise with the congregation and then the deacon calls them to attention at this awful hour when the Spirit descends. The priest bows his head and secretly prays for the descent of the Spirit, waving his hand over the water.

Priest. O Almighty Father God, have mercy upon us. From thy dwelling place on high and from thy presence in every place send thy Holy Spirit upon us and upon this water which is purified. He who is a person (*knūma*), he who is pre-eminent, he who is Lord and life-giver, he who spoke through the law and the prophets, and the apostles, who is present in all places, who fills all space, who perfects holiness in those who obey thy perfect will, not as a servant but as a lord, pure in nature, working in many ways, the spring of spiritual gifts, in essence like to thee, proceeding from thee, taken from thy Son; he is co-heir with thee and with our Lord and God and Saviour Jesus Christ, thine only Son, of thy kingly throne.

Raising his voice he three times asks the Lord to grant answer to him, and the people respond with a threefold Kyrie.

O Almighty Lord God, make this water to be water of comfort, water of joy and gladness, water which sets before us the death and resurrection of thy only Son, water of purification.

Make it to be cleansing from impurity of flesh or spirit, release from all bondage, forgiveness of sins, and light of souls and bodies. Make this to be baptism of a fresh birth, the adoption of sonship, the garment of incorruption, the renewing of thy Holy Spirit.

He then takes the vessel of consecrated oil (*mūron*) *in his hand and lifts it up three times in the form of a cross.*

O God, the waters saw thee;
O Lord, the waters saw thee, and were afraid.

Deacon. Hallelujah.

Priest. The voice of the Lord is upon the water,
The glorious God thundered,
The Lord sits upon the great waters.

Deacon. Hallelujah.

Priest. Glory be to the Father and the Son and the Holy Spirit.

All. As it was in the beginning. . . .

Then the priest pours mūron *into the font in the form of a cross saying*: We pour this holy oil into this water of baptism that the

old man may be renewed into a new man, in the name....
Amen. Hallelujah.

Deacon. Kyrie eleison.

Then again the priest prays secretly for the candidates, and blesses the water in the name of the Trinity. He places the child in the font facing east and puts his right hand on the child's head. With his left hand he takes water first from the front of the child, then the back, then the right side and then the left and pours it over his head, saying:

> With the hope of life and for the forgiveness of sins, receive thou baptism for eternal life in the name of the Father, for eternal life in the name of the Son, for eternal life in the name of the Holy Spirit.

The child is then taken from the font and handed to the sponsor, while the deacon chants a song. One verse of this song which magnifies the Church as the king's daughter is very pleasant. The deacon sings:

> O new lamb born from water in the name of the Trinity, born from the font of baptism, we greet thee. As Gideon chose his men at the river, so our Lord chose his in the water of baptism.

The priest then anoints the child three times on the forehead in the form of a cross, as a sealing in the name of the Trinity.

Then he anoints the child's entire body, from top to toe, giving meanwhile an exhortation about the Christian life reminiscent of the bishop's final charge in the 1928 revision of the English Confirmation Service. As he anoints the child, he first declares: 'N. is sealed with holy *mūron*, the fragrant scent of the Messiah, as a seal and sign of true faith, and for the fullness of the gift of the Holy Spirit in the name....'

The child is then taken to the sanctuary and a crown placed on its head. This is, in practice, a woollen bonnet. The priest carries a boy three times round the altar, as a sign of joy, but a girl is crowned at the gate of the sanctuary. There is a special hymn sung at the crowning. The child is sent away with a blessing, and the crown ought to be worn for seven days afterwards, and taken off with a special prayer.

The Wedding Service

On their wedding morning a bride and bridegroom are expected to attend the *kurbāna*, although on this occasion they do not meet or stand near each other. Later in the day, at the time of the actual wedding, the small table is placed in the northern part of the *katastroma* and priests who have come to assist gather round it wearing their ordinary clothes, except for the celebrant who puts on his vestments. The couple stand side by side in front of the table, the bride at the right side of the bridegroom with her attendant on her right. (This attendant is a woman member of her own family until after the blessing of the ring, when she is replaced by a woman member of the bridegroom's family.) The best man stands just behind the bridegroom on his left. The wedding service lasts about an hour and consists of two parts, the blessing of the rings and the blessing of the crowns. In both parts most of the ordinary prayer forms of the Church find a place. Both start with a *kauma*, and there are *prūmions* and *etros* with incense in each part. Many hymns are sung in Syriac, most of which praise Christ as the heavenly bridegroom and extol the beauty of his bride the Church. The prayers are related to the same theme and references to the couple being married are made in this context.

The blessing of the ring starts with an ascription of glory to God and prayer for God's blessing. Then Ps. li is said and prayers and three hymns lead to *prūmion* and *sēdra*. Part of the hymn that follows will show the general line of thought and its insistence on the sacredness of the mystery:

When the heavenly bridegroom was betrothed to the faithful Holy Church,
He called Simon and he called John, and entrusted her and gave her to them both,
He appointed Simon as the head of the house, and John as the preacher;
He called and commanded them to guard with great care the Church which he had bought with his precious blood;
The faithful Church shouts aloud, 'My Lord, My God, has prepared a feast for me;
The fat bullock that has been sacrificed for me cannot be approached by a stranger;

For thus hath he commanded and thus hath he spoken to me';
Everyone who comes to thee apart from me who begat thee with water,
Thou shouldst not allow him to learn the mysteries which are kept sacred among the faithful.
Glory be to the Father, and to the Son and to the Holy Spirit.
Tamar was victorious by means of the ring, the staff, and the veil,
David was victorious over the Philistine by means of the bag, the sling, and the stone;
By three things Tamar was exalted, and by three things David became great;
The holy faithful Church sings glory and praise to the Trinity who has saved her.

The priest then prays for the betrothed couple and blesses two rings. He places the first on the third finger of the groom's right hand and the other on the corresponding finger of the bride with appropriate blessings. That said to the bride is as follows:

> May the right hand of our Lord Jesus Christ which is full of blessing be stretched out in secret upon thee. Receive thou this ring of thy betrothal from the hands of the holy priests as if from the hands of the holy apostles. In health of soul and body, and with heart-felt joy, mayest thou offer up praise to him and to his Father and to his Holy Spirit now and for evermore.

Another prayer is followed by a most beautiful hymn glorifying the Church:

I am the Church, I am the Church and the Bride of the Most High,
Blessed am I, whom he has betrothed to himself;
I worship that Bridegroom who came down and betrothed himself to me.
In the day when I was betrothed by him all creation was amazed at me,
Who was poor and who suddenly became rich.
Blessed am I because I have been exalted.
He prepared for me a bridal chamber on high that I might rejoice with my friends;
I entered in and sat down. Blessed am I who have confessed him.
He took me away from the midst of idols
And showed me hidden mysteries,

And promised that he would abide with me,
Till the end of the world.
The King's Son gave me all the gifts
Which he brought from the Father's Home;
Therefore I worship him.
Woe unto the evil one who deceived me
Through the worshipping of idols,
And shot his arrows against me.
Thanks be to Jesus who saved me.
Blessed am I, for I have been made worthy.
He clothed me with the armour of the Spirit,
Through the water of baptism,
And he placed on my finger as a ring,
His holy body and blood.
The Bridegroom is like unto the sun,
And the Bride is like unto the daylight,
And the feast is like unto a tree putting forth sweet fragrance.
I heard the fame of his good news;
I fell in love with him;
Just before I saw him, I confessed him.
I went round by sea and land;
None could tell me where he was;
I searched for him in Bethlehem;
They said to me, 'He has departed to Egypt'.
I rejoiced and started out for Egypt following him;
When I reached there, they told me,
'He has departed to Nazareth of Galilee'.
I followed him along the way to Nazareth,
When I reached there, they told me,
'He has departed into the river Jordan'.
Without being afraid or being terrified of the robbers on the way,
I went after him to Jordan and searched for him among the multitudes,
I slumbered a little, poor I was, weary and sleepy,
When I arose, they told me, 'The Bridegroom has invited thee to the bridal chamber'.
I resolved to go and see my Lord at that feast;
When I entered, they gave me to drink the excellent wine which he had changed from water;
The Bridegroom and all his attendants answered and said unto me,

'O holy woman, whom art thou seeking?
Thy Lover departed to the wilderness'.
The sweet odour of his love blew towards me;
He made my face to shine and I rejoiced,
And followed after him to the wilderness,
I searched for him among the multitudes.
I heard the sweet voice of one speaking from the crowd,
'The Lover of this holy woman has been crucified on the Tree on Golgotha'.
I wept bitterly and followed him to Zion;
When I entered the city they told me,
'The Jews have placed him in a sepulchre'.
I wept bitterly leaning my head against the Tree;
An angel answered me and said, 'Weep not! He is risen from the tomb'.
I heard his voice and rejoiced;
My face shone and I was full of joy,
I held him and embraced him,
He answered me lovingly and said:
'Peace be unto thee, O worthy woman,
Who hast been betrothed to me on the Cross,
I ascend to the Father and I send to thee the Holy Spirit'.

The blessing of the crown follows exactly the same plan as the first part of the service. There is some doubt whether actual crowns were used in Malabar.[1] Now a gold chain with a cross is used instead, held out in the priest's fingers in the form of a crown. One of the hymns praises the beauty of Christ's Church as she sings glory to God holding in her hands the harp of David, the harp of 150 strings, that God may shower his mercies on all the world, like a bird singing glory to the most high God in the early morning. There is in some of these hymns a most apparent love of nature which is not a characteristic of the people of Malabar. In this service Epistle and Gospel are read, the Epistle being Eph. v. 20–6, 31; and the Gospel Matt. xix. 1–12; both are introduced in the usual way, including the *Benedictus qui venit* before the Gospel. Then the priest blesses the gold chains and cross, the cloth to be given to the

[1] Fr Placid says that the bridegrooms used to wear a gold crown called *venthamudi* (king's crown) and that the custom goes back to the tradition of the golden crown presented by Cerumān Perumāḷ to Thomas of Cana as a reward for bringing back the king's offended artisans from Ceylon.

bride, and the *minnu*. Taking the chain he raises it three times above the bridegroom's head, waving it round as the crown and singing a blessing. Finally he places the 'crown' on the bridegroom's neck. Then he acts in a similar manner for the bride. A distinctively Indian feature now follows, and this is still, for most of the Syrian Christians, the decisive moment of the wedding. The priest places the thread with the *minnu* round the bride's neck and the bridegroom standing behind her ties it in a knot. The cloth which is his present to the bride, woven with a gold thread in the case of a rich family, is then thrown over the bride's head. There are no special prayers for this part of the ceremony except that the priests say:

> The cross is the sign of peace
> And the cross is the standard of victory:
> We are saved through the cross;
> In it we all glory.

The service finishes with a prayer and a hymn and an exhortation during which the priest joins the hands of the couple together and says: 'Behold from this time forward, we entrust you each to the other, God be the witness between me and you, that if ye break any of the laws of God, I am guiltless.' Then the Lord's Prayer is said, the register is signed, and the people leave for the feast in the bridegroom's house.

Thanksgiving after Child-birth

The primary purpose of this service is the purification of the woman from the defilement of child-birth and much of it takes place outside the church proper, in the porch. For forty days after the birth of her child the woman has rested in the house,[1] but now she comes to church with two candles as an offering.

The first prayer throws light on the meaning and purpose of the service, which is for God's acceptance of the child as well as for the purification of the mother.

> Our Lord God, born from God of Mary, who, after forty days were accomplished, for the fulfilling of the law, brought thee her son to the temple. At that time Simeon the priest took thee up

[1] The custom of staying in the house during menses was formerly universal. It has now changed, and the Catholicos has ruled that there is no sin, as was previously held, in receiving Holy Communion during this time. The Hindus formerly (still in country districts) observed pollution rules with great strictness.

in his arms and said 'O Lord, receive this child which we have at this time brought before thee'. O Creator of all, do thou bless this child and bring him up in all virtue of character according to thy holy will. With the sign of the cross put to flight from this child all the host of the enemy, because thou, O Lord, art the guardian of thy children. Give to this infant through holy baptism an inheritance in thy kingdom with thy saints and thy elect. By the grace of the holy Trinity, one in essence, and without change, may he be saved.

The *prūmion* which follows speaks of 'this time of the purification of God's handmaid' and the *sēdra* 'Cleanse her from all sins. Purify her from all uncleanness. She has come to thy holy house to be made fit to receive thy holy sacraments without sin.'

Incense is offered, and at the end of the *etro* the woman is made to enter the church and taken in front of the altar, at the entrance to the *katastroma*. The book of the Gospels is placed on her head and after Hallelujahs, Luke ii. 22–37 is read. A song (a prayer, of Mar Ephraim) and a long prayer of blessing complete the service.

Service of Anointing

The service starts with the reading of James v, as a warrant, and then a *kauma* is said and a prayer for the sick. Part of Ps. vi is followed by a *prūmion* and *sēdra* which plead for the remission of the sick man's sins. In the course of the hymn which follows the following stanza is sung, comparing the oil of the woman of Magdala with the oil of anointing:

> Give oil to me. Do thou receive gold as its price. Do thou give to me oil better than hers, mingled with my tears, to anoint the first-born. I take refuge in God. The voice of a woman who was a sinner as she spoke to the seller of spices was heard, saying, 'By this oil which I receive from thee my trespasses and sins will be forgiven'. When she took oil our Lord saw her faith and forgave her sins.

The prayer of incense prays for the healing and cleansing of the sick person. Then there are readings[1] and, after Hallelujahs and Psalm, the Gospel.[2]

[1] James v. 13–16; Rom. xiii. 11–14. [2] Matt. x. 5–10.

The hymn which follows praises the medicine bought without price which is freely given by the great Physician, and prays that he will give medicine to strengthen the soul of the sick man. Then the priest prays directly for the patient's healing, lays his hands on his head and prays again for healing and strength.

After this the sick man himself says a prayer of confession and then the priest anoints his forehead, breast, and knees with olive oil, saying:

> Mayest thou be cleansed and sanctified. May the sins and trespasses which you have committed willingly or unwillingly, knowingly or unknowingly, be forgiven. May all evil thoughts and all works of the devil be far from thee. May this be for eternal life in the name of the Father (*Amen*), and of the Son (*Amen*), and of the Holy Ghost (*Amen*).

Next, both eyes are anointed and signed, the right eye twice, the left once.

> By his mercy and by this fragrant oil may all sins which you have committed through your eyes be forgiven, for eternal life in the name. . . .

Similarly the ears, nose, lips, are to be anointed twice, the tongue, hands and navel once.

The service finishes with praise of the Virgin and the saints, with petition for their prayers, a *hūtōma* and the seven penitential Psalms.

Burial Service

The funeral service of a dead Syrian is long and is made up of four services, said one after the other. Some or all of the first three may be said in the house, where the corpse remains until the time of the funeral, laid upon a bed and wrapped in new cloth, with a cross at the head and candles burning all round. Under the bed there is usually a small bowl of charcoal on which incense is thrown from time to time, to sweeten the atmosphere. The body is brought to church in a coffin either on a litter or in a hearse, with the face exposed, accompanied by the men of the family and friends of the dead person. Formerly relatives would take no part in handling the coffin, but now it is considered an honour to undertake this duty. At least the last of the four services is said in church. There are different offices for a man, a woman and a child, and there are seven services for the burial of a priest or a bishop, of which five are obligatory.

The first three services are made up of chants based on Scripture describing Christ's victory over death, and prayers for the departed. Frequent references are made to the Eucharist which has been received as food for the journey and which gives entrance into heaven. In the same way baptism is mentioned as the means by which we have been made partakers of Christ's death and therefore also of his resurrection, in which we have put on the new man which will not see corruption. I think there is no reference anywhere to the personal faith of the departed; it is enough that he has been sacramentally incorporated into the believing Church. The ministry of angels in helping the passage of the spirit to a happier land is also mentioned many times. In the course of these prayers the dead person is apostrophized, and bidden to depart without fear, for the Lord will make him dwell in the land of light, and the cherubim will guide him thither. In one or two prayers the soul of the departed addresses his body. In all three services there is an *etro* in which petition is made that by the incense there may be remission of sins, acceptance by God of the dead man, and that the offering may be received on his behalf. The fourth service follows the general lines of the first three, but there are lections from the Bible,[1] and, after the prayer with Hallelujahs, a Gospel is read.[2] This is followed by a litany said by the deacon, the people responding with Kyries.

A hymn follows sending the departed away in peace. It begins thus:

My dear ones, why do you stand far off?
Come near me and give me peace and pray for me, and lament for me with sighing.
For behold, today has death struck me down and made me fall at the gate of hell.
When the angel of death came after me I looked everywhere, but I found no one to help me....

After this prayer the priest pours oil on the corpse and prays:

O Lord God, who by his holy commandment and according to his royal pleasure has taken away his servant from this passing life, do thou send from thy presence ministering angels to his

[1] Deut. xxxii. 48–52; xxxiv. 1–6; II Pet. iii. 8–13; I Cor. xv. 34–53.
[2] John v. 19–29.

help. Through this oil which is poured on his body give him grace, that he may not be taken by the hostile armies which lie in wait in the heavenly sphere to attack the souls of men, or by the host of the enemy, and may be freed from all error. Bring him to the dwelling of light and to bliss with the saints. May he with joy and gladness give thanks and praise to thee and to thy Father and to thy Holy Spirit, now and for ever.

Then the priest makes the sign of the cross with oil on the face, breast and knees of the dead man and says:

This oil is poured out for everlasting life, with rest from toil, peace from warfare and joy with the saints, in the name of the Father (*Amen*), in the name of the Son (*Amen*), and in the name of the living Holy Spirit (*Amen*).

Then the coffin is taken from the church to the cemetery, and songs are sung while it is lowered into the grave. The priest takes earth into his hand and lets it fall on the coffin in the form of a cross, saying:

Our Lord, who didst say, thou art earth, to earth shalt thou return and again shall be renewed, behold thy holy will is accomplished.

The grave is then filled with earth, while the mourners stand around and chant more songs. A prayer is said:

Our Lord who didst come and save us and wilt come to raise us, make me go out of the prison house that I may praise thy holy name. O our Lord and our refuge for ever, to thee be praise. *Barekmore*.

More hymns and chants follow, a *kauma*, and the Creed, and the service finishes with a long prayer.

When a bishop dies, his body is dressed in full episcopal robes and seated in a chair, with his pastoral staff tied in his left hand and his small hand-cross in the right. Candles and crosses are arranged round the body and the faithful come to say farewell to their bishop, kneeling to kiss the cross he is holding. From the time of death until the funeral service priests must be in the room with the body, chanting hymns and prayers and reading from the Scriptures. At the time of the funeral the body is carried in procession in the chair to the church, with robed priests holding a canopy over it and many crosses and state umbrellas, and incense. The service at the church is long and complicated. A most moving moment is when the dead bishop, through the lips of the officiant, is made to take leave of his flock and commend them to God. The body is lifted high, to the east and west and north and south, so that all his flock may be blessed, and before it is buried, all the priests present come to kiss the bishop's hand. The body is buried still seated in the chair, and the grave is filled with incense before being sealed up. Formerly bishops were buried within the churches, but this practice is less common than it was. The local explanation of the sitting posture is that Hindu *sannyasis* also are buried in that way. In the popular mind there is no doubt that the bishop's unmarried state invests him with a sanctity greater than that of his married clergy, and the head-dress he wears, as a mark of the order of St Anthony, is said to mark him as a *sannyasi*.

Other Occasional Offices

The other occasional offices provided in the book ordinarily used are the blessing of a house, confession, and an office for the consecration of sacred vessels and ornaments.

Great importance is attached to the laying of the foundation stone of a house, and its dedication when completed. Usually, following the Hindu custom, the housewife boils milk on the fire as the first dish to be prepared in the new house, and there is a house-warming feast.

Ordination Service

All bishops in the Syrian Church have a sacramentary, or book containing those offices which must be conducted by a bishop. They are in Syriac and I think no Malayāḷam version exists.[1] An important part of this book is the *hamalogion*, or confession of faith, which is read and publicly accepted by the candidates at the time of ordination. They are further required to seal their acceptance by making the sign of the cross, in ink, in the book.

Ordinations are given on days when the *kurbāna* is celebrated.

[1] I had the privilege of seeing the sacramentary of the locally canonized bishop, Mar Gregorios. An English translation of ordination services is given in Hough, IV, appendix, pp. 650–72. The *hamalogion* is taken from the same source, and has been checked with an independent translation from another sacramentary. Both ordination services and *hamalogion*, as given in the text, contain references to the Patriarch which are now omitted by the Orthodox section.

Readers are ordained by the bishop, signing their foreheads three times with the cross, and pronouncing them ordained to be readers of the word of everlasting life in the holy Church, 'in the name...', and by prayer. Exorcists are appointed by the bishop's order, not by the laying-on of hands. Singers and subdeacons are ordained by prayer. In all these services the archdeacon has a part to play, for he stands on the chancel step, holding the bishop's staff, and bids prayer for those to be ordained. In the case of subdeacons, they prostrate themselves, and after this prayer the bishop places the stole round their necks and raises them up, making them stand on the steps of the sanctuary while he stands in front and prays for them. Then he signs each candidate three times in the name of the Trinity to be a subdeacon (or singer) in the holy Church. He delivers a book of the Epistles to the subdeacon, giving him authority to read them in the church. Singers are given the book of Psalms.

The structure of the ordinal is the same for deacons and priests, but the content of the prayers is different, reflecting the differences of status and function between the two orders. Both orders are given after the celebration of the holy *kurbāna* before the post-communion. If deacons are to be ordained priests they stand in a row across the steps at the entrance to the sanctuary during the celebration. At the end they kneel on both knees, as a sign that they have received the two talents of purifier and enlightener. The stole on one shoulder is said to show that they have traded faithfully with the one talent they received as deacons. Those who are to be ordained deacons kneel down on the right knee, in token that they are purifiers. The bishop starts the ordination service with the *Gloria* and prayer for the candidates. Then follows a chant based on Ps. xv but expanding it and changing quickly into an act of pure praise, the people responding with fourfold Hallelujahs. The content of this chant is slightly different in each service. Then the bishop again prays for the candidates: if deacons, he prays for the coming of the anointing Spirit upon them; if priests, he prays an expanded version of Ps. li, ending up in both cases in the same way:

> It is an infinite wonder that God should be held with pure hands, and come down to bestow gifts on the bishop, as on Aaron. Glory and praise be unto the name of the only true God and Holy Trinity, the Father, the Son and the Holy Ghost.
>
> As it was....

> O ye children, glorify with reverence him who is over all, and whom the angelic hosts continually serve. Ye priests praise him at all times; and ye Gentiles give thanks unto him, and bless his name for ever.

The bishop continues his prayer, that the candidates may receive God's gifts, deacons to praise God with angelic songs, and priests to minister to God's holy name with fear. The *prūmion* and *sēdra* are both concerned with petition that the candidates may be empowered from on high for their ministry.

The lections are introduced by a chant which praises God for the establishment of a ministry in the Church. That used at priests' ordinations finishes thus:

> O priests, who have received this high and priestly office of binding and loosing according to the command of the Creator of all creatures, be mindful of what you have obtained. Behold the keys of heaven and hell are placed between your brethren. Blessed will ye be if ye perform the will of your Lord and Master, that ye may enter with him into the bride-chamber.

Then the *etro* is said, and incense is put on, with joyful singing from the congregation. The lections over,[1] Ps. cl is sung in an expanded form:

Praise the Lord in his holiness: praise him in the firmament of his power.

May the Holy One who dwelt on Mount Sinai, and sanctified it, descend upon his servants, and sanctify them.

Praise him for his mighty acts: praise him according to his excellent greatness.

The Most High descended on Mount Sinai, and laid his hands upon Moses: Moses laid his upon Aaron: and thus it was carried on till John.

Praise him with the sound of the trumpet.

May the Holy Spirit, which spake by the prophets, and abode on the Apostles, come and abide upon these thy servants, and sanctify them.

[1] At a deacon's ordination: Acts ii. 16–21, 38, 39; x. 34, 35, 44–6; I Tim. iii. 8–15; iv. 6–10; Ps. xxvi. 8, 11; John xii. 24–6, 35–6; xiii. 31, 34, 35; Luke xi. 13; John xx. 19–23. At a priest's ordination: I Pet. ii. 1–10; I Tim. iii. 1–7; Tit. i. 9; ii. 1–4; I Tim. iv. 14–16; John xiv. 15–20; xx. 19–23.

Praise him with the psaltery and harp.
May the Holy Spirit, who rested upon the Apostles in the upper room, come and rest upon these thy servants, and sanctify them.
Praise him with the timbrel and dance.
O thou Holy Spirit, who didst commit unto the Apostles power in heaven and earth, cause thy tranquillity and peace to dwell in the four quarters of the world.
Praise him upon the loud cymbals.
May the Holy Spirit, who endued the Apostles with wisdom to understand all languages, come and rest upon these thy servants, and make them wise, and sanctify them.
Praise him with a loud voice.
May the right hand which was stretched out upon the Apostles, and blessed them, come and rest upon thy servants, and bless and sanctify them.
Glory be to the Father, and to the Son, and to the Holy Ghost.
Glory be to the Holy Father, who sent his Holy Son, and sanctifies the saints by the Holy Spirit.
As it was in the beginning, is now, and ever shall be, world without end.
May the Holy Spirit, who descended in the form of a dove, and rested upon the head of the Son, come and rest upon thy servants, and sanctify them.

Then the Creed is sung. The bishop then prays secretly as he proceeds to the act of ordination. The archdeacon goes to the south side of the sanctuary, and standing upon the step, with the bishop's crozier in his hand, faces north and says:

May the grace of our Lord Jesus Christ, which always supplies what is wanting, with the good pleasure of God, and the power of the Holy Spirit, be on these who are here present, and with fear, trembling and true faith, stand before the altar bowing their heads, and inwardly looking unto thee who dwellest on high, and waiting for thy heavenly goodness.

Bishop. Which calls some of the assembly of the brethren to the office of deacon.

Archdeacon. *N*. is ordained deacon for the holy and divine altar in the church of... (*he names the saint of the church*) and of Mary the Mother of God, and the twelve Apostles, and the forty victorious martyrs, at such a place under the jurisdiction of the apostolical seat of Antioch in Syria which loves Christ and is loved by him.

The archdeacon then bids prayer:

...for those who are here present, that the grace and influence of the Holy Spirit may rest upon them, from this time and for evermore, and that all may say with a loud voice, Lord, have mercy upon us: Lord, have mercy upon us: Lord, have mercy upon us.

The bishop again prays for the candidates, and all the priests present join in, saying:

O our Saviour, may the Holy Spirit come and rest upon each of them according to thy promise. O Lord, deprive them not of the gift of the Holy Spirit. We beg this of thee who hearest prayers. We also pray to the Holy Spirit, saying, thou art holy, O Spirit the comforter. Thou art holy, O Spirit the author of everlasting life. Thou art holy, O Spirit whom we have obtained. Glory be unto thee, O Lord of all, for the gift of the Holy Spirit, and for thy great and unspeakable mystery, and thy wonderful works to our race.

A preliminary blessing of the candidates follows, which seeks to impart the holiness of the altar and the sacrament lying on it to them. The bishop lays his hands twice on the host, and appears to take his hands full and put the contents into the cup, then he places his hand on the cup and appears to take its spiritual content and place it on the host. Then he turns, with his hands full from the host, but covered with the corner of his cope held over them by a priest, and blesses the candidate, lifting his hands as high as possible, while his cope covers the candidate's head. Then the bishop brings his hands down and waves them over the head of the candidate, passing them down his face, shoulders and arms, as low as his arms can reach. Then he covers the candidate again with his cope, and lays his right hand on his head, while he moves his left backwards and forwards over his shoulders, and earnestly prays secretly for the candidate. When he first raises his hand to bless, a deacon removes the veil from the bishop's head, and others hold the 'angels' over his head during the whole ceremony. The bishop prays aloud and then turns to the candidate, lays his right hand on his head, and says:

Bishop. Thou art ordained in the holy Church of God.
Archdeacon. *N*. as deacon [*or* priest] to the holy and divine altar at the church dedicated to Mary the Mother of God, the twelve holy Apostles, and the forty victorious martyrs and to... (*patron saint*).
Bishop. As a deacon [*or* priest] to the holy altar of the holy Church erected at the place of the orthodox persons named above.
Archdeacon. *Barekmore*.

The bishop then seals (signs) the newly ordained man three times on the forehead in the name of the Trinity for everlasting life.

After this the bishop prays for God's blessing on the person he has ordained and, taking him by the right hand, raises him from his knees. Then he waves the vestments (the alb, stole and cap) three times over the sacrament, and then over the head of the deacon in the form of a cross. Then he is vested, and given incense to offer in the censer. The bishop gives him the Gospel and says:

> Receive power to read the Gospel in the house of God for the quick and the dead, in the name....

Then they kiss the altar and the bishop's hand and are given the Peace by all the priests present, who join in a chant of joy.

The ordination of priests differs only in the last ceremonies. The vesting comes first and the bishop gives him the sacred vessels with the host, and wine in the chalice saying:

> Receive power to offer oblations unto God, and to perform Christian sacrifice for the quick and the dead, in the name....

Then he lays his hand on his head and breathes on him in the form of a cross, saying:

> Receive the Holy Ghost. Whosesoever sins thou remittest, they are remitted unto him. Whosesoever sins thou retainest, they are retained.

He repeats these words three times; the third time he takes the censer and waves it three times over the sacrament and over the head of the new priest and delivers him incense to offer. Then, as with the deacons, the priest receives the Cross, Gospels, purse and seals. All the priests present, with the bishop, give them the kiss of peace. As the people go out at the end of the service they kiss the hands of the newly ordained priests.

The *hamalogion*, or statement of faith, accepted and sealed by the candidates for priests' orders before the service:

Brethren in Christ, beloved in the right faith, spiritual children and members on God's right hand, know this: you are now desirous to take upon you the ministry of the high God, and an office which cannot be estimated nor compared. When you receive this great, invaluable, and incomparable gift at my hands, who am myself weak, and feeble, and unworthy of such a high office, you must take heed to the quickening mysteries of Christ.

Now, first of all I make known to you, my sons, how you ought to accept this very high office, and conduct yourselves without offence and without blame, agreeable to the vocation to which you are called, and as becomes those who receive the mysteries of our Lord Jesus Christ. It becomes you, my sons, first of all to keep, without any mixture of error, the true faith, which is, to believe in the Father, and the Son, and the Holy Spirit, three persons and one God, according as our Lord Jesus Christ, in his holy Gospel, has commanded his pure disciples, and as they, by the holy Apostles, delivered to the holy Church, and according as all the fathers and orthodox teachers, unitedly appointed, preached and taught. This, your faith, must be in your mouths and words, and heart, in public and private. Ye must acknowledge and confess aloud that onc of the persons of the Trinity, the eternal Word of God the Father, descended from heaven, of his own will and that of his Father and of the Holy Spirit; that he abode in the Virgin Mary the Mother of God; that of his love to mankind he took a body from her; that he sat on his throne at the time he abode in the womb of the Virgin; and that he is perfect God and perfect man, for whose mercies be glory.

Again, you must acknowledge and believe the right faith. You must adhere to St Peter the chief of the Apostles, and his companions, the seventy-two preachers, the fire-like Mar Ignatios, Julios, Dionysios, Athanasios, Basilios, Gregorios, Dioscoros, and Severios, called the key of the mouth of the fathers and teachers. You must submit to Mar Ignatios, Patriarch, our present ruler and father, and to me also, who though weak, walk in their paths. Ye must abjure the heathen, astrologers, Jews, Nestorios and his company, Leo, the synod of Chalcedon, Paul of Samosata, Yehebah of Uraha, Bardaisan, Julian the Apostate, Barsolee of Nicebene, Arios, Eunomios, Eutyces, Marcion, and all those who adhere to their doctrine, and every heretical departure from the true faith. Ye must abjure all whom we abjure. You must renounce all whom we renounce.

The candidates shall answer: We do abjure and renounce.

Bishop. You must receive all whom we receive.

Answer. We receive all whom you receive.

Bishop. You must believe as we believe, and confess what we confess.

Answer. We believe and confess.

Then the bishop commands them, saying: Now I exhort you, my sons, not to be slothful nor weary, but to be diligent in the divine service of the High God, as is meet, and to keep your souls from concupiscence, drunkenness, adultery, uncleanness, lasciviousness, idolatry, witchcraft, hatred, variance, emulation, wrath, malice, strifes, seditions, schisms, envy, murder, covetousness, perdition, and from all such things. The blessed Paul has said: Of which I now tell you plainly, as I have also told you in time past, that they who do such things shall not inherit the kingdom of God. These are the things which keep men from the door of God.

As the Apostle Paul has said, a priest of God should be faultless, not contentious nor passionate, but blameless, vigilant, sober, of good behaviour, given to hospitality, apt to teach, not given to wine, and whose hand is not quick to strike. Again, he must be meek, not covetous, one who ruleth well his own house, having his children in subjection with all gravity (for if a man know not how to rule well his own house how shall he be able to govern the Church of God?); not a novice in doctrine, lest, being lifted up with pride, he fall into the condemnation of the devil. Moreover, he must have a good report of them who are without, lest he fall into reproach and the snare of the devil. He must not open his mouth to reviling, cursing, and swearing, nor cherish in his mind revenge to his adversaries. He must refrain himself from usury and gain, which consume worldly possession; for these things are abominable in the sight of the high God. Be ye diligent in fasting, in prayer, in supplication, and intercession without ceasing before our Lord Jesus Christ, for yourselves and all the people connected with you. Ye must be kind to strangers and the needy; and live in unity, love, peace, long-suffering, gentleness, goodness, faith, meekness, and patience toward all men; for these are the fruits of the Spirit, that you may be worthy to minister before God, that you may obtain comfort to your souls, and that you may stand with boldness before our Lord Jesus Christ at his second coming to judge both the quick and the dead. I shall be free from your offences. Let us unitedly ascribe glory to the Father, and to the Son, and to the Holy Spirit, for ever.

Here the bishop commands the candidate to make the sign of the cross, thus ✠, and says, Now my sons, mark on this paper the sign of the cross, as a witness to yourselves before God and his Angels, and before the throne of the Lord, and these elders now present, that I and you may stand with boldness before the throne of our Lord Christ at his second coming. You must keep inviolate the faith which I have delivered to you, and not alter any of the things which I have commanded you. If you do alter my commands, and disobey my word, let God judge between me and you in the day of judgment. For I being the intercessor, by his command do now stand and lift up my hands toward heaven, that the Holy Spirit may descend upon you. I now admit you to this high and important office, to be obedient to God in all humility. Be not proud, nor rebellious, lest God be in any way angry with you. Behold, now we stand before God and his Angels, before the martyrs, saints, and this present congregation. Let these be a witness unto you, that you will not alter any of these things which I have delivered to you: if you should alter them, ye will be deprived of and dismissed from the office entrusted to you, and removed from this excellent gift which you have received. Should you oppose me, a poor weak person, or any of the metropolitans, my brethren, ye shall be excommunicated, removed, and rejected from the holy Church, and deprived of these mysteries which I have entrusted to you: and everyone who shall assist you in wickedness, subtlety and fraud, shall, in like manner, be excommunicated, etc. Moreover, the most high God also will be witness to you, that you will keep the regulations of the Apostles and true faith delivered to you.

Be it known unto you, that the sign of the exalted Cross will prove a witness between me and you, that ye shall be deprived of the free gift which I have bestowed on you, on the day in which you resist my weakness, and transgress my orders.

I now supplicate and pray to our Lord Jesus Christ to deliver me and you from all deceit and sins, and to make you worthy to stand before him with joy, having improved the talent entrusted to you this day, through the prayers of the Virgin Mary, the Mother of the Light, St John the Apostle, all the prophets, apostles, preachers, martyrs, saints, and confessors.

Here the bishop will clip the candidate's hair of the head in the form of a cross, behind and before, on the right side and left, in order, saying, Now, my sons, first of all I exhort you, that when you enter the house of God ye do so with fear and trembling as becomes you, not with pride, passion, envy, deceit, enmity and reproach. Take care that ye provoke not God to wrath, but rather enter the house of God with cleanliness, purity, humility, purity of mind and heart, and peace, having the head uncovered, and having on a scarf, as it becometh the priests and ministers of God. Do not admit any unlawful thing with you into the chancel, nor eat anything in it but the holy mysteries. Avoid pride, drunkenness, and every thing which is unbecoming the priests of God. Do not appoint or inflict fines upon any of the believers through ignorance; but pass judgment without respect of persons. Make use of such bread as is proper, and mix wine and water in the cup as is meet. Perform the service of the Lord with fear and trembling. Do not leave here and there the linen, towels, covering cloths, or any of the ornaments belonging to the altar table; for to do so shows carelessness in this service. You must know that Christ is always watching over you, to accuse or reward you as you deserve. You must also know that no one has authority to leave the altar at which he is accustomed to minister, and go to minister at another altar, without the permission of the bishop of the place. When you shake the vessels of the altar, you must take care that none of the consecrated crumbs fall on them or on to the ground. Beware of the blessing in your mind. If you do not perform all according as I have commanded you, you yourselves will have to give account before our Lord Christ. I am innocent of your transgressions. If you keep my words, I shall acknowledge you as the ministers of God.

Let us now pray to our God to deliver you from deceit and contention, to cause you to walk righteously in his sight with humility and purity, to make you worthy to present to him on the great day of account, with boldness, with joy, and with much profit, the talent entrusted to you, and to deliver you from all offences, through the prayers of the Virgin Mary, the Mother of the true Light, and our Mother, all the prophets, apostles, martyrs, and saints. Amen.

O believers, let us now beseech our Lord and Creator Jesus Christ to make these priests and ministers newly ordained for you this day worthy to be blessed for you, and that through their prayers he may shower his blessings and goodness upon you; bring you joyful seasons and fruitful years, and grant you abundant gifts; that he may bless you with his right hand full of imperishable blessings, defend you from all anxiety, deliver you from all afflictions, and make you worthy to perform good works; that we may all arrive at that good end promised to all the saints and holy men who do his will; that he may grant you his grace to be dutiful and obedient, bestow his grace upon you, shower down his mercies upon you all, and put away from you contentions, and the hosts of the cursed enemy; that he may protect your children, and raise up from among them sincere, righteous, and holy ministers and priests; that he may deliver you from temptations, comfort and bless your dead, and make them stand at his right hand with the martyrs and saints; that he may put you in possession of the delights of paradise, cause you to hear the joyful words, Come, ye blessed of my Father, inherit the kingdom prepared for you from before the foundation of the world, through the prayers of the Mother of God, the prophets, apostles, martyrs and saints. Amen.

Other Features of the Religious Life of the Syrians

In the long ages when the life of the St Thomas Christians centred in the parish church, festivals were eagerly looked forward to, and celebrated with enthusiasm and an almost reckless disregard of expense, remarkable in a community marked, on the whole, by industry and thrift. The special observances of the great festivals are dealt with elsewhere; we have here to consider dedication feasts of local churches, and the like, which were socio-religious occasions. Many churches before Diamper were dedicated to the legendary bishops, Mar Sapor and Mar Aproth, who were believed to have come with the second influx of Syrians to Quilon in the ninth century. After Diamper most were rededicated to the Blessed Virgin, but the bishops are still venerated at Quilon, Kāyamkuḷam, Ankamāli, Akaparāmpu and Paṛavūr.

The festival day starts, according to the usual Syrian reckoning, the previous evening, when people come to church and, after prayers, go in procession round the church with silver crosses, lights, processional umbrellas and other insignia of royalty and a band, the progress marked by loud reports of 'bombs', charges exploded to show joy rather than to scare any lurking devils. The procession goes to the churchyard cross and there incense and prayers are offered. The procession returns to the church for more prayers, and afterwards the priests and senior men of the congregation have a feast. The following morning the *kurbāna* is celebrated by a packed congregation and a sermon preached on the life of the saint. Then all place offerings, which go to church funds, in a vessel standing in the church in front of a cross; and rice *kanji* is given to everyone. In the evening another procession is held.

These festivals are very colourful affairs, for almost all the paraphernalia of Hinduism is used in the procession, apart of course from the actual idols.[1] Many Syrian churches have a flagstaff outside the west end, as do Hindu temples, and the festival begins with the hoisting of the church flag, usually a red pennant marked with a white Greek cross. The worshippers often present certain kinds of cakes or sweetmeats to the church, some of which are given back to the givers, and devoutly eaten, like *prasādam* in temples. In certain churches, like Kōtamamgalam, Paṛavūr and others which keep a yearly festival in honour of the bishop buried there, or Pālayūr, with its St Thomas associations, the chief festival is a very big affair, attended by Hindus as well as Christians, an occasion for members of the community from different places to meet each other, and to buy articles they need from the temporary shops and stalls erected, which lend something of the atmosphere of an English fair to the occasion.

Rather similar occasions are commemorations of departed members of the congregation or thanksgiving for some special benefit, at which the family concerned gives a *nercca* or vow,

[1] The following are some of the articles used: two kinds of royal state umbrellas, drums, Tamil music, the iron tubes for explosion of gunpowder, metal torches carried on a stick, ceremonial flywhisks, and a round fan carried usually on an elephant.

usually taking the form of a feast for all who care to come.[1] A great feast of this description is held annually at the end of the three days' fast before Christmas at Piṟavom and the immense flight of steps leading down to the church on the east side is completely covered with feathers by the time all the fowls destined for curry have been plucked. At this festival, however, all the worshippers bring their own food, which they cook in the church compound.

These vow feasts are not celebrated today on the same scale as they used to be, because of the wide scatter of many Syrian families and the increasing adoption of Western culture. A rich man would engage three priests to concelebrate the *kurbāna*, with a hired band in attendance. Afterwards the priests would be escorted back to the house under a canopy and a great feast would be served with quantities of meat and fish, the dishes being given in a special order. Sometimes toddy was served at the end of these feasts and by some was drunk to excess.[2] After the feasting the priests rose and sang prayers in Syriac and Malayāḷam, assisted by their *kappiars* with censers. Priests and *kappiars* were paid fees for coming, and these fees formed an important part of their income.

An even more expensive and elaborate vow was called the 'feet-washing' from the similar ceremony performed by bishops on Maundy Thursday. The offerer would give new clothes to all the priests taking part on the Friday evening. On Saturday morning he arranged that nine bearded old men should have an oil bath, and afterwards bathe. Then he gave them a new set of clothes and sent them to church, where they assisted at the *kurbāna*. After the service the priests and old men returned to the house, and at the gate very carefully washed their feet from two great water pots set there for this purpose. Then they walked on strips of cloth laid down as a path to a *pandal* erected in the yard and sat on benches. The offerer, usually the head of the house, then came with a brass vessel of water and a large flat dish, and standing in front of the priests and old men poured water over their feet, catching it as it ran off in the flat dish, and drying their feet with the cloth tied round his waist. One of the priests poured the water from the dish

[1] L. Duchesne, *Christian Worship*, p. 49. There is a theory that these are essentially Nestorian observances in origin.

[2] Patriarch Peter in his Bull of 1877 strongly condemned holding *nerccas* in churches and profaning Sundays with processions like the Hindus, with bands and groups of dancing, leaping youths. He excommunicated all who took part. But his influence was not strong enough to stop the custom.

into a bottle, without losing a drop, and gave it to the offerer. It was considered of very great importance that no one should touch the water between its collection and its bottling by the priest, for its efficacy and purity would thus be lost. The Syrians believed that this was no ordinary water, but had divine power in it; they used it to relieve the mother at child-birth and would rub diseased limbs with it. After this a special feast was given to the priests and old men (twelve in all) who stood in the place of the Apostles for the fulfilment of the vow, and afterwards twelve children were fed.

Vows nowadays are generally in the form of the promise of a gift to the church if the desired boon is granted.

We read of these vows being celebrated in Portuguese times, and one account speaks of a river pilgrimage to the site of St Thomas's landing on 21 November from the church at Paṛavūr, and then of the return to Paṛavūr and the feast eaten in the churchyard.[1]

Fasting had an importance in life greater even than that of feasting. Gouvea in one place contrasts the seriousness of the Syrian Christians, and their rigidity in fasting, with the laxity of many European Christians. It is true that recent years have seen this custom, as almost all others, relaxed; but in country places the fasts are still kept by all, and they are everywhere rigidly kept by the clergy. The ordinary fasts are the great fast of fifty days before Easter, the fast of twenty-five days before Christmas, the fifteen days' fast in honour of the Virgin, the twelve days' fast in honour of the Apostles, eight days before the Nativity of the Virgin (8 September), and the three days' fast of Jonah.[2] All other Wednesdays and Fridays are officially fast days. During the fast no animal products were taken (even milk and eggs being excluded) and no toddy drunk. Chewing betel was also forbidden, and in the old days only one meal would be taken, after sunset. From noon on Maundy Thursday until Holy Saturday adults used to fast completely and spend the time in silence. The rigour of these observances can be judged by the fact that formerly on the day before Lent everything in the house was cleaned and the floors newly plastered with cow dung; all the metal vessels were discarded and new ones bought, so that no trace of any animal food was left in the house.

A special ceremony connected with the great fast was held in

[1] Fr Correa Amander, S.J., writing from Cochin, 20 January 1564; quoted in Fr Placid's MS. History.

[2] Codrington, *Syrian Liturgies*, p. 47.

the middle of it, on the Wednesday; there was also one on the fortieth day and, most particularly, one on Maundy Thursday. On these days a special bread was made, not leavened by toddy (the usual yeast substitute) but made with black gram, and in the middle of the loaf a cross was made of palm leaf. A special drink was also prepared of coconut milk, molasses and plantain, which represented the wine of the Last Supper. As far as possible the whole family was expected to come together for this special meal, including married daughters living away from home with their husbands. In each house, after supper, the head of the family would take cakes of the bread, divide each into thirteen pieces and give a piece, and a little of the drink, to each member of the household. This was considered a means of blessing, and a kind of re-enactment, in each family, of the Last Supper. Newly married girls would usually return to their father's house, in readiness for this ceremony, just before Hosanna Sunday, for which also a special sweetmeat was prepared, balls of rice with coconut and sugar inside.

Apart from these set fasts old people often fasted for their spiritual good; and sometimes women would fast for a year, taking no food before mid-afternoon, to atone for a death caused by drink or some crime, or to correct some evil tendency they thought they saw in their children.

The fast before receiving Communion is strict, and priests commonly used not to speak to non-Christians before the *kurbāna* on a day when they were celebrating, and would even avoid travelling in vehicles driven by non-Christians.

There were many penances of various kinds offered to show penitence or to avert some evil, besides fasting. These included fines, which had to be paid to the church, or such exercises as walking round the church on one's knees on Good Friday. I do not know whether the excessive devotion shown by those who rolled round the Kōtamamgalam church at its festival and aroused the comment of the more conservative Protestant writers like Whitehouse, originated in penance or out of religious fervour. The bitter drink on Good Friday in church is said by Fr Placid to be of the nature of a penance.

The Portuguese remarked the absence of images in the Syrian churches and their great reverence towards the Cross. This is reflected also in the *Thoma Parvam* song of the seventeenth century with its recurring story of St Thomas erecting crosses in the places where he preached the Gospel, before buildings could be put up. (This reflects a common state of things today: someone erects a cross, as a votive offering, and after some time a thatched shelter is put up in front of it, then replaced by walls and a roof and soon a small chapel is to be seen there.) Most churches have a large granite cross standing near them, at the west or the east ends, either in the churchyard or else by the roadside, marking the site of the church. A box for alms is often placed in front of these crosses, and sometimes the base or pedestal on which they stand is beautifully carved, as at Ceṅannūr, and studded with many small lamps, either of stone or metal. They are supplied with oil and wicks and lit on festivals. Many of these crosses are most beautiful in design, and have the form commonly found in Kēraḷa, with the titulus bar.

Syrian houses are often marked with the cross, and so are certain possessions, like bullock carts. The cross is greatly venerated inside the church, and this probably is a tradition going back to Nestorian times. The altar cross is the principal ornament of the church, and represents the presence of Christ.[1] The Portuguese found many stone crosses in the churches, of which some survive. The placing of the cross on the *thronos* is a culminating ceremony in the dedication of churches.

The sign of the cross is constantly used by Syrians, in public worship and in private prayers. Every priest uses a small hand-cross with a silk handkerchief or *sudarion* tied to a ring at the end of the handle, to bless the people, signing the congregation with it or giving it to priests to kiss. When bishops and priests die, a wooden replica of this blessing cross is always placed in the folded hands.

A local parallel is to be found in the Hindu custom, practised until a generation ago, of signing with a cross the palm of the hand of the man to whom one was talking, to asseverate a statement. At morning worship the Hindus sign themselves with the swastika.

In ordinary illness recourse was had to the ordinary *vaidyan*, or physician using the Ayurvedic system of medicine, but hysteria and

[1] Gouvea mentions that the Syrians did not approve of image worship but that pictures of saints over the altar had been introduced through Portuguese influence in churches near the factories.

fits and madness were attributed to the influence of evil spirits. It was noted that some fits occurred always on Wednesdays and Fridays. The best way to treat these was to burn the palm cross made in the church on Hosanna Sunday, and drink the ashes mingled with water. To prevent further attacks a prayer book was placed under the patient's pillow. If the symptoms recurred the priest was called to exorcize the spirits. This he did by placing a Gospel book on the patient's head, opening it and reading a portion. Then he signed the patient with the cross on the forehead, and all present recited the Creed, after which he ordered the devil to go out. If this treatment proved ineffective he would write the word 'faith' in Syriac, burn the paper and give the patient the ashes to drink in water, and he might write out the Lord's Prayer and tie it on his arm as an amulet, inserting it in a little gold or silver cylinder or locket. This custom was noted by the early Jesuit missionaries, and has persisted until recent times.[1]

The Bible was not available in the language of the people, and although the Church authorities at first co-operated with Church Missionary Society missionaries in preparing a Malayāḷam translation of the Gospels, conservative opinion was for a long time against the Bible being read in houses where there were women and children. The custom of saying the whole *kurbāna* service in Malayāḷam, except for Syriac hymns and the *Gloria*, is increasing, but even where much is read in Syriac the lections are always translated into Malayāḷam, and there is now no objection to the widest possible use of the Scriptures in private houses.

Diamper insisted on the revision of the Peshitto version in use in the churches, criticized the canon as defective and accused the Syrians of deliberately altering the text to support false Nestorian doctrine, and also, in the case of Luke vi. 34, to allow their common practice of usury.[2]

I have heard from old people that formerly, before the Malayāḷam Bible was available or modern primary education started, children learned a good many Old and New Testament stories in the form of songs.

[1] Letter of Fr Campori, S.J., to Fr Francis de Oliveira of 20 August 1618 quoted in Ferroli, p. 419.

[2] Session III, decrees 2, 3.

CHAPTER XI

THE WORSHIP AND FAITH OF THE ST THOMAS CHRISTIANS BEFORE 1600

It is not difficult to discover the way in which the Indian Church worshipped before Menezes intervened. Indeed most of our information comes from Menezes himself who, in the Diamper decrees, very carefully states those Indian practices and errors which he considers were to be condemned. It is clear that the Indian Church followed the use of the East Syrian Church, with a number of observances of perhaps more local origin. The Portuguese found nothing to indicate a connexion with the Jacobite Church; but the liturgy in common use, which they corrected and printed in its corrected form at the end of the decrees of the synod (and which was reprinted by Gouvea in all his editions), is identical with the liturgy of the Apostles Addai and Mari. The variations apart from those introduced by Menezes are two only. The formula of the Institution is found in the Malabar liturgy and not in Addai and Mari, and according to the version printed by Gouvea, the whole section from the lections to the Creed (which includes litanies of intercession, the expulsion of the catechumens and the setting of the mysteries on the altar) is entirely different in the order of these elements of the service. Comparison of the Malabar and East Syrian liturgies was first made by Fr Peter Le Brun in 1716.[1] R. H. Connolly did the work again very thoroughly in 1914 and left no doubt about the identity of the two liturgies.[2] Fr Placid believes that the corrected rite as printed by Gouvea was never in actual use by the Church. There are ancient Romo-Syrian manuscripts which contain the ordinary of the mass and rubrics for the *raza* (most solemn celebration) which mention the Diocesan Synod of Ankamāli celebrated by Archbishop Roz in 1603. In these manuscripts we find the order of the prayers is the same as in the

[1] P. Petrus le Brun, *Liturgiae Chaldaeo-Malabarica et Chaldaeo-Nestoriana comparatae* (Explication littérale historique et dogmatique des prières et des cérémonies de la Messe). Parisiis, edito anno 1716 de quo altera editio (jam exhausta) an. 1843 excusa fuit. See Matthew, *Subsidium ad bull. patron. Portugalliae*, p. 15.

[2] R. H. Connolly, O.S.B., 'The work of Menezes on the Malabar Liturgy', *Jour. Theological Studies* (April and July 1914).

present missal used by the Romo-Syrians. Their rite was discussed in 1757 by Propaganda, who considered reprinting the draft Menezes had left, but ten years later decided that the opposition to the change would be too great for it to succeed. In 1768 Propaganda ruled that the name of the Pope should be inserted in place of the Patriarch and that there should be elevation immediately after the consecration. With these additions the missal printed in Rome in 1774 was substantially that of Archbishop Roz and this agrees with Addai and Mari more closely than that printed by Gouvea.

Fr Placid believes that the Syrians who had accepted Mar Gregorios and the Jacobite obedience in 1665 nevertheless continued to use their old rite for some years afterwards. He has in his possession a book containing the divine office copied in 1734 under Mar Thoma V which is the same as the Romo-Syrian except for some slight verbal changes which indicate relations with the Jacobites. Mar Gregorios celebrated mass when he first arrived, using the Jacobite liturgy of St James, which demonstrated he was different from the eastern bishops that they had received before, and so caused some suspicion among the people. It is said that Mar Thoma I begged him to change his rite.[1] Even when the West Syrian rite was used it was written in Syro-Chaldaic script and there are still copies extant. Some believe that the Syro-Chaldaic script and rite were given up in favour of West Syriac (Maronite or Jacobite) only in the middle of the nineteenth century. Perhaps Mar Kurilos was the bishop who brought about the change. At all events the change-over is now complete and almost everyone in the Church believes that the present rite has been in use for many centuries. Pre-Diamper manuscripts include those in the Buchanan collection in the University Library, Cambridge, and a book of canonical offices in the possession of the Chaldean Syrians of Trichur. This book is entirely Nestorian in its memorials and in its address to Mary as Mother of Christ.[2]

Duarte Barbosa, who left India in 1518, gives the following note about worship: 'These Armenians [that is, the bishops of Syrian

[1] Letter of Fr Azevido, S.J., dated Ampalacat, 28 July 1666. A translation of his letter was published by Fr Heras in *The Examiner* (Bombay, 14 May 1938), p. 294.

[2] The book was written by Matthai, son of Joseph Kassisa, and finished on 6 Kanni 1585 at St Mary's Church, Kōtamamgalam. It was given by Mar Eustathios to Mar Timotheos, a Nestorian bishop who came to Trichur in 1910.

Christians] are white men, they speak Arabic and Chaldee. They have the Church law and recite their prayers perpetually. Yet I know not whether they recite the whole office as do our Friars. They wear their tonsures reversed, hair in the place of the tonsure, and the head around it shaven. They wear white shirts, and turbans on their heads, they go barefoot and wear long beards. They are extremely devout and say mass at the altar as we do here, with a cross facing them. He who says it walks between two men, who help him, one on each side. They communicate with salted bread instead of the host, and consecrate thereof sufficient for all who are present in the church; they distribute the whole of this as if it were blessed bread, and every man comes to the foot of the altar to receive it from the priest's hand. And the wine is in this wise. As at that time there was no wine in India they take raisins brought from Mecca and Ormuzd, and leave them for the night to soak; the next day when they go to say mass they press out the juice and say the mass with that. These men baptized for money, and when they returned from Malabar to their own country they had great riches, and thus for lack of money many went unbaptized.'[1]

There are other references besides the above which show that the Indian Church always used unfermented wine for the Eucharist. Fermented wine was one of the articles of trade brought in Western ships in the days of Roman trade. It is probable that there was never very much demand for it on the coast and it may be that the Moors were unwilling to import it. However this may be, Joseph the Indian in Novus Orbis in 1451 also mentions how they made their wine. Menezes forbade this at Diamper and the synod petitioned the King of Portugal to supply wine enough for all the needs of the Church.

The Portuguese spoke of the Church as Nestorian. This is abundantly evident from the decrees of the Synod of Diamper and from the book written by Fr Roz and published in 1586, *De erroribus Nestorianorum*.[2] The books written before Diamper which are still extant are in the Nestorian script and all contain references to Diodoros, Theodoros, and Nestorios, and describe the Virgin Mary as the Mother of Christ. The oldest of such manuscripts was written in 1301 in Cranganore under Mar Jacob, 'Metropolitan of the See of St Thomas and the whole Church of the Christians of

[1] Duarte Barbosa, *Description of the Coasts of E. Africa*, book II, pp. 600–1.
[2] Ed. in *Orientalia christiana*, XI (1928).

India, and under Mar Jabalha VIII the great ruler of the holy catholic church of the East, head of the pastors and prelate of prelates, prince of princes and father of fathers. . ., Patriarch of the East which is the head place of all other parts of the world'.[1] The extreme distaste of the Indian Christians for the images shown them by the Portuguese, and their veneration for the Cross, strongly supports the view that the Church was Nestorian.

Although the evidence seems conclusive that the worship of the Church was Nestorian in form before Diamper, the doctrinal and ecclesiastical affiliation of the Church is rather perversely disputed. We have seen that the first certain historical reference to the Church was made by Cosmas, and it is reasonable to suppose that it, like the Church in Ceylon, was administered by bishops from Persia. That means an East Syrian connexion. It is, however, all too easy, in ecclesiastical controversy, to imagine that it is sufficient to label a Christian of a tradition different from your own, and that you have then dealt conclusively with him. Although the Persian Church in the sixth century is labelled Nestorian, it certainly does not mean that it wilfully and knowingly had rejected the Catholic faith. The subsequent history of the Indian Church shows plainly that it did not understand minutiae of doctrinal formulation and the confusing relations of the East Syrian Church with Rome suggest that even the guardians of the Nestorian faith were more concerned with ecclesiastical authority and political standing than with the purity of their tradition. It must be understood, therefore, that the doctrinal positions implied by the names of schismatics mentioned in this note were probably never held strictly by the Malabar Church as a whole, whose faith was always more a way of life than an attachment to a particular doctrinal position.

A section of Romo-Syrians maintains that the Portuguese were mistaken in calling the Church Nestorian.[2] They state that the

[1] For a lectionary of St Paul's Epistles for all Sundays and principal feasts, including those of Diodore, Theodore and Nestorios (that of Nestorios being erased), see Vatican Syrian MSS. 22, XII; 'written by Zecharias, son of Joseph, son of Zecharias, of the town of Schengale'. I owe this reference to Fr Placid.

[2] The first statement of this position was *The Syrian Church in Malabar*, by Fr Panjikaran, O.C.D., who pointed out that Francis Xavier, in commending Mar Jacob to the King of Portugal, made no suggestion that he and his people were not Catholics, and says that the fact that Menezes could command attendance at the Synod of Diamper on pain of excommunication, and could order all the Syrian priests to say mass for its success, proves they must all have been Catholics, though in error on certain points. But it seems more probable that Mar Jacob was living under Portuguese protection and had

Malabar Church received its bishops from a section in the East Syrian Church which had always been in communion with Rome. They say that the letter sent to the Patriarch in 1504 must have been to a uniat Patriarch or it would not have got into the Vatican Library. They mention also the statement of Marignolli that he received money from the Christians of Quilon.[1] The latest and most persuasive statement of this view is in an unpublished book of Fr Placid, a Carmelite of the Malabar congregation.

Fr Placid believes that the Church held the Catholic faith from the time of St Thomas, and was subject to Rome from the beginning (for if she was not, she was not, *ex hypothesi*, Catholic). But he distinguishes this relation from the Portuguese idea of 'obedience to Rome', as implying full acceptance of the Latin rite and system. He traces a great deal of the quarrelling and other troubles which came upon the Syrians to ill-advised Portuguese policy. Fr Placid lays great stress on the fact that, from the first contact of Portuguese and Syrian Christians, whether Indian or coming from the Patriarch, they seem to have had communion *in sacris*. He quotes a Jesuit Annual Letter of 1581[2] which says the inhabitants of Ankamāli were for the most part infected with the Nestorian heresy, that they received communion under both species and that they were gradually drawn from heresies to the truth of the Roman Church. It goes on to say that they were very kind to the Jesuits and wanted them at all feasts, and when the Jubilee granted by the Pope was published in 1581 at Ankamāli 'many thousands of people flocked thither and most of them received *rite* the body of Christ'. Placid says this shows that they could not have been Nestorians, but were Catholics, though of Chaldean rite. The

conformed to Rome because of this—this is the natural explanation of the words 'in his old age he conforms to the Roman Church'. Menezes considered himself, as Primate of the Orient, the bishop of all Christians in the East and it is likely that Rome's views of the orders of the schismatic Eastern Churches questioned their regularity rather than their validity. This would account for Menezes's attitude described above. See also C. J. George Kaṭṭanar, *The Orthodoxy of the St Thomas Christians*. In *Kēraḷa Soc. Papers*, series 10 (1932), Fr G. Schurhammer, S.J., in 'The Malabar Church and Rome', tries to prove the thesis that the pre-Portuguese Church in Malabar was Roman Catholic (pp. 291–306). He is answered in the same issue of the magazine by K. N. Daniel in 'Rome and the Malabar Church', pp. 307–40.

[1] This is sufficiently explained by the hypothesis, for which there is evidence, that traders in Quilon had established a Church of the Latin rite there. In any case, as the Mutalāḷi family of Quilon now say, Syrian Christians would always treat a visiting bishop as an honoured guest, even though not of their rite. They say he did not receive money *ex officio*, as papal legate.

[2] Kept in the Torre do Tombo at Lisbon; 28, fos. 34 v–38 w.

Jesuits misunderstood this. Placid also quotes Portuguese reception of the bishops sent by the Patriarch and St Francis Xavier's commendation of Mar Jacob to the King of Portugal—a matter about which there was much controversy. As an example of Jesuit misunderstanding, Fr Placid quotes *De erroribus* which has to admit that the Indians professed the Roman Catholic faith though they had with them books containing Nestorian heresies. Fr Abraham di Giorgio, S.J., a Maronite, wrote in October 1593 from Vaipikoṭṭa to the Father-General, S.J., many accusations against Mar Abraham, who had become a 'public Nestorian'. In a further letter of December he gives ten particular points of accusation.[1] Roz mentions the archdeacon weeping when required to strike out the mention of the Patriarch Simon from the liturgy, and Placid says that it was no wonder, as he claimed he was Simon Denha who received the *pallium* from the Pope in 1585. Placid also maintains that the Pope did not approve of the latinization carried out by Diamper, because diocesan synods were not encouraged, and he points out that the Pope never congratulated Menezes in so many words for bringing in heretics, because the Malabar Christians were, in fact, Catholic.

Barbosa, early in the sixteenth century, speaks of the Christians of Cranganore as very devout, only deficient in doctrine.[2] The Syrians had left Cranganore because of Portuguese interference with their customs, especially their allowing fish and liquor in Lent—both abhorrent to the Syrians.

But from the earliest times the East Syrian Church had no close relationship, if indeed it had any connexion at all, with the West. The mendicant orders made the first close contact with the separated Nestorian and Jacobite Churches, and it was through their influence that the Patriarch Sulakha made his submission to the Pope in 1551. His successor Abd'iso also received the *pallium*, but his attachment to Roman doctrine was not unquestioned. It was he who sent Mar Joseph and Mar Elias to Kēraḷa in 1556, with two Dominicans. The Portuguese were apparently not altogether reassured by the presence of Bishop Ambrose, for they detained the party at Goa, but this was probably more due to jealousy of encroachment on an area they considered part of the *Padroada* jurisdiction than to doubts of their orthodoxy. They were called

[1] G. Beltrami, *La Chiesa Caldea nel secolo dell' Unione*, pp. 114, 115, 291.
[2] K. P. P. Menon, *History of Kerala*, I, p. 315.

'Nestorians' by the Portuguese and objected to this appellation.[1] The dispute about jurisdiction was dealt with by the sixth session of the Council of Trent, which said the Portuguese could institute prelates only in places for which the Holy See had not appointed them.[2] It is to be noted that the first Council of Goa apparently did not convict Mar Joseph of heresy, though the Portuguese became more and more doubtful of his sincerity in doctrinal matters. Mar Abraham, Mar Joseph's successor, had been consecrated (or re-consecrated) at Rome, but remained under the jurisdiction of the Chaldean Patriarch, Denha Simon, who had succeeded Abd'iso. Such is the connexion of the Malabar Church with the uniat East Syrians, or Chaldeans. Before 1556 the bishops must have been Nestorians, and the Portuguese were correct in calling them by that name.[3]

An entirely different view of the doctrinal position of the Malabar Church was brought forward by E. M. Philip.[4] He says that the Church was Nestorian at the beginning of the sixteenth century, but that this was only a recent development: its attachment through the centuries was to the Jacobite Patriarch of Antioch, through the Jacobite Church of Persia. He finds proof of his view in Rae's interpretation of Burnell's translation of the Pahlavi inscription on the Kottayam cross. But, as a very different translation is now accepted, this evidence is of no value for his case. He adduces the Estrangelo Syriac Bible in the Buchanan MS. at Cambridge, which was written at the close of the twelfth century and is marked into liturgical readings according to the Jacobite calendar. The Metropolitan Dionysios who gave it to Buchanan in 1807 said that they had kept it, as some thought, for a thousand years. Philip is of the opinion that this excludes the possibility that the book was brought by Jacobite bishops in 1665, 1685 and 1751. But plainly the 'thousand years' is inaccurate, and there is no firm ground for Philip's statement. Great antiquity is commonly attributed to buildings and objects in Malabar which are more than a century old. Philip also tries to argue his case on the ground that ceremonies condemned by Diamper were in reality not Nestorian, but Jacobite;

[1] Report of Mar Elias at Rome, quoted by Fr Placid. He says they should be called 'Chaldeans.'

[2] Bull of Pius IV, 1562.

[3] Bishop Medlycott, *Catholic Encyclopaedia*, XIV, pp. 682, 683, art. 'St Thomas Christians'.

[4] *The Indian Church of St Thomas.*

but examination of his arguments does not induce confidence in them.[1]

The Rev. P. T. Geevarghese (afterwards the Most Revd. Mar Ivanios, Roman Catholic Archbishop of Trivandrum) wrote a thesis in 1918 restating Mr Philip's contentions, but he was answered conclusively in 1919 by Mr K. N. Daniel.[2] It is difficult to believe that the Jesuits would not speedily have identified peculiarly Jacobite errors in the Malabar Church, and the absence of any condemnation in their writings as well as the absence of any specifically Jacobite episcopal names is strong evidence against the view that the Church has always been Jacobite, apart from temporary aberrations. My own conclusion should be clear from the first section of this book.

[1] Philip argues that the condemnation of a liturgy of Dioscoros must be a mistake for that of Theodoros Rabban, a Jacobite, as a liturgy of Dioscoros is not known. He says that the commixture and signing condemned in Session V, decree 3, is a Jacobite and not a Nestorian ceremony. G. P. Badger, *The Nestorian Churches*, II, p. 235, does not support Philip in this.

[2] Mr Daniel's pamphlet is to be incorporated as chapter XIX in his unpublished MS. *History of the Syrian Church in South India.*

CHAPTER XII

THE FAITH OF THE ST THOMAS CHRISTIANS TODAY

UNTIL the Portuguese came the Malabar Church held the Nestorian faith, but it is doubtful how clearly the Indians understood the *differentia* of the Nestorian theological position. Indeed, with their education (even in Christian prayers) often in the hands of Hindu teachers and with no Malayāḷam translation of the Scriptures, it is probable that most Christians were very ignorant indeed.[1] When the Roman mission came it started teaching the faith at once. The first Malayāḷam book ever printed in India was a catechism of Christian doctrine,[2] and the decrees of Diamper show the importance attached to Christian instruction by the Jesuits. But this instruction did not cause undue alarm, for the Jesuits very wisely retained the accustomed services of the Nestorian rite, correcting them as necessary. The Western rite was never introduced, though Western vestments and other ornaments were. Gradually, systematic teaching had its effect; customs were changed and devotional habits altered. The most obvious and striking change was probably in the use of the *Ave*. The Virgin had been greeted as Bearer of Christ, but no prayer was made to her, asking for her intercession. Only at evening prayer was any petition addressed to her. The Roman custom was very different, and in this matter the Jacobite Church approximates to Roman practice. In the Jacobite daily office the *Ave* is said eighteen times, following the Lord's Prayer whenever this is recited, except during the celebration of the Eucharist. In the liturgy of St James frequent supplication is made that the prayers of the Theotokos and of the

[1] Session VIII, decree 18, Synod of Diamper, 'The Christians of Malabar welcomed and venerated foreign bishops, episcopas or metrans and allowed them to take part in the spiritual affairs of their Church, whatever might be their creed or belief. In other words, the Syrians had not much attachment to one creed or aversion to another'; majority judgment, Seminary Case, 1879–89, p. 60.

[2] *Doctrina Christia a maneyra de dialogo* (feyta en Portugal pello padre Marcos Iorge da Companhia de Iesu. Tresladada en lingua Malavar Tamul pello padre Andrique Anriquez da Mesma Companhia. Impressa com approvacao do Ordinario et Inquisidor et com licenca do Superior. Em Cochin, no collegia da Madro da Dios, aos quatorze da Novembro do anno de MDLXXIX).

There is a copy of this book in the Sorbonne.

saints may be a stronghold for us. We know that for some time, at least in the seventeenth century, the newly arrived Jacobite prelates used a corrected version of the Roman correction of the Nestorian rite. It is therefore clear that the bewildering shift from Nestorian to Roman and Roman to Jacobite allegiance was not, for the mass of the people, marked by any sudden and therefore unacceptable changes in the externals of religion. Kidd's description of the transition as a *volte-face* without parallel in the history of the Church may be justified strictly; but the theological implications of the change of allegiance were certainly not realized at the time by many, if by any, Indian Christians.[1]

The standard of faith of the Jacobite is the Nicene-Constantinopolitan Creed and the common tradition of the community about the Church, the sacraments, the after-life and other things, which finds its sanction in the liturgy rather than in the Bible. The Peshitta was in use, but was an unknown book to the laity until a Malayāḷam version was published in the nineteenth century. The Hudaya canon has authority for the Jacobite Church, but there is no copy of this in Travancore accepted as genuine by all sections of the Church.

In 1869 a booklet by Fr E. Philipos called *The Syrian Christians of Malabar*[2] gave a statement of faith in the form of question and answer; it was written in response to a suggestion of the Rev. G. B. Howard. Two or three books have been published in this century expounding the Faith, mostly with controversial needs in view. The first and most important was called *The Articles of Religion*[3] by Wattasheril Geevarghese Malpān, published in 1892. (The author was consecrated in 1909 as Mar Dionysios.) The most recent book, and the most ambitious, is *The Truths of Holy Religion* by Augen Mar Timotheos.[4] The bishop tries to expound the Faith, basing his work on Syriac writers but trying to interpret their teaching in Malayāḷam, a task in which he does not seem to be uniformly successful, because of the great difficulty of finding Malayāḷam (or in fact Sanskrit) equivalents for the Syriac terms in which his theological thinking has been done. For example, in some places he translates *persona* by the word *satvam*, in others by *āḷ*. The latter

[1] B. J. Kidd, *Churches of Eastern Christendom*, p. 44.
[2] See Bibliography below, p. 310.
[3] See Bibliography below, p. 307.
[4] See Bibliography below, p. 312. Unfortunately no references are given to other authors in this book.

can be defended, but the former means undifferentiated existence. In another place he uses the word *mūrtti* to translate *persona*.[1]

Jacobite prayers are rich in Biblical references, but most of these are typological. In the wedding service almost every triad of things mentioned in the Old Testament, such as the ring, bracelet and staff which Judah gave to Tamar, is treated as a type of Trinity. Almost every mention of water in the Old Testament is used as a type of water in baptism, including the water in which Bathsheba was washing when David saw her. (Bathsheba is then reckoned a type of the Church, as David of Christ.) At the prayer of the veil the priest apostrophizes the elements saying: 'Thou art the rock of flint, which sent forth twelve streams of water for the twelve tribes of Israel. Thou art the hard rock, which was set against the tomb of our Redeemer.' When the priest makes his communion he says: 'The propitiatory live-coal of the Body and Blood of Christ our God is given me.' Although this typology is characteristic of the liturgical life of the Church, in the theological books mentioned we find an effort to prove all points made by direct reference to the Scriptures, a use of the Bible learned from the Church Missionary Society missionaries, which was the basis of their own appeal and of the Mar Thoma reform movement. Such a use, however, is a modern development, although the spread of Western theological education is likely to make it normal.

The teaching of the Indian Church about the Person of Christ is in no way different from that of the Jacobite Church in Syria, and Indian Jacobite apologists have been concerned to show that their faith is, in fact, more orthodox than that of the Chalcedonian Definition. While Chalcedon is not recognized as a General Council, Eutyches is anathematized as a heretic in the confession of faith made by every priest before his ordination. They believe that the two natures of perfect Godhead and perfect manhood inhere in Christ without change or diminution or confusion, but go on to use the questionable simile of the mingling of wine and water. Mar Timotheos quotes Cyril of Alexandria as expressing exactly the doctrine they hold when he said: 'We do not preach a man made God but a God in flesh—this is our preaching and our faith.'

Philipos answers the question about the Jacobite view of the union of Christ's divinity with his humanity thus: 'Not like oil and water but like wine and water they are joined together and are

[1] Augen Mar Timotheos, *The Truths of Holy Religion*, pp. 77, 179, 180.

become one; and they believe in him as perfect God and perfect man both at his conception and birth, his sufferings, death and resurrection, and at his coming on the last day, and that he had not destroyed his humanity by his divinity, nor his divinity by his humanity.'[1]

Later he explains that God first descended into the womb of the Virgin and there took flesh. And in reference to the first occurrence, viz. the descent of God, the Syrians believe that God was born, that God died, and that the Virgin Mary is the Mother of God.[2] The same writer says: 'The Word of God, one of the Holy Trinity, came down from heaven, and was begotten in the flesh of the Spirit of holiness, and of the blessed Mary, the Virgin, the Mother of God. And he is perfect God and perfect man. And after that the two natures were united in him..., it cannot be that they shall be separated or divided for ever.... But the Syrians believe that the nature in Christ is one: that the two natures were united one with another; because in Christ the two natures were mingled together—the nature of the Godhead and the nature of the manhood—like wine with water. And whereas it is said that there is one nature in Christ, it is for the confirmation of the unity of the two natures one with another.'[3]

Mar Dionysios emphasizes the union of the perfect Godhead and perfect manhood, so that they could never afterwards be separated. This union is a great wonder, he says. After the union neither the two natures (*svab-hāvam*) nor the two persons[4] can be separated but are one nature, one person, one *parsūppa* or face,[5] one will, one in his action. He is perfect God and perfect man. When at the time of death his soul separated from the body, his Godhead, without separating from his soul or body, inhered in both. Because in the resurrection he made his body incorruptible, thenceforward neither death nor any affliction had power over him.[6]

Mar Timotheos expounds the above statement with no significant differences. He is at pains to state and answer Nestorius's views; however, this is largely a bookish argument, since the two groups have never come face to face in Travancore until recent

[1] Philipos, *The Syrian Christians of Malabar*, p. 2.
[2] *Ibid.* pp. 10, 11. [3] *Ibid.* p. viii.
[4] He uses the Syriac word *knūma* but puts the Malayāḷam *āḷukaḷ* in brackets.
[5] I.e. Lat. *persona*.
[6] Dionysios, *Matōpadēsaṅaḷ*, pp. 4, 5. See also the Prayer of the Fraction in the *kurbāna*.

times.[1] He thinks that Eutyches fell into heresy by postulating a Christ who was neither perfect God nor perfect man; for, if two things join and are mixed the particular properties of both will be destroyed and they will become something else, as lime and sand become mortar, a third thing. At the same time Mar Timotheos attacks Flavian who divided Christ's nature in his reply to Eutyches. Timotheos says that the natures of the body and spirit of a man are distinct yet the two combine to form one man. So also is Christ; he has one unified nature. The second Synod of Ephesus in 449 decided against Flavian's views and supported the view of Christ's single nature, in which the natures of Godhead and manhood are joined together without the possibility of separation, or of turning into any new, third, thing. Dioscoros, who was condemned at Chalcedon, was no heretic, and the cause of his fall was not any theological error on his part, but jealousy of the primacy of his see on the part of Rome and Constantinople. Mar Timotheos maintains that a nature cannot be conceived apart from the person in whom it finds its existence and expression. So the Chalcedonian definition must lead to belief in two persons in Christ, and thus, logically, to worship of a Quarternity.[2]

The *communicatio idiomatum* is very clearly taught by Timotheos, who says that one can speak of God undergoing human experience, such as thirst, and can also properly speak of man rising from the dead and sitting at God's right hand. After reading Timotheos, who gives the fullest treatment of these questions ever published in India, one is left with the impression that a great part of the difficulty lies in the meaning given to the Syriac terms *kyōno* and *knūma*, and the question whether or not one can exist without the other. Timotheos often seems to be fighting for the truths which the Chalcedonian definition seeks to safeguard, but which he cannot recognize in that verbal expression. It is also open to question whether his use of *satvam* to translate *knūma*, and in another place *mūrttitvam*, does not confuse the issue. The word used for *kyōno* is *svab-hāvam*. Often, however, as in the liturgy, the Syriac word itself is transliterated into Malayāḷam. It is in the light of the above interpretations that one has to judge such expressions as 'Christ's

[1] They are now more conscious of their common danger from Rome than of mutual doctrinal incompatibility. The small Nestorian diocese is in Trichur. It represents a secession from the Romo-Syrians.

[2] In this connexion Howard quotes Xenajas (British Museum, Addl. MSS. 14, 529, fos. 65, 68, 69); Philipos, *The Syrian Christians of Malabar*, ix, x.

temporary manhood', which occurs in the office of the first Monday in Lent.[1] The whole Jacobite Christological position is often judged and condemned by the simile of the mingling of water and wine, repeated frequently, as in the preparation of the chalice at the *kurbāna*, but it is questionable whether the intention behind these doubtful expressions is not, in the last resort, orthodox.

Unfortunately nothing remains to indicate if there was ever any Indian theological thinking in Nestorian times. In all likelihood there was not. The theology of Cyril of Alexandria must have been in every way more congenial to the Indian environment, with its many stories of the *avatārs* of God, as familiar to Christian children as to Hindu, but the Church seems to have been saved from wholesale adulteration of Christian doctrine in this regard by the fact that the Creed and liturgy were in Syriac, and the Sanskrit terms with their Hindu connotation were not used at all by the Syrian Christians until modern times.

The service for Pentecost and every sacramental rite witness to the Jacobite belief in the personality of God the Holy Spirit. All sacramental grace is believed to be mediated by him. The Creed confesses that the Holy Spirit proceeds from the Father alone, but he is said to be *eṭukkappeṭṭavan*, that is, the one taken from the Son. It may be that the Malayāḷam word is an inadequate translation, for the action of the Holy Spirit is generally taken to be 'receiving' or 'receiving substantially' from the Son. The opinion has been expressed by Indian Jacobite divines that the controversy about the double procession is not important, and may be a mere logomachy.[2]

The Church is the sphere of the Spirit's working, the company of those living as God's people, in the covenant made by Christ. There was no sense of evangelistic responsibility towards non-Christians at all, either when the Portuguese tried to arouse such a sense, or when the Church Missionary Society missionaries preached their conviction that the Syrian Church was called to take the Gospel to the whole of India. This attitude depends on the equation of Church and community never questioned by the Syrians. There are frequent thanksgivings in the offices for the Cross, or baptism, whereby people have been delivered from

[1] *Āndutaksā*, ed. Fr Punūs, p. 53.

[2] See Seminary Case, Judgments, II, p. 105; the twenty-fifth witness for defendant, Ipe Thoma Kaṭṭanar.

heathen darkness and idolatry, but the praise seems set against a Syrian and not an Indian background. The Holy Spirit operates through baptism and gives a child re-birth into the spiritual sphere, into the Church. Through the Cross, the power of the devil was shattered like a broken piece of glass, and baptism brings the child into that victory and to enjoyment of eternal life. The place of personal faith is never emphasized, it is enough to be incorporated into the faithful, worshipping, believing Church. The anointing of baptism had a greater importance in the eyes of most people than the actual water baptism; by this one was anointed with the Holy Spirit and made God's child. Without the anointing there can be no Holy Spirit, the baptism is as John's baptism.[1]

Man was redeemed by the incarnation of Christ and his death, and redemption is made available to men through baptism and eucharist. The idea of Christ's death being vicarious or penal does not, I think, find expression anywhere; it is regarded as the moment of victory and triumph against the devil and all the powers against God.

There is a very lively belief in the Church Triumphant and the efficacy of the prayers of the Blessed Virgin and the saints. The whole atmosphere of worship is in the heavenlies where Christ reigns at the right hand of the Father. Always the resurrection is connected with the death of Christ, which is never dwelt on in abstraction. The Syrians look for a literal bodily resurrection at the Last Day. For this reason cremation is viewed with abhorrence and old people used to keep any teeth which fell out and have them buried with them, that they might not be toothless on the resurrection morning.[2] The Syrians do not have any articulated doctrine of purgatory, but they believe that prayers and sacrifices for the dead are necessary and efficacious.

The whole of Syrian worship may be understood as sacrificial. It is all, in a way, *kurbāna*, or offering. The *kauma*, or canonical daily prayer, is regarded as a devotion which effects something, and may be offered with special intention. So were *nerccas*, or memorial feasts, parallel to the Hindu ancestor sacrifices. As has been shown in an earlier section, it was and is a universal custom among the Syrians to offer the *kurbāna* for the departed on certain fixed days

[1] Bull of Patriarch Peter III, 15 Makaram 1887.

[2] English Christians who encourage cremation are looked on as Hindus, about whose destiny the Syrian Church keeps its own counsel.

after death and every year on the anniversary of the death. Votive *kurbānas* are frequent and sometimes they were offered in support of plans which were somewhat questionable from a Christian point of view. The name 'vow' was given not only to a feast, always held with the assistance of clergy, but to other things like crosses, candles, oil, or vestments, which might be presented to the church with special intention. The word in common use to describe a sacrament, or act of worship, and especially the Eucharist, was *karmmam*, and the priest was described as *karmmi*, both words deriving directly from Hindu ideas of offering. An interesting example of this sacrificial tone is the place of incense in Jacobite worship. It is often spoken of as the reconciling or propitiatory incense and each *etro*, or prayer of incense, in the offices speaks of some special effect of its offering. The following is part of the prayer of incense in the preparatory service of the *kurbāna*:

> We offer before thee this incense after the pattern of Aaron the priest who offered pure incense unto thee in the tabernacle and stayed thereby the plague from the people of Israel. We beseech thee, O Lord, to receive this savour of spiritual sweetness which in our weakness we offer unto thee for our sins and offences and in behalf of our father Adam and our mother Eve, in behalf of the holy Mother of God, Mary, the prophets and apostles, the righteous and the just, the martyrs and confessors, the orthodox doctors and fathers, the solitaries and cenobites, the orphans and widows, the distressed and afflicted, the sick and the oppressed, and all those who have spoken and charged us to remember them in prayers to thee, O Christ our God, and in the behalf of the living and departed and the repose of their souls in the heavenly Jerusalem.... Receive, O my Lord, in thy mercy the incense of thy servants. By the incense of thy priests be thou reconciled to us....

APPENDIX I

SYSTEM OF TRANSLITERATION

The system of transliteration from Malayāḷam to English characters used in this book is as follows:

അ	ആ	ഇ	ഈ	ഉ	ഊ	
a	ā	i	ī	u	ū	
എ	ഏ	ഐ	ഒ	ഓ	ഔ	അം
e	ē	ai	o	ō	au	am
ക	ഖ	ഗ	ഘ	ങ		
k	k-h	g	g-h	ṅ		
ച	ഛ	ജ	ഝ	ഞ		
c	c-h	j	j-h	ñ		
ട	ഠ	ഡ	ഢ	ണ		
ṭ	ṭ-h	ḍ	ḍ-h	ṇ		
ത	ഥ	ദ	ധ	ന		
t	t-h	d	d-h	n		
പ	ഫ	ബ	ഭ	മ		
p	p-h	b	b-h	m		
യ	ര	ല	വ	ശ		
y	r	l	v	ś		
ഷ	സ	ഹ				
ṣ	s	h				
ള	ഴ	റ				
ḷ	l̤	ṟ				

APPENDIX II

SPELLING OF PLACE-NAMES

IN the text I have usually transliterated the Malayāḷam form of place-names, but certain places are often called by an anglicized form of their name, which I have employed in the following cases: Cranganore, Cochin, Quilon, Cape Comorin, Calicut, Diamper, Cannanore and Mylapore.

The place-names on the map are printed as on the Tour Map published by the Survey Department of Travancore-Cochin. As the transliteration appears quite arbitrary the following table is given to show the present place-names transliterated according to the system used in the text. In a few cases names in use in Portuguese times are added in brackets.

MAP	TEXT
Alangad	Ālaṅāṭ
Alleppey	Ālappul̤a
Alwaye	Āluvā
Angamali	Ankamāli
Anjengo	Aṇcuteṅu
Anjur	Āññūr
Arttat	Ārttāṭ
Chalisheri	Cālaśśēri
Changanacheri	Caṅanaśśēri
Chengannur	Ceṅannūr
Chennamangalam (Vaipikkoṭṭa *or* Rapolim)	Cendamamgalam
Cheppadu	Cēppāṭ
Chowgat (Palayur)	Caukkaṭ
Cranganur	Koṭuṅaḷḷūr
Edapalle	Iṭappaḷḷi
Edathva	Eṭatvā
Ernakulam	Eṛaṇākuḷam
Kaduthurutti	Kaṭutturutti
Kaladi	Kālaṭi
Kallada	Kallaṭa

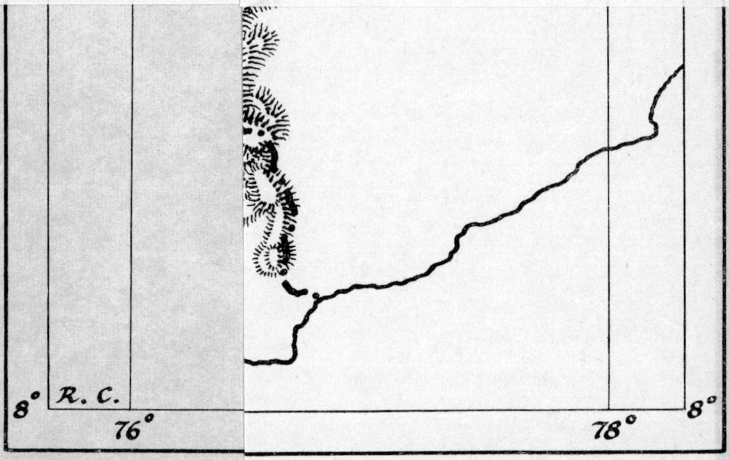

NTRES

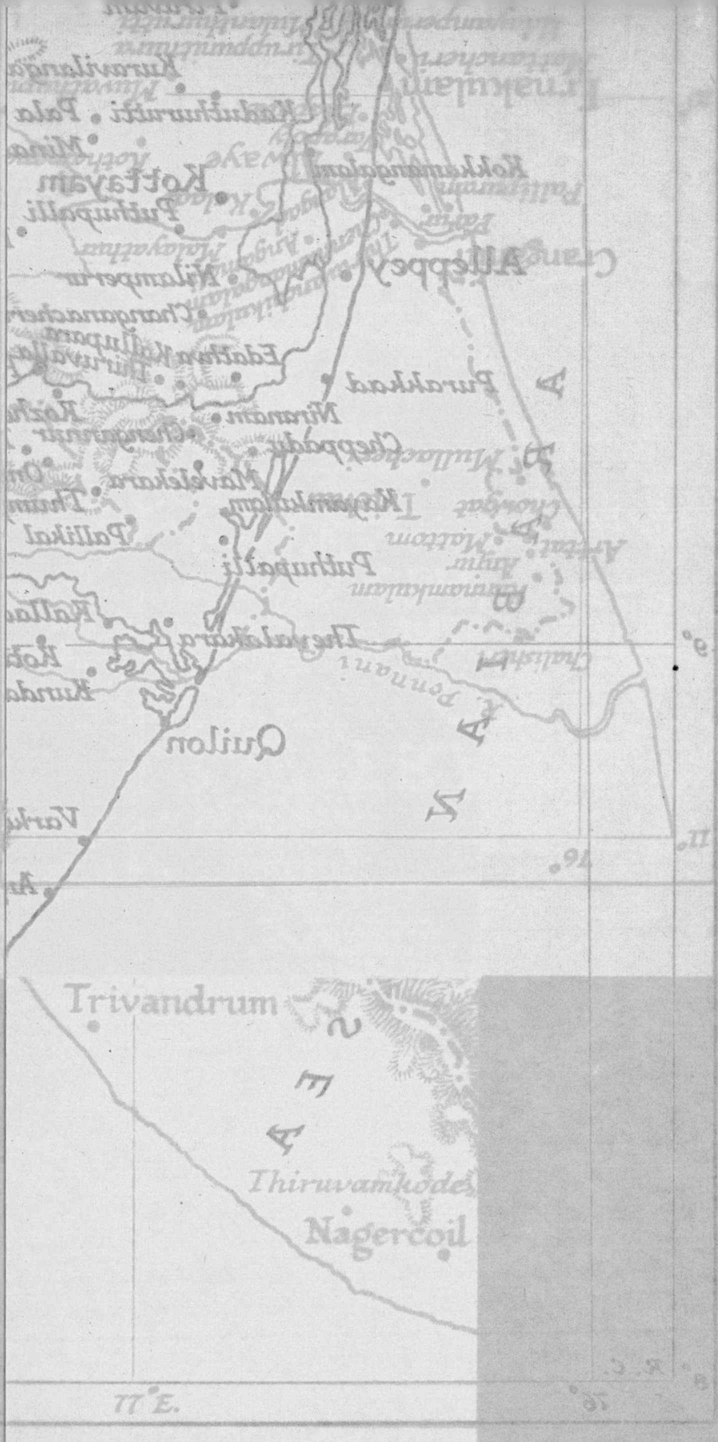

CHRISTIAN CEN

MAP	TEXT
Kallupara	Kalluppaṛa
Kanjirapalli	Kaññirappaḷḷi
Kayamkulam	Kayamkuḷam
Kokkamangalam	Kōkkamamgalam
Kothamangalam	Kōtamamgalam
Kottarakara	Koṭṭarakkara
Kottayam	Kōṭṭayam
Kozhencherry	Kōḻaṇcēri
Kundara	Kuṇdara
Kunnamkulam	Kunnamkuḷam
Kuravilangad	Kuravilaṅāṭ
Malayathur	Malayāṛṛūr
Mattancheri	Maṭṭāncēri
Mattom	Maṛṛam
Mavelekara	Māvēlikkara
Minachil	Mīnaccil
Mulanthurutti	Muḷanturutti
Mullacheri	Mullaśśēri
Muvathupuzha	Mūvāṛṛupuḻa
Nagercoil	Nagarkōvil
Nilamperur	Nilampērūr
Niranam	Niraṇam
Omallur	Ōmallūr
Pala	Pālā
Pallikal	Paḷḷikkal
Pallipuram	Paḷḷippuram
Parur	Paṛavūr
Pathanamthitta	Pattanamtiṭṭa
Piravam	Piṛavam
Purakkad	Purakkāṭ
Puthupalli (North and South)	Putuppaḷḷi
Quilon	Kollam
Ranni	Rānni
Thevalakara	Tēvalakkara
Thiruvalla	Tiruvalla
Thiruvamkode	Tiruvāmkōt
Thiruvanchikulam	Tiruvaṇcikuḷam
Thumpamon	Tunpamaṇ
Tiruppunithura	Tiruppuṇittura

APPENDIX II

MAP	TEXT
Trichur	Trichūr (Trśśērippērūr)
Trivandrum	Tiruvanantapuram
Udayamperur (Diamper)	Udayampērūr
Varapoly	Varāppoḷi
Varkala	Varkkala

APPENDIX III

GLOSSARY

(*Words which are immediately explained in the text and do not recur are not included in this list*)

Ācārya head of a Hindu religious community, hence a Christian bishop or priest.

Agni the Hindu goddess of fire, fire.

Aḻi the barrier separating nave from chancel in a Syrian church.

Amma mother.

Amouques a word used by Gouvea to describe men under a vow to do some desperate deed. The word is not used now.

Anamnesis the liturgical commemoration of Christ's acts of redemption.

Anaphora the canon or great eucharistic prayer of consecration.

Annaprāśanam the ceremony of first feeding a child with rice.

Aṅāṭi same as *cānta*, bazaar.

Appan (or *Accan*) father.

Aṛa strong-room for storing grain and valuables.

Āśān a teacher.

Avatār a form in which, according to Hindu mythology, God manifested himself on earth from time to time.

Barekmore bless, O Lord (Syriac).

Basmalka a prayer in praise of Mary.

Bauddha name given in ancient Hindu stories to men of other faiths, including probably Christians.

B-hartāva husband.

B-hārya wife.

B-hasmam a paste for smearing on the forehead made of the five products of the cow.

Cakram a Travancore coin worth about a halfpenny.

Cānta a street of shops, bazaar.

Catholicos the bishop with semi-patriarchal powers in the Nestorian Church, latterly used in the Malabar Church.

Cāttam a feast.

Ceṭṭi a caste of Hindu traders.

Cīnacaṭṭi a kind of iron frying-pan believed to have been introduced from China.

Copper plates: grants of land or privileges by Hindu rajas inscribed on copper plates.

Curuṭṭu a cake made of flour and plantains.

d'hanam drum played from the back of an elephant.

d'hobi a washerman.

Diwan the chief minister of a hindu State.

Ekbo a short collect.

Epiclesis the invocation of the Holy Spirit on the Elements in the consecration prayer.

Epimanikia cuffs of silk material worn over the sleeves of the eucharistic alb.

Etro prayer used with the offering of incense.

Fanam four *cakrams*.

Golgotha a stand holding cross and candles used in certain ceremonies in church.

Haikkala nave of the church.

Hamalogion a confession of faith.

Iḻava a community of Hindus.

Jacobite name given to monophysite Christians in the East who followed the teaching of Jacob Baradeus (mid sixth century).

Kaiyyasūri the Peace, a 'kiss' given with the hands.

Kamissa a kind of cassock in everyday use outside the church worn by Syrian priests.

Kaḷari school for traditional Hindu education; now obsolete.

Kanniyān an astrologer.

Kāppa a cope, the Eastern form of chasuble.

Kappiar a church sexton.

Karmmam lit. work; used for a Hindu sacrifice.

Karnnavan the head of a family.

Katastroma 'chancel' enclosure in a church.

Katina an iron shell in which gunpowder is exploded to make a cheerful noise.

Kaṭṭanar a Syrian priest.

Kauma a Jacobite form of praise.

Kavaṇi a woman's veil thrown over the head and top half of body.

Kēraḷa the Malayāḷam-speaking area: Malabar, Cochin and Travancore.

Kharosttic Sanskrit in Semitic script.

Knūma perhaps 'personification' is nearer than 'person'; later the word seems to mean 'individual' (Syriac).

Kshatriya the warrior and kingly caste of Hindus.
Kukkoyo a Syriac song.
Kurava a noise expressive of joy made by women with their forefingers in their mouths.
Kurbāna an offering, the Eucharist.
Kuthino a white eucharistic vestment, alb.
Kuṭumi the single lock of hair formerly kept by a Brahmin, the rest of his head being shaved.
Kyōno nature (Syriac).
Madbaha the sanctuary space in a church.
Mahācandrikā a book of traditional Hindu rules for house-placing and construction.
Makaram one of the Malayāḷam months.
Malpān a Syriac instructor.
Mammodisa baptism.
Mantram a spell or incantation.
Manusyalaya a book similar to *Mahācandrikā.*
Maphrian a bishop with special powers under the Jacobite Patriarch.
Mar (*Maron*) Lord; courtesy title given to bishops.
Marggam the way.
Marggamkali a dance celebrating origins of the Malabar Church.
Marumakkattayam system of matrilineal inheritance.
Marwah'tho metal fans surrounded by bells used to make a noise during the Eucharist.
Metran Metropolitan or ruling bishop.
Metropolitan see *Metran.*
Minnu a small gold ornament worn round the neck by married women.
Mūron holy oil.
Mūrttitvam existence in form, hence as a person; but the idea of personality is hardly implied.
Mutaḷāli courtesy title used by Hindus of some Christians.
Nampūtiri a Malabar Brahman.
Nasrāṇi Māppiḷa an ancient name of the Syrian Christians of Malabar.
Nāyar a Hindu caste from which the rajas of Travancore were selected.
Nercca a vow; often used of a memorial feast.
Neyyappam a kind of cake made with rice flour.

Ōḷa a palm leaf strip for writing on with an iron stylus.
Ōṇam the national (Hindu) festival of *Kēraḷa*.
Padroada the right of Portuguese kings to appoint to ecclesiastical office in their Asian dominions.
Pahlavi old Persian written in Semitic characters.
Pallium the woollen vestment bestowed by the Pope as a sign of archiepiscopal authority.
Pālpustakam the Book of Lots used by Syrians for divining the future.
Pandiada a Hindu woman's gold ornament.
Paṇikkar a teacher of the art of warfare; also given as an honorific title.
Pantal a palm-thatched shed with open sides.
Paradēśi a foreigner.
Paṭi overlord.
Paṭippuram gate-house.
Passāram the percentage of dowry payable to the Church.
Pērunāḷ a festival.
Peshitto ancient Syriac version of the Bible.
Phaino same as *kāppa*.
Pir a Moslem holy man.
Prakāram a porch of church or temple.
Prasādam sweet food given to the worshippers in Hindu temples after being offered to the god.
Propaganda: the college at Rome concerned with the extension of the Church in the world.
Prūmion a preface used in the Eucharist service.
Pulakkuḷi the feast which marked the end of the period of ritual pollution after a death.
Pulayan a section of the depressed classes in a community.
Pūnnūl a sacred thread worn by Brahmans and Kshatriyas.
Rambān a monk in the Jacobite Church.
Rassisa tax due to the Patriarch from the Church.
Śakunam omen.
Sannyesi a Hindu wandering ascetic.
Schema the black cap embroidered with crosses and with a veil at the back worn by *rambāns* (and bishops).
Seal as used on p. 228 it means the Host. As a verb it refers to signing with the Cross.
Sēdra a long fixed form of prayer.

Serra the mountains; a name given to the inland regions of Kēraḷa by the Portuguese.
Sirkar the Government.
Slība the Cross.
Ślihanmar Apostles.
Ślokam a Hindu aphorism (der. slogan).
Sosafa the veil with which the Elements in the Eucharist are covered.
Statikon a bishop's letters of appointment from the Patriarch.
Star Pagodas a coin of the East India Company. The phrase refers in the text to an endowment given to the Church in 1808 and subsequently the object of prolonged litigation (see p. 127).
Stoumen kalōs stand properly.
Sudarion a silk handkerchief attached to the handle of a hand cross.
Śudra lowest caste of Hindus.
Sūmmoṛo a chanted versicle.
Tablitho consecrated slab of stone or wood on which the eucharistic vessels must be placed.
Tāḷi same as *minnu*; the sign of married women.
Taravāṭ the Hindu joint-family; almost 'clan'.
Thronos the high altar.
Tiraśīla curtain cutting off the sanctuary of a church.
Trisagion the angelic praises; same as *Kauma*.
Tubdon a section of intercessory prayer.
Tulasi a labiate plant considered sacred by Hindus.
Vaidyan practitioner of Ayurvedic system of medicine.
Vaisya Hindu trading caste (or which *Nāyars* are a branch).
Vina Indian stringed musical instrument.
Yavana Westerner, foreigner.
Yōgam a society or association.

No attempt has been made at a systematic or scientific transliteration of Syriac words, which are transliterated from the Malayāḷam in accordance with the local, eclectic usage.

BIBLIOGRAPHY

ALEXANDER, MALPĀN MAṬṬAYKKAL. *Kurbāna Taksā* (Eucharistic Order), (Kōṭṭayam, 1940).

Analecta Ordinis Carmelitarum Discalceatorum (1937, 1938).

ASSEMAN, J. S. *Bibliotheca orientalis Clementini Vaticana* (in qua manuscriptos codices syriacos, arabicos, persicos, turcicos...Bibl. Vat. addictos recensuit), (4, vols. Rome, 1719–28).

ASTLEY, THOMAS. *A New General Collection of Voyages and Travels* (4 vols. London, 1745).

AYYAR, ANANTA KRISHNA. *Anthropology of the Syrian Christians* (Ernakulam, 1926).

BADGER, G. P. *The Nestorian Churches*, II (London, 1852).

BADGER, G. P. Ed. *Travels of Ludovico di Varthema...A.D. 1503–1508* (Hakluyt Soc. London, 1863).

BARBOSA, DUARTE. *A Description of the Coasts of E. Africa* (Hakluyt Soc. London, 1866).

BAUER, W. *Rechtgläubigkeit und Ketzerei im ältesten Christentum* (Tübingen, 1934).

BELTRAMI, G. *La Chiesa Caldea nel secolo dell' unione* (Rome, 1933).

BERNARD, Fr. *Mar Thomma Kristyānikaḷ* (The Mar Thoma Christians), (St Thomas Press, Palai, 1916).

BIRCH, W. DE G. *Commentaries of the Great Affonso de Albuquerque* (4 vols. Hakluyt Soc. London, 1875–84).

BUCHANAN, CLAUDIUS. *Christian Researches in Asia* (8th ed. Cambridge, 1811).

Bulletin of Rama Varma Research Institute (Trichur, July 1946).

BURKITT, F. C. *Early Eastern Christianity* (London, 1904).

BURKITT, F. C. 'St Thomas and his feasts', in *Kēraḷa Society Papers* (1930), series 6.

BURKITT, F. C. 'Three St Thomas documents', in *Kēraḷa Society Papers* (1932), series 9.

CHARPENTIER, JARL. *St Thomas the Apostle and India* (Uppsala, 1927).

CHAZHIKAN, J. *The History of the Southists* (in Malayāḷam), (Catholic Mission Press, Kōṭṭayam, 1940).

CHERIYAN, P. *The Malabar Syrians and the Church Missionary Society, 1816–1840* (Kōṭṭayam, 1935).

CHURCHILL, AWNSHAM AND JOHN. *Collection of Voyages and Travels*, III (London, 1704).

CODRINGTON, H. W. *Studies of the Syrian Liturgies* (Geo. E. J. Coldwell Ltd. London, 1953), reprinted from *Eastern Churches Quarterly* (1936–7).

COLERIDGE, H. J. *Life and Letters of St Francis Xavier* (1872).

CONNOLLY, R. H., O.S.B. 'The work of Menezes on the Malabar liturgy', in *Jour. Theolog. Studies*, XV (April–July 1914).

CORREA, GASPAR. *Lendas da India* (4 vols. Lisbon, 1604,.

(CORREA, GASPAR.) *The Three Voyages of Vasco da Gama from the 'Lendas da India' of Gaspar Correa.* Trans. H. E. J. Stanley (Hakluyt Soc. London, 1859).

DE COSTA, A. *Indian Church Quarterly Review* (April, 1895).

D'CRUZ, F. A. *St Thomas the Apostle in India* (Mylapore, 1929).

CURETON, W. *Ancient Syriac Documents* (London, 1864).

CURIAN, G. *Prize Essay on the Syrian Church* (Kōṭṭayam, 1872; reprinted, Kōṭṭayam, 1940).

DAHLMANN, J., S.J. *Die Thomas-Legende* (Freiburg, 1912).

DANIEL, K. N. *A Critical Study of Primitive Liturgies* (2nd ed. Tiruvalla, 1949).

DANIEL, K. N. *Dissertations on the Copper Plates in the possession of the St Thomas Christians* (Bombay, 1925). Reprint from *Indian Antiquary*, LIII (1924).

DANIEL, K. N. 'Rome and the Malabar Church', in *Kēraḷa Society Papers*, II, series 10.

DIONYSIOS, Mar. *Matōpadēśaṅaḷ* (The Articles of Religion), (1892; 4th ed. Kōṭṭayam, 1914).

DRURY, Major HEBER. Trans. *Letters from Malabar* (of J. C. Visscher, 1743), (Madras, 1862).

DUCHESNE, Mgr L. *Christian Worship* (London, 1927).

Encyclopædia Britannica (14th ed.), II, p. 819, 'Axumite kingdom'.

FARIS, N. A. *The Arab Heritage* (Princeton, 1944).

FARQUHAR, J. N. *The Apostle Thomas in North India* (Rylands Library Bulletin, 1926).

FARQUHAR, J. N. *The Apostle Thomas in South India* (Rylands Library Bulletin, 1927).

FERROLI, D., S.J. *The Jesuits in Malabar* (Bangalore, 1939), vol. I.

FORTESCUE, A. *Lesser Eastern Churches* (London, 1913).

GARBE, R. *Indies und das Christentum* (Tübingen, 1914).

GEDDES, MICHAEL. *History of the Church of Malabar* (London, 1694).

GEORGE, C. J. KAṬṬANAR. *The Orthodoxy of the St Thomas Christians* (Kōṭṭayam, 1900).

GIAMIL, S. *Genuinae relationes* (Rome, 1902).

GOODSPEED, E. J. *History of Early Christian Literature* (Chicago, 1942).

DE GOUVEA, ANTONIO. *A Diocesan Synod of the Church and Bishoprick of Angamale* (trans. by M. Geddes; Coimbra, 1606).

DE GOUVEA, ANTONIO. *Jornada do Arcebispo de Goa, Dom Frey Aleixo de Menezes...* (Coimbra, 1606). *Histoire orientale des grans progres de l'eglise catholique en la reduction des chrestiens de S. Thomas par le revme Don Alexis de Menezes, archeveque de Goa* (Fr. trans. by J. B. Glen, Antwerp, 1609).

GUNDERT, H. In *Madras Jour. of Literature and Science*, XIII (1844), pt. 2.

Heras, Fr H., S.J. *The Two Apostles of India* (Bombay, 1944).
Heras, Fr H., S.J. In *Esplendores da religio* (Goa, April 1930).
Heras, Fr H., S.J. In *The Examiner* (Bombay, 14 May 1938).
Heras, Fr H., S.J. Review of *St Thomas the Apostle in India* (d'Cruz) in *Jour. Bombay Hist. Soc.* (Sept. 1929).
Heras, Fr H., S.J. In the *Malabar Mail*, 6 and 9 July 1938.
Herzfeld,—. In *Epigraphia Indica*, xix (1914–15).
Hosten, Fr H., S.J. *Antiquities from San Thome and Mylapore* (Calcutta, 1936).
Hosten, Fr H., S.J. 'Thomas of Cana and his copper-plate grant', in *Indian Antiquary*, lvi (July 1927).
Hosten, Fr H., S.J. In *Kēraḷa Society Papers* (1930), series 4.
Hough, James. *History of Christianity in India* (4 vols. London, 1839).
Howard, G. B. *Christians of St Thomas and their Liturgies* (London, 1864).
Howard, G. B. (ed.). *See* Philipos, Fr E.

Indian Antiquary, xxxii (1904), lvi (1927), lvii (1928).
Ittoop, Joseph. *Malayāḷuttuḷḷa Suriyāni Kristyānikaḷuṭe Caritram* (History of the Syrian Christians of Malabar), (Kōṭṭayam, 1869).
Ittoop, Pukadiyil. *Suriāni Kristyānikaḷuṭe Sabhacaritram* (Church History of the Syrian Christians), (2nd ed. Kōṭṭayam, 1906).
Ivanios, Mar. *The Order of the Holy Qurbana of the Orthodox Syrian Church of Malabar* (S.P.C.K. London, 1934).
Iyengar, P. T. S. *History of the Tamils to A.D. 600* (Madras, 1929).
Iyer, C. V. Narayana. *Origin and Early History of Saivism in S. India* (Madras, 1938).

James, M. R. *The Apocryphal New Testament* (Oxford, 1924).
du Jarric, P., S.J. *Histoire des choses plus memorables adventues tant ez Indes orientales, que autre pais de la desconverts des Portugais, en l'établissement et progrez de la foi chretienne et catholique* (3 vols. 1600, 1610, 1614); (Latin trans. 1615), *Thesaurus rerum indicarum.*
Joseph, T. K. *Malabar Christians and their Ancient Documents* (Trivandrum, 1929).
Joseph, T. K. *Malabar Miscellany* (Bombay, n.d.), reprint from *Indian Antiquary*, lvii (1928), pp. 24ff. and lviii (1929), pp. 13ff.
Joseph, T. K. *Malankara Nasranikaḷuṭe nāluceppēṭukaḷ* (The Four Copper Plates of the Malankara Nasranis), (Trivandrum, 1925).
Joseph, T. K. *South India's St Thomas* (Ceṅannūr, 1952).
Joseph, T. K. In *Indian Antiquary* (Bombay), lvii (1928), pp. 24ff., 46f., 103, 117, 160, 209; lviii (1929), pp. 13ff., 21, 113, 178.
Joseph, T. K. 'Citerior India and extra-Indian Indias', in *Journal of Indian History* (Trivandrum, Aug. 1947).
Joseph, T. K. In *Kēraḷa Society Papers* (1930), series 3.
Joseph, T. K. 'St Thomas in Parthian India', in *National Christian Council Review* (Jan. 1952).
Joseph, T. K. 'A Hindu date for Thomas in Malabar' in *Powra Dhvani Annual* (Kōṭṭayam, 1944).

JOSEPH OF ST MARY, Bishop. *Mémoires.*
JOSEPH OF ST MARY, Bishop. *Seconda Speditione* (Rome, 1666).
Journal of Madras Literary Society, VII (1838), pp. 41–74; VIII (1838).
Journal of Rama Varma Archaeol. Society, XV (1949).
Journal of the Royal Asiatic Society, I (1834), pp. 171–92, II (1835), pp. 51–62 ('Memoirs of the Primitive Church of Malabar', by Capt. Charles Swanston); VII (1841), p. 343 (Facsimiles of Kōṭṭayam copper-plates); IV (n.s.) (1870), pp. 79, 90 (interpretation of copper-plates in an article by E. W. West).

KEAY, F. E. *History of the Syrian Church in India* (Madras, 1938).
KER, R. *A General History and Collection of Voyages and Travels* (Edinburgh, 1824).
Kēraḷa Society Papers (Trivandrum), series 1 (1928); series 2 (1929); series 3, 4, 5, 6 (1930); series 7, 8 (1931); series 9, 10 (1932); series 11 (1933).
KIDD, B. J. *The Churches of Eastern Christendom* (London, 1927).
KIELHORN, F. In *Epigraphia Indica*, VI (1900–1).
KOCHUTHOMMEN APOTHECARY. *Pariśkkārapāti* (Trivandrum, 1926).
KODER, S. S. 'A Hebrew letter of 1768', in *Jour. of Rama Varma Arch. Soc.* (Trichur), XV (1949).
KURIAKOSE, KAṬṬANAR. *Malabar Kristyānikaḷ* (The Christians of Malabar), (Kunnankulam, 1910).
KURMANAKAN, J. *The Southists and the Northists* (in Malayāḷam), (B.V.M. Press, Alleppey, 1941).
KURUVILLA, K. K. *The History of the Mar Thoma Church* (Madras, 1951).

LA CROZE, V. *Histoire du christianisme des Indes* (2 vols., 2nd ed. La Haye, 1758).
LAND, J. P. N. *Anecdota syriaca* (4 vols. Leiden, 1862–75).
LE BAS, CHARLES WEBB. *Life of Bishop Middleton* (2 vols. London, 1831).
LE BRUN, PETRUS. *Liturgiae Chaldeo-Malabarica et Chaldeo-Nestoriana comparatae* (1st ed. Paris, 1716; 2nd ed. 1843).
LE QUIEN, Fr M. *Oriens christianus* (3 vols., 1740).
LUCAS, P. V. *Suṛiānipurātanapāṭṭa* (The Ancient Songs of the Syrian Christians of Malabar), (1st ed. 1910; Kōṭṭayam, 1935).

McCRINDLE, J. W. *Christian Topography of Cosmas Indopleustes* (Hakluyt Soc. London, 1907).
MACKENZIE, Col. G. T. *State of Christianity in Travancore* (Trivandrum, 1901).
Madras Journal of Archaeology I; IV (n.s.), IX, XIII, XXI.
MAFFEI, Fr JOHN PETER. *Historiarum indicarum libri* XVI (Cologne, 1589).
MAJOR, R. H. *India in the Fifteenth Century* (Hakluyt Soc. London, 1857).
MARCELLINUS, Fr. *Kēraḷattile Satyamarggatīnṭe Caritram* (History of the True Religion in Kerala), (Kuneanevu, 1872).

MATHAN, KONAṬṬ, Malpān. *Nitya Prart-hana Kraman* (Daily Office translated into Malayāḷam), (7th ed. Pampakuda, 1948).

MATTHEW DE OLIVEIRA XAVIER, Dom. *Some Elucidations* (Ernakulam, 1903).

MATTHEW DE OLIVEIRA XAVIER, Dom. *Subsidium ad bullarium patronatus Portugalliae* (Alleppey, 1903).

MEDLYCOTT, Right Rev. A. E. *India and the Apostle Thomas, an Inquiry* (London, 1905).

MEDLYCOTT, Right Rev. A. E. Art. 'St Thomas Christians', in *Catholic Encyclopaedia*, XIV, pp. 682–3.

MEDLYCOTT, Right Rev. A. E. Art. in *Voice of Truth*, 11 and 21 June 1902.

MEILE, P. *L'Inde classique* (Paris, 1949).

MENON, C. ACHUTHA. *Cochin State Manual* (Ernakulam, 1911).

MENON, K. P. PADMANABHA. *History of Kēraḷa* (4 vols. Ernakulam, 1934–7).

MEREDITH, D. O. 'How the Romans worked the world's sole source of porphyry', in *Illustrated London News* (16 Dec. 1950).

MINGANA, ALPHONSE. *The Early Spread of Christianity in India* (Rylands Library Bulletin, Manchester, 1926).

Monumenta Xavierana (Madrid, 1912).

DE PAIVA MANSO. Ed. *Bullarium patronatus Portugalliae regum in ecclesiis Africae, Asiae atque Oceaniae* (bullas, brevia, epistolas, decreta actaque sanctae sedis ab Alexandro III ad hoc tempus usque amplectens). (Lisbon, 1868–79.)

PANIKKAR, K. M. *Malabar and the Dutch* (Bombay, 1931).

PANIKKAR, K. M. *Malabar and the Portuguese* (Bombay, 1929).

PANIKKAR, R. N. *Kēraḷa B-hāṣa Sāhitya Caritram* (History of the Kerala Language and Literature), (Trivandrum, 1941–9).

PANJIKARAN, Mgr J. C., C.D. *Christianity in Malabar* (Trichinopoly), reprinted from *Orientalia Christiana*, VI (1926).

PANJIKARAN, Mgr J. C., C.D. *The Syrian Church in Malabar* (Trichinopoly, 1914).

PARAMEAKKAL, Administrator. *Journey of the Archbishop Kariyaṭṭil* (in Malayāḷam), (Aterampula, 1936).

PAUL OF ST BARTHOLOMEW, Fr, C.D. *India orientalis christiana* (Rome, 1794).

PAUL OF ST BARTHOLOMEW, Fr, C.D. *Viaggio alle Indie orientali* (Rome, 1796); Eng. trans., *Voyage to the East Indies* (London, 1800).

PHILIP, E. M. *The Indian Church of St Thomas* (Malayāḷam ed., Tiruvalla, 1929; Eng. ed., Nagercoil, 1950).

PHILIPOS, Fr E. *The Syrian Christians of Malabar* (ed. G. B. Howard; Oxford and London, 1869).

PHILIPPS, W. R. *Annual Report* (1902–3) of Archaeological Survey of India, I (Calcutta, 1904).

PHILIPPS, W. R. 'Translation of Notes on the Indo-Scythians by Sylvain Levi', in *Cambridge History of India*, I.

PHILIPPS, W. R. In *Indian Antiquary*, XXXIII (1904).

PIMENTA, Rev. P. NICHOLAO, S.J. AND AQUAVIVA, Rev. P. Cl. *Nova relatio de rebus in India orientali a patribus Soc. J. anno 1598–9 gestis* (Mainz, 1601).
PLACID, Fr, T.O.C.D., D.D. 'The social and socio-ecclesiastical customs of the Syrian Christians of India', in *Eastern Churches Quarterly*, VII (1947), no. 4, pp. 222ff.
POONNEN, T. I. *The Rise of Dutch Power in Malabar* (Trichinopoly, 1948).
POPE, G. U. *The Sacred Kurral* (London, 1886).
PUNŪS, Fr. Trans. *Āṇdutaksā* (Order for the Year), (Tiruvalla, n.d.).
PUNŪS, Fr. Trans. *Kūdāśakramangaḷum Anīdāyum* (The Sacraments and Observance of the Syrian Christians), (Tiruvalla, 1935).

Quatorzième Continuation des missionnaires danois de Tranquebar.

RAE, G. M. *The Syrian Church in India* (Edinburgh, 1892).
RANCINOTTO, LUIGI. *Gubernatis: storia dei viaggiatore italiani.*
RAO, T. A. GOPINATHA. In *Travancore Archaeological Series*, II (Trivandrum, 1916).
RAULIN, JOHN FACUNDUS. *Historia ecclesiae malabaricae*, cum Diamperitano Synodo apud Indos Nestorianos S. Thomae Christianos nuncupatos coacto ab A. de Menezes, 1599. (Rome, 1745.)
RAWLINSON, H. G. *Intercourse between India and the Western World* (Cambridge, 1916).
RENAUDOT, E. *Anciennes Relations des Indes et de la Chine* (Paris, 1718).
Report of the Christian Committee on Inheritance (Trivandrum, 1912).
RICHARDS, W. J. *Indian Christians of St Thomas* (London, 1908).
ROCCA, Fr. 'La leggende de S. Tomaso Apostolo' in *Orientalia Christiana*, XXXII.
ROZ, Fr FRANCIS. *De erroribus Nestorianorum* (1586); ed. in *Orientalia Christiana*, XI (1928).

SANKER, K. G. In *Indian Antiquary*, LVI (1927).
SAULIÈRE, Fr, S.J. In *Indian Athenaeum* (Aug.–Sept. 1923).
SCHAAF, Dr. *Relatio historica* (Leiden, 1714).
Selections from the Records of the Madras Government. Dutch Records, no. 13 (Madras, 1911).
SMITH, V. A. *Early History of India* (3rd ed. Oxford, 1914).
DE SOUSA, MANUEL Y FARIA. *Asia Portugesa.* (Eng. trans. by Capt. J. Stevens, *Portuguese Asia* (2 vols. 1695).)
DE SOUZA, Fr FRANCIS. *Oriente conquistado a Jesu Christo pelos padres da Companhia de Jesus da provincia da Goa* (Lisbon, 1700. Reprinted in Bombay, 1888).
STRABO. *Geography*, trans. by Hamilton and Falconer (3 vols. Reprint, London, 1892–3).

TARN, W. W. *The Greeks in Bactria and India* (Cambridge, 1951).
TAYLOR, W. *S. Indian Christian Repository* (Madras, 1837), I.
THAMPARAN, KAUJIKLETTAN. *Kēraḷam.*

THOMAS, Dr P. J. *Kēraḷattile Kristīya Sāhityam* (Mannanam, 1935).

THOMAS, Dr P. J. *The Marriage Customs and Songs of the Christians of Malabar* (in Malayāḷam), (Madras, 1936).

THOMAS, P. J. 'Roman trade centres in Malabar', in *Kēraḷa Society Papers* (1932), series 10.

THOMSON, J. O. *History of Ancient Geography* (Cambridge, 1948).

THURSTON, E. *Castes and Tribes of Southern India* (7 vols., esp. V and VI; Madras, 1909).

TIMOTHEOS, AUGEN Mar. *Viśud-ha Matōpadeśaśatyaṅaḷ* (The Truths of Holy Religion), (Kōṭṭayam, 1950).

Travancore State Manual (1st ed.), II.

TROTTER, R. A. 'The history of Christianity in Sind' in *Conference* (Journal of the Foreign Missions Dept. of the Church of Scotland, published in Edinburgh), (February 1947).

VARMA, E. A. RAVI. In *Kēraḷa Society Papers* (1932), series 9.

(DI VARTHEMA, LUDOVICO.) *Travels of Ludovico di Varthema in Egypt, Syria, Arabia Deserta and Arabia Felix, India and Ethiopia, A.D. 1503–1508*, trans. J. W. Jones; ed. G. P. Badger (Hakluyt Soc. London, 1863).

VINCENT MARY OF ST CATHERINE OF SIENA, Fr. *Viaggio all' Indie orientali* (Rome, 1672; Venice, 1683).

VINE, A. R. *The Nestorian Churches* (London, 1937).

VISSCHER, JACOB CANTERS (1743). Eng. trans. *Letters from Malabar* by H. Drury (Madras, 1862).

WARD, B. S. AND CONNOR, H. *Memoir of the Survey of Travancore and Cochin* (Trivandrum, reprint 1898).

WARMINGTON, E. H. *Commerce between the Roman Empire and India* (Cambridge, 1928).

WELLANIKKARAN, Fr A. F. In *Caritas* (Alwaye, 1939).

WHEELER, R. C. M. AND OTHERS. 'Arikamedu', in *Ancient India* (July 1946).

WHITEHOUSE, T. *Lingerings of Light in a Dark Land* (London, 1873).

WINCKWORTH, C. P. T. In *Kēraḷa Society Papers* (1930), series 6.

WINCKWORTH, C. P. T. In *Jour. Theological Studies*, XXX (April 1929).

WINSLOW, J. C. *The Eucharist in India* (London, 1920).

YULE, Col. Sir HENRY. Ed. (revised by H. CORDIER). *The Book of Ser Marco Polo* (Hakluyt Soc. London, 1903).

YULE, Col. Sir HENRY. Ed. (revised by H. CORDIER). *Cathay and the Way Thither* (3 vols. Hakluyt Soc. London, 1913).

YULE, Col. Sir HENRY. Ed. *Mirabilia descripta* (by Jordanus), (Hakluyt Soc. London, 1863).

ZALESKI, L. M. *The Apostle St Thomas in India* (Mangalore, 1912).

ZALESKI, L. M. *The Saints of India* (Mangalore, 1915).

INDEX

Abdalla, Jacobite Patriarch of Antioch, 151, 175
Abdiso, Nestorian Patriarch, 20, 286
Abdul Massih, Jacobite Patriarch, 151 n. 1, 153–4, 155, 157 and n.
Abraham Malpān, 140–1, 172
Abraham, Mar (arrived in India, 1568), 23, 24, 25, 26, 93
Acts of St Thomas, 43–5
Addai and Mari, Liturgy of, 281
Ahattalla, Bishop, 99–100
Angelus, Bishop, 114–15, 116
anointing, service of, 260–1
architecture, 202–4, 213–14
astrology, 200
Athanasios, Mar (arrived in 1825, Jacobite), 137
Athanasios, Mar Mathew, 141, 142–7 *passim*, 182, 184
Athanasios, Mar Paulos, 152, 155
Athanasios, Mar Thomas, 145, 148

Bailey, Rev. B., 133–5, 136
baptism, 250–4
Baselios, Mar (arrived in 1751, Jacobite), 120, 172
Beliarte, 13, 14 n.
Bible, Malayāḷam translations of, 132, 137 and n. 4, 280
birth customs, 184–6, 259–60
bishops consecrated in recent years, 158–61
Brito, Fr de (second archbishop), 95, 96–8
Buchanan, C., 1, 125–6
burial service, 261–4
Buttigeg, Bishop Ambrose, 20, 21, 286

Cabrol, Admiral Peter Alvares, 11, 12
Carmelite mission, 101–7, 110
caste, 167–8
Catholicos (of the Indian Church), 2, 154 and n. 2, 155, 158
Chandy, Bishop Parampil (Alexander de Campo), 107, 109
Christmas, ceremonies of, 236–7
Church Missionary Society, 76, 126, 132, 135, 138–40, 160, 291, 294
Cochin, 19, 33, 104, 125
copper-plate grants, 74–5, 85–90
Cosmas Indicopleustes, 68, 69
Cranganore, 11, 19, 25, 38, 52, 73, 94
Cross, reverence to the, 278–9
crosses, stone, 79–81

Dancing, religious, 202
death, 205–7; *see also* 261–4
Diamper, Synod of, 5, 11, 32 ff., 281, 283
Dionysios I, Mar, 122–7 *passim*
Dionysios II, Mar, 129
Dionysios III, Mar, 135, 136
Dionysios IV, Mar, 136, 137, 141–3
Dionysios V, Mar (Pulikkot Joseph), 144–8 *passim*, 150–1
Dionysios VI, Mar, 151, 152–6 *passim*, 290, 292
Dioscoros, Mar (arrived in 1807, Jacobite), 126
divisions among Syrians, 174–6
Dominicans, 96–7
dowry, 177–8
dress, 199–200, 205–6
Dutch, the, 3, 107–13 *passim*, 169

Easter, ceremonies of, 246–7
education, 186–7
Elias, Jacobite Patriarch, 155, 156
England, Church of, 126, 135
Ephraim I, Jacobite Patriarch, 156
Epiphany, ceremonies of, 237–40
Eucharist, 216–32
Eustathios, Mar (Patriarch's delegate), 151

Farquhar, J. N., 48
fasting, 199, 277–8

Gabriel, Mar (arrived in 1708 or 1705), 73, 115–17 *passim*, 118
Gama, Vasco da, 12, 13, 109
Garcia, Fr F., S.J. (third archbishop), 98–105, 107
Geddes, M., 1
George, Archdeacon, 27, 28, 94–8
Goa, Councils of, 23, 25
Good Friday, ceremonies of, 205, 244–5, 278